POLITICAL PARTIES AND IDEOLOGIES IN CANADA

Third Edition

POLITICAL PARTIES AND IDEOLOGIES IN CANADA

Third Edition

William Christian
Department of Political Studies
University of Guelph
Guelph, Ontario

Colin Campbell
Barrister & Solicitor
of the Ontario Bar

McGraw-Hill Ryerson Limited

Toronto Montreal New York Auckland Bogotá Caracas Hamburg Lisbon
London Madrid Mexico Milan New Delhi Paris San Juan São Paulo
Singapore Sydney Tokyo

ISBN: 0-07-549621-6

1 2 3 4 5 6 7 8 9 0 W 9 8 7 6 5 4 3 2 1 0

Printed and bound in Canada

Care has been taken to trace ownership of copyright material
contained in this text. The publishers will gladly take any
information that will enable them to rectify any reference or credit
in subsequent editions.

Sponsoring Editor: Susan Erickson
Supervising Editor: Carol Altilia
Copy Editor: Jane Lind
Interior design: Christopher Griffin
Typesetting: Dana Murray
Printing & binding: Webcom Limited

Canadian Cataloguing in Publication Data

Christian, William, date
   Political parties and ideologies in Canada

(McGraw-Hill Ryerson series in Canadian politics)
3rd. ed.
ISBN 0-07-549621-6

1. Political parties - Canada.   2. Ideology.
3. Canada - Politics and government.   I. Campbell,
Colin, date   . II. Title. III. Series.

JL195.C4 1989   320.971   C89-095395-3

In Memoriam

George Parkin Grant 1918–1988

Δ

Δ

CONTENTS

Δ

FOREWORD

It is a pleasure to welcome the third edition of *Political Parties and Ideologies in Canada*. The first two editions were fine books but this revision is even better. The authors have updated the material and refined their thinking further. The result is a significant work that makes an important contribution to political science, not merely because it describes and explains the ideological positions of Canada's three major political parties but because it argues a hypothesis about politics and Canadian culture.

In the second edition of their book, Christian and Campbell traced the development and ideologies of Canadian political parties and nationalism from their beginnings to 1983. This third edition brings the account up to date. Reading it, one is struck by how much happened in this relatively brief interval of six years. Pierre Trudeau disappeared from the scene as prime minister and gave way to John Turner as leader of the Liberal party and short-lived prime minister. The Conservatives replaced Joe Clark with Brian Mulroney, who then won an overwhelming electoral victory, became prime minister, and confirmed his position by achieving a second solid victory. The New Democratic Party retained Ed Broadbent as its head but the party rode a roller coaster in its standings in public opinion polls. Nationalism was put to the test in a celebrated general election fought on the issue of free trade with the United States. While special interest groups continue to press their own claims vociferously, the courts have begun to render judgements on the issues by interpreting the relevant clauses in the new Canadian constitution. The constitution itself was subjected to examination, and the Meech Lake

Accord proposes significant admendments that would recognize Quebec as a distinct society and grant the provinces greater powers. This move engendered disputes that have been accentuated by Quebec's use of the notwithstanding clause in the *Charter of Rights* to override a Supreme Court decision protecting language rights in the province.

Christian and Campbell explain how each party, within the parameters of its own ideology, has tried to grapple with these and other recent developments. The author's reviews of the various leadership candidates' positions at recent party conventions are particularly useful, as are the reviews of the positions of the parties themselves during the past two elections. What is revealed, of course, is that the federal Liberal Party has been split between what the authors call business liberalism and welfare liberalism. The party's new leader, John Turner, started out in 1984 espousing business liberalism and ended up in both 1984 and 1988 supporting welfare liberalism. This shift gave the Conservatives the opportunity to capture the business interest vote, which the party has consolidated by advocating free trade. It is the Conservatives who are now the business party, rather than the Liberals who enjoyed that position in the late 1940s and 1950s under Prime Ministers King and St. Laurent. Christian and Campbell are right in noting that this constitutes a major change in Canadian national politics. They are also correct in pointing out that the two major parties have realigned themselves by exchanging their historic positions on nationalism. The Liberals, who traditionally preferred free trade and continentalism, are now exponents of nationalism while the Tories, who supported tariffs to build a nation on an east-west axis, are now free traders accepting economic integration with the United States. Meanwhile, the NDP still seeks to reconcile its conflicting ambitions to retain its social democratic ideals and at the same time to reach out to a broader audience.

Reflecting on the history of parties' ideologies in Canada and the impact of recent developments upon them, Christian and Campbell draw certain conclusions that are significant and provocative. They argue that Canada is not a "fragment society" in the Hartzian sense, that is, a mere offshoot of some other culture. They believe that Canadian politics "exhibits the ideological diversity of European societies, although it has a more liberal cast." The latter makes it tolerant and receptive to intellectual influences from elsewhere, whether the ideas come from Britain, the United States, France, or other European countries. While such eclecticism adds richness to Canadian political thinking, it inhibits indigenous creativity and limits our individuality. This impoverishment is all the more regrettable because ideology is essential to politics. Without it, the authors believe, politics becomes a vacuous struggle for power.

This latter assertion encapsulates the essence of Christian's and Campbell's book and demonstrates its greatest contribution to political science. Although *Political Parties and Ideologies in Canada* is an excellent descriptive account of

Canadian political parties and nationalism, it is not a mere recital of historical developments and beliefs. It is a forthright statement that ideology in politics is important and that contrary to the popular brokerage theory, Canadian politics has been ideological. The activity has not been just a game of the ins and the outs or of pragmatic catch-as-catch-can. Canadians have struggled and died for matters of substance in politics, not least of which is the integrity and preservation of their country. In short, political beliefs have been important in Canada, and this is as it should be.

Christian and Campbell have not only written a very useful book but they have rendered a signal service by pointing out the importance of ideology in Canadian politics.

January 6, 1989   Paul W. Fox
Victoria College   General Editor
University of Toronto

Δ

PREFACE TO THE THIRD EDITION

Since the first edition of this work appeared in 1974 our task of charting the course of Canadian ideologies has been made much easier in two important respects. First, there has been a steady, but mounting, production of books that have added fuel to our arguments. These include memoirs and books of analysis by politicians, both active and retired, as well as academic analysis on the various topics that have interested us.

The second important change has been the general, though not universal, acceptance of the main thread of our analysis: namely, that there are now and always have been ideological concerns at the heart of Canadian politics. Of course, this does not mean that we deny the importance of other factors affecting the course of our political life. Although our parties sometimes steered their ship by the pole star of ideologies, at times clouds obscured their vision, and they headed off by instinct. At other times a mutinous crew seized the rudder and forced the captain to walk the plank. Sometimes they simply ran aground on unforeseen shoals; and all too often they abruptly changed course to dock in some bustling port in the hope of turning a quick profit. Most of the crew joined the ship's company because they liked the chosen destination; but many signed on simply for hope of adventure; and some were merely unlucky to be in the village square when the press gang happened by.

Of all the debts we accumulated over the years, we will mention only the greatest, to the late George Grant, whose brilliant mind and generous character were fundamental in the formulation of our argument. Sine quo non. Paul Fox has given us good advice and active encouragement from what seems by now time immemorial. More recent helpers have been George Alkalay of Trent University who contributed a valuable analysis of the manuscript and suggestions for improvement, and Susan Erickson of McGraw-Hill Ryerson who consistently supported this edition. The authors would particularly like to thank Miss Vanessa Maguire, a graduate student at the University of Guelph, who showed great dedication and enthusiasm over the tiresome business of proofreading and preparing the index.

Guelph/Toronto   William Christian
August 1, 1989   Colin Campbell

CHAPTER I

Δ

INTRODUCTION:
THE APPEAL OF IDEOLOGY

Party is a body of men for promoting by their joint endeavors the national interest upon some particular principle in which they are all agreed.

It is the business of the speculative philosopher to mark the proper ends of government. It is the business of the politician, who is the philosopher in action, to find out proper means towards those ends, and to employ them with effect.

Edmund Burke, *Thoughts on the Cause of the Present Discontents (1770)*

A QUIET COUNTRY

There are few things that most Canadians deplore more than the pursuit of grand dreams. We pride ourselves on being a sensible and practical people, whose visions run to matters such as airlines and oil companies, which might be expected to show a satisfactory profit. The veneration of political excess is for other times and other places. It has a kind of foreign feeling to it. The United States might have its life, liberty and the pursuit of happiness, the French their liberty, equality and fraternity, and the British Labour Party its dream of building a New Jerusalem. Our founding fathers, blacksuited Victorian businessmen and lawyers, contented themselves with the modest phrase that we would have a constitution similar in principle to the United Kingdom; they did not even think it necessary or desirable to spell out in any detail those principles that were going to define the terms on which we would share a common life as fellow citizens. We have not greatly changed since those distant days of colonial moderation.

The *Charter of Rights and Freedoms* set out in the *Constitution Act* of 1982 guarantees the rights and freedoms set out in it, "subject only to such reasonable limits prescribed by law as can be demonstrably justified in a free and democratic society." And if our panache were not sufficiently restrained by this cautious beginning, the operative part of the Charter concludes with the turgid declaration that "Subsection (3) applies in respect of a reenactment made under subsection (4)." This would be an unlikely rallying cry to send the starving to the barricades in the hope of building a heaven on earth.

Few Canadians see anything wrong with such restraint. We have been pleased, for the most part, that intense and bitter ideological confrontations have not often threatened the unity of the country or the security of its inhabitants. Although there have been some who have seen the course of history as the stuggle of contending classes or as the effort of women to free themselves from male subjugation, most Canadians are proud that the profound questions of politics have not weighed heavily on our minds. Sir John A. Macdonald mirrored the spirit of the new country when he admitted, with considerable satisfaction, that he had felt it unjustified to "waste the time of the legislature and the money of the people in fruitless discussions on abstract and theoretical questions of government."[1] Canadians today would generally agree that the right approach to politics was practical, pragmatic, common-sensical. Many would even reject entirely the suggestion that Canada's politics are in any important way ideological, or even that ideology should play a minor though important role in our national life.

THE END OF IDEOLOGY
AND THE BROKERAGE THEORY

In the late 1950s and early 1960s, it was fashionable in Canada and elsewhere to think that ideas had ceased to play an important role in politics. Books were published with titles such as *The End of Ideology,* and serious philosophers speculated that political philosophy might be dead.[2] In Canada, of course, political scientists had been teaching for years the famous "brokerage theory" of politics. This theory claims that political parties are elements in the larger political system and that they play their proper role when they balance competing interests and the varied regions within the country. To do this makes compromises, taking into account such factors as the number of people involved and the intensity of their desires. If the politicians were effective in this activity, the stronger or more numerous would get enough to keep them reasonably content, and the losers would be reconciled that they had fought the good fight. The brokerage theory was useful because it took seriously the existence of such factors as interest groups and regional difference in Canada; but it failed as a comprehensive theory. There were simply too many things that it could not adequately explain.[3]

Any theory can appear to be both useful and consistent by reducing everything to its own terms, and the brokerage theory was no exception. Thus, it is possible to treat the 1926 constitutional crisis as a series of domestic political manoeuvres and to ignore the serious divisions about fundamental issues such as Canada's proper role in the British Empire or the constitutional position of the Governor-General. In this view, R.B. Bennett's victory of 1930 was a deviation and his New Deal a fraud because they seemed to offer an alternative view of Canada. Even the CCF and Social Credit could be dismissed as "third parties," curious and probably temporary growths on the two-party system. Mackenzie King patronized the CCF as "Liberals in a hurry" whose demise as an independent party awaited only the propitious time for him to adopt as much of their platform as he found desirable. If both the Liberals and the Conservatives (fundamentally indistinguishable except for the fact that one formed the government and the other the official opposition) were honest brokers addressing an appeal to all men of good will, of what possible use were ideological parties except to distort the patterns of politics? The brokerage theory taught us what to see, and its lesson was that there were no significant ideological divisions within the country.

This understanding of Canada and its politics was the basis for what might be called the Mackenzie King system of politics. King was so skilful a master of conciliation and compromise that he persuaded his main rivals to compete with him on his own terms. He imposed a style of politics on Canada, which took such deep root that people mistook a way of practising politics for politics itself. Interest group politics and the politics of regionalism became the prevailing orthodoxy, the Canadian way. For the greater part of the time from King's first election victory in 1921 until the defeat in 1957 of his successor, Louis St. Laurent, this version of Liberalism almost changed the country into its image. But it was a country without imagination or vision: it was in danger of atrophy.

Faced with what seemed to be an unbeatable political formula, the other parties paid King the high compliment of imitation; each sought, in its own way, as Arthur Meighen put it, to "out-King King."[4] Yet the spreading predominance of Canadian Liberalism never succeeded in eradicating competing ideologies. Since the 1950s, toryism, socialism and nationalism have revealed that they still can make an important contribution to the debate about what kind of country Canada should be. Our argument in this book is that Canada was in its origins and is still a country of rich ideological diversity; and that the explicit expression and acknowledgement of these differences give our country a much greater chance to resolve the question of the kind of social life we wish to share as fellow citizens.

It is, then, our contention that Canadian politics is, at present, and has been in the past, influenced by ideology. It is difficult to state this proposition without being misunderstood, since we have evolved in Canada a reasonable prejudice against the sort of extreme doctrines that are normally understood by the word "ideology." Some of these have even intruded in a minor way on the Canadian experience. The anarchistic terrorism of the FLQ exploded briefly in the late 1960s, and sophisticated versions of Marxist doctrine have had an allure for a minority of professors in political science, sociology and history departments, and for a small but vocal number in the NDP and in the trade union movement. None of these views, however, has ever appealed to more than a handful of Canadians when put to an electoral test. Ironically, the most superficially amusing of all the small parties is the Rhinoceros Party, whose humour conceals a dangerously shallow and empty nihilism. Others, like the Western Canada Concept Party or the Libertarians, reveal the existence of serious discontent with the vision of the overwhelming majority. Only in Quebec, with the rise to power of the Parti Québécois in 1976, did a new party seriously threaten the ideological equilibrium of the country, and the significance of that development will be explored in greater detail in Chapters V and VI.

A CANADIAN APPROACH

The ideologies that concern us in this book are all deeply rooted ones: liberalism, conservatism, socialism and nationalism. True, like all things Canadian, their ancestors once came from somewhere else to settle in the northern half of North America, and like many, they have relatives and friends throughout the world, especially in Europe and in the United States. These similarities with other ideologies have often misled those who have tried to study them. Canadian politicians have, on the whole, been the sort Edmund Burke called philosophers in action. They have not written neat and concise treatises outlining their assumptions about the nature of man and his relationship to the physical and social world. Consequently, it has often been easier to study the more readily available explicit ideological statements from Europe or the United States, where different traditions and needs have produced clear and articulate doctrines, and then to assume casually that the ideologies with similar names in Canada are in all essentials comparable. Some have conceded that the Canadian variant differs in some respects, though others have been thoroughly critical of Canadians and their politicians for sullying the pure heart and essence of the doctrine.

Our approach has been unashamedly Canadian. We have studied these beliefs as they have existed in Canada, from their roots in the seventeenth and eighteenth centuries, through their slow but steady evolution in the nineteenth and twentieth. The dynamics of Canadian ideological development, and the unique Canadian ideological mix, which we describe in the next chapter, encourage us in our adherence to this historical method.

We are all the more encouraged because our study has not led us to the conclusion that there have been radical or dramatic turning points that shifted any of the major doctrines we studied onto totally new and unforeseen courses. What we have observed instead is a slow and steady adaptation of the ideologies in response to a variety of circumstances: economic, electoral, social, diplomatic, military and others. But in all cases there has been an inescapable element of continuity, provided in the case of liberalism, conservatism and socialism by the institutional structures of major and electorally successful political parties. However radically the leaders of these parties might have wished, on occasion, to depart from the settled traditions of their predecessors, they have found themselves restrained by the need to retain the support of their colleagues, to encourage the enthusiasm of their party's activists, and to seek the broad support of a populace that has never been united in the belief that major, radical changes were needed.

No one would ever deny, though, that Canadian ideologies are members of larger families; they often bear family resemblances, at times striking, to their British, European and American namesakes. There are two important reasons for such similarities. First, when the French and the British made the long physical and spiritual journey from the Old to the New World, they did not and could not abandon all the political ideas with which they had lived at home. Second, Canadians live in North America. Their ancestors thought of themselves proudly as both British and North Americans.

Moreover, Canada has always been open to influences from abroad. Ideas in the air elsewhere have often found their adherents here. The writings of Lord Keynes and Sir William Beveridge, architects of the British welfare state, had a profound influence on the thought of Canadian Liberals as to the role and social responsibilities of the federal government. The New Deal of President Roosevelt during the Great Depression, the radicalism of Barry Goldwater in the 1960s, and more recently, Reaganomics, monetarism and neo-conservatism have had their impact on segments within the Conservative Party. The legacy of the British Tory party has also been profound. As Canada's greatest political philosopher, George Parkin Grant, has observed, "One cannot understand the conservatism of Canada (Macdonald, Whitney, Borden, Ferguson, Bennett, Diefenbaker) without thinking of Disraeli."[5]

Canada's youngest ideology, socialism, has been perhaps the most open and receptive. One historian describes Salem Bland, the philosopher and mentor of the Social Gospel Movement in Canada, as:

> an omnivorous reader, and in the decade of the 1890s when he seems to have first formulated a social gospel outlook, [he] was especially influenced by Carlyle, Tennyson, Emerson, Channing and Thoreau, by the historical critics of scripture, and by Albert Ritschl, the great German theologian....At least as significant for Bland was the literature of evolution. The notes for his first socialist lecture, "Four Steps and a Vision," acknowledge various works of Darwin, Drummond's *Ascent of Man,* and Kidd's *Social Evolution,* as well as *Fabian Essays,* Arnold Toynbee, Edward Bellamy, and Henry George.[6]

Many subsequent leaders and theorists of Canadian socialism, such as J.S. Woodsworth, M.J. Coldwell and David Lewis, were either born or educated in England; and the eyes of many CCFers were on the spirited debates concerning the revision of socialist doctrine in which the British Labour Party was engaged in the 1950s. The lessons they drew were applied to the development of the doctrines of the New Democratic Party when it was founded in 1961. Subsequently, that party studied carefully Sweden's successful socialist government, and later, in the 1970s, turned its attention, although with less intensity, to see what it could learn from Germany's moderate Social Democrats. In the early 1980s it directed its attention to France's President Mitterand.

These influences, important though they have been, should not be exaggerated. What we have borrowed, we have usually adapted to our needs as we thought most appropriate. To assume, without investigation, a similarity between, say, American conservatism and the ideology of a Canadian political party bearing the name "Conservative," is to be ensnared by the powerful but primitive magic of names. This approach must be shunned. A true understanding of our political doctrines will come only after we have read the pamphlets and speeches of our politicians and the platforms of our parties. We shall never understand ourselves if we turn our eyes always outward, either across a border or beyond an ocean.

Let us, then, put aside most foreign comparisons, and take seriously the integrity and coherence of Canadian political ideas. Instead of comparing Canadian ideologies with their counterparts in other cultures or different political traditions, it is appropriate to bring them together for examination. Just as is the case of a family photograph, we will notice striking family characteristics they share; and we will also observe that each one enjoys its own individuality.

THE LIBERAL MAINSTREAM

The main component in the ideological structure of all three of our major parties is a profound belief in liberal values. Liberalism celebrates the individual and his liberty: the best person is the one who directs and determines his or her own life to the fullest possible extent. The best society is that in which every individual, in full consciousness, can choose for oneself the kind of life to lead, with external social restraint kept to the minimum necessary to preserve society from the aggressive and invasive behaviour of a lawless minority. Globally, this view vies with Communism as the leading understanding of how people should associate in political communities. It has many different national incarnations, many strains, many variants.

In our analysis of Canada we will consider only the two most important, which we call business liberalism and welfare liberalism. Both agree that the proper end of political action is the furtherance of a society in which each individual's freedom is extended to the utmost; but they differ in their assessments of the most serious threat to individual liberty, and in their views of the most effective means of enhancing it.

Business liberalism, the older doctrine, stresses the original concerns of liberalism to remove restraints on each person's freedom, historically most often imposed by government through laws, regulations and ownership. Thus it tends to view the state with suspicion as the association with the greatest concentration of coercive power, a virtual monopoly on law making and on the use of organized and institutionalized force to exact obedience. It fears that the state shows a remorseless tendency to expand into the lives of private individuals. Business liberals, therefore, usually draw the conclusion that each extension of the role of government must be carefully weighed, balancing immediate benefits against the long-term dangers of future oppression.

Welfare liberals see these matters somewhat differently. For them the emergence in modern capitalist society of large business organizations exercising considerable control over the theoretically free markets of the classical economists presents a disturbing paradox. For such business organizations are at the same time the result of the liberated energies and talents of the enterprising, but also pose a threat to the freedom and self-determination of others. The trade union movement, once seen by welfare liberals as a liberating form of social organization, has grown in strength to the point where it, too, is potentially oppressive. The conclusion welfare liberals draw is that the liberation of economic activity, the legacy of Adam Smith, David Ricardo and the other great liberal economists, has produced distortions by restricting other liberties. The small businessman who cannot compete with the large monopoly, the reformist political party that can make no progress against opponents financed with big-business money, the poor who have only the freedom to be poor, lie on the consciences of welfare liberals. Their response is to assert a hierarchy of rights, in which economic or property rights rank lower than human rights. In consequence, the negative liberty of classical liberalism, the removal of restrictions on human activity, by itself is no longer adequate. To protect the more important human rights, it is justifiable to restrict economic rights by such devices as progressive taxation, extensive government intervention to regulate economic life and social-welfare programs.

All of these provide a positive face to liberalism. Thus, welfare liberalism, while agreeing with business liberalism that liberty should be protected by charters of rights, a politically neutral civil service and the fair and impartial administration of justice, protests that such formal guarantees do not go far enough. Although they might provide equal liberty in a legal sense to all, they do not assure that each human being will be able to exercise that liberty in such a way as to be able to develop human potential to the fullest possible extent.

To redress the balance, welfare liberals look to the state, which they see as an effective counterweight to the large corporations and trade unions. The state can also give substance to the formal liberty of all by ensuring an acceptable minimum standard of social resources by the redistribution of wealth through the taxation system and social-welfare programs. Some commentators confuse welfare liberalism with another doctrine called corporatism, an ideology that insists that the greater corporate entities in society, the state, producers and workers, should be organized in such a way as to form a coherent and harmonious whole. These writers claim that corporatism has been a significant contributor to the ideological conversation of twentieth-century Canada.[7]

This suggestion about the importance of corporatism is one which we do not find persuasive. Although we do not deny that Canadian liberals such as Mackenzie King attached a high value to consensus and social peace, our analysis leads us to conclude that they did so because of the importance of tranquility and security for individual liberty. We suggest that if one pays attention to the reasons why most of the supposedly corporatist politicians pondered the questions of the relationship between the state and the other major associations, it will be clear that their ideas were inspired by the new ideas of welfare liberalism rather than by corporatism. We do suggest, though, that corporatism had a minor role to play in the development of Canadian Conservatism, a matter that is discussed in Chapter IV. Instead of having a link with Canadian Liberalism, we see corporatism as an extreme development of the tory element in Canadian Conservatism, erupting in response to the crisis of the Great Depression of the 1930s.

No major Canadian political party is ideologically pure or doctrinaire, though the Liberal Party comes the closest as a partnership between two interpretations of the significance of liberalism for Canada. The Conservative Party and the New Democratic Party are more heterogeneous, each consisting of a coalition between compatible, but distinct, ideologies.

CANADIAN CONSERVATISM

In Canadian Conservatism, the two leading beliefs are those of business liberalism and toryism, though even other strains of liberalism such as progressivism and welfare liberalism have been espoused by a relatively small number of important figures in the party. Liberal individualism was a major idea in nineteenth-century Canada and it is not surprising to find that political Conservatism, which also took root in the mid-nineteenth century, shares this feature with Liberalism. Yet, in the history of Canadian Conservatism, we can also identify as a tory element a commitment to the values of collectivism and a belief in the enduring value of hierarchy as an element of social life. As George Parkin Grant has observed, "This may be a tradition that has decayed in Canada before the ravages of capitalism and liberalism, but it was a great part of this country."[8]

We think that toryism was a significant element in Canada Conservatism before the Port Hope Conference of 1942 and the selection of John Bracken as leader of the newly renamed Progressive Conservative Party. Nevertheless, although it has subsequently become a recessive strain in the party's ideology, we argue that the tory belief in a society that places social order and collective or community values before individual rights is alive, if not exactly thriving, in the modern Conservative Party. In the era since John Diefenbaker became leader of the party in 1956, toryism has increasingly appeared in a democratic tory form. Although this variant is often confused with populism, the belief that the interests of the common people are the only real subject matter of politics, it draws more on a tradition that acknowledges the responsibility of those with privileges to use their advantages for the benefit of the less well-off in the community. Its survival, however, is currently being threatened by the party's tough, confident and aggressive business liberals, who at times show considerable impatience with the demands of ideological compromise. Curiously this tradition draws its present strength from the Quebec caucus rather than from the English, a factor that promised to become more significant after the 1988 election in which David Crombie did not run and Flora MacDonald was defeated.

There is one final element that deserves a mention as part of the modern Conservative Party, and that is libertarianism. In its extreme form, this ideology verges on anarchism, and has spawned a political party of the same name, which runs candidates in federal and some provincial elections. As the name suggests, liberty is the sole value with which these thinkers are concerned, and they consistently identify the state as a malign influence. Although the more extreme libertarians want to restrict the state to the mere maintenance of law and order, those within the Conservative Party are normally found pressing the government to withdraw from the more prominent areas of the welfare state.

What makes this identification even more difficult is that, over time, toryism has increasingly lost its character as an outright defender of privilege, and has more and more become what we might call democratic toryism. What distinguishes this from the older form of toryism is a strong sense of *noblesse oblige* — the privileges of those who are well-to-do are justified only to the extent that they serve the poorer elements of the community. In earlier times this tradition was manifested particularly in the charity work of the wealthy, but with the rise of the welfare state, tory democrats have accepted this instrument in partnership with progressive taxation as an appropriate instrument for serving the interests of the poor. All these differences will be discussed in depth in subsequent chapters.

CANADIAN SOCIALISM

The New Democratic Party has comparable difficulties and has, at times, such as during the early 1970s, revealed equally serious signs of internal ideological dissension. Here, again, it is liberalism that ties the NDP securely into the main-stream of Canadian political life, but in this case it is the welfare rather than the business variant. Just as the business liberalism of the Conservative Party takes on its unique character as a consequence of passing many years in the company of toryism, so in the NDP does welfare liberalism take on a more radical guise by dint of an engagement of more than half a century in partnership with social-ism. Curiously, socialism and toryism are more closely related than might appear at first glance, for socialism was a rival interpretation of the significance of col-lectivism. It spurned what it considered the tory's unrealistic belief in the value of the nation, and claimed instead that a true sense of community could be grounded only in the common experience of the working class, or the trade un-ion movement. Moreover, in its commitment to social equality, it was responding antithetically to the tory commitment to society as a graded order of ranks. As toryism diminished in strength and in electoral appeal, its concerns resurfaced, transfigured, in socialism.

NATIONALISM

Of the ideologies considered in this book, only nationalism has not found con-sistent institutional embodiment, though even here such movements as Henri Bourassa's Nationalists, or the *Bloc Populaire* of the Second World War achieved a transitory success in federal politics. In 1976, of course, the Parti Québécois rose to power in Quebec. Because of the very interesting questions it raises for the study of Canadian ideologies, in Chapter VI we will turn our atten-tion briefly away from our focus on federal parties and their ideologies to con-sider the PQ's unique ideological mix. More usually, Canadian nationalism, whose popular appeal has ebbed and flowed over time, has been grafted, when the need arose, more or less convincingly onto the ideologies of the three major parties. All three of the major ideologies — toryism, liberalism and socialism — can, for varied reasons, be induced under the right circumstances to agree that foreign domination is both pressing and undesirable. Nationalism's collectivism is often closer to the modern socialist conception of the composition of society. How-ever, in contemporary Canadian politics, nationalism has forged close ties with welfare liberalism; and for the immediate future, it is this alliance that is likely to prove the most important, politically.

THE HISTORY OF IDEOLOGY

The very idea of studying ideology is a relatively novel one. The word ideology originated in France at the end of the eighteenth century, in the aftermath of the revolution of 1789. It was at this time that "the people" set out on the path that was eventually to develop throughout the Western world as democracy with universal suffrage. Of course, people had always had their opinions about their rulers. Some they loved, others they hated or despised. One king might be a father to his subjects, another a bloody, rapacious tyrant. The lower classes, especially in the capital, might give vent to these feelings, now with a spontaneous outburst of enthusiasm, again with surly mutterings of discontent, or even a full-scale riot. However, politically relevant public opinion was largely restricted to the nobility and landed gentry, and in some countries to the large merchants and manufacturers. Popular opinion, although volatile, was not organized, and rarely affected the day-to-day affairs of state.

Regimes changed slowly, some with more and others with less social upheaval. The transition was smoothest in the English-speaking countries. Although a handful of reformers in England in the late eighteenth century envisaged a form of government in which all adult males would have the franchise, even this state of affairs was not reached for another century. The suffragette movement secured for women a place on the electoral lists during the First World War, but it was only in the 1960s that Canada became a country in which all adult citizens were allowed to vote. In the history of our civilization, there were other examples of democracies. Athens, in the age of Pericles, considered itself such, though it allowed only adult male citizens to be politically active and, much like modern Switzerland, made citizenship a difficult attainment for even a wealthy, male foreigner.

The development of a society in which the opinions of all adult citizens were politically important on a continuing and institutionalized basis required the creation of new forms of social organization of control, by means of which large numbers of people of varied background and diverse interests could be moved to action. Individual parliamentarians increasingly lost their independence, and their freedom of action was constrained by the need to associate with other like-minded individuals to persuade as many citizens as possible, when the time arose, to perform one vital act, namely voting in favour of the candidate of a particular political party. The analysis of voting behaviour has become a technically sophisticated subject, which seeks to account for voter preferences by correlating voting with salient personal characteristics, such as age, sex, religion, occupation, family income or education. It usually avoids any discussion of the rightness or justice of the voter's choice, on the grounds that such a topic is not susceptible to scientific analysis.

In this book, we affirm that Canadians have long held strong opinions on questions involving liberty, individualism, social coherence, hierarchy and equality. By framing their policies to appeal to some of these values, and by persuasion that their proposals are fair, just and reasonable, political leaders in this country have sought to win the favour of a majority of the electorate.

TWO LEVELS OF IDEOLOGY

Political leaders have had to take into account that there are two main levels of ideology operating in any political community, the one more subtle and tacit, the other more obvious and articulate.[9]

The deeper level of ideology is found in the rules, procedures and practices of the country's social and political institutions. Edmund Burke exalted this as a kind of hidden wisdom, and he took the view that political theory should be derived by bringing to full consciousness the principles implicit in the constitution.[10] If society is coherent — if it is operating to the satisfaction of its members, who show neither a disposition to alter it in any fundamental way nor even a desire to offer comprehensive theories about the way it works — then ideology derived from it will be incomplete, a mere expression of some of its salient and more problematic features. The full theory, known consciously and fully by no one at all, will lie embedded in the actual operation of the institutions, and need never be extracted.

A second level of ideology, which is more on the surface, is the one with which this book is principally concerned: the kind that Michael Oakeshott describes as "an abstract principle, or set of related abstract principles, which has been independently premeditated. It supplies in advance of the activity of attending to the arrangements of a society a formulated end to be pursued, and in so doing it provides a means of distinguishing between those desires which ought to be encouraged and those which ought to be suppressed or redirected."[11] To illustrate, he compares ideology to a scientific theory or hypothesis, which he suggests is not "a self generated bright idea," but rather the outcome of "the traditions of scientific inquiry from which it was abstracted."[12]

It has been suggested that the ideologist is to politics what the drama critic is to a play. From the performance in question, he extracts principles which, taken as a whole, make it a successful drama, or whose inconsistencies or inept implementation make it a failure. The canons of criticism, however, are not ideas independent of previous theatrical performances, but instead flow from a tradition of dramatic writing. It may be possible to set them down in abstract form, as Aristotle does with the unities in his *Poetics,* but this abstraction remains dependent upon the actual practice of drama that preceded it.[13]

To return to Oakeshott's formulation, "a political ideology must be understood, not as an independently premeditated beginning for political activity, but as knowledge (abstract and generalized) of a concrete manner of attending to the arrangements of society."[14] All ideologies presuppose, Oakeshott is saying, that there already exists in the world the practical knowledge necessary to execute political skills well. Part of that knowledge is then articulated in a summarized form in the ideology, which might get part of it wrong.

This last example shows us something else about ideology. Once ideas are separated or distilled from the complex reality of human society, they can be expanded as a set of abstract ideas — an ideology, in fact. In our next chapter we will examine more closely this process of intellectual migration, and offer a hypothesis as to why some ideas, which did not take root in the United States, found the Canadian climate more hospitable.

An ideology does not need to originate in political activity. One can abstract from the practice of war, religion, or as Oakeshott believes Marx had done, from the conduct of industry. Ideologies have a certain usefulness to the extent that they highlight particular features of a country's political tradition and thus serve an educational function. However, as a guide or blueprint to the functioning or direction of a whole society, they are quite deficient. For since they present or lay stress on only a few strands ("intimations") of a political tradition, they are apt to be seriously misleading.

Curiously enough, Oakeshott's view of ideology as derivative of some concrete activity is similar to the Marxist view of ideology as merely a reflection of a particular set of economic or productive relationships. So Marx puts it in *The German Ideology*: "Men are the producers of their conceptions, ideas, etc. — real, active men, as they are conditioned by a definite development of their productive forces and of the intercourse corresponding to these, up to its highest forms. Consciousness can never be anything else than conscious existence and the existence of men is their actual life-process." Thus the Marxists see particular ideologies as the abstract expression or rationalization of the economic position of a particular group in society; and the dominant ideology at any point is the expression of the class interest of the ruling class, in the guise of the general interest of all.[15]

Ideology need not be wholly derived from an activity or practice. It can also come from thought or reflection, from philosophy. Thus, in Chapter VI we will consider Elie Kedourie's contention that nationalism has its root in certain philosophical notions about the nature of moral behaviour and of the state, ideas not formulated with any practical application in view, but were later invested, by the passage of events, with an apparent immediate political significance.[16]

Can we now come to an understanding of the nature of ideology and its role? We shall view it as a doctrine or a set of ideas that claims to provide an adequate explanation of political arrangements. It will seek either to justify an existing state of affairs, and hence preserve it from change; or else it will seek to reveal inadequacies in the arrangements and consequently propose a better political system to replace the old one. In this, ideology is unlike social criticism, which is content to point out incoherences, injustices, miseries and the like without formulating solutions or new social orders. Ideologies provide model understandings of politics, which facilitate attacks on or defence of existing institutions by analyzing the whole through concepts such as liberty, equality, privilege or the collectivity, or activities — religious, economic, cultural — which have played an important role in the political tradition of the community, or in some other community with which the first has close intellectual ties.

Ideology will attempt to abridge the political practices of the community in conformity with the organizing central ideas. If these central ideas have been historically important to a segment of the community, they will, if a crisis of some sort leads to dissatisfaction with the existing political organization, provide an immediately appealing and familiar guide to the nature of the crisis and the outlines of a possible solution. For example, the farmers in Western Canada had long practised co-operation in the rough and isolated frontier communities in which they lived. This aspect of their life could be seen not only in their projects of mutual self-help, but also in such institutions as the communally organized telephone services. They also had a rough sense of equality as a consequence of the agricultural organization of the prairie-wheat economy, which followed from the government's policy of offering equal plots of land to all settlers. Therefore, when these farmers, among others, were faced with the droughts and the ruinous decline of agricultural prices in the Depression of the 1930s, they were open to the proposals for regeneration put forward when the Co-operative Commonwealth Federation was founded in 1932. The collectivism and egalitarianism of that movement's socialism appeared as sound principles upon which to reestablish the country's political life. Farther west, in Alberta, the Depression further increased the collective sense that Albertans were oppressed by the operation of the Eastern financial system. The doctrines of Social Credit suggested solutions to these grievances, and Albertans defiantly returned fifteen Social Credit MPs in 1935.

An ideology also serves to narrow the range of relevant social and political information. As European politics became increasingly democratic from the middle of the eighteenth century on, reformers there began to indict existing governments for their complexity. They claimed that governments were unnecessarily confusing to the common people, and that this complexity served only to allow rulers to impose on the ignorance of the people. Complexity, they felt, led to quietism; it was critical to establish a new way of looking at politics, stemming from certain simple principles easily comprehensible even to the uneducated. Ideologies, then, were born in order to establish which political institutions and beliefs were valuable and which could be discarded. The organizing ideas, whether they were collectivism, privilege, equality, liberty, or any other, were set to their task of purification and simplification.

HOW IDEOLOGIES SUCCEED

To gain acceptance, an ideology does not need to appear striking, novel or unprecedented. The contrary is probably true: it is most likely to be successful if it contains familiar elements, transformed, or presented in a new light. Most effective is an old organizing idea put to a new use, or put to use in novel circumstances. Thus, Social Credit's success in Alberta in the 1930s was due in large part to its ability to redirect the religious enthusiasm William Aberhart had stirred up through the Calgary Prophetic Bible Institute and his radio broadcasts. The expectation of religious salvation through a belief in the Bible was transmuted into a hope for economic rehabilitation.

The choice between rival ideological understandings is "a choice between incompatible modes of community life."[17] Ideological changes are rare events. To reject one ideology without adhering to another is a serious matter; it is, in effect, to abandon all hope of influencing political developments. Often, the average citizen is moved to vote for a particular candidate because skilful leaders have appealed to certain strains of ideological vision; shared beliefs lead to an effective basis for co-operative action. But a citizen who merely despairs gives up politics. Aberhart did not counsel his followers to await the millennium and take what they were given today. He advised them first to try to influence the old parties, and later to create one of their own. The founders of the CCF did more than simply hope for the eradication of capitalism; they offered a program that they expected would lead to the establishment of the co-operative commonwealth. René Lévesque, dissatisfied with the policies of the Quebec Liberal Party, offered the prospective supporters of his new Parti Québécois the option of sovereignty association.

How people convert from one ideology to another is difficult to explain satisfactorily. The American political writer, Eric Hoffer, has suggested that it is a phenomenon analogous to a religious conversion.[18] This is a wise observation. Just as the latter change involves the replacement of one set of metaphysical and theological presuppositions for another, so an ideological shift entails the substitution of one set of social and political beliefs for those that previously had appeared persuasive. It was one of Burke's great insights that this might be a rare event for entire countries. What he called the "capital of nations and ages" involved both concepts and institutions. In the intermediate stage of a revolution, existing institutions and beliefs lose their legitimacy, but new ones have not yet arisen or been created. The energy and imagination of society is disorganized and diffused, and much social energy has to be spent on creating a new complex of organizations and practices before each citizen can return to the business of individual living.

This process of conversion can never be strictly rational. Each ideological vision purports to offer a fundamental understanding of the individual and society, and there cannot consequently be a more fundamental standard by which to judge the other two. Each ideology offers its own standards of evaluation, coming off best, naturally, by its own criteria. An individual, unhappy with a previous understanding of politics, might be prepared to accept a rival interpretation explaining those features that had been especially puzzling or painful before; then the person will be able to understand, retrospectively, certain inadequacies in a former approach. Thus, it was not surprising that Pierre Vallières's *L'Urgence de Choisir*, written after he had repudiated the FLQ and its terrorist road to an independent Marxist state for Quebec, would more or less satisfy the criteria that it dictated for itself. Needless to say, it fell short of satisfying old comrades such as Charles Gagnon, who remained loyal to the doctrines Vallières had set forth in *White Niggers of America*. Although Vallières's arguments did not immediately convince his former associates, his example shook their confidence. The subsequent electoral success of the Parti Québécois confirmed for many the correctness of his new position. Just as in science a single experiment can prove decisively the superiority of a new hypothesis over the accepted orthodoxy, so the election results of November 1976 gave hope to many former Felquistes and their fellow travellers that an independent Quebec could be attained by democratic means. The failure of a majority to support sovereignty association in the 1980 referendum, however, made the experimental results more ambiguous, and opened the door once again to some who interpreted the available evidence as showing the necessity of more radical measures if Quebec were ever to become a sovereign country.

Such ideological shifts are, interestingly, more common when the ideology is articulated in some detail and intensely held. They are less likely with the more diffuse ideologies between the parties, as studies in Canada consistently indicate, but this evidence does not invalidate our central argument. It is not our contention that the major Canadian political parties have ever been doctrinaire. As we argued earlier in this chapter, each of the three main parties represents a coalition of ideologies. Far from undermining our position, this observation highlights the fact that there has been a conversation of ideologies in Canada; we also believe that this diversity has been a valuable source of new ideas about the Canadian polity which has, and will continue to open up a wider range of political options than is available in a country with only a single ideology. Indeed, the complaint that Canadian politics are tiresome stems from the monologue that occurs when liberalism attains such a dominant position that it no longer has to take time and listen attentively to its rivals.

There can be little doubt about the usefulness of ideology. It simplifies the world, forecloses options, points the way to a restricted range of solutions. Nonetheless, as useful as ideologies are in political life, they do have their weaknesses. Our position in this book is neither for nor against the ideologies we have identified and described; we believe in their limited value, but we are fearful when they threaten to become the sole mode of understanding politics. Let us then look at some of the deficiencies of the ideological mode of understanding.

THE LIMITS OF IDEOLOGY

An ideology can isolate a political group from many urgent problems that it either ignores, or for which it cannot provide, on its own terms, an acceptable solution.

We touched earlier on the difficulties that Quebec nationalism poses for Canadian Liberalism. Lacking the conceptual category of a cultural nation, Liberal leaders such as Lester Pearson and Pierre Trudeau have taken the view that the grievances felt by French Canadians arose because, as individuals who happened to be French-speaking, they had been denied certain rights in education, in the courts, in the armed forces, in the civil service. Once the problem has been identified in this way, it can be resolved by the provision of simultaneous translation facilities, bilingual documents, and the promotion of francophones to prominent and responsible positions in the bureaucracy and Crown corporations. These solutions do not even begin to address the problems that concern the nationalist, for whom the preservation of the French language and the culture of Quebec is a powerful moral right belonging to the French-Canadian nation that has found its home in Quebec for over three centuries. For the federal government to provide French-language services wherever there happens to be a sufficient concentration of francophones to make the expense justifiable only exacerbates the problem: it encourages the dispersion of French Canadians and weakens their attachment to their homeland.

The debate over the Meech Lake Accord was a case in point. Although all three major parties supported it, they did so for different reasons. The Conservatives were most drawn by its contribution to national unity and its decentralizing implications. The NDP found the collectivism inherent in the acknowledgement of Quebec as a distinct society its most alluring feature. The Liberal Party was the one most divided on the issue. The business liberals agreed with the Conservatives, but the welfare liberals, for whom former Prime Minister Trudeau spoke, were not prepared to accept what they considered a serious weakening of the powers of the central government. They also objected to precisely what the NDP admired, the recognition of Quebec as a collective unit.

Similarly, the NDP is too enthusiastic a partisan of the trade unions for the taste of most Canadians. It is clear that the socialist strain in the party has a continued commitment to trade unionism as an expression of collectivism; but most Canadians pay serious attention to the activities of unions only when they impinge directly on them, either because a strike has made goods or services unavailable, or because they attribute a rise in prices or in taxes to excessive wage claims.

Ideology has these sorts of inadequacies because it is always intent on acting in the world. It is not disinterested, and ideologies generally take little time for that philosophic reflection Oakeshott has said ought to be "without presupposition, reservation, arrest or modification."[19] Ideologies do not gain adherents who are interested in the pursuit of truth for its own sake. Marx observed in his *Theses on Feuerbach* that previous philosophers had only interpreted the world; the point was to change it. This attitude, widely prevalent in the modern world, is preoccupied with action. Nor is this position entirely new. As Plato has Callicles tell Socrates:

For philosophy, you know, Socrates, is a charming thing, if a man has to do with it moderately in his younger days; but if he continues to spend his time on it too long, it is ruin to any man. However well endowed one may be, if one philosophizes far on into life, one must needs find oneself ignorant of everything that ought to be familiar to the man who would be a thorough gentleman and make a good figure in the world. For such people are shown to be ignorant of the laws of their city, and of the terms which have to be used in negotiating agreements with their fellows in private or in public affairs; and, in short, to be utterly inexperienced in men's characters.[20]

The second weakness of ideology is that it tends to be rather smug and self-satisfied. It takes itself very seriously, and, more dangerously, it takes at face value its own claim to be a satisfactory account of political experience. A more satisfactory understanding is more tentative — and more ambitious. The driving need to understand all experience as part of a whole is an enterprise frightening in both its scope and in its difficulty. The enormity of the task helps explain why most people prefer ideology. Great nobility of character is required, combined with wisdom to recognize the limits of one's knowledge. For this, among other reasons, politics is not really an activity for the young. Plato recognized this fact in his *Republic* and insisted that only after a man of exceptional talents had undergone a long and arduous process of education could he be deemed fit to rule others. Nor is this requirement limited to classical political thought. Both the Canadian and American constitutions require members of their Senate to be at least thirty years old, and the American president must be at least thirty-five years old. Ideology is a shortcut that busy or lazy people take to avoid the rigours of philosophy; ideologies are of necessity partial explanations, valuable for those who want to get on with the job at hand.

The third weakness of ideology is that it is not sufficiently self-critical. Ideologies purport to make direct sense out of the empirical world. They rarely excel in that second-order activity, which is the province of philosophy, namely, making a world of ideas more coherent. "(P)art of the task of political theory is to clarify concepts, to engage in analysis and make distinctions."[21]

Ideology is to us what rhetoric was to the ancient Greeks: a tool used for the sake of persuasion. "Thus rhetoric, it seems," Socrates says in the *Gorgias*, "creates conviction based on trust, rather than educating about what is just and unjust."[22] Or, as Aristotle put it in the *Rhetoric*:

The political orator aims at establishing the expediency or the harmfulness of the proposed course of action; if he urges its acceptance, he does so on the ground that it will do good; if he urges its rejection, he does so on the ground that it will do harm; and all other points, such as whether the proposal is just or unjust, honorable or dishonorable, he brings in as subsidiary and relative to his main consideration.[23]

The classical orator and the modern ideologist are alike because both claim to know what is right and just, but in practice, justice and goodness are not matters they have considered deeply. What they say might very well be true, but at heart their attitude is indifferent to truth. Ultimately, they are dependent on the opinions of the majority, whose behaviour they are trying to affect. Plato described this relationship as follows:

> It is as if a man were acquiring the knowledge of the humours and desires of a great strong beast which he had in his keeping, how it is to be approached and touched, and when and by what things it is made most savage or gentle, yes, and the several sounds it is wont to utter on the occasion of each, and again what sounds uttered by another make it tame or fierce, and after mastering this knowledge by living with the creature and by lapse of time should call it wisdom, and should construct thereof a system and art and turn to the teaching of it, knowing nothing in reality about which of these opinions and desires is honorable or base, good or evil, just or unjust, but should apply all these terms to the judgement of the great beast, calling the things that pleased it good, and the things that vexed it bad, having no other account to render of them, but should call what is necessary just and honorable, never having observed how great is the real difference between the necessary and the good, and being incapable of explaining it to another.[24]

There is, as this metaphor suggests, a difference between the ideology of the political leaders and that of the average citizen. Those who speak for parties are usually more articulate, more able to manipulate political words and political ideas; but at bottom, they are dependent on the ideological beliefs of the ordinary citizen, and especially in a mass democracy with universal suffrage, they cannot depart too far from the popular conception of right and wrong without losing their influence. Ultimately the leaders are no better off than their followers. "Without political philosophy politics might well go on as merrily as ever. The only trouble is that it would not be understood, it would be a practice without consciousness of the norms which inform its activity, ignorant even of its own identity or nature....But if the day ever comes when political philosophy is really dead, the triumph of information over knowledge will be complete."[25]

Ideologies are to political philosophy what the *Reader's Digest* condensed book is to the original: a pale imitation for the man of affairs. But as Maurice Cranston has observed, one of the many disagreeable features of the twentieth century is that it is an age of dogma; and ideological disputes are to us what religious controversies were to earlier ages, or continue to be in Northern Ireland or the Islamic world. Political philosophy has a twofold interest in ideology. First, ideologies are sometimes corruptions of philosophy, and philosophy must constantly purify and repurify. Second, ideologies are part of the world of political experience, and consequently, if philosophy is going to account comprehensively for all the phenomena relevant to an understanding of politics, it has to enfold ideology in its coherent account of the whole.

What, then, are we to conclude from all this? It seems likely that ideologies are of complex parentage; they may embody abstractions from both practical activity and from philosophy. All the same, they are essentially limited and partial, and present a correspondingly constrained view of the world. We must especially remember their practical nature: they are meant to have an affect in and on the course of events. Before we can turn to an analysis of the ideologies that have been most important in Canada, we will first consider how ideologies, and a unique ideological structure, have developed in Canada.

---

1. Quoted in H. Macquarrie, *A Brief Record of the Progressive Conservative Party of Canada* (n.p., n.d.), p. 1.

2. Daniel Bell, *The End of Ideology* (Glencoe: Free Press, 1960). P. Laslett, *Politics, Philosophy and Society*, First Series (Oxford: Basic Blackwell, 1956), p. vii. See also S.M. Lipset, "Ideology & No End," *Encounter*, XXIX, No. 6, pp. 17–22.

3. Gad Horowitz, "Toward a Democratic Class Struggle," *Agenda 70*, T. Lloyd and J.T. McLeod, eds. (Toronto: University of Toronto Press, 1968), pp. 241–255.

4. Quoted in J.L. Granatstein, *The Politics of Survival* (Toronto, 1967), p. 135.

5. George Grant, *Globe and Mail*, Saturday May 8, 1982, p. 15.

6. Richard Allen, "The Social Gospel and the Reform Tradition in Canada," in S.D. Clark, J.P. Grayson and L.M. Grayson, eds., *Prophecy and Protest: Social Movements in Twentieth-Century Canada* (Toronto: Gage, 1975), p. 47.

7. See, for example, the discussion of corporatism in R.J. Van Loon and Michael Whittington, *The Canadian Political System*, 3rd. edition (Toronto: McGraw-Hill Ryerson, 1981), pp. 103–106. As they explain it: "Thus, the corporatist component of our political culture conceives of society as a collection of interest groups and hence it has an anti-individual bias." They further go on to conclude that "there is a clear corporatist streak in our political culture."

8. Grant, *Globe and Mail*, May 8, 1982, p. 15.

9. S. Wolin, "Paradigms and Political Theory," in *Politics and Experience*, B.C. Parekh and P. King, eds. (Cambridge: Cambridge University Press, 1968), p. 149.

10. Burke, in *Parliamentary History*, XXIX (London: 1817), p. 1324.

11. Michael Oakeshott, "Political Education," in *Rationalism in Politics* by Michael Oakeshott (c) 1962 by Michael Oakeshott (Methuen & Company Limited, London) (U.S.: Basic Books, Inc. Publishers, New York), p. 116.

12. *Ibid.*, p. 119.

13. M.W. Cranston, "The Mask of Politics," in *The Mask of Politics and other Essays* (London: Allen Lane, 1973), pp. 1–2.

14. Oakeshott, p. 120.

15. The problem with Marx's own view, of course, is that ultimately it is itself uncommonly similar to ideology — an abstraction from a limited form of human activity, economic production, applied without reserve to all human activity.

16. E. Kedourie, *Nationalism* (London: Hutchinson, 1961), p. 10. Much of the following discussion is indebted to T.S. Kuhn, *The Structure of Scientific Revolutions* (Chicago: University of Chicago Press, 1962), but since the debt takes the form of a free gloss, rather than a direct borrowing, it will have to suffice here to note the source of inspiration for many of the following ideas.

17. Kuhn, p. 93.

18. Eric Hoffer, *The True Believer* (New York: Harper Bros., 1951).

19. M. Oakeshott, *Experience and Its Modes* (Cambridge: Cambridge University Press, 1966), p. 2.

20. Plato, *Gorgias*, 484CD, trans. W.R.M. Lamb (Cambridge, Mass.: Harvard University Press, 1925).

21. John Rees, *Equality* (London: Macmillan, 1971), p. 58.

22. Plato, *Gorgias*, 455A, our translation.

23. Aristotle, *Rhetoric* 1358b 20-25, trans. W.R. Roberts (New York: Random House, 1941).

24. Plato, *Republic*, 493A-C, trans. P. Shorey (Cambridge, Mass.: Harvard University Press, 1935).

25. M.W. Cranston, "The Mask of Politics," p. 25.

CHAPTER II

Δ

THE CANADIAN SETTING

THE ORIGIN OF CANADIAN IDEOLOGIES

We have suggested that ideologies present limited or incomplete explanations of politics; and that ideologies can be distinguished one from another in terms of the central or organizing idea or ideas around which each is constructed. Thus, concepts such as liberty, equality, privilege, individualism, collectivism or nationality have been used as the focal points of political ideologies. We have also suggested that there are four main ideologies to be found in present-day Canada — liberalism, toryism, socialism and nationalism. Why should there be four ideologies? Why not six, or ten? Why not only one? Why these four in particular? Why not fascism or communism? Even if these questions are answered, the relationship of these political ideologies to practical politics in Canada, to political parties and elections, is still unclear. We have a Liberal Party, a Conservative Party, and, in the NDP (in part, at least), a socialist party, but we have no Nationalist Party, though we have politicians of various stripes who call themselves nationalists.

The answers to these questions must be sought in the past. Our ideologies, like our political parties or any other part of our political tradition, did not simply appear, full-grown, in their present form. Rather, they developed from the slow marriage of European ideas and the Canadian environment, an environment that at first was a clean slate, but became progressively more complicated and sophisticated as the marriage bore fruit. This process of development is similar in its pattern to the theory of Canadian economic development propounded by the Canadian economic historian, Harold Innis.[1] He argued that successive waves of European technology acting on the Canadian environment had produced a progressively more complex and distinctive Canadian economic system. Thus, the techniques of making felt hats from beaver pelts produced the fur trade; the development of fishing vessels and the process of salting cod led to the growth of the fisheries; and the introduction of railway technology made possible the development of the wheat fields of the West.

These few examples are sufficient to make the point that these imported techniques produced, over time, a distinctive Canadian economy. The process was cumulative and self-perpetuating; the influence of external developments declined. Application of railway technology, for example, raised domestic demand for iron and steel products and encouraged the growth of a Canadian steel industry. A similar process is evident in the history of political ideas in Canada. Successive waves of immigrants brought different political ideas with them. Each contributed to the ideological richness of Canada and each affected the other, creating a distinctive Canadian matrix of political ideas. It is necessary, then, to establish which political ideas came to our shores, and which took root. This is not a simple question, for the reception of a political idea depends not only on its inherent ideal characteristics, but also on contemporary social and economic circumstances. To give an extreme example: Marxist socialism had very little appeal in the predominantly rural and prosperous Ontario of late Victorian times; but in the Ontario of the 1930s, increasingly urban and industrial, and stricken by the Great Depression, it was a very real option.

THE HARTZ THESIS

The "raw materials" of the Canadian political tradition, the European political ideas brought to Canada, did not simply replicate the political traditions of their homelands for two reasons. In the first place, many settlers came to Canada at times when the political ideas of their home countries were in nothing like their present form, from pre-revolutionary France or pre-industrial Britain. In the second place, those who chose or were forced to emigrate did not constitute a perfect microcosm of their home countries. Louis Hartz[2] has made this point in *The Founding of New Societies*: the new countries thrown off by Europe were only, in ideological terms, "fragments" of their parent societies. Hartz's argument is that the European countries exhibited a diversity of ideological beliefs, which produced a dialectical process of development in their political ideas. Europe entered the modern age dominated by feudal, or, to use the British term, tory, ideas about the nature of society. The tory viewed society as a collective whole, an organic unity within which different groups or classes of people had distinct but harmonious functions. One group, the aristocracy, by its education, experience, birth and property was especially fitted to govern, and all classes in society benefitted if it was allowed to carry out its proper role. The proper attitude for the rest of society was obedience and for the aristocracy, a responsibility for the welfare of those over whom they ruled. This tory ideology directed attention to collectivism, the group rather than the individual, and privilege or hierarchy as the salient features of social and political life.

By the seventeenth century, new political ideas were developing in Europe and came into conflict with feudal or tory ideas. Hartz labels them "bourgeois" or "liberal" (the more common British term); their distinguishing characteristic was their emphasis on the importance of the individual and the necessity and benefits of individual freedom. These ideas had a close relationship both with Protestantism and with capitalism. Protestant theology exalted the individual and ultimately solitary nature of the relationship of man to God and denied the authority of institutions such as the Catholic Church. Similarly, capitalism encouraged individual enterprise and initiative and rebelled against collectivist economic organizations such as the medieval guilds and collectivist economic theories such as mercantilism. Politically, liberal individualism found its clearest expression in the writing of Thomas Hobbes and John Locke, who argued that society was essentially an atomistic collection of individuals, and that government was a device to serve primarily individual ends, rather than group or collective ends. Along with this went arguments for individual freedom of conscience, expression and so on. Thus, liberalism is characterized by the ideas of individuality and liberty.

Hartz's point is that liberalism did not supersede or eliminate, but co-existed with, feudal or tory ideas. The resulting conflict of ideas was fruitful in two respects. First, because neither became completely dominant, driving out all competing ideas, the way to further development was left open. Second, the stock of "raw materials" for future growth was that much greater. Out of this conflict of toryism and liberalism developed socialism, the youngest of the European ideologies. It joined elements of both its warring parents, the collectivism, or concern for the communal or group aspects of human life, of the feudal or tory tradition, and the liberal ideas of individuality and liberty in the form of the idea of equality. Thus, the socialist believes the moral liberty and equality of individuals requires not only the liberal expedient of removing external restraints on individual action, but also, the collective action of individuals, acknowledging their fundamental equality and working through collective entities, the union, the co-operative, the local community, and pre-eminently, the state, which increasingly organize life in a modern industrial society.

Hartz argues that the new societies, which developed from European settlement such as the United States and Canada, did not reproduce in themselves this ideological diversity and the consequent process of development. For example, New France was settled at a time when "feudal" or collectivist and hierarchical views were dominant in France, particularly among the peasants and artisans from whose ranks the settlers were drawn. Liberal political thought developed later in

France, after emigration to New France had ceased, and so the process of ideological conflict and development was blocked in New France by the absence of liberal ideas.

Hartz's original thesis was directed (in *The Liberal Tradition in America*) more specifically to the United States. His conclusion that the United States possessed a single, dominant ideology, liberalism, is supported by two main arguments. The first is that the early settlers in the American colonies were predominantly liberal or bourgeois in their political beliefs. Indeed, the individualistic and sometimes libertarian views they held about religion and government were often the cause of their departure from England, which, in the seventeenth century, was still powerfully affected by tory beliefs. Thus, the society that developed in the United States represented in the main only a "fragment" of its parent society: the liberal or bourgeois fragment. Furthermore, such non-liberal elements as were present were largely driven out at the Revolution and routed in the Civil War — the Tory Loyalists in the former, the quasi-feudal Southern planter aristocracy in the latter.

The second argument is that ideological uniformity, once achieved, is self-perpetuating by creating a climate of ideological intolerance that repels all foreign ideas. Liberal ideas of individualism, economic free enterprise and suspicion of government intervention so dominated the United States that they became an integral part of the American national identity. That is, to be an American came to mean accepting liberalism as part of the "American Way of Life." Conversely, to believe in some other system of political ideas was to reject the United States itself; in short, to be un-American. This, Hartz argues, placed irresistible social pressures on new immigrants to conform to these liberal ideas and to abandon tory ideas of privilege and tory and socialist ideas of collectivism.

Hartz's argument goes a long way to explain the dominance of liberal individualist thought in the United States, though there are other factors, such as the incongruity of privilege or hierarchy in a frontier society, and the immense natural wealth of the country, which allowed it to proceed through the early stages of economic growth without great hardship for its citizens. His argument makes intelligible the hostility, verging at times on paranoia, that American society has demonstrated toward socialism, from McCarthyite witch hunts in the 1950s to Ronald Reagan's label of Russia as an "evil empire." It also explains the desire of the United States to "export" American ideas and institutions to totally dissimilar cultures in the four corners of the earth. These are the reactions of a culture that cannot accept non-conforming ideas, nor understand why others would willingly do so. The confidence with which this was done, which Canadians sometimes reproach themselves for not having imitated, reflects the certainty of Americans that no alternative was worth considering. The increasing realization during the twentieth century that other societies are profoundly different, and prefer to remain so, has been a traumatic experience for Americans.

Some writers have attempted to apply without modification or adaptation the Hartzian analysis to Canada and to argue that Canada is virtually the same, ideologically, as the United States. The leading exponents of this view are Hartz's collaborator in *The Founding of New Societies*, Kenneth Macrae, David Bell and Lorne Tepperman[3] who see Canada as basically uniform in ideology, sharing with the United States a common North American liberalism. A Canadian historian who likewise stressed the essential sameness of American and Canadian political values, but outside the Hartzian framework, was the late F.H. Underhill.[4] Although Underhill was a principal author of the *Regina Manifesto* of 1933, with its call for the eradication of capitalism expressed in Marxist rhetoric, it became evident that the benchmark he preferred for evaluating political change was the reformist capitalism of the Roosevelt New Deal. This essentially continentalist way of thinking about North America is also shared by many Canadian economists and businessmen, who see Canada not as a single economic unit, but as a series of regions, each of which is part of a transborder north-south economic unit. Thus, the "natural" economic affinity of the Maritimes is with New England; Ontario and Quebec with New York and the Midwest; the Prairies with the American prairie states; and British Columbia with California.

THE HOROWITZ THESIS: THE UNIQUENESS OF CANADA

This continentalist approach is opposed by a vigorous nationalist school, which concentrates not only on those aspects of Canadian life that are shared with the United States, but those that are distinctive to Canada. One of the most important of these is the Canadian relationship to Europe and to European ideas. We shall look first at a nationalist application of the Hartz thesis to Canada. As we have seen, Hartz argued that American society is completely permeated by the ideology of liberal individualism, and Macrae extended this judgement to Canada, arguing that it, too, was a liberal "fragment," though with "minor imperfections." Gad Horowitz's now-famous reply[5] was that these flaws or imperfections in the otherwise pure liberalism of Canada were neither minor nor insignificant, but sufficient to invalidate Macrae's argument and to point to a specifically Canadian political identity.

Hartz argued that the United States "purified" itself ideologically by escaping from, or expelling, its tory elements and thus inoculated itself against the future development of socialism. In Canada, Horowitz saw evidence of tory and socialist ideas reflecting ideological diversity closer to that of Western Europe. These rivals do not have to dominate or to displace liberalism, for all the Western nations have strong strains of liberal individualism in their political culture. What distinguishes the United States is the exclusive position of the liberal ideology, and what differentiates Canada, in a North American context, is the existence of a meaningful ideological diversity.

It is not difficult to find sources for tory ideas in Canadian history. Leaving aside French Canada (with which Horowitz does not deal), there are the Loyalists who rejected the American Revolution, and the massive wave of British immigration in the nineteenth century. Horowitz's point is that although these people were by no means unalloyed tories, they were sufficiently unliberal[6] to produce a different political culture. The evidence Horowitz cites is persuasive: Such well-known features of Canadian history as the absence of the lawless, individualistic and egalitarian American frontier; the preference for Britain rather than the U.S. as a societal model; the weaker emphasis on social equality; the greater acceptance by individuals of the facts of economic inequality, social stratification, and hierarchy.[7]

This, in turn, contributes to the greater willingness of Canadians (compared to Americans) to defer to constituted authority and to the value that is placed on the maintenance of order and stability in society (witness the general reaction of the Canadian public to the October crisis of 1970 and the proclamation of the *War Measures Act*, which ranged from passive acceptance to enthusiastic support for the Trudeau government's actions).

These tory ideas have also contributed to the long-standing Canadian willingness to use the power of government to effect certain common goals or objects; and, moreover, to use it with equanimity and often with enthusiasm. This can be seen in a multitude of instances from the railway and canal building of the last century to the initiation in more recent times of public enterprises such as the CBC, Air Canada, Ontario Hydro and Petro-Canada.

This difference in attitude is crucial and cannot simply be explained away, as Macrae attempts to do, by arguing that Canada is smaller and poorer than the United States and cannot indulge itself in fixed principles on this sort of issue. The question of government intervention in economic matters has simply not been a matter for deep heart-searching by Canadians because of a differing set of political values. This is underlined by George Grant's observation that a good deal of such government intervention has been undertaken by Conservative governments (Ontario Hydro, the CNR, the Bank of Canada, and the CBC, for instance); for the Conservative Party is the resting place for tory influences, and such action on its part is proof of their existence. Furthermore, it highlights the differences with the United States because American conservatism is diametrically opposed on this point: it is inconceivable that such policies would be tolerated, let alone adopted, by Ronald Reagan.

The presence of this tory strain in Canada in turn contributed to the growth of socialism in Canada, a development that further set us apart from the Americans.

This, Horowitz argues, happened in two ways. On the one hand, the existence of a collectivist toryism provided the potential within the Canadian political culture for a collectivist socialism.

> Since toryism is a significant part of the political culture, at least part of the leftist reaction against it will sooner or later be expressed in its own terms, that is in terms of class interests and the good of the community as a corporate entity (socialism) rather than in terms of the individual and his vicissitudes in the competitive pursuit of happiness (liberalism).[8]

On the other hand, it helped to keep Canada open to imported socialist ideas because through collectivist toryism, socialism had a ready-made point of contact, or introduction, to Canadian society. Socialism was not an exotic foreign growth; it "fitted" into the Canadian ideological structure. Because of the collectivist element in toryism, Canadians were receptive to collectivist approaches, albeit in a different form. This was important, because socialist ideas had no such point of reference in the United States; they were, as we have seen, regarded and rejected as profoundly un-American. To become true Americans, immigrants had to check their socialist ideas at the Statue of Liberty, so to speak. In Canada, on the other hand, socialist ideas were already potentially present. In addition, the fact that liberalism did not reign unchallenged in Canada prevented the identification of ideology and nation that prevailed to the South, and left the way open for further ideological development.

Horowitz attempts to assess the relative weight of the two factors by using Hartz's notion of "congealment." Hartz argued, and Horowitz accepted, that a new society will "congeal" or gel at some point, forming a peculiar national mould, which would assimilate all future imports of ideas to its shape. The idea is an obvious reflection of the American experience of an ideologically intolerant and assimilationist society; it is applied uncritically by all the Hartzians to Canada. In fact, there is no reason why any society should necessarily "congeal" at any particular point, although when a society is in its formative stages it may be more open to outside influences. We feel that this openness is a matter of degree, however, and that while Canada is a good deal more settled in this respect than it was in the early nineteenth century it is still open to outside ideological influences.

This is relevant to our discussion of Canadian socialism because the notion of congealment, as used restrictively by Macrae, tends to rule out any outside ideological influence after the early nineteenth century, and as used more indeterminately by Horowitz, means nothing at all. It is best forgotten: excluding cataclysmic changes, succeeding imports of political ideas, like imports of technologies, will probably have lesser effects on a country that has been developing over a long period of time than on an entirely undeveloped one; but it is unlikely they will have no effects at all. The United States, with the peculiar mechanism it has erected to sift out non-liberal ideas, is distinctly atypical in this respect in the Western world. Thus, Canadian socialism has profited not only from the openness of the Canadian political culture to collectivist as well as to individualist politics, but from a continuous influx of immigrants, predominantly but by no means exclusively British, bearing collectivist ideas and loyalties, an influx which has had as much effect in the 1950s as in the 1850s.[9]

It might be useful at this point to sum up what we have learned about ideologies in Canada. In the first place, we have identified three distinct ideological approaches to politics that Canada has inherited from Europe: liberalism, organized around the two concepts of individuality and liberty; toryism, built upon collectivism and hierarchy or privilege; and socialism, sharing tory collectivism, but seeking to replace privilege by equality. Second, we have seen that all three have found permanent, albeit unequal, places in the Canadian political culture. Third, we have seen how this ideological diversity sharply distinguishes Canada from the United States.

Horowitz was not the first theorist to recognize the significant ideological differences between Canada and the United States, though in our view his adaptation of Hartzian ideas provides by far the most satisfactory explanation. Seymour Martin Lipset, an American social theorist whose study of prairie socialism[10] investigated one facet of Canada's ideological diversity, used the ideas of the American sociologist Talcott Parsons to characterize Canadian society as both more collectivist and more elitist than its American counterpart.[11] His catalogue of the products of this recognizably tory strain includes greater deference to authority figures and particularly to public authorities such as the courts and police, greater tolerance for dissent, less aggressiveness and optimism in business and other facets of economic life, a peaceful and orderly frontier, less lawlessness and corruption and greater ethnic cohesiveness and particularism. All this is remarkably similar to Horowitz's evidence for a tory strain in Canada.

Lipset correctly locates the roots of these differences in the Loyalist influence and its counter or anti-revolutionary tradition, though he appears to ignore the importance of the ideas brought by nineteenth-century immigrants from Britain. He places considerable emphasis on the Canadian religious tradition, dominated by hierarchically-organized churches closely related to, though formally separated from, the state. Lipset took a sympathetic view of Canada, finding the country particularly appealing because of its toleration of dissent arising from its diverse and generally anti-populist tradition.

Similar evidence came from Canadian sociologist S.D. Clark,[12] who characterized Canada as the "bureaucratic society," of which the typical member is not, as in the United States, an entrepreneur but an office-holder. Stability and order, provided by large-scale bureaucratic organization, replace the American values of competition and egalitarianism. Clark's analysis agrees with Horowitz's in certain of its conclusions, and with regret, for Clark clearly prefers the American values to Canadian; but this preference of Clark's gives us all the more reason to accept his evidence about the nature of Canada.

At least one notable attempt has been made to explain these distinctive features of Canadian political culture while denying any real ideological distinctiveness.[13] Tom Truman's argument is that the perceived differences between Canada and the United States are due to a combination of inherited institutional factors and the openness of Canadian society, which arose on account of long-standing British connections. Greater social order and government intervention in Canada are products of a centralized and strong system of cabinet government, and Canadian socialism was accepted because, as a British import, it could not be rejected.

We disagree with Truman's conclusions, because we think that he ignores the extent to which political institutions themselves embody and reflect political ideas, and perpetuate them as they accustom participants in the political system to the values that are implicit in the institutions. Modern cabinet government, for example, with its executive dominance over the legislature, draws deeply on tory values going back to Elizabethan times.[14] The tory ideas that a government derives its existence and legitimacy not primarily from the electorate but, rather, from the Crown, and that concepts of national interest and duty are more important than passing popular majorities are used to justify government actions directly contrary to popular will (for example, on abolishing capital punishment). These attitudes are shaped by the tory collectivist values embedded in our institutions.

Generations of Canadian politicians and voters have learned their political values within these institutions and the implicit tory and collectivist ideas that the institutions embody have restrained the influence of liberal ideas. It is also clear that the values embedded in institutions must be compatible with the values held by society, generally, if these institutions are to endure for any time. The successful operation in Canada of a tory-collectivist constitution for well over a century supports our conclusion that such values are acceptable and legitimate to large numbers of Canadians. We conclude that this system of strong cabinet government and the tradition of state intervention with which it is associated is both an indication and a cause of the ideological diversity we have described.

NATIONALISM — A DEPENDENT IDEOLOGY

Though we have so far only identified three ideologies—liberalism, socialism, and toryism — another ideology, nationalism, has had and is having an important effect on Canadian politics. Nationalism as a consciously thought-out political doctrine is also a European import, yet it draws on sentiments less coherently expressed and more universal: patriotism or xenophobia, for example. Nationalism, too, is less comprehensive in scope than the other ideologies — it provides answers to fewer practical political questions than its broader rivals. Consequently, it is almost always found in combination with one of them. A nationalist in Canada is usually a conservative, liberal, or socialist as well, but the reverse is not necessarily true. Thus, a study of nationalism requires the extraction of nationalist elements from the wider groups of ideas in which they are found. For instance, the Waffle faction within the NDP claimed to be both nationalist and socialist, and the student of Canadian nationalism must disentangle the two for purposes of analysis. This is a particular problem in Canada, because liberalism pervades most areas of political thought and practice to some degree or another and this has led some commentators to lose sight of its competitors, and even to forget that liberalism itself is an ideology.

To understand nationalism, it is important to note the range of nationalist ideas. Nationalism might be provisionally defined as the belief that political boundaries should coincide with the territory occupied by a particular "nationality" or "nation" — in short, belief in the "nation state." Nationalist policies seek either to achieve this end, or to protect it once arrived at. There are two important criteria for distinguishing different varieties of nationalist ideas: one is the means of defining the "nation"; the other the priority that achievement or protection of the nation state, the ultimate nationalist end, is given in relation to other political ends such as equality or liberty.

What might be called classical European nationalism defines the nation in terms of linguistic and cultural uniformity and favours the demands of the nation rather than the individual. English-Canadian nationalism has followed a different path. While flirting in the late nineteenth century with the notion of Canada as a unilingual, anglophone state, it has steadily moved away from this position. The ideal of linguistic unity implied a closer union with one or other of the major English-speaking countries, Britain and the United States, and Canadian nationalists have rejected both. On the contrary, nationalists have come to value Canada's bilingual and multiethnic makeup as a factor that distinguishes Canada, particularly from the United States. In any case, the pursuit of linguistic uniformity would disrupt the foundation of the Canadian state. English-Canadian nationalism has therefore rejected language and turned to political institutions, culture and economic concerns, such as ownership of industry and natural resources, as the focal points of national differentiation. It has also differed from European nationalism by giving the demands of the nation a relatively lower priority than individual concerns. This is not surprising in view of the dominant liberalism of English Canada.

THE SPECIAL STATUS OF QUEBEC

The ethnic uniformity of French Canada is more compatible with the European model, and there has been a strong strain of French-Canadian nationalism stressing linguistic uniformity in Quebec, and greater autonomy for Quebec within Canada. The historical absence of a strong liberal strain in French Canada also allowed a higher priority to be given the ends of the French-Canadian *nation*. This is connected with the process of ideological development in French Canada to which we now turn.

In English Canada, ideologies developed from the interaction over time of waves of immigrant-borne ideas. In French Canada, the last significant franco-phone immigration took place before 1760, and bore a single, "feudal" and conservative set of political ideas. Succeeding ideological influences were foreign or external to French Canada in a way not experienced by the rest of the country. In particular, they were the ideas of a conqueror and were both liberal and Protestant, and so were doubly repugnant to New France's conservative Catholicism. This ensured that their reception would be neither entirely congenial nor their acceptance assured. Thus, the ideological situation in Quebec was rather more like that in the United States or Latin America than in the rest of Canada, with the identification of a particular ideology with the society itself, and consequent intolerance and rejection of differing beliefs. This has a long history in Quebec, from clerical attempts in the nineteenth century to destroy the free-thinking *Rouges*, to Premier Duplessis's *Padlock Law* of 1937, which authorized the closing of premises used by "subversive" groups.

The attempt by Quebec to insulate itself from the rest of British North America was never successful to the same degree as were similar attempts in the United States, for Quebec did not possess the political and economic power necessary to enforce its wishes. It was forced to tolerate an English-speaking minority within its borders and was impelled by a mixture of choice and circumstance to enter into a federal union with an English-speaking majority, both of which were alien in language and ideology. Quebec was unable to escape entirely from the presence of its unwelcome rivals, and the process of ideological development was slower at first and less even in pace.

Economic liberalism, the ideas of individual free enterprise and entrepreneurship, entered Quebec with the British and American merchant community that set itself up after the Conquest (which in turn was merely an outpost of the burgeoning liberal capitalism of Britain and English North America).[15] The conservative, Catholic and rural society of Quebec was brought, however unwillingly, into contact with the dynamic and secular capitalism of English North America. The primary response of Quebec was to reject the new ideas and retreat behind the ramparts of tradition — the so-called "siege" or "fortress" mentality. This was due to the understandable distaste of a Catholic society for the capitalist ethos, and to differences of attitude and education that made equal participation difficult for French Canadians. In a negative sense, this reaction meant a tenacious defence of Quebec's conservative ideology and values, and a refusal to adapt existing institutions, such as the church-controlled education system, to the new challenge. Thus was perpetuated the long neglect of technical, commercial and scientific education in French Canada. More positively, attempts were made by both church and state to provide a workable alternative to an urban and industrial capitalist society by encouraging agriculture and rural settlement (through the colonization movement of the nineteenth and early twentieth centuries) and by encouraging co-operative collective action, such as the *caisse populaire* (credit union) movement and the Catholic trade-union movement.

Political liberalism, too, fell at first on stony ground in Quebec. The demands of the English minority for representative institutions, granted in 1791, met little francophone response, and the new institutions were used (or abused) by the *Canadiens* for nationalist or conservative ends. The rebellions of 1837 in Upper and Lower Canada are often viewed as attempts to introduce a greater degree of liberal democracy. This is a serious over-simplification. William Lyon Mackenzie and his followers in Upper Canada may have had this aim but the *Patriots* in Lower Canada were fighting not for self-government *per se*, but for freedom from anglophone rule — the immediate issue was merely the occasion presented by circumstances. Later in the century, the *Rouge* group developed, influenced by European liberalism and sharing to some degree its anti-clericalism (though apparently not its religious scepticism). This won it the bitter hostility of the church and effectively prevented it from having any real political success. Political liberalism only achieved respectability in Quebec with Laurier's repudiation of continental liberalism and its anti-religious bias in favour of the more moderate British variety.

In the long run, French Canada was not able to maintain its isolation. Grant has pointed out[16] how difficult it is for a conservative society to defend itself against the dissolvent effects of a dynamic, technologically-sophisticated liberal society, and Quebec had the further disadvantage of possessing only limited political sovereignty. It was able to protect its educational system from technological and liberal values, but was not able to prevent the expansion of the North American economic system into the province. So urbanization and industrialization proceeded apace, a process the French Canadians were not trained to master. The result was the anglophone domination of the Quebec economy, which was a major political issue in Quebec until very recently. The frustration resulting from this situation was one cause of the Quiet Revolution of the 1960s and may still contribute to social and political unrest in Quebec today. The triumph of liberal capitalism thus put pressure on French Canada to abandon the "feudal" or conservative ideology of the past, at least as the dominant ideology of Quebec, and to search for a more effective and comprehensive alternative.

One answer to this dilemma was to come to terms with the invader; to accept liberal values, and to develop Quebec as a liberal society like the rest of North America. The leading advocates of this approach are, understandably, Laurier's heirs in the Liberal Party. Intellectual liberals such as Trudeau, Gerard Pelletier and Jean Marchand, who argued for liberal ideas and policies against the Duplessis regime from a political wilderness in the 1950s, came into their own in the late 1960s. Provincial Liberals such as Jean Lesage and Robert Bourassa attempted to integrate Quebec more effectively into North American capitalism, and enabled Quebecers individually to compete on more equal terms by initiating reforms in a wide variety of areas including education, transportation, social welfare schemes and various government initiatives to promote economic development. The remarkable development in the past twenty years of an effective and dynamic business elite in Quebec and the growth of business enterprises owned and managed by francophones is proof of the attraction and effect of this alternative.

These changes were designed to enable the province and its people to participate with the maximum reward in a liberal, capitalist economic system but have not, by any means, signalled the complete triumph of liberalism in Quebec. While anglophone liberals were quick to praise the steps taken in the Quiet Revolution to reduce political corruption, secularize education, stress technical and business training and encourage economic development, they were sometimes shocked by measures that favoured neither individuality nor liberty, the pillars of liberalism. Nationalist policies, which favoured a collectivity, the French Canadian *nation*, have been pursued by all governments in Quebec — Liberal, Union Nationale and Parti Québécois alike. Particularly alarming to anglophone liberals have been the measures to promote the French language, culminating in *Bill 101*, the Charter of the French Language, in 1977. The continuing battle over *Bill 101* and the apparent renewal of the language issue in the late 1980s under the Liberal Bourassa government testify to the continuing strength of collectivism in Quebec society. Growing concern over the effect on the French-Canadian nation of a low birth rate and advocacy of government action to reverse it (such as the financial incentives for large families contained in the 1988 Quebec budget) is another contemporary manifestation of this collectivism. This should not, however, surprise us, for the idea of community or collectivity is, as we have seen, deeply rooted in Quebec's past and has clearly tempered imported liberal ideas.

The continuing effect of the past in French Canada is also evident in the rapid growth of socialism. That socialism should develop in Quebec in reaction to the incursions of liberalism and capitalism is hardly surprising from a Hartzian viewpoint, for socialism is the primary collectivist answer to modern industrial society, and Quebec's stock of political ideas includes a strong collectivist element. This collectivism is deeply embedded in Quebec's institutions: from the earliest days of New France, the government actively intervened on a broad scale in economic affairs; after the Conquest this activity declined, except for promoting colonization, but government action in social and cultural affairs remained. The church, by its nature a collectivist institution, has long encouraged community enterprise, whether in establishing charitable or educational institutions or, in more specifically economic terms, in encouraging land settlement and parish credit unions.[17]

Socialists drew on this collectivist tradition and concluded that state action is the correct response to modern industrial society. Quebec's collectivist past provided receptive and fruitful soil for socialist ideas once the invasion of liberal capitalism had broken the monopoly of the old conservative ideology as the rapid growth of the Parti Québécois in the 1960s attests. The decline in the power of the old "feudal" or conservative ideology has been both rapid and revolutionary. In retrospect, it seems clear that it was the facade that collapsed in the Quiet Revolution of the 1960s — the underlying substance must have already been deeply eroded. This is the only conclusion consistent with the more or less simultaneous collapse in Catholic belief and practice and the position and authority of the church in Quebec, for the foundation of these ideas in Quebec was the church. This decline is a testament to the dissolvent effects of liberal capitalism; it is probably also proof that reliance on power alone cannot save a system that has lost its authority. Whatever its cause, the effects are very clear. The remnants of the *ancien regime*, in the *Union Nationale* or the *Creditiste* movement, are like the inhabitants of a large but ruined mansion, seeking shelter in what remains of their habitation. Their attacks on the "permissive" society, support for authority and order in the community and their populist espousal of the "little man" are but fragmentary reflections of the shattered whole.

Whether, as Grant has wondered (in *Lament for a Nation*), Quebec can survive in the long run as a distinct society after abandoning the Catholic world-view on which it was founded is an open and unresolved question. The *péquiste* Jacques-Yvan Morin (in his introduction to the recently-published French translation of *Lament for a Nation*) has recognized the seriousness of the question but hopes that the collectivist strain in Quebec has been perpetuated in socialism in Quebec and in secular nationalism. Regardless of the ultimate answer, in the shorter term, Quebec has developed a lively, and sometimes explosive, ideological diversity, which is quite outside of any brokerage theory of politics.

THE IMPACT OF THE CHARTER

The system of political ideas Canada has developed as a result of the process we have described is distinctive in North America for its variety and diversity. This diversity has been evident in all three of the major political issues Canada faced in the 1980s: the patriation of the Canadian constitution and adoption of the *Charter of Rights and Freedoms* in 1982, the Meech Lake Accord of 1987 and the Canada-United States Free Trade Agreement ratified in 1988.

The idea of a written, constitutionally-entrenched codification of customary rights such as the Charter is an eminently liberal notion, reflecting the liberal position that individual rights exist independent of any society or government. As the American *Declaration of Independence* argues, men are endowed by their Creator, not by society or government, with certain inalienable rights, which are to be immune from restriction by government or society. The thought that such a constitutional document might be necessary reflects the liberal tendency to distrust government, seeing it as a potential source of undesirable restrictions on individual rights. Hence, Pierre Trudeau's advocacy of the Charter was the product of his liberalism (which we will explore further in Chapter III).

The Charter is not, however, a purely liberal document. First, it reflects the internal ideological divisions within liberalism, especially between business liberalism, seeking to minimize government restriction (especially in the area of economic activity), and welfare liberalism, the "human" rights variant of liberalism, which accepts the restriction of economic liberties in the interests of a more humane society. The original version of the Charter, reflecting the predominance of welfare liberalism in the modern Liberal Party, contained no reference to property rights, as opposed to rights such as freedom of speech or assembly. The Conservative proposal to entrench protection for property rights constitutionally reflected the strain of business liberalism within the Conservative Party, which we will explore more fully in Chapter IV. Initially, the Trudeau government agreed to this addition, perhaps for tactical reasons, but doubtless also because of the perseverance of business liberalism as a minority strain within the Liberal Party. The NDP's hostility clearly reflected both the welfare liberalism in that party, and the socialist fear that any protection of property rights would make the introduction of a more egalitarian society more difficult. The opposition of the NDP and lukewarm support of the Liberals was sufficiently strong to prevent the clause's adoption.

By contrast, the success of the campaign mounted by women's groups to ensure the entrenchment of equality rights, reflects the inherently liberal nature of the demands of the mainstream of the women's movement. The Liberal government, as well as the liberals within both the Conservative Party and the NDP, had little difficulty supporting the measure.

The collectivist strain in Canadian politics was evident in efforts to entrench native-group rights in the constitution. The reluctance of the Trudeau government to do more than guarantee traditional native rights was a product in part of liberal reluctance to recognize such collective rights.

The persistence of collectivism in Canada was also reflected in the entrenchment of other group rights, including rights to denominational schools in some provinces. The original Trudeau proposals would have diminished the position of the provinces by use of the referendum to overcome the opposition of provincial governments to proposed constitutional amendments. This reflected the liberal view that regional or provincial differences were relatively unimportant, given the fundamental uniformity of all people. The more traditional collectivist view that Canada is a federation of provinces and that regional identities and loyalties are legitimate and important was reaffirmed by the unyielding opposition of the federal and provincial Conservatives and the decision of the Supreme Court in the Constitutional Reference Case in 1981 that these values were embedded in the basic constitutional structure of the country.

Although the Charter takes a basically individualistic approach to language rights, it made important concessions to group language rights. Rights to the use of French were not extended uniformly across the country, but were adapted to provincial wishes and local conditions, and within Quebec, rights to have immigrant children educated in English were restricted.

THE MEECH LAKE ACCORD

The debate on the Meech Lake Accord continues the original arguments about the Charter. This is not surprising since the Accord was seen as an attempt to correct certain shortcomings in the 1982 provisions and to overcome the opposition of Quebec, which led it to reject the Charter and the other 1982 constitutional amendments. The thrust of the Accord is to strengthen certain group rights, particularly those of Quebec, but also those of other regions. Hence, the constitutional recognition of Quebec as a "distinct society," the granting to the provinces of certain rights to participate in appointments to federal institutions such as the Senate and Supreme Court and possible restrictions on the federal spending power in relation to shared-cost programs.

The strongest opposition has come from the authors of the Charter, Pierre Trudeau and his former colleagues such as Donald Johnston, and from women's groups opposed to any restriction on the equality rights provision of the Charter. In each case, opposition is ideologically-based. So, paradoxically is some opposition from the labour movement, which sees the Accord as weakening the federal government's ability to intervene in economic and social welfare matters. Labour opposition also reflects the tendency of English-speaking socialists to look for intervention at the federal rather than the provincial level. The Quebec labour movement has supported the Accord, which is compatible both with French-Canadian nationalism and with a socialism that looks to the provincial government as the main source of government intervention.

The support by Quebec women's groups for the Accord underlines the strength of nationalist and collective sentiment in Quebec in contrast to the otherwise strongly liberal cast of the women's movement in Canada. Women are seen as individuals whose rights as individuals have been restricted by gender-based discrimination. While minority socialist voices in the movement might see women as a special part of an oppressed class in a capitalist society, or even as a separate collectivity of its own, they are outside the liberal mainstream. In a liberal society, differences of gender, as of region, are ultimately unimportant. The liberal woman wants to be treated as a man, not as a member of the proletariat or of a separate sisterhood. In Quebec, as the debate on the Accord shows, women at least wish to be treated as members of the French-Canadian nation.

THE FREE TRADE DEBATE

The free trade debate has raised similar issues. The free trade agreement is correctly perceived as reducing in a significant, and perhaps irreversible way, the federal government's ability to intervene in certain areas of economic activity — tariffs, subsidies, energy policy, controls on U.S. investment. Not surprisingly, it is hailed by business liberals. The enthusiasm in the Conservative Party for the trade pact is an indication of the eclipse of the tory element in the party, which could not view it but with considerable misgiving. In the Liberal Party, it is business liberals such as Don Johnston who support the pact. The dominant welfare liberals are generally opposed, because of the limits placed on government intervention. To the socialist element in the NDP, the agreement is anathema — it runs directly contrary to its collectivism and is seen as preventing government action to promote genuine equality. This view is also entirely congruent with welfare-liberal opposition to the agreement. This ideological unity explains the degree of NDP party unity on this issue, notwithstanding regional factors that might have produced some support for the agreement, among western New Democrats, for example.

Because socialists and some welfare liberals have become the main bearers of nationalist ideas in Canada, their opposition to the pact has been redoubled, for it is difficult to reconcile with the nationalist ideal of the primacy of the nation-state and its distinctiveness.

Only in Quebec is this analysis not applicable. Quebec nationalists and socialists tend to view the pact as inoffensive if not desirable — it does not affect the ability of the Quebec government to act, and may even make Quebec more economically independent of the rest of Canada. The powerful force of Quebec nationalism has thus muted the appeal of its collectivist cousins in English Canada on this issue. This, together with the support of business liberalism for free trade, accounts for the relative lack of opposition to free trade in Quebec.

CONCLUSION

We have now examined the origin and nature of political ideologies in Canada and their relevance to the principal issues of the 1980s. Before turning to a detailed examination of each, it is worth noting the criticism that ideological diversity divides and weakens Canada, depriving us of the certainty that fathers decisive action. Like Hamlet, we are "sicklied o'er with the pale cast of thought," unlike the Americans. The answer of the historian or the patriot is simple: the situation is defensible because it is *ours*; some other state of affairs might be preferable, but it would not then be Canada. In short, Canada's existence is its own justification. For the philosopher, who cannot take into account such considerations of contingency or sentiment, the justification is different, and we have suggested it already. Ideologies, we have argued, provide only limited or partial views or explanations of reality. The philosopher seeks a view without partiality or limitation, and this is more likely in a situation of ideological diversity, where the competition of ideas points out the weaknesses of each system, and the absence of an exclusive ideology fosters both questioning and tolerance.

---

1. Innis is best known for such works as *The Fur Trade in Canada* (New Haven: Yale University Press, 1930), *The Cod Fisheries* (Toronto: The Ryerson Press, 1940), *A History of the Canadian Pacific Railway* (1923), *The Bias of Communication*, and *Empire and Communications* (1950).

2. See also Hartz's *The Liberal Tradition in America* (New York: Harcourt, Brace, Jovanovich, 1955).

3. David Bell and Lorne Tepperman, *The Roots of Disunity: A Look at Canadian Political Culture* (Toronto: McClelland and Stewart, 1979).

4. See, for example, Frank H. Underhill, *In Search of Canadian Liberalism* (Toronto: University of Toronto Press, 1960).

5. Gad Horowitz, *Canadian Labour in Politics* (Toronto and Buffalo: University of Toronto Press, 1968), Chapter 1.

6. This is the main point of contention between Bell and Horowitz; in particular, Bell argued that the Loyalists were only Lockean liberals with a sentimental attachment to Britain.

7. Horowitz, p. 10.

8. *Ibid.*, p. 16.

9. For a perceptive and convincing analysis of the effect of settlement patterns on ideological development in a regional context, see Nelson Wiseman, "The Pattern of Prairie Politics," *Queen's Quarterly*, Volume 88:2, Summer 1981, pp. 298–314. Wiseman's explanation of differences in political culture in Manitoba, Saskatchewan and Alberta is an excellent example of the analytical power of the Hartz thesis in general and of the Horowitz adaptation to Canada in particular. While provincial or regional politics are outside the scope of this book, we note that Wiseman's conclusions are generally compatible, and support the conclusions of our analysis.

10. S.M. Lipset, *Agrarian Socialism.*

11. S.M. Lipset, "Revolution and Counterrevolution: Canada and the United States," in Thomas Fond, ed. *The Revolutionary Theme in Contemporary America* (Lexington: University of Kentucky Press, 1965), pp. 21–64.

12. S.D. Clark, "Canada and the American Value System," *La Dualité Canadienne à L'Heuve des Etats Unis* (Quebec: Les Presses de L'Universite Laval), pp. 93–192.

13. T. Truman, "A Critique of S.M. Lipset's Article: Value Differences, Absolute or Relative: The English Speaking Democracies," *CJPS*, IV:4, 497–525.

14. See S.H. Beer, *Modern British Politics* (London: Faber, 1965).

15. For an interesting, if heavily coloured, view of this system, see Pierre Vallières, *White Niggers of America*, translated by Joan Pinkham (Toronto: McClelland and Stewart, 1971), pp. 123–142.

16. In George Grant, *Lament for a Nation* (Toronto: McClelland and Stewart, 1965).

17. *The Manifesto of Le Parti Acadien* (Petit Rocher, N.B., 1972) in New Brunswick is a classic example of this mixture of traditional collectivism and socialism.

CANADIAN LIBERALISM

INTRODUCTION

By the late eighteenth century, liberal political ideas were firmly entrenched in the English-speaking world. The liberal beliefs in individual freedom and the primacy of the individual over the collectivity had triumphed in the American colonies and were elegantly encapsulated in the American *Declaration of Independence*. In Britain, liberal ideas were increasing in political influence and were being reinforced by persuasive arguments in favour of economic individualism like Adam Smith's *Wealth of Nations* (1776).

The ideological conversation, which now forms an established part of the Canadian political tradition, began with the Conquest. Not only did British policy guarantee religious toleration in the new colony of Quebec, but there was immediate pressure from the growing British and American merchant community for the establishment of more liberal political institutions. Although the political ideas that the English-speaking merchants and settlers brought with them in the late eighteenth and early nineteenth centuries were, as Horowitz has argued, not exclusively liberal, they were predominantly so. Even the United Empire Loyalists, as we shall argue in the next chapter, were tories who had accepted the Whig principles of 1688.

These liberal ideas at once ran against two main obstacles. First, liberals were frustrated by the form of colonial administration the British North American colonies enjoyed at the time, which placed executive power in the hands of an appointed governor and council who exercised it without responsibility to the popularly-elected assembly. This lack of popular control was perceived as an infringement of the liberties of the citizen, and groups of "Reformers" emerged in the colonial assemblies seeking greater local control of the executive; these men were the ancestors of the Liberal Party.

The second obstacle was the social, religious and political ideas of the French Canadians. Here, also, a direct ideological clash occurred. The *Canadiens* possessed deeply conservative or feudal ideas and were simply not all that interested in individual liberty. While English-speaking liberals wanted reform to free themselves from local oligarchies and imperial government policies, which hampered individual liberty (such as the attempt to establish the Anglican Church), the French-speaking wanted control over the colonial government to protect the collective interests of French Canadians. This often conflicted with the pursuit of individual liberties by English Canadians. For example, the French majority in the legislature of Lower Canada obstructed efforts by English Canadians to further economic development, and persisted in supporting a *de facto* establishment of the Roman Catholic Church, which liberals saw as an infringement of individual Protestant rights and an improper exercise of the power of the state.

This clash of French social conservatism and English liberalism helped to bring about the division of the colony of Quebec in 1791 into Upper and Lower Canada but this did not fully solve the problem, for an English minority remained in Lower Canada. English liberals were thus placed in a paradoxical situation, for the achievement of the liberal goal of more local self-government would, in Lower Canada, result in the rule of the non-liberal French. The racial conflict to which these ideological differences contributed came to a violent head in the rebellions of 1837, and resulted in the subsequent mission and report of Lord Durham. The insurrections and Durham's reflections upon them bear examination for the light they shed on the nature and subsequent development of Canadian liberalism, as well as the immediate antecedents of the Liberal Party.

THE REBELLIONS OF 1837
AND THE DURHAM REPORT

In Durham's view the troubles in Canada arose from an ideological struggle between the French, an "uninstructed, inactive, unprogressive people" in an "old and stationary society"[1] and the English, representing the "liberal and enlightened movement," of "a new and progressive world."[2] Durham's sympathies, as a prominent English liberal, were clearly on the side of the English minority who sought changes in land tenure and a more comprehensive program of public works to give freer rein to the individual initiative and enterprise valued by the English settlers with their liberal ideas.

Durham's aim was to create an ideologically uniform colony. To do so he would have to persuade the imperial government to destroy the profoundly con-

servative society of Quebec, based on French political, economic and social institutions dating from the seventeenth century, which "more than those of any
other European nation, [were] calculated to repress the intelligence and freedom
of the great mass of the people."[3] Durham was clear that "the sympathies of the
friends of reform are naturally enlisted on the side of sound amelioration which
the English minority in vain attempted to introduce into the antiquated laws of
the Province."[4]

The English "immigrant and enterprising population" had quickly secured a
dominant position in the commercial life of the province and a strong position in
its agriculture and they naturally[5] sought, according to Durham, a government
whose chief business it was "to promote, by all possible use of its legislative and
administrative powers, the increase of population and the accumulation of property."[6] But this conflicted ideologically with the more static and conservative
views of the French, who saw Quebec "not as a country to be settled, but as one
already settled" and who preferred its government "to guard the interest and feelings of the present race of inhabitants."[7]

The reaction of the English population to the conservatism of the French Canadians shows how widely they shared liberal assumptions. Faced with a choice
between a liberal polity — responsible government — that would only serve to
protect and perpetuate a static, non-liberal society, and a non-liberal polity that
nonetheless promised liberal ends, the English of Lower Canada unhesitatingly
chose the lesser evil and made "common cause with a government which was at
issue with the majority on the question of popular rights."[8] Their predicament was
all the greater in comparison with Upper Canada, which did not face this ideological division over the nature of society.

The Upper Canadians largely agreed that society would be organized to secure
a high degree of individual liberty and enterprise, and the various groups in the
legislature there had generally co-operated, in spite of lesser ideological differences, to enact measures directed to this end. Without a common ethnic and
ideological opponent, English-speaking Upper Canadians were more concerned
with lesser distinctions between tory and liberal, which had been pushed into the
background in Lower Canada. These distinctions were not unimportant; on the
contrary, they are, as Horowitz argued, the source of a good deal of Canada's
ideological diversity. But they must be seen in the context of a strong and per-
sistent substratum of liberalism, clearly discernible in the English settlers' support
for a society that would allow them to employ their initiative and energies to the
greatest possible extent. The presence of liberal ideas is hardly surprising, given
the strength of liberalism in the United States and Britain, whence the English-
speaking population originated, and gives a distinctive flavour to both conservatism and socialism in this country, as we shall argue in some detail when we
consider those ideologies.

Ideological and ethnic conflict in Lower Canada pushed the English there into an equivocal position, for they opposed the extension of personal liberty in the political sphere in the form of responsible government, which would place power in the hands of the conservative French majority. In Upper Canada, a general consensus on economic development allowed more subtle differences to come to the fore on specifically political issues like responsible government. A small group, composed of longer-settled and more wealthy residents, and known popularly as the Family Compact, dominated the government and enjoyed a privileged position in the colony:

> The bench, the magistracy, the high offices of the Episcopal Church, and a great part of the legal profession are filled by the adherents of this party; by grant or purchase, they have acquired nearly the whole of the waste lands of the Province; they are all powerful in the chartered banks, and, shared among themselves almost exclusively all offices of trust and profit.[9]

The most visible sign of this was in the attempts to establish the Anglican Church by endowing it with large tracts of strategically placed land, the Clergy Reserves.

Many in the colony felt that such privilege was a denial of political liberty, for it effectively excluded them from full participation in government: hence their demand that the government should be responsible to the legislature (and hence responsive to the wishes of the majority party) and their opposition to an established church. Despite the support of the greater part of the population for some reform, Mackenzie's rebellion of 1837 was a dismal failure, for only a small and extremist minority wished to import the American practices of direct election of judges and the executive to increase popular control of government, and were willing to resort to rebellion to obtain it.

The majority took a more moderate position, favouring responsible government on the British model, but wishing neither to imperil the imperial connection by rebellion nor to contribute to the "revolutionizing"[10] of the province by overly radical measures for popular control. They preferred to "assimilate the Government of Upper Canada, in spirit as well as in form, to the Government of England, retaining an executive sufficiently powerful to curb popular excesses, and giving to the majority of the people, or to such of them as the less liberal would trust with political rights, some substantial control over the administration of affairs."[11] George Brown, for example, one of the founders of the Liberal Party and an important Reform figure from the late 1840s, was bitterly opposed to any extension of American-type radical democracy to Canada. His experience of such measures in New York led him to state that the newspaper he intended to found in Toronto would be "thoroughly conservative";[12] conservative, that is, by American standards.

This conservative streak has not been uncommon in Canadian liberals, and is undoubtedly one reason why other liberal movements, like the Progressives, have sprung up outside the Liberal Party, and why some liberals continue to find their political home in the NDP. It is significant that this tendency to moderation was brought largely by British immigrants like Brown and Alexander Mackenzie, men who reflected something of the ideological diversity of British society. Their ideological stance found fertile soil in a land that had attracted so many of their compatriots and which, partly as a consequence, had a strong conservative strain. Horowitz has remarked on these centrist, middle of the road tendencies of a liberal party in an ideological spectrum, which provides it with enemies on both left and right, and which, correspondingly, limits its freedom of action. It has a long history in Canada, from the rebellion of 1837 to the vacillations of the Trudeau government in the early 1980s between conservative monetarism and liberal Keynesianism.

THE ORIGINS OF THE LIBERAL PARTY

The Union of Upper and Lower Canada in 1841 led to a curious alliance between the Reformers and the conservative French Canadian *Bleus*, in an attempt to curb the privileges of the Family Compact and its equivalent in Lower Canada, the Chateau Clique. Despite the rhetoric at many a Reform banquet, this alliance remained a marriage of convenience, for the aims of the partners were at ideological opposites. The natural allies of the *Bleus* appeared to be the English-Canadian Tories, but two factors stood in the way of this coalition. In the first place, the English never entirely lost their suspicions that the French were disloyal to the British connection. In the second, they were divided on the question of responsible government. For the English Tories, it meant an end to at least some of their privileges; for the *Bleus*, it allowed the establishment of their own system of French and Catholic privilege.

With the accomplishment of responsible government in 1848-1849, the rationale for the Bleu-Reform alliance was undermined. The early 1850s saw a fundamental realignment of political forces that laid the foundations for the present Liberal and Conservative Parties. The question that brought matters to a head was the issue of the separation of church and state.

The Reformers viewed state churches as infringements on the liberty of conscience, and supported voluntaryism, the principle that each church or sect should be supported in all its activities solely by the voluntary aid of its adherents. By 1850 the Reformers had largely defeated attempts to establish the Anglican Church in Canada West, when they were faced with a powerful attack from another quarter. Demands from Roman Catholics for a Catholic school system in Canada West and for public incorporation of a variety of Catholic institutions in Canada East were met with warm support from the majority of French-Canadian members of the legislature. The support for these measures from their erstwhile allies in Canada East was disturbing to many of the Reformers, but hardly surprising in view of their conservative and Catholic disposition. What made it particularly galling was that the most contentious issue, that of separate schools in Canada West, was being decided largely by the solid French bloc from Canada East, who held a powerful position in the legislature of the United Province, where seats were divided equally between the two Canadas (despite the now-superior population of Canada West). To their protests against separate schools, the reformers again took up the cry for political reform, this time for representation by population.

Protest against domination of the nominally Reform government by the conservative French came first from the more radical Clear Grits of Canada West. They included the more extreme radicals from 1837, and their agitation for American-style democracy at first alienated Reformers like Brown. The strength of the church-state issue was so great, however, that many of the English Reformers, Brown at their head, finally broke with the Reform government. When the crisis surrounding the disintegration of the last Reform government (the Morin-Hincks ministry) cleared in 1854, a new political configuration had appeared. The conservative *Bleus* were allied with English conservatives, led by John A. Macdonald, and with some of the moderate Reformers who had been satisfied by the institution of responsible government in 1849 in the Liberal-Conservative Party, which today exists as the Progressive Conservative Party.

This was opposed by another coalition, liberal in policy, and soon to be Liberal in name. United by a common commitment to individual equality of status and opportunity expressed in their opposition to any church-state link and support for "Rep. by Pop." were two unequally matched partners. In Canada West, the Clear Grits and many of the English Reformers, strongest in Western Ontario, provided most of the party's support. Although the Grits' support for separation of church and state was carried over into the new Reform party, other aspects of their radicalism were muted by moderates like Brown, who maintained his opposition to any policy of radical democracy. The centrist, middle of the road position established by Brown and his supporters has remained a hallmark of the Liberal Party to this day.

This group from Canada West was joined with English Reformers from Canada East and a group of French Canadian radicals, the *Rouges*. These were the descendants of the *Patriotes* of 1337, and Papineau himself for a time was their leader. Their position in some ways was similar to that of the Clear Grits. They favoured more radical, American-style political reform and opposed any church-state connection.[13] They were very much a minority group in French Canada and were bitterly opposed by the church and much of the population. This weakness posed a serious problem for the Liberal Party, which was not solved until Laurier's time.

It would be wrong to suggest that the division of 1854 was only a product of ideological differences, for more pragamatic concerns also existed.[14] Nevertheless, we are arguing that clear ideological divisions did exist, and that they played an important role in this realignment. The two main principles on which the liberal ideology was based were the commitment to liberty — freedom from restriction — and the related belief in individualism — the desire for a society in which individual initiative, opportunity and enterprise were given the fullest possible scope. These continued to guide Reform politics after 1854. This is particularly evident in the liberal response to the constitutional problem in the Province of Canada. The Reformers of Canada West chafed under the rule of conservative governments who owed their existence to the support of the Bleus and who supported separate denominational schools in Canada West.

The liberal Reformers also opposed the tendency of the Conservatives to meddle in economic matters which, by orthodox liberal economic doctrine, ought to have been left to the natural laws of economics. Reformers thus opposed the sharp increase in protective tariffs in 1859 because it would tend to channel the import trade of Canada West through Montreal, rather than through its "natural" and cheaper route in the United States.[15] Similarly, they supported the Reciprocity Agreement of 1854. The liberals in Canada West objected that the conservative willingness to suborindate economic rationality to politics favoured the sectional interest of Canada East and threatened the economic liberties of the inhabitants of the western section of the province. This commitment to *laissez-faire*, and the desire to maintain close economic ties with the United States as the "natural" market for Canada, has continued in various degrees in the modern Liberal Party.

The platform of the Reform Party (which quickly adopted the name Liberal) for the first Dominion elections in 1867 asserted that it was the "duty" of the Canadian people to "cultivate the most friendly relations with the neighbouring people of the United States, and especially to offer every facility for the extension of trade and commerce between the two countries."[16]

THE LIBERALS AND CONFEDERATION

The Liberals' sympathy for continentalism and the rejection of any comprehensive economic program (save free trade) was connected with Reform support for sectional rights and opposition to the existing union of the Canadas, which subjected them to the rule of a French-dominated Conservative majority. The initial reaction of the Reformers to the union had been that of Lord Durham, to assimilate the *Canadiens* and cement the union with cultural and ideological uniformity. Twenty years of experience had taught the Reformers tolerance, or at least convinced them that the French were too tough to swallow, and the Liberals abandoned simple political unification[17] as a solution by itself.

Instead, the Liberals sought to replace the union of 1841 with a looser, federal union, which would grant its constituent parts autonomy over local matters. The exact nature of the new federation was a matter of some contention in Liberal ranks. There was a strong desire to maximize provincial independence to allow the farmers and businessmen of Canada West to exploit the resources of the West. These Liberals saw the new national union as a chance to enhance the opportunities for individual enterprise and profit. At the same time, there was a streak of nationalism among Reformers like Brown, which produced the vision of a new continental nation and moderated the demand for decentralization. Thus, Reform proposals for a very loose confederation with an amorphous "joint authority"[18] to deal with matters common to two virtually autonomous states were modified to the point where Brown, at the Quebec Conference in 1864, virtually agreed with Macdonald that the provincial governments were to be merely quasi-municipal bodies. This mixture of nationalism and liberalism in Brown's thinking is but another example of the way in which practical politics tend to be not unideological, but ideologically fuzzy. The tension between the two has never disappeared from the Liberal Party and has remained a permanent feature of Liberal politics in Canada, resurfacing with particular vigour in the 1970s and 1980s.

The final form of Confederation owed a good deal to the force of Ontario separatism and its political expression in the Liberal Party, which doomed plans for a centralized legislative union. Indeed, the desire of Quebec for more autonomy, often cited as an important factor in the making of Confederation, was as much an effect as a cause of the British North America Act. As long as most powers were vested in the central government (as in the union of 1841), the French Canadians had a compelling interest in maintaining their influence in it. This, in turn, required political accommodation with at least some of the English, and an effort to moderate more extreme sectional demands. When this sytem broke down because of the refusal of Western liberals to accept the limitations it imposed on certain of their individual liberties, and provincial governments with significant powers were established, the loyalties of the French were given a compelling new focus.

These nationalist impulses in Canadian Liberalism weakened after 1867, particularly as the party developed provincial organizations, which stimulated separatist leanings. Oliver Mowat, Liberal Premier of Ontario from 1872 to 1896, led a provincial assault on Dominion power that substantially changed the intent, if not the letter, of the original plan of Confederation.

In many respects, Confederation made little difference to the goals of Canadian liberalism or the policies of the Liberal Party. Until Laurier's day the party remained the same loose grouping of Ontario Grits and *Rouges*, with only a leaven of Maritime Reformers and anti-Confederates. Its policies retained the same bias towards an individualistic organization of policies and the removal of restrictions on individual liberty. Alexander Mackenzie and his successor as Liberal leader, Edward Blake, maintained an unyielding opposition to protective tariffs as an unjust restriction on individual liberty. As Blake put it in the 1883 election campaign, "I do not approve of needless restrictions on our liberty of exchanging what we have for what we want, do not see that any substantial application of the restrictive principle has been or can be made in favour of the great interests of the mechanic, the labourer, the farmer, the lumberman, the shipbuilder, or the fisherman." This led the Liberals to oppose not only that part of the National Policy dealing with tariffs but also Macdonald's railway policy. Blake described the contract that the Conservative government made with the CPR for the construction of the transcontinental railway as "improper," "indefensible" and "premature." The political functions of the Canadian Pacific as a means of tying East to West in a national economic system were, for the Liberals, subordinate to the economics of the line. The "true policy," said Blake, was to build only the cheaper and more profitable Prairie section at first, "to give value to our lands and a traffic for the road before contracting for the completion of the eastern and western ends."[19] This, as Joe Wearing has remarked, "was in the best tradition of Gladstonian public frugality"[20] and, it might be added, public acquiescence in the untrammelled operation of a market economy.

The growth of manufacturing, which the protective policy of the Conservatives encouraged, was also disturbing for Liberals. It introduced a collectivist form of social organization: the factory with its system of factory discipline. This ran counter to liberal individualism and created a gap between employer and employed, encouraging class distinctions and conflict. Mackenzie blamed the growth of the "Communistic movement" in certain American centres on protection, which he thought tended to impoverish the working classes at the same time that it enriched a few manufacturers, driving the workers to the conclusion "that the only remedy was an equal distribution of property."[21] Thus, Mackenzie reasoned, interference with the individual's freedom of action through protection eventually produced an equally non-liberal demand to curtail individual freedom by equalizing wealth. This new world of collective action was an unfamiliar one for liberals and eventually required a minor revolution in liberal thinking in the aftermath of the Great War. For the moment, however, Liberals contented themselves with damning protection and, like Brown and Mackenzie, bitterly opposing as limitations on individual liberty collectivist strike action taken by nascent trade unions.

THE CANADA FIRST MOVEMENT
AND GOLDWIN SMITH

The early years of Confederation also witnessed one of the periodic eruptions of the Liberal left in the "Canada First" movement of the 1870s. Radical liberalism was not new in Canada — William Lyon Mackenzie's followers in 1837 and the Clear Grits of Canada West in the 1850s had pushed liberal ideas to extremes. Individual issues such as the church-state question disappeared as time passed, but radical liberal ideas remained, producing the great Progressive revolt during and after the Great War and contributing to the growth in NDP support in the 1960s. This has had important repercussions for Canadian Liberalism, either in swinging more conservative mainstream Liberals to the left, or in the formation of new liberal political groups outside the Liberal Party, such as the Progressive Party in the 1920s. This existed independently only for a short time before it was reabsorbed into the Liberal mainstream, but other radical liberal elements have found a permanent political home outside the Liberal Party by allying with labour and socialist groups in the CCF and NDP.

The Canada Firsters never became more than an intellectual pressure group on the fringes of Canadian party politics. Their ideas had no sectional appeal, and Canadian society in the 1870s was too stable to allow any disruption of the emerging party system. The combination of the new society of the Prairies and the turmoil of war that blessed the Progressives had no parallel for their predecessors in 1874. Nevertheless, the movement is of interest, for the Canada Firsters made an important contribution to the development of Canadian nationalism. They felt that Canada was ready to have a greater say in its affairs and resented restrictions imposed by the imperial relationship. As Edward Blake, who was close to Canada First in sentiment, if not an actual member, put it, Canadians were "four millions of Britons who were not free."[22] The Canada Firsters were not uniform ideologically, though, and the remedies that they proposed varied.

The more conservative favoured imperial federation, aiming to raise Canada's status in the world by increasing its influence and autonomy within the empire. Their contribution is discussed in detail in Chapter VI. These conservative nationalists, seeking greater Canadian participation in imperial affairs, soon parted company with their more liberal allies, who distrusted imperialism in any form and sought to increase Canadian autonomy by reducing to a minimum Canadian ties or participation in the Empire. Their calls for "independence" for Canada were greeted with open hostility from more conservative, pro-British Liberals like Brown and Mackenzie who feared that Canada was in no position at its current stage of development to stand alone against the United States. They also realized that liberal anti-imperialism could not necessarily be equated with nationalism. Opposition to the British connection did not automatically mean support for a stronger Canada. The truth of this proposition can be seen in the thought of

Goldwin Smith, the intellectual mentor of the anti-imperialists in Canada First and a thorough liberal in his social, political and economic views.

A convinced individualist, Smith was bitterly opposed to collectivism in any form, whether the remaining vestiges of toryism in Britain or the rising forces of socialism, which were sounding the "trumpet of industrial war."[23] His dogmatic liberalism led him to advocate complete continentalism. The forces of "geography, commerce, identity of race, language, and institutions" were bound to triumph over sentiment favouring a separate Canadian identity.[24] Canada was an integral part of the liberal and democratic society of North America, despite attempts to import feudal institutions like the monarchy from Europe. Only by integrating with the United States could Canada attain "The glorious era of perfect order and civilization."[25] This continentalist outlook was even more strongly expressed in Smith's economic views. Trade ought, and in the long run was bound, to flow without any political interference, and protective tariffs were a "desperate war against nature."[26] Smith noted the degree to which Canadian voluntary organizations, businesses, magazines and sports were integrated, controlled or influenced by their American counterparts and concluded that English Canada and the United States were "in a state of economic, intellectual, and social fusion."[27]

Smith's analysis of what he called the Canadian Question revealed the weaknesses of this sort of liberalism. He had a contempt for politics, especially in an ideologically diverse country like Canada in which a number of rival ideological understandings intermingled. He revealed the intolerance that Canadian Liberalism has displayed to rival ideological voices. His desire was to crush the diversity that Cartier lauded. This hope comes out clearly in his attitude to Quebec. Annexation, as he knew, would speed the elimination of the non-liberal and ideologically unwelcome conservative society of Quebec. Smith understood well the powerful homogenizing capacity of the dynamic, liberal society of the United States: "Nationalities are not so easily ground down in a small community as they are when thrown into the hopper of the mighty American mill."[28]

Smith was able to carry liberal individualism to its logical end point, untrammelled by the exigencies of practical politics or by nationalist sentiment. His contemporaries in the Liberal Party were inhibited both by sentiment and calculation from going more than part way down the road from liberal anti-imperialism to outright continentalism. The demand for the primacy of economics over politics, seen in Smith's pejorative use of "political," and his contrast of the artificiality of decisions based on political considerations to the naturalness of those based on economic "reality" has remained important in Liberal thinking. Similarly, the demand for greater Canadian autonomy, in terms of separation from Britain and withdrawal from European affairs rather than participation on a basis of greater equality, became a constant theme of Liberal policy.

The goal of economic rationality and greater economic integration with the United States has since been pursued by Laurier in the reciprocity campaigns of 1891 and 1911, by King in the 1938 trade agreement with the United States, by St. Laurent and Howe in the resource export boom of the 1950s and by Pearson in the *Automobile Pact* of 1965. The logical end of such policies, which Smith saw clearly, has either been obscure to, or obscured by, many Liberal politicians, and the conflict between continentalist and nationalist policies has never been fully resolved. The most recent of these conflicts, which began in the 1960s, is still a major theme of Liberal politics in the 1980s, and will be examined at greater length later in this chapter.

WILFRID LAURIER

When Laurier succeeded Blake as Liberal leader in 1887, the party was still a sectional rather than a national force, based largely in Ontario. Perhaps Laurier's greatest political achievement was to broaden the party's support in Quebec and give it a genuinely national basis. The Liberal Party's victory in a province that had in no way abandoned its social and religious conservatism at first sight presents difficulties for any account that purports to see certain ideological positions running through Canadian politics. However, it was precisely the liberalism of the party that enabled it to accommodate Quebec until habit and history hardened the mould.

In particular, the Liberal Party supported provincial rights, historically as a result of the liberal demands of Ontario to be free from the restrictions of a central government in which the more conservative French had considerable influence. This had little attraction for Quebec before Confederation. With Confederation, Quebecers were given a choice between a provincial government they controlled, and a Dominion government now dominated by the English. When the central government acted against the interests of the French minority, the attraction of the provincial government became irresistible. Such a situation occurred in the aftermath of Louis Riel's rebellions and subsequent execution in 1885.

The Liberal platform of 1882 declared: "Our provincial rights are amongst the chief jewels of our constitution; and on their preservation rest the prosperity and the permanence of the Confederation";[29] and that of 1887 called for "full recognition of provincial rights."[30] Even before Laurier became leader, Liberal representation in Quebec had doubled, and the attraction of a French Catholic leader gave the Liberals a majority of seats in the province by the election of 1891.

Laurier sought to hasten the *rapprochement* between the Liberal Party and Quebec by repudiating the electorally damaging anti-clericalism both of the old *Rouges* and of continental European liberalism. In an historic speech to the Club Canadien in Quebec on June 26, 1877, he declared that in Europe there was

...a class of men who give themselves the title of Liberals, but who have nothing of the liberal about them but the name, and who are the most dangerous of men. They are not Liberals; they are revolutionaries....With these men we have nothing in common, but it is the tactics of our adversaries always to identify us with them.[31]

Laurier described the *Rouges* of the 1840s as "young men of great talent and still greater impetuosity of character who not satisfied with wanting to revolutionize their own country...greeted with transports each fresh revolution in Europe." They soon perceived their immense error:

Since that time the party has received new accessions, calmer and more thoughtful ideas have prevailed in it; and, as for the old programme, nothing whatever remains of its social part, while, of the political part, there only remain the principles of the English Liberal party.[32]

In the same speech, Laurier made clear his belief that ideological differences lay at the root of partisan politics: "What is the bond of cohesion to unite each individual of the different groups?...It is the Liberal principle or the Conservative principle....those who were attracted by the charm of novelty or the charm of habit respectively." Laurier's preference for the former was based on a view of human nature that combined the Hobbesian view of human society as a constant struggle between competing individuals, and the more recent meliorist view that human nature was ultimately perfectible and essentially good. The resulting idea that human happiness and perfection were best realized in a society that maximized individual liberty to compete and thereby to make constant change and improvement is fundamental to Canadian liberalism (and Liberalism). Thus, Laurier stated that the principle of liberalism was inherent in

...that desire of happiness with which men are all born into the world, which pursues us throughout life and which is never completely gratified....We only reach the goal we have proposed...to discover new horizons opening up...(Man's) desires will always be greater than his means and his actions will never rise to the height of his conceptions. He is the real Sisyphus of the fable: his work once finished has always to be begun over again.
   This condition...condemns him irrevocably to movement, to progress: our means are limited, but our nature is perfectible....there is always room for improvement of our conditions, for the attainment by a larger number of an easier life.[33]

Here is Hobbes's "restless search for power after power which ceaseth only in death" tempered by Laurier's sunny ways. Laurier's explication of the central dynamic of liberalism should belie any attempt to explain Canadian politics as a mere calculus of interests.

Laurier's skilful disavowal of liberal radicalism was joined with support for provincial rights. This was clearly seen in the Manitoba schools crisis of 1896. Despite intense pressure from Quebec and especially from the Catholic bishops to support central government intervention to protect separate schools, Laurier refused. The Conservative government had "outrageously misinterpreted"[34] the constitution and disregarded provincial rights when it introduced remedial legislation. Laurier's victory in 1896, based on a Liberal sweep in Quebec, vindicated his stand and further lessened the faith of French Canadians in the readiness of the central government to protect their rights.

Although Laurier came into conflict with a series of provincial governments seeking to restrict French language and religious rights, he refused to use the Dominion powers of disallowance or to enact remedial legislation. Thus, in 1905, when the new provinces of Alberta and Saskatchewan were established, he attempted to provide for separate schools but backed down in the face of strong territorial disapproval. Even more explosive was the controversy over the infamous Regulation 17[35] in Ontario (which banned the use of French in Ontario schools), which reached its height in the shadow of the 1917 conscription crisis. Despite this direct attack of Premier Howard Ferguson on French-language rights, Laurier refused to support Dominion intervention: in a speech in Toronto in 1916 he declared himself to be "of the old school of Mowat and Blake, the parent school of Provincial Rights. By that doctrine I stand. The province of Ontario, and the province of Ontario alone, will and shall determine for herself the decision."[36]

The Liberal Party's successful wooing of Quebec was not without its ideological price. Quebec had never shown any sympathy with the free trade principles of liberalism, and the growth of manufacturing in the province under the wing of the National Policy had confirmed this position. Such was the commitment of the party as a whole to economic liberalism that this acted as a restraining rather than a determining force on Liberal economic policy, and there was no fundamental change in Liberal policy in Laurier's time. The party in 1882 disapproved of "needless restrictions on our liberty of exchanging what we have for what we want," rejected the proposition that "any substantial application of the restrictive principle has been, or can be, made in favour of the great interests of the mechanic, the labourer, the farmer, the lumberman"[37] and in 1887 called for "an earnest effort to promote reciprocal trade with the South."[38]

Depression in the late 1880s brought forth fresh Liberal demands for freer trade, this time in the form of a continental common market or "commercial union." Sir Richard Cartwright, Laurier's chief lieutenant in Ontario at the time, indicated the lengths to which some Liberals were willing to take their belief in the primacy of economics:

> I have no hesitation in saying frankly that if the United States are willing to deal with us on equitable terms the advantages to both countries, and especially to us, are so great that scarcely any sacrifice is too severe to secure them. I am as averse as any man can be to annexation or to resign our political independence, but I cannot shut my eyes to the facts.[39]

Laurier did not go so far, preferring the simple elimination of tariffs with the United States:

> The hostility which now stains our long frontier will disappear, the barriers which now obstruct trade will be burst open, and trade will pour in along all the avenues from the north to the south and from the south to the north, free, untrammelled and no longer stained by the hues of hostility.[40]

The 1891 election was fought and lost by the Liberals on the issue of "unrestricted reciprocity" or all-out free trade. Defeat killed the idea of commercial union but reciprocity persisted, and the party again promised a "fair and liberal reciprocity treaty" in the 1896 election.

The Liberal victory did not bring free trade. The Americans were cool; protectionist elements within the party were opposed; and a growing wave of prosperity blunted criticism of the National Policy. For the time being, Laurier maintained the existing protective system with some modification, but the idea of free trade persisted and when, in 1910, the American government expressed its support of a new reciprocity scheme, Laurier jumped at it. The resulting agreement was the main issue in the 1911 election.

This attempt to realize free trade precipitated not only Laurier's defeat and resignation as prime minister, but an ideological split within the Liberal Party. A group of Toronto Liberals, led by Clifford Sifton, broke with the party and repudiated reciprocity. This "Revolt of the Eighteen," together with the crushing defeat suffered by the Liberals in Ontario, brought home the degree to which Central Canada was bound to protection — a lesson not lost on Mackenzie King. The reciprocity campaign of 1911 was the last appearance of simple free trade under Liberal colours. The economic liberalism of the party was to be recast in a different form in the future, although the old free trade doctrines reappeared for a time in the 1920s in the more radically liberal Progressives.

Laurier's approach to the issue of Canadian autonomy was more durable. As we have seen, there were two ways of dealing with Canada's position in the world. The isolationist policy was to reduce the ties that bound Canada to the outside world and to Britain in particular so as to maximize Canadian freedom of action or inaction. A more positive and interventionist policy sought to promote greater and more equal Canadian participation in imperial and world affairs so as to maximize Canadian influence and promote a different sort of national freedom.

Borden's Conservatives adopted the latter course; Laurier and the Liberal Party chose the former. Canadian Liberals inherited from English liberalism a hostility to imperialism and colonial subordination, regarding them as an unjustified restriction of their liberty. Canadian Liberals also developed a typically North American distrust and sometimes hostility for Europe, which resulted in pressure not only for independence, but isolation. Many liberals like Goldwin Smith saw Europe as the home of an old and disreputable class-ridden society, a hive of militarism and the worst sort of power politics, in sharp contrast to the liberty and egalitarian promise of the New World.[41]

This attitude was encouraged by the Quebec wing of the party, since French Canadians had few emotional ties to Europe, and tended to be isolationist. English Canadians, however, many of them born in Britain, had personal ties and loyalties, which could outweigh the strictly liberal view. This created continuous tension within the party, and split it entirely in 1917; but in the long run the declining power and prestige of Britain and the traumatic experience of the Great War tipped the scales in favour of isolation.

Laurier faced strong pressure both in Canada and from Britain for "Imperial Federation," a closer association of Britain and the self-governing Dominions on the basis of a federation giving greater colonial participation. For a brief period in 1897 Laurier showed some sympathy for the idea,[42] but when the question of Canadian participation in the Boer War arose, Laurier refused to make any commitment to a common imperial policy: "I claim for Canada this, that in future she shall be at liberty to act or not act, to interfere or not interefere, to do just as she pleases."[43] At the Colonial Conference of 1902, his objections to a common imperial foreign and defence policy were cast in familiar liberal terms: "There is a school in England and in Canada which wants to bring Canada into the vortex of militarism which is the curse and blight of Europe. I am not prepared to endorse any such policy."[44]

The possibility of Canadian participation in a general European war sharpened the conflict. Laurier's autonomist position was demonstrated in the *Naval Service Bill* of 1910, which provided for the gradual establishment of a separate Canadian navy rather than an immediate contribution to the Royal Navy and a larger share in imperial decision-making. Laurier's isolationism was offset during the war by a wave of patriotic fervor among English Liberals who felt that the contribution conscription might make to Canada's war effort justified the cost in terms of domestic unity. Laurier and the French Liberals, along with some of the English Liberals, would not accept conscription and the party temporarily split in 1917. Thus, Laurier entered politics in a predominantly English Liberal Party, and left as the head of a largely French parliamentary faction.

THE RISE OF THE PROGRESSIVE MOVEMENT

When Mackenzie King succeeded Laurier in 1919, he inherited the leadership of a party divided not only by race and language, but also by a revolt of liberal radicalism that the Liberal Party had been unable to contain. The election of 1921 brought sixty-four Progressive members to Parliament from all provinces except Quebec, Prince Edward Island and Nova Scotia, and revealed the seriousness of the ideological fragmentation. Party splits were not a new thing; Henri Bourassa led a nationalist secession from the Liberals twenty years before, but it had not survived 1921, for nationalism by itself is rarely a sufficiently comprehensive ideology to sustain a continuing political party. Liberalism is more comprehensive, and those Progressives who rejected King's blandishments to return to the Liberal fold carried elements of their radical liberal ideology into both the CCF and Social Credit parties.

Progressivism was an agrarian movement, strongest in the West and in the old Clear Grit areas of Western Ontario. Its roots can be traced to an American farmer organization, the Grange, which began to organize in Canada in the 1870s at much the same time as trade unions were beginning to organize the workers. The radical liberalism underlying these farmers' movements was reflected in J.W. Dafoe's comment on Laurier's defeat in 1911:

> I should be very well content to see the Liberal party remain in opposition for the next fifteen or twenty years, if it will devote itself to advocating real Liberal views and building up a party which, when it again takes office, will be able to carry out a programme without regard to the desires and feelings of the privileged classes.[45]

W.L. Morton spoke of the "search for such a purged and radical Liberal party," though curiously he goes on to argue that such a party would be a "sectional third party"[46] rather than an explicitly ideological and national party.

There were three main elements in the thought behind the Progressive movement: "faith in democracy, hatred of corporate wealth, and distrust of the political system."[47] Each was significant, but the ideology as a whole contained contradictory elements. Their faith in democracy entailed a collectivist view of the people. They viewed people primarily as co-operators, not as competitors. It was for the people as a whole to speak with a single voice through such techniques as the initiative, the referendum and the recall. The political system as a whole could not be trusted because the members of parliament spoke as individuals and were susceptible to corruption by Eastern financiers and corporations.

On the other hand, their hatred of corporate wealth was neither based on envy nor on a dislike for privilege in itself. The privilege of the Eastern interests was objected to, not because it was inherently wrong, but because it imposed limitations on the farmers' freedom. As R.C. Henders, president of the Manitoba Grain Growers Association put it in 1912:

> We are governed by an elective aristocracy, which in its turn is largely governed by an aristocracy of wealth. Behind the government and the legislators are the corporations and trusts and behind the political monopolists are the industrial monopolists.[48]

Therefore, if the wishes of the people could be directly expressed through a reformed electoral system, the people would be able to "break the hold of the 'bosses.'"[49] The Progressives sought to use their collective political power, made effective through political reforms, to further their position as independent individual producers. Their radicalism was a mixture of collectivism and egalitarian individualism, a halfway house to socialism, which eventually found a foothold in all the parties, and more than a foothold in the Western Conservatives and in the CCF/NDP.

This liberal individualism was expressed also in hostility to protective tariffs. Although the Liberal Party had, in 1891 and 1911, supported free trade, it had been rebuffed by the electorate, in spite of almost solid support from Saskatchewan and Alberta in 1911. In 1921, under the leadership of Thomas A. Crerar, the Progressives ran as an independent political party bent on achieving free trade in foodstuffs and agricultural equipment and "an immediate and substantial all round reduction of the customs tariff." The protective tariff, according to the Progressives, "fostered combines, trusts and 'gentlemen's agreements' in almost every line of Canadian industrial enterprise," made "the rich richer and the poor poorer" and,

has been and is a chief corrupting influence in our national life because the protected interests, in order to maintain their unjust privileges, have contributed lavishly to political and campaign funds, thus encouraging both political parties to look to them for support, thereby lowering the standard of public morality.[50]

Although Mackenzie King attempted to bring the Progressives into his government,[51] negotiations broke down, and the Progressives refused even to form the official opposition, confident that they would retain their ideological purity and best serve the interests of their constituents by taking an independent stand. King and the Liberals were ideologically closer to the Progressives than were the Conservatives and generally could count on their support in Parliament.

In Parliament, the Progressives were riven by ideological disputes. Supporters of Henry Wise Wood, mainly from Alberta, distrusted the party system generally, and were "in concept revolutionaries."[52] Supporters of Crerar from Manitoba were less hostile to traditional party and parliamentary tactics, and wanted to see the Progressive movement take the form of a reformist political party. The ascendancy of this group was demonstrated by the election of Robert Forke as leader in 1922.

The ideological moderation of this Manitoba faction proved to be its great electoral weakness. These men were the first "Liberals in a hurry." There was no significant ideological difference between them and King's Liberals and, as a consequence, there was little lasting excuse for them to continue as a separate political party. In the 1925 election campaign, Forke continued to attack the protective tariff and to hold out the Progressive Party as a "promise of salvation." But the Progressives were on the defensive and Forke felt called upon to defend the necessity of "maintaining our independence as a group and freedom of judgment and action in the parliamentary arena."[53] Large numbers of voters returned to their traditional old party allegiances and the Progressives were reduced from sixty-five to twenty-four MPs.

After the 1926 election, the absorption of most Progressives into the Liberal Party was almost complete. Nine members were elected as Liberal-Progressives and only thirteen as Progressives. The more radical Albertans broke with the main body of the Progressives and founded their own party, the United Farmers of Alberta. While the remaining Progressives continued to press for such policies as reciprocity with the United States in natural products, the UFA demanded more radical political reforms to break the hold of the Eastern financial interests and to make Parliament directly responsive to the wishes of the constituents. It was not until the founding of the CCF in 1932 that the ideological confusion was temporarily resolved, with the more collectivist elements finding a home in the CCF and the reformist liberals returning the mainstream of Canadian Liberalism.

MACKENZIE KING

The challenge facing Mackenzie King in 1919 was to reunite the Liberal Party, a process that required both King's very considerable talents of political conciliation and a recasting of the party's ideology. This was not necessary in all areas—King's policy on Canadian autonomy and foreign relations was a logical extension of Laurier's. The problem area was social and economic policy, for the postwar depression, the problems produced by rapid industrial and urban growth and the general social malaise following the war produced widespread unrest and dissatisfaction, of which the Progressive revolt and the Winnipeg General Strike of 1919 were the most spectacular examples. The traditional Liberal policy of *laissez-faire* economic liberalism was not acceptable to unemployed and exploited workers and farmers facing ruinously low prices.

King proposed two major changes in Liberal ideas. In the first place, he tempered the *laissez-faire* view that the essence of economic liberalism was "negative" in nature, consisting of the removal of restraints (particularly by government) on economic activity, with the new idea of "positive" liberalism developed by such English liberals as L.T. Hobhouse. Hobhouse argued, in his *Liberalism*, that individual liberty was restricted as much by the lack of such things as adequate food, housing, or medical care as by external restriction. Positive government action to fill these needs through a variety of social welfare programs was not only consistent with, but central to, liberalism in the modern world.

It is this "positive" liberalism, which we call welfare liberalism in contrast to the older, "negative" kind of liberalism, which we call business liberalism, and which we discussed in Chapter II. At the 1919 Liberal leadership convention, King committed the Liberal Party to the eventual achievement of a welfare state, including medicare, old age pensions and unemployment insurance. The ease with which this was done, and the importance of King's new ideas to his convention victory, reflected general dissatisfaction with the status quo, a readiness to seek new solutions and the fact that these ideas were within the canon of the Liberal ideology and were seen as a creative adaptation of the Liberal tradition rather than a leap in the dark.

Welfare liberalism still saw society in individualistic terms, and approved collective action only as a means of maximizing individual initiative and opportunity. King clearly recognized the difference between this and genuine socialism. In supporting legislation against sweatshops and cartels he argued that

> it is the business of the state to play the same part in the supervision of industry as is played by the Umpire in sports to see the mean man does not profit in virtue of his meanness, and on the other hand that nothing should be done which will destroy individual effort and skill. Some may term this legislation Socialism, but to my mind it is individualism.[54]

The justification for such measures was that they ultimately maximized liberty. "Most effort to promote human welfare necessitates some interference with individual liberty. Where wisely applied and enforced, it is an immediate restriction, that a wider liberty in the end may be secured."[55] To this end, the convention of 1919 resolved that,

> in so far as may be practicable, having regard for Canada's financial position, an adequate system of insurance against unemployment, sickness, dependence in old age, and other disability, which would include old age pensions, widows' pensions, and maternity benefits, should be instituted by the Federal Government.[56]

This commitment to welfare liberalism was not fully realized until the 1960s but it marked a permanent change of direction in Liberal thinking.

King's other major contribution was in recasting the Liberal view of class and industrial strife while preserving continuity with traditional liberal thinking. Liberals viewed society as a collection of individuals, and the common interest of society as the sum of those individual interests. Subordinate groups within society, such as trade unions, were viewed as potential enemies of the common good. King accepted the basic analysis: economic conflicts were not based on objective group or class interests but on the selfishness or stubbornness of individual persons, which blinded them to their more important common interests.[57]

Thus, King rejected socialism to the extent that it involved a theory of class conflict: the Progressives may have been "Liberals in a hurry," but the CCF in the 1930s could not "be regarded in any sense as allies."[58] However, he realized that individual interests in an industrial society could often best be realized through joint action, and accepted unions as the workers' legitimate representatives, ending the old liberal hostility. Government was to mediate between unions and employers, inducing each to moderate its own position, and leading them towards the common good. As the first Deputy Minister of Labour, King organized the federal Department of Labour and introduced government conciliation services. The 1919 convention endorsed the Labour Convention of the League of Nations, and called for the introduction of labour and community representation in industrial control, and the safeguarding of labour and community interests in the shaping of industrial policies.[59]

King's position was not revolutionary. He wanted no fundamental changes in the distribution of economic power in society, which socialists sought by nationalization or worker control, and no basic change in the capitalist, private enterprise economy. His aim was to improve the lot of the poorest and to reduce industrial strife, all within the existing system through the welfare state and reforms in industrial relations. This made the Liberal Party more attractive to those, particularly in Progressive or Labour groups, who had left it after 1918, and had an immediate political relevance in 1919, a fact not lost on the delegates to the convention. King's reinterpretation of liberalism for an urban, industrial society was a major achievement, leading to the return of most of the errant Progressives through the 1920s. It was perhaps his greatest legacy to the Liberal Party.

King also developed the notion that the Liberal Party was somehow the party of "national unity." The idea originated with Laurier, when the party had successfully combined English and French support across the country. This alliance was in ruins by 1919, but King assiduously set out to rebuild it. As an anti-conscriptionist, he enjoyed the sympathy of Quebec, whose support was vital to the Liberal claim to be the national party. In the fight to retain it, King had an important ideological advantage in the Liberal commitment to Canadian independence along isolationist lines. Isolationism was attractive to French Canadians who lacked strong emotional attachments to Europe, and allowed the Liberals to place the accommodation of French-Canadian interests ahead of wider Canadian interests, in the name of national unity. Thus, in 1917, the Laurier Liberals placed Quebec's opposition to conscription ahead of Canadian military commitments. During the elections of the 1920s and 1930s, French-Canadian voters did not (and were not allowed to) forget that the Conservatives had conscripted their sons in 1917; at the beginning of the Second World War, King specifically repudiated conscription. When circumstances and mismanagement forced the abandonment of this policy in 1944, King took every possible opportunity to delay the event and reduce the effects of conscription.

Other aspects of King's foreign policy showed a similar bias. He equated any imperial connection with the sort of colonial subordination against which his grandfather William Lyon Mackenzie had rebelled in 1837, and avoided any international commitments. The differing attitude of Meighen and King to the Chanak crisis in 1922 was a case in point. Through the 1930s he avoided any

Canadian involvement in the collective security plans of the League of Nations. The repudiation of the commitment of the Canadian Ambassador to the League of Nations to resist fascist Italian aggression in Ethiopia in 1935 marked the zenith of King's retreat into the "fireproof house" of North America. The Liberal platform in 1940 boasted of King's avoidance of any prior national commitments; "The King Government — wisely interpreting the wishes of the Canadian people — refused to commit this country, in advance, to a policy of fighting wars at unpredictable times, at unknown places and for undetermined causes."[60]

Closely connected with King's isolationism was his inclination to see Canada in a North American or continental, rather than a European, context. This was a common Liberal view, derived from the liberal tendency to give economic factors free play. King had modified this belief in *laissez-faire* by endorsing welfare liberalism but remained committed to freer trade, particularly with the United States. The platform for the 1921 election supported tariff reductions and commended the ill-fated Reciprocity Agreement of 1911.[61] In office, King had to step gingerly in order to maintain his support among Quebec protectionists, but was able to give the Progressives sufficient satisfaction on the tariff question that they were induced to return to the fold. In any event, King never lost his faith in the virtues of free trade. In 1935, despite the example of Roosevelt's New Deal, King clung to what he terms the "Liberation of External Trade" as the primary solution to the economic problems posed by the Depression:

> I cannot stress too strongly the importance the Liberal party attaches to getting rid of prohibitory tariffs and other restrictions which have been strangling Canada's trade. It believes that upon the development and expansion of our domestic and foreign trade depends the only ultimate solution of the problems of unemployment, railways, debt and taxation, and the establishment of substantial measures of social reform.[62]

On resuming office in 1935, the Liberal government made no attempt to rescue the Bennett New Deal legislation from its constitutional problems.

Not surprisingly, King was willing to allow economic forces to take their course in integrating Canada with the United States. The form of the National Policy was maintained, but the policies of 1879 were no longer relevant to maintaining a separate Canadian economy in the situation after 1920. New resource-based industries serving American markets weakened the national, East-West orientation of the Canadian economy and American ownership of Canadian business began to rise sharply. At no time did King interfere with either of these trends. This process of economic integration went along with an increasingly continentalist defence policy. King's decision in 1940 to accept extensive Canadian collaboration with the Americans in a common continental defence scheme (the ancestor of NORAD) was of a piece with a 1938 agreement to reduce tariffs with the United States, and with the continued drift to continental economic integration.

This continentalist orientation was inherent in the Liberal commitment to a high degree of economic liberalism and the resulting tendency to place the demands of economics before those of politics. It has been a constant factor in the liberal ideology since at least the 1850s, though it has sometimes been offset by strong national or imperial loyalties held by liberals and often been rejected by the voters. It also accorded with Liberal sympathy for provincial rights, for the new resource industries fell largely under provincial jurisdiction, and any attempt to alter their course would have involved an extension of central government control. King's position was consistent with the Liberal past and was carried on by his successors.

THE SHIFT AWAY FROM PROVINCIAL RIGHTS

The traditional orientation of the Liberal Party as the champion of provincial rights and its reliance on *laissez-faire* free trade policies for purposes of economic management were soon to be eclipsed, however, by the unfolding internal logic of welfare liberalism and the pressure of outside events. For if it was consistent with liberal principles for the state to provide welfare services for its citizens to enhance their real liberty, could it be any less consistent for the state to manage the economy to provide jobs and enhance the people's real economic liberty? The "negative" liberty of the unemployed was no less empty than that of those requiring other government services, and in Trinity College, Cambridge, the giant of liberal economic theory, John Maynard Keynes, was arguing convincingly that a capitalist economy could be managed by government manipulation of the level of demand in the economy.

While King was apparently never convinced, Keynesian economic theory soon came to dominate the thinking of senior civil servants in the Department of Finance. Almost at the same time the Second World War began. Prosecution of the war effort required unparalleled federal domination of the economy and by 1945, the federal government completely overshadowed the provinces in taxing and spending. During the war, the commitment of the federal Liberal government to welfare liberalism was deepened and took concrete form under pressure from a rapidly rising CCF and a demanding electorate. The Marsh Report of 1943 heralded a complete welfare state; family allowances were begun in 1944; and the Green Paper of 1945 promised a full-scale welfare state and central management of the economy along Keynesian lines.

All this required the federal government to maintain its position of dominance and not to retreat as it had after 1918. Keynesian theory presupposed a unitary state and, it was thought, could not be applied without complete central control of both fiscal and monetary policy. In any case, if a federally-dominated welfare state were to come into existence, the position of wartime dominance had to be retained. The war-swollen bureaucracy in Ottawa (and its political masters in the Liberal Party) had become used to power. Finally it was clear that Canada was to play a larger role in the postwar world, a role that by 1949 and the beginning of the Cold War involved unprecedented levels of peacetime defence spending.

The factors came together in the 1940s to transform the federal Liberal Party into the protagonist of the central government, a position it has maintained ever since and which continues to influence the party over issues such as free trade and the Meech Lake Accord. This policy shift was followed, not surprisingly, by a significant realignment of the party's electoral base. In King's heyday, the pillars of the Liberal Party outside Quebec were Nova Scotia and Saskatchewan. With the identification of the Liberal Party with the central government, and with those areas of the country that identified most closely with the central government, Liberal support in the hinterland began to ebb, though the realignment was not substantial until after the 1949 election and did not reach its full extent until the late 1970s.

Given the shift or reemphasis of party ideology towards welfare liberalism, the abandonment of the party's traditional provincial rights position posed few strictly ideological difficulties. The party had originally supported the position because it was believed that personal liberty was maximized by restricting the power of the federal government. Now, maximization of real personal liberty required a greater degree of government intervention, and Keynesian economic theory and the habit of power dictated that it was the federal government that would best act to maximize individual liberty. The universalism inherent in liberalism ruled out any defence of provincial rights based on the grounds that there were differences of real significance between Canadians in different regions that were worth protecting at the expense of federal power.

In addition, Liberalism had always approved of Canadian capitalism (if deploring some of its excesses) and during King's years in power developed a close relationship with the Canadian business community. Business, in turn, while deploring certain types of government intervention, was always sympathetic to government action that favoured its interests. In the interwar period, most of the demands of business on government fell at the provincial level, because the growth industries, like pulp and paper and mining, required specifically provincial assistance in developing, for example, hydroelectric power. After the war, as corporate integration on a nation-wide basis increased, business came to depend more on assistance from Ottawa in areas such as subsidies, development assistance, transportation and communication regulation, energy policy and financial industry regulation. The tendency of the Liberal Party to accommodate itself to business interests eased the transition from the traditional provincial-rights position. Businessmen reconciled themselves to a more active central government, in part on the grounds that some government intervention, such as welfare measures or steps to control unemployment, was necessary to secure public acceptance of the continued existence of capitalism. In short, these measures were a form of inoculation against the far more serious threat of socialism and, in addition, many directly benefited specific business interests.

The policy shifts consequent on this ideological reorientation took a number of forms: the rapid expansion of the shared-cost programs — the Trans-Canada Highway scheme and hospital insurance, for example — as a means of increasing federal influence in areas of provincial jurisdiction under the constitution; continued federal dominance in the taxing area through the continuance of the wartime tax-rental arrangements; financial aid to universities and to cultural activities. From 1945 until well into the 1950s, federal Liberal politicans turned a deaf ear to provincial requests for greater participation in decision making in those areas.

LOUIS ST. LAURENT

Liberal identification with the Canadian corporate establishment reached its highest point under King's successor, Louis St. Laurent, Prime Minister from 1948 to 1957, and was personified in C.D. Howe, his aggressive, American-born (and self-made millionaire) Minister of Trade and Commerce. However, though Howe and other Cabinet colleagues, such as Robert Winters and Walter Harris, dramatized this aspect of Liberal policy, there was no real ideological change in the transition from King to St. Laurent, and the latter contributed little to Liberal thinking. The 1948 Liberal convention, which ratified St. Laurent's succession, restated its fundamental belief in liberty and individualism in fuller terms than at any time since 1919:

> Liberal policies are those which protect, sustain and enlarge the freedom of the individual. The liberal...believes in freedom because he believes the resources of human personality and endeavour to be rich and varied beyond calculation or prediction. Liberalism rejects the unreasoning preservation, in the name of freedom, of outworn existing arrangements and measures. It rejects the maintenance of privilege however historic. Liberalism equally rejects the theory that state ownership of the instruments of production in itself constitutes progress and a solution of social problems.[63]

St. Laurent continued King's mixture of welfare liberalism and anti-nationalist economic policies. Such nationalist feeling as did exist in the Liberal Party was expressed in policies that were largely the product of King's anti-imperialism. The institution of separate Canadian citizenship in 1947, the abolition of remaining judicial appeals to the Privy Council in 1949 and the promise of a new Canadian flag whittled away at the few remaining formal ties with Britain, but increasing dependence on the United States was ignored. The military alliance with the United States was strengthened, and the government's refusal to support Britain during the Suez crisis in 1956 marked the final passage of Canada from the diplomatic orbit of Britain into that of the United States. St. Laurent also maintained King's approach to centralization even though it involved a continuous and bitter confrontation with Quebec, as the federal government expanded shared-cost programs and continued the wartime tax-rental system of revenue-sharing between Ottawa and the provinces into the 1950s.

THE PEARSON YEARS

The outward calm, not to say torpor, of the party was shattered by the Conservative victories of 1957 and 1958, and the questioning that ensued raised ideological questions that persisted after the Liberals returned to office in 1963 under the leadership of Lester Pearson. The criticism was part of a general upsurge of radical liberalism finding expression both in Diefenbaker-style populism in the Conservative Party and in the growth of the New Party movement.

The Liberal critics, chief of whom was Walter Gordon, argued that the party organization was not democratic enough, and did not allow for rank and file participation in party decision making. Its policies were too business-oriented and required more emphasis on extending the welfare state. The traditional Liberal commitment to continentalism was criticized on nationalist grounds, and policies of economic and cultural nationalism were called for. The party's postwar policy of centralization was challenged by both the resurgent Quebec wing of the party and by many of the provincial governments.

Pearson met this situation with much the same ideological stance as his predecessors. Liberalism's primary concern remained with the individual: "The fundamental principle of Liberalism is belief in the dignity and worth of the individual. The state is the creation of man, to protect and serve him; and not the reverse"; and particularly, with individual liberty: "the first purpose of government (is) to legislate for the liberation of human personality." Pearson restated the distinction between business and welfare liberalism, between merely removing restraints on individual action and providing citizens with the means to exercise their abilities to the fullest:

> Liberalism includes the negative requirement of removing anything that stands in the way of individual and collective progress.
>
> The negative requirement is important. It involves removal and reform: clearing away and opening up, so that man can move forward and societies expand. The removal of restrictions that block the access to achievement: this is the very essence of Liberalism.
>
> The Liberal Party, however, must also promote the positive purpose of ensuring that all citizens, without any discrimination, will be in a position to take advantage of the opportunities opened up; of the freedoms that have been won....[64]

Pearson made it clear, however, that welfare liberalism was not to be confused with socialism; its purpose was only to provide equality of opportunity — a common starting point in the race — and not to guarantee equality at the finishing post.[65]

In office, Pearson shifted the policy emphasis towards welfare liberalism by instituting the Canada Pension Plan and promoting Medicare. He was distinctly cool to nationalism: his liberalism and his diplomatic experience had made him a convinced internationalist and had led him to downgrade national differences that might impede international integration. His government placed a high priority on restoring the closest possible trade and diplomatic relations with the United States after 1963, and pursued the traditional Liberal policy of continentalism. Defence-production-sharing agreements with the United States encouraged continental integration in the aircraft and electronics industries, and the *Automobile Trade Pact* of 1965 effectively ended any hope of a separate Canadian automobile industry. When the United States government threatened to disrupt the free flow of capital within North America in 1965, the Pearson government hastened to Washington to seek exemption.

Nevertheless, Pearson's habit of acting as a mediator between the different factions in the government allowed him to accept certain measures (restricting foreign ownership in the financial and communications industries) that were advocated by the Gordon group in the party. When, however, Walter Gordon precipitated a major debate on economic nationalism in the party during 1966, Pearson stood on the sidelines while Mitchell Sharp led the majority of the party into a decisive rejection of nationalist policy.

In the area of federal-provincial relations, the Pearson government attempted to carry on where the St. Laurent government had left off in 1957. It ignored the steady drift to political support to the provinces and the concessions made to the provinces by the Conservatives, who pioneered opting out in 1961 with respect to university financing in Quebec and replaced the tax rental system in 1962 with a tax-sharing mechanism that allowed the provinces to set their own tax rates and still have the federal authorities collect the taxes. The proposals in 1963 to set up a Municipal Loan Fund, under which municipalities could borrow directly from Ottawa, and to establish a Canada Pension Plan controlled by the federal government produced a head-on collision with the provinces, particularly Quebec, which was in the throes of the Quiet Revolution. Quebec's opposition was fatal; at meetings in Quebec City in April 1964, the original Canada Pension Plan was dropped and replaced with one that did not apply to Quebec and gave control over accumulating pools of capital to the provinces. This was closely followed by substantial transfers of fiscal resources to the provinces and by the adoption in 1965 of opting out legislation, which allowed Quebec not to participate in a national shared-cost program and yet not lose the equivalent amount of federal money.

At the time, this appeared to be a return to the Liberal provincial rights position of the period before the Second World War, but in retrospect, it is clear that it was merely a tactical retreat from a temporarily indefensible position. The longer-term response was to strengthen the Liberal position in Quebec and resist further concessions. To accomplish the former and increase the party's appeal to Quebec, Pearson recruited the "three wise men," Jean Marchand, Gerard Pelletier, and Pierre Trudeau, for the 1965 election, and espoused the cause of bilingualism. The latter was a genuinely liberal response to nationalist demands in Quebec for greater recognition of the French-Canadian nation. The federal government and civil service would protect and encourage the rights of individual French Canadians to use their own language in dealings with the federal state. To this end, the Laurendeau-Dunton Royal Commission on Bilingualism and Biculturalism was established in 1964 to assess the position of the French language in Canada and to make recommendations for protecting and encouraging it. Having taken steps to make the federal government more attractive to French Canadians, the Pearson government stiffened its attitude to the provinces.

It is probably no coincidence that this followed by a matter of months Pierre Trudeau's election to parliament and his appointment as Parliamentary Secretary to Lester Pearson. In September 1966, the federal government unilaterally terminated the technical education shared-cost program and replaced it with a comprehensive cost sharing plan to fund post-secondary education. This new program ended Quebec's opting out in respect to university grants and put an end to any suggestion of special status for the Province of Quebec. At the first of a series of first ministers conferences on constitutional reform in February 1968, Trudeau, then Minister of Justice, imperiously rejected the Quebec position, with the consequence that he was soon celebrated in English Canada as a champion of national unity who knew how to handle the impertinent demands of his native province.

PIERRE ELLIOT TRUDEAU

The candidates at the Liberal leadership convention of 1968 displayed in microcosm the spectrum of thinking in Canadian Liberalism, from business liberals like Paul Hellyer, Robert Winters and Mitchell Sharp to welfare liberals like Paul Martin and Allan MacEachen. Pierre Trudeau confounded all of them with a skilfully conceived and executed flanking movement: by clever exploitation of his engaging lifestyle, his leadership campaign succeeded in convincing a great many delegates (and voters two months later) that he was on an entirely different plane from the other candidates. The categories of right and left were a remnant of the old-style politics of ideology and emotion: Trudeau, the New Man of Canadian Politics, was beyond all this.

The promised novelty of 1968 was delivered in full measure: Trudeau as Prime Minister never lost the ability to shock, to inspire, to enrage and, above all, to surprise. Yet the novelty was of style and of personality, not of ideology. Through the twists and turns and seemingly endless opportunism of so many of the Trudeau government's actions ran a clear thread of ideological consistency, a consistent and powerful core of liberal principle. This commitment to liberalism paradoxically caused apparent inconsistency, for in pursuing the central core, Trudeau was often willing to sacrifice the peripheral. While some have interpreted this as unprincipled manoeuvring to retain power at any cost, certain key decisions, particularly his single minded and ideologically driven pursuit of constitutional reform in 1980-1982, suggest otherwise.

This central core is the familiar liberal concern with the liberty of the individual and the commitment to individualism, which is fundamental to Trudeau's thinking and comes from longstanding personal inclination: "I have never been able to accept any discipline except that which I imposed upon myself....I found it unacceptable that others should claim to know better than I what was good for me."[66] From this premise, Trudeau draws several conclusions. One is the value of the rights of individuals and the consequent need for tolerance.[67] Another is that the "primordial responsibility" of the liberal to foster individual freedom entails an open-ended commitment to change:

> The first visible effect of freedom is change. A free man exercises his freedom by altering himself and — inevitably — his surroundings. It follows that no liberal can be other than receptive to change and highly positive and active in his response to it, for change is the very expression of freedom.[68]

The notion that freedom means change or movement is connected with the view that the human essence is activity or movement — to be human is to be active, competitive, in motion and comes from the deepest roots of liberalism in the writing of Thomas Hobbes. Trudeau put it in terms strikingly reminiscent of the author of *Leviathan*: "Life is confrontation, and vigilance, and a fierce struggle against any threat of intrusion or death."[69] This statement was made within a few weeks of the imposition of the *War Measures Act* in the October Crisis of 1970, and exposes an aspect of liberalism rather different from the "bleeding heart" variety Trudeau repudiated at that time.

This commitment to liberal individualism can be seen most clearly in Trudeau's approach to the twin problems of French Canada's place in Confederation and of constitutional reform. There are two theoretical approaches to these issues, one more individualist, the other more collectivist in nature. Under the former, French Canadians are viewed as individuals who have rights to use the French language, denial of which is wrong in principle and a threat to Confederation. The solution from this standpoint is to safeguard these individual rights, and the Trudeau government proceeded in this direction through the *Official Languages Act*, which extended bilingualism in the federal bureaucracy across much of the country, through administrative action to increase the use of French in the civil service and through extension of individual language rights in the *Charter of Rights and Freedoms*. The Trudeau bilingualism policy thus had a distinct individualist bias.

Under the collectivist approach, the real question is not the rights of French-speaking individuals, but the rights of the French-Canadian collectivity, the nation, and the solution lies in extending and safeguarding the rights of that collectivity. This collectivist argument is based on a perception of the primarily emotional or non-rational group loyalties of French Canadians, on their deep attachment to their own collectivity, and on the assertion that the preservation and transmission of a culture can be successfully accomplished only within a sympathetic social milieu.[70] Thus, the preservation and extension of French culture depends not on preserving the legal rights of individuals so much as on the strength of the collectivity (the nation) and, for obvious reasons, the province of Quebec has generally been identified as the political embodiment of that nation: hence, the demands that have been made for special status and powers for Quebec to enable it to fulfil its role as the protector of French Canada.

The gist of this position, then, is that Quebec *n' est pas une province comme les autres* because of its special relationship to the French-Canadian nation, and therefore deserves "special status" with respect to the central government and the other provinces. Demands of this sort have been made by both Liberal and Union Nationale provincial governments in Quebec and by the Parti Québécois, which carries the argument to its extreme conclusion. The federal Conservative and New Democratic parties have briefly flirted with similar ideas and for a time it seemed that the federal Liberals, under Pearson, would move in this direction, following the retreat on the Canada Pension Plan and the passage of opting-out legislation in 1964-65.

Trudeau's opposition to this approach was, in part, that of a constitutional lawyer concerned with the problems involved with special status: the anomalous position of French-Canadian representatives in a Canadian Parliament (which would have less jurisdiction over Quebec than the other provinces) and the position of non-French minorities in Quebec. Underlying this is a deep hostility to the notion that the state should be organized on any primarily collective or group principle, whether of class or nationality. For Trudeau, the state exists to serve primarily individual ends. "Men do not exist for states; states are created to make it easier for men to attain some of their common objectives."[71] Thus, while agreeing that Quebec could rightfully take steps to promote the French language and culture above others, he insisted that this was based on the state's obligation to serve the individual interests of its citizens, who in this case happen to be largely French-speaking: "It is inevitable that its policies will serve the interests of ethnic groups, and especially of the majority group in proportion to its numbers; but as a special privilege of the largest group."[72]

Trudeau's longstanding hostility to nationalism is based partly on the familiar case against nationalist excesses:

> The tiny portion of history marked by the emergence of the nation-states is also the scene of the most devastating wars, the worst atrocities, and the most degrading collective hatred the world has ever seen....the nation-state idea has caused wars to become more and more total over the last two centuries; and that is the idea I take issue with so vehemently....In days gone by religion had to be displaced as the basis of the state before the frightful religious wars came to an end. And there will be no end to wars between nations until in some similar fashion the nation ceases to be the basis of the state.[73]

Trudeau pointed out that many states contain ethnic minorities and that the attainment of the nationalist ideal of each nationality embodied in its separate nation-state, would mean such disruption that "the very idea of the nation-state is absurd."[74]

Beyond the practical consequences of nationalism, however, Trudeau argued that the element of collectivism in nationalism, the attachment it demands to the national group, is repugnant to the liberal preoccupation with individuality. In asserting that the lone individual is the ultimate moral unit, Trudeau approvingly quotes Renan's assertion that "man is bound neither to his language nor to his race; he is bound only to himself because he is a free agent, or in other words a moral being."[75] Thus, even while recognizing the desirable qualities fostered by the nation and sustained by national feeling — "a cultural heritage, common traditions, a community awareness, historical continuity, a set of mores, all of which go to make a man what he is" — he insisted on their purely temporary value —they are valid only "at this juncture of history" — and contended that they ought to be superseded in the long run:

> Certainly, these qualities are more private than public, more introverted than extroverted, more instinctive and primitive than intelligent and civilized, more self-centred and impulsive than generous and reasonable. They belong to a transitional period in world history.[76]

The hostility to nationalism explained Trudeau's enthusiasm for federalism. Like his mentor, the nineteenth-century English liberal Lord Acton, Trudeau saw federalism as the ideal means to tame and eventually eliminate nationalism. By dividing sovereignty between different levels of government in one state, federalism allows the accommodation of different nationalities within one political framework. This not only gives nationalist feelings an outlet at a level where the harm they can do is minimized, but in the long run teaches toleration, and works toward the elimination of nationalism.

One of the corollaries of the idea that federalism is essentially anti-nationalist is that attempts by federal governments to hold together federations by encouraging nationalist sentiment at the federal level may be self-defeating. Trudeau's description of the nature of such policies is close to the sort of program advocated by contemporary Canadian nationalists:

> Resources must be diverted into such things as national flags, anthems, education, arts councils, broadcasting corporations, film boards; the territory must be bound together by a network of railways, highways, airlines; the national culture and the national economy must be protected by taxes and tariffs; ownership of resources and industry by nationals must be made a matter of policy.[77]

Trudeau objected that national feeling fostered in this way may not reflect the aspirations of all the groups within the state and may exacerbate separatist feelings. More important, the ultimate basis of a federal state is not emotional loyalty to the nation but a rational and calculated compromise of conflicting regional interests. A federal state is maintained by the gradual and prosaic alteration of the "terms of the federative pact," "by administrative practice, by judicial decision, and by constitutional amendment."[78] Appeals to nationalist or patriotic emotions create an "inner contradiction" in a federal state for "in the last resort the mainspring of federalism cannot be emotion but must be reason."[79] Trudeau, then, looked to the complete displacement of nationalism and nationalist emotion:

> Thus there is some hope that in advanced societies, the glue of nationalism will become as obsolete as the divine right of kings; the title of the state to govern and the extent of its authority will be conditional upon rational justification; a people's consensus based on reason will supply the cohesive force that societies require; and politics both within and without the state will follow a much more functional approach to the problems of government. If politicians must bring emotions into the act, let them get emotional about functionalism.[80]

Trudeau's use of "reason" and "rationality" in this connection illustrates the liberal tendency to see people as essentially homogenous beings despite differences of culture or history, a tendency arising from the atomistic individualism of liberalism. If what is really important for a person is that which pertains solely to her or him as an individual, differences which are the result of collective influences — linguistic or cultural, for instance — are only secondary. For Trudeau, this common core in every individual is "reason" or "rationality." The basis for national differences is thus emotional and irrational and, one hopes, also transitional and temporary. Indeed, Trudeau equated any sort of "emotional" response to political questions with superstition, and left no doubt that such sentiment, nationalist or otherwise, should ideally be discarded in the future:

> No doubt, at the level of individual action, emotions and dreams will still play a part; even in modern man, superstition remains a powerful motivation. But magic, no less

than totems and taboos, has long since ceased to play an important role in the normal governing of states. And likewise, nationalism will eventually have to be rejected as a principle of sound government.[81]

This liberal bias against cultural differentiation has allied itself with the liberal inclination in favour of technology and rapid technological innovation. Technology is a natural companion for the liberalism that seeks to maximize human freedom since technology, by extending natural human powers, works to the same end. Furthermore, technologies, whether of production or of business organization, operate best with the maximum of standardization and the greatest possible economies of scale. The combination of liberal attitudes and a highly developed technology thus produces a dynamic set of social forces, for liberalism demands the maximization of freedom or liberty and technology promises this in direct proportion to the degree to which it is employed. There is thus constant pressure to extend the scope and speed of technological innovation. At the same time, as we have noted, technology tends to standardize and simplify, much like a production line, so that a liberal technological society has a powerful dissolvent effect on pre-existing cultural or national differences. The constant impetus to standardization across national boundaries given by multinational corporations, and the production and marketing of those goods on a continental or global scale are examples of this process at work.

Trudeau recognized this homogenizing force ("...if technology is free to enter, the country must irrevocably step into the era of great communities of continental economies,"[82]) and is sympathetic to this sort of dynamic, dissolvent, technological society. For Trudeau, the mastery of technology is the key to the future — the "banana republic" of tomorrow is the state that has not mastered the "cybernetic revolution," — and to political progress:

> [T]he state — if it is not to be outdistanced by its rivals — will need political instruments which are sharper, stronger, and more finely controlled than anything based on mere emotionalism: such tools will be made up of advanced technology and scientific investigation, as applied to the fields of law, economics, social psychology, international affairs, and other areas of human relations: in short, if not a pure product of reason, the political tools of the future will be designed and appraised by more rational standards than anything we are currently using in Canada today.[83]

Reason no longer seeks, as in the classical view, to know the ultimate ends or purposes of the state and its citizens, but merely to master the techniques or tools necessary to the limitless expansion of human freedom.

Once Trudeau's secular rationality led him to espouse technology, he readily accepted the corollary that barriers should not be placed in its path and he argued that cultural values, like technologies, should be exposed to a maximum degree of competition. A special, protected position for Quebec within Confederation "can only tend to weaken values protected in this way against competition. Even more than technology, a culture makes progress through the exchange of ideas and through challenge." In "advanced societies," "cultural differentiation is submitted to ruthless competition" and "the road to progress lies in the direction of international integration."[84] The message is clear: technological forces ought to be given full play, and cultural or national values that succumb to their dissolvent effects are not worth having anyway.

This theoretical framework developed by Trudeau before he entered political life in 1965 has found concrete expression in language policies aimed at protecting individual language rights, the rejection of group rights in the form of special status for Quebec and, its greatest monument, the *Charter of Rights and Freedoms* incorporated in the Canadian constitution in 1982. Trudeau consistently advocated a constitutionally entrenched bill of rights, and although he was apparently willing to accept patriation without it in the early 1970s, in the face of provincial opposition, after 1980 he insisted on its inclusion.

As we noted in Chapter II, the Charter in its final form is not a purely liberal document. Strong opposition from the provinces, the federal Conservatives and some New Democrats, fortified by the Supreme Court of Canada's decision in the Constitutional Reference of 1981, forced the Trudeau government to accept the provision that either the federal or the provincial governments could enact legislation contrary to certain sections of the Charter, as long as they made it explicit that the legislation was to take effect notwithstanding the provisions of the Charter.

While the Trudeau government and some of the provincial governments announced their intention to use this override provision sparingly, if at all, it clearly allows a significant restriction on the Charter rights in favour of collective goals decided by democratically elected legislatures. The Parti Québécois government of René Lévesque during its period in office opted out of the Charter to the maximum degree possible.

Limited recognition of group rights for native peoples was also added and, from the beginning, the individual rights of immigrants to free choice of the language of education was restricted. The persistence of non-liberal elements in Canadian society also produced major changes in the other component of the Trudeau constitutional reform proposal, the amending formula.

The original amending formula would have allowed the federal government to call a referendum to override the opposition of provincial governments to proposed constitutional amendments. This option was available only to the federal government and was seen by most provincial premiers as a centralist attack on the provinces. In the version enacted the referendum, with its implications that the provincial governments were ultimately secondary to the individual voters and the federal government, disappeared entirely and amendments now require the approval of both parliament and the legislatures of two-thirds of the provinces, representing 50 percent of the Canadian population and, for certain amendments, unanimous provincial consent.

Trudeau's rejection of nationalism, as we have seen, was quite fundamental. The collective loyalties and sentiments on which it is based were, he thought, ultimately irrational and therefore to be rejected. Federalism was merely a means of blunting its impact; for Trudeau, federalism did not involve any recognition of any ultimate value accorded to the constituent parts of the federation. Thus, while Trudeau's chief enemy was French-Canadian nationalism, he was no more kindly disposed to other regional loyalties. It is this double focus that consistently directed Trudeau's approach to federal-provincial relations.

Any suggestion of special status for Quebec was rejected out of hand, and a like fate met similar demands from the Dene people of the Northwest Territories in the late 1970s. Attempts were made to eliminate existing manifestations of Quebec's special status, both by terminating programs from which the provinces could opt out and by foregoing opting out in new programs. The Established Programmes Financing (EPF) scheme originally set up in 1977 moved in this direction. In addition, provincial attempts to carry on quasi-diplomatic relations with foreign jurisdictions, or to encroach on federal financial resources were consistently rejected.

The refusal of the Trudeau government to introduce any new cost-sharing programs, the termination (Trans-Canada highway grants) and consolidation (Canada Assistance Plan) of others and the EPF scheme, which lessened direct federal financial control and provincial accountability, have been seen as an anti-centralist return to the classical federalism of clearly defined federal-provincial boundaries. Such a view is consistent with Trudeau's criticism in the 1950s of the expansion of federal power[85] and his advocacy of a balance or equilibrium within the federal system[86] and it may be asked why, if Trudeau was at heart a centralist, the position of the federal government relative to the provinces apparently continued to decline after 1968. The answer was that Trudeau faced economic and political forces, including Quebec nationalism and western alienation, of an intensely centrifugal nature, and had to respond from a base of political support that had narrowed to Quebec and parts of Ontario and the Atlantic provinces. The measure of Trudeau's defence of central power was perhaps the degree to which he held provincial demands in check. The defeat of the Parti Québécois referendum on sovereignty association in May 1980, the imposition of the National Energy Programme between 1980 and 1982 and the reduction in federal transfer payments in the 1982-1987 tax-sharing legislation all bear witness to this.

Some of the retreats were clearly tactical, in response to Trudeau's obsessive preoccupation with defeating Quebec nationalism. Patriation of the constitution and the Charter were seen as a major means of enhancing the legitimacy of the federal government in French Canada; abandoning the centralist amending formula and allowing the provinces to opt out of parts of the Charter are a price he was willing to pay. Reduction of federal involvement in shared-cost programs was acceptable because it ended special status for Quebec. Ultimately, the federal system itself was for Trudeau a price for accommodating French-Canadian nationalism because the functionalism Trudeau espoused could have been achieved by administrative rationalization or decentralization and does not require a federal division of power among quasi-sovereign entities.

Given Trudeau's views on federalism and nationalism, it was hardly surprising that the Meech Lake Constitutional Accord reached in 1987 attracted Trudeau's attention, disapproval and, ultimately, vitriolic condemnation. The Accord's recognition of Quebec as a "distinct society," and of the role of the Government of Quebec in preserving and promoting it, raised the spectre of special status for Quebec and a recognition of group rights, which might override individual rights. Trudeau was quick to claim that the Charter's promise of protection for individual rights was undermined by the Accord:

> For those Canadians who dreamed of the Charter as a new beginning for Canada, where everyone would be on an equal footing and where citizenship would finally be founded on a set of commonly shared values, there is to be nothing left but tears.[87]

The restrictions in the Accord on the federal government commencing new shared-cost programs in areas of provincial jurisdiction would produce the "balkanization of social services," a statement that is proof indeed of the tactical nature of Trudeau's earlier retreats in this area.

Trudeau's opposition to the Accord was entirely predictable and his description of Brian Mulroney as a "weakling" and Robert Bourassa and the other "prominent politicians" in Quebec as a "bunch of snivellers" was another manifestation of the verbal brutality and hyperbole that presumably reflected Trudeau's view of life as a "fierce struggle against intrusion."

Some opponents of the Accord in the Liberal Party, particularly among ethnic communities in Southern Ontario, would obviously have welcomed Trudeau's return to active politics to fight it. If he had done so, he would have found other allies within the party, including supporters of women's rights, for his attack appealed directly to the core of liberal individualism in the Party. He chose not to do so, and the federal Liberals under John Turner blessed the Accord with some reservations, primarily because of broad support in Quebec. This is yet another indication of the presence of non-liberal strands in the Canadian political culture and of the way in which the Liberal Party has been forced, as Horowitz observed, to modify its ideological orientation in the face of competition from other ideologies.

Perhaps the most surprising development in Liberal policy and attitudes under Trudeau was the drift toward interventionist and nationalist economic policies typified by the Foreign Investment Review Agency (FIRA) and the National Energy Programme (NEP). As we have seen, Trudeau is no friend of nationalism, and in the debates in the Liberal Party in the late 1960s over economic and cultural nationalism he was not identified with the nationalist wing of the party. He never showed any particular interest in economic policy as such and until the energy crisis, beginning in 1973, and the resulting upsurge in inflation, his government had continued the economic policies of its predecessors.

Our argument is that the excursion of the Liberal Party under Trudeau into the unfamiliar terrain of nationalism was a product of several factors. One is that nationalism, as we argue more fully in Chapter VI, can co-exist with different ideologies, and powerful nationalist sentiments have developed in Canada since the mid-1950s which have affected the Liberal Party. Some of Trudeau's strongest supporters in cabinet and in the party, including Allan MacEachen, Marc Lalonde, Herb Gray, Senator Keith Davey and Jim Coutts inclined to nationalism. Their role in supporting and encouraging Trudeau in his return to power after the fall of the Clark government in 1979 unquestionably strengthened their position.

Liberalism itself has an area of contact with nationalism because foreign domination arguably limits the economic or political freedom of citizens and therefore threatens the most fundamental of liberal values. In addition, the consistent argument of Canadian economics-nationalists has been that, in the long run, foreign control over the economy makes Canadians less, rather than more, wealthy. The corollary that a welfare liberal can easily draw is that foreign domination ultimately has the consequence of diminishing the worth of liberty in Canada. Paradoxically, Trudeau's very hostility to nationalism contributed to the Party's modest nationalist inclination, for the alternative to Canadian nationalism was seen to be not internationalism but the powerful nationalism of the American empire. This new realism is more reminiscent of Macdonald's analysis in the 1880s of Canadian vulnerability to the United States than the myopic liberal nationalism of Laurier and Mackenzie King.

Since 1956, increasing awareness of the problems created by American economic and cultural penetration of Canada clearly allowed some Liberals to justify nationalist measures on liberal grounds. Nationalist policies are advocated as a means of achieving autonomy, a goal which, in the political sphere, has been a fixture of liberal policy since at least the time of Laurier. The 1980 Liberal Convention was told:

> If we are...to increase our economic autonomy as an industrialized nation and ensure that a larger measure of the return on investment accrues to Canadians, then our dependence on foreign investment must diminish.[88]

The habit of resorting to government intervention, which was a product of Keynesian economic policies and welfare liberalism and which was firmly ingrained in

Canadian Liberalism by the 1970s, undoubtedly also smoothed the way for nationalist intervention. Finally, nationalist sentiment in the electorate, and parliamentary and electoral pressure from the more nationalist NDP strengthened the internal forces in the party favouring nationalist policies.

The result was a number of measures, most notably FIRA, the establishment of Petro-Canada and the NEP, which imposed significant limitations on foreign investment in Canada and went beyond any measures taken in the 1960s. In addition, cultural nationalism was manifested in federal support for Canadian-content rules in broadcasting and in the application of FIRA powers with particular stringency for publishing companies.

The growth of nationalism, generally, which is examined in Chapter VI, contributed to the drift of the Trudeau government to interventionist economic policies. We have argued that liberals, unlike socialists, have no automatic commitment to such policies. However, the rise of welfare liberalism and the decline of business liberalism in the Liberal Party in the 1970s lowered the threshold at which intervention was accepted. The result was the willingness of Liberals to resort to government intervention to deal with problems caused by the energy crisis and the chronic inflation and unemployment, which developed in the late 1970s. The response to the energy crisis was a government-imposed pricing regime for oil and natural gas, the establishment of Petro-Canada and the NEP. The response to inflation was wage and price controls in 1975, and the mixture of restraint and suasion that was the "six and five" solution of 1982. In general, these policies outraged pure business liberals such as the National Citizens Coalition led by the late Colin Brown, and Sinclair Stevens in the Conservative Party. They encouraged the drift of business liberals away from the Liberal Party without satisfying the socialists of the NDP. It is our argument that these policies were ideologically consistent with the welfare liberalism that has become an increasingly important component of Canadian Liberalism. Trudeau's seemingly erratic changes of direction in this area, for example, on wage and price controls in 1974-1975, were only movements within the bounds of liberal ideology. Since the time of Mackenzie King, the Liberal Party has accommodated both strands of liberalism, but when Trudeau left the party leadership in 1984, the apparent strength of business liberalism had never been so low.

JOHN TURNER

Because the Liberal Party is an ideological coalition, a change in party leadership provides a revealing picture of the shifting balance and relative strengths of different components in its ideological structure. This tendency is strengthened by the dominant position of the party leader and where a party leader like Trudeau was both conscious and capable of clearly articulating ideological positions, his particular view of the party's ideological mix will be reinforced. With a change of leadership the established ideological balance is temporarily in abeyance, awaiting the imprint of the new leader. During a leadership campaign there is a tendency for the component elements in the party ideology to become more visible as different candidates emphasize different aspects. Just as a physicist resolves a complex motion into its component forces, a party leadership campaign often has the effect of resolving the party's ideological mixture into its components until a new leader restates the party ideology.

This was particularly true in the leadership campaign following Pierre Trudeau's decision to resign in 1984. In 1968 Trudeau had defeated Robert Winters, the chief proponent of business liberalism within the party, and although Trudeau often disappointed welfare liberals, business liberalism played a secondary role in Liberal ideology during Trudeau's leadership. Trudeau's brand of economic nationalism, his growing reliance on the federal bureaucracy to direct the economy and, after 1980, the acceptance of staggering budgetary deficits to blunt the impact of economic recession, all pointed to the secondary position of business liberalism in the party ideology. Empirical studies support this conclusion. Opinion surveys of delegates to the 1968 and 1984 Liberal leadership conventions conclude that business liberals made up between one-quarter and one-third of party activists, and welfare liberals the remainder.[89]

Despite the apparent eclipse of business liberalism during the Trudeau years, his successor, John Turner, was generally perceived by delegates to the 1984 leadership convention as a business liberal,[90] and his success an indication that business liberalism remained a significant force within the Liberal Party, although the perception of Turner as a potent vote-getter clearly influenced many delegates to the convention.[91] The view of Turner as a business liberal found support in the 1984 leadership campaign. The policy measures Turner proposed would have produced a government more in tune with the thinking of Robert Winters and Mitchell Sharp, or even C.D. Howe, than Trudeau and Lalonde.

Turner implicitly criticized past Liberal policy, stating that dealing with Canada's economic problems

> means a restructuring of our standard basic industries and competitive stance with the rest of the world....It means a climate for better investment. It means predictability of economic policy and stability of economic policy.[92]

He praised the entrepreneurial tendencies of Westerners as Canada's chief "risk-takers"[93] and promised to simplify the taxation system to encourage business and to cut the federal deficit in half within seven years.[94] Turner's view that Canadian oil prices should rise to world market price levels implicitly rejected a major aspect of the NEP ostensibly designed to benefit lower-income Canadians.[95] In a speech to a Liberal meeting in Ottawa, Turner explicitly set out his view that the primary function of government was to establish a mix of economic policies that would favour business investment and enterprise:

> I start from the proper position that there are many things that only government can do and the first priority is to get these right — fiscal policy, tax policy, trade policy, monetary policy. Then, the government must provide a safety net for those who are unemployed, ill, aged, disadvantaged.[96]

His business liberalism was further reflected in his call for the sale of some Crown corporations and a general reduction of government regulation of business.

Turner also retreated from the centralist position taken by Trudeau, which has become associated with an interventionist position generally, promising to restore greater harmony in federal-provincial relations by restraining federal actions that conflicted with provincial policy or strayed into provincial jurisdiction. His most controversial position in the leadership campaign was that the controversy over French-language rights in Manitoba should be solved within the province and not imposed externally by legal action taken or encouraged by the federal government:

> Because of the fragility of the issue, certainly in historical terms for Canadians...provincial services for French languages within a province should be a matter of provincial initiative and should be negotiated within the province and should be a matter of provincial political resolution and not a matter imposed by judicial decision.[97]

Similarly, Turner stated, in relation to the extension of French language services in Ontario, that:

> It is up to the Government and Legislature of the province to find a solution acceptable to the people of Ontario.[98]

Turner's position on the language issue was widely criticized and he subsequently modified it somewhat. In retrospect, this dispute foreshadowed the disagreement within the Liberal Party, which later developed over the Meech Lake Accord. However, the extent of his departure from party policy under Trudeau was clear. Turner stated that he was "in principle, for the Charter [of the French language]...it's a question of provincial rights,"[99] and that Newfoundland should have greater control over its off-shore mineral resources than under existing Liberal government policy. From this position, it is not difficult to understand Turner's willingness to accept the Meech Lake Accord in 1987.

At the same time, Turner made it clear that the welfare liberal component of Canadian Liberalism was to remain, though in a less powerful role, and he reiterated his support for the existing system of social welfare programs. Indeed, in the 1984 election campaign Turner emphasized the Liberal Party's commitment to the principles of welfare liberalism more than business-oriented issues such as deficit reduction, which he had stressed in the leadership campaign. This was both an act of desperation in the face of an impending electoral disaster and a reflection of the welfare liberal bias of party *apparatchiks* such as Senators Grafstein and Davey on whom Turner was forced to rely in managing the election campaign. It is worth noting that Turner has also restated the fundamental combination of individualism and meliorism — the belief that human nature can be improved, if not perfected — that underlies, as we have seen, both business and welfare liberalism. In a speech to a Liberal policy conference in 1985, Turner declared that:

> ...first of all, liberalism extols the supremacy of the individual and the rights of the individual over the rights of the state. Liberalism seeks to allow every individual to develop to the full limit of the law and the full limits of his or her potential. We believe in equality of opportunity....[100]

In the same speech, he evoked (properly) Laurier in restating Liberal meliorism:

> To paraphrase those great words of Sir Wilfrid Laurier, we accept change and we seek it — we believe in reform and we fashion it, and we believe most of all that human beings can improve themselves. We believe that the world can become a better place if only we try hard enough. We really do believe that it is perfectible.[101]

The tension between business and welfare liberalism not only illustrated the way ideologies interact in Canadian political parties, but also the importance of a leader remaining within the boundaries of the party's ideological universe. While Turner emphasized business liberalism, he avoided pressing it to extremes and made it clear that welfare liberalism still had a role to play within the party. Thus, it was possible for delegates to the leadership convention to favour Turner on personality grounds or as the candidate most likely to win, while holding predominantly welfare-liberal views because he remained within the boundaries of the established Liberal ideology.

Donald Johnston's dilemma was that of a candidate who was perceived to be much closer to those boundaries. Johnston's views were in many ways similar to Turner's. Like Turner, Johnston was critical of certain aspects of the NEP and proposed that Canadian oil prices rise to world price levels, advocated selling certain Crown corporations and reducing government regulation of business. Johnston, however, perhaps because he was not a front runner, and in order to distinguish himself from the other candidates, spelled out his ideas in much greater detail. Johnston named specific Crown corporations to be sold. While Turner talked in general terms of reducing the deficit and government regulation, Johnston suggested scrapping the entire industrial and regional development grant and incentive program because it distorted the normal forces of market competition. In its place, he proposed tax-based incentives that would be distributed as a result of market forces rather than the decision of government officials.

While Johnston reaffirmed the party's traditional commitment to a "safety net" for the disadvantaged, he restated that commitment in radical terms, calling for the replacement of existing welfare programs with a guaranteed annual income, under which universality of benefits would be replaced by an impersonal means test administered through the tax system. While such a plan would likely increase the level of assistance to the poor (because of the redistribution of money made available by reducing benefits paid to middle- and upper-income groups) the proposal was perceived as a significant departure from the canons of welfare liberalism and contributed to Johnston's image as the "right-wing" candidate. Thus, while Johnston doubtless remained inside the boundaries of Liberal ideology, the language he used and the way in which he stated his proposals created a perceived threat to move outside those boundaries. This may have improved Turner's position by suggesting to welfare liberals that he, by comparison, was well within the boundaries of the Liberal ideology.

The apparent resurgence of business liberalism produced an equal and opposite reaction from the welfare-liberal wing of the party. Two minor candidates, John Munro and Eugene Whelan, based their campaigns on opposition to the business liberalism of Turner and Johnston, criticizing the banks, and corporations in general, and resisting any suggestions that Canadians should pay world prices for oil. Both suggested that the federal government should be stronger and Whelan criticized those advocating greater power for the provinces, making it clear that he would not hesitate to interfere with provincial jurisdiction.[102] Munro painted himself as the defender of a Liberal tradition under attack from the right: "...I am a candidate because I say 'never' to any tendencies that would take the Liberal Party away from its traditional centrist position."[103] Their welfare liberalism was, however, as far to one end of the Liberal spectrum as Johnston was at the other and their main function may have been to act as stalking horses for the main champion of the status quo in the Liberal Party, Jean Chrétien.

From the beginning, Chrétien committed himself to maintaining the ideological mixture of the party under Trudeau against an attempt to move the party to the right by giving a greater importance to business liberalism. He criticized "the new reform fad [that] would have the country move to the right"[104] and in defending the record of the Trudeau government, stated that "we did not succumb to the doctrinaire policies of the new right."[105] In almost every area of policy, Chrétien supported the Trudeau government's position and, both directly and by implication, attacked Turner. On the Manitoba language rights question he stated:

> Constitutionally protected minority language rights in every province have become a Canadian responsibility. This achievement is the proud heritage of all Liberals. On this I shall not compromise. I pledge to maintain this heritage intact and to work to expand it.[106]

Chrétien opposed concessions to Newfoundland on the offshore jurisdiction question, [107] disagreed explicitly with Turner on improving federal-provincial relations by reducing federal aggressiveness ("I don't buy peace at any price"), and rejected Turner and Johnston's proposals for changes in the National Energy policy.[108]

The polarization of support between Turner and Chrétien made it difficult for the two other candidates, John Roberts and Mark MacGuigan, to establish a position in the centre. MacGuigan described himself as part of the "reforming centre," opposed Turner on the Manitoba language rights question[109] and attacked Turner's plans to cut the deficit ("Canadians don't want Reaganomics whether it is offered by Tories or Liberals,")[110] and proposals that Canadian oil prices should go to world market levels.

Roberts echoed the criticism of Turner and Johnston's business liberalism made by other candidates, stating that some unnamed candidates were "tiptoeing to the right"[111] and that he did not believe that "Canadians wanted the Liberal Party as a carbon copy of the Conservative Party."[112] He attempted to stake out his "new liberalism" by advocating a mixture of policies, some of which, such as tax reform designed to encourage capital formation and assistance for small business, might have been perceived as business liberalism; others, such as equal pay for women, better day care, more retraining for displaced workers and expanded protection of the environment, might have been considered as welfare liberalism.

Roberts restated the traditional liberal justification for social-welfare policies, of providing equality of opportunity as a means of redressing social injustice, rather than the equality of condition produced by state intervention favoured by socialism:

> [the Liberals are] not conservatives who are ready to simply hold back and let the fittest fight for survival and status because we know that in the race for life not all start with equal chances. And we are not socialists. We reject the omni-present state. We want to encourage the spontaneity, the initiative and the enterprise of the individual Canadians.[113]

In fact, as we have argued, the *laissez-faire* philosophy Roberts criticized is not a tenet just of Canadian conservatism, but of the business liberalism that is an element in the ideologies of both the Conservative and the Liberal Parties. Roberts's comment is perhaps best seen as an argument for an ideological balance within the Liberal Party, which gives greater emphasis to welfare liberalism than business liberalism.

The Liberal defeat in the election of 1984, the worst showing (either in terms of seats or popular vote) in the party's history, contributed to maintaining the ideological flux following Trudeau's resignation. As a defeated leader, in any circumstances Turner would have had greater difficulty in imposing his ideological vision on the party. Turner's difficulties in the party leadership between the 1984 and 1988 elections, the open challenge to his leadership in 1986, and his perceived leadership shortcomings made this task more difficult. At the same time, however, Turner's problems were attributed by his detractors to ideological causes. As early as the 1984 election campaign, as we discussed above, Turner retreated from the business liberalism evident in the 1984 leadership contest, apparently at the price for the help of champions of welfare liberalism such as Senator Keith Davey. The decline in party support during the 1984 election campaign was also thought by some to have resulted from lack of emphasis on the welfare liberalism that had become a hallmark of the party over the previous twenty years.

Turner's position was not made easier by the emergence of two central issues before the 1988 election: the Meech Lake Accord and the Canada-United States Free Trade Agreement, each of which raised ideological questions.

MEECH LAKE, FREE TRADE
AND THE 1988 ELECTION

The Meech Lake Accord directly challenged the individualist and anti-collectivist assumptions that Trudeau so rigorously applied, by suggesting that a particular collectivity, the French-Canadian society within Canada, had certain rights that could override individual rights in some circumstances. We have looked at Trudeau's own reaction to the Accord; it was followed by reactions of a significant group within the Liberal party, ranging from liberal academics and women's groups concerned about restrictions on the application of the Charter to ethnic groups concerned perhaps because they enjoyed no such collective rights. Many of these Liberals joined together in ALARM, the Association of Liberals for the Amendment and Reform of Meech Lake, the honorary president of which was John Roberts. For the opponents of the Accord, it also threatened the ability of the federal government to intervene in certain areas of social policy by means of shared-cost programs. This ran counter to the centralizing tendencies of the Liberal Party in the post-1945 period which, as we have seen, were closely connected with welfare-liberal demands for such policies. The two lines of criticism were not, however, necessarily linked together. The individualist rejection of French-Canadian collective rights was equally congruent with business liberalism and opponents of Meech Lake were not, as we discuss below, always opponents of free trade.

Turner's support of the Accord clearly also enjoyed support in the Liberal Party, particularly in the provincial Quebec wing. On an issue with fewer ideological overtones, and led by a leader in a stronger position, one might speculate that the party would have accommodated its differences more easily. The Liberals eventually proposed amendments to the Accord designed to ensure that the Charter of Rights would override the Quebec "distinct society" clause, and to protect Northern and aboriginal and other minority rights, as well as move toward an elected senate. At the same time, the Liberal Party decided to approve the Accord in parliament even if such amendments were not made (as was certain to be the case).

The New Democratic Party faced somewhat similar problems but found the issue generally less divisive. One might speculate that the collectivist, socialist element in the NDP gave the party a point of reference to the principles underlying the Accord, which made it easier to accept than it was for some Liberals. The NDP's collectivism also appears to have given it a more positive view of the provincial governments as instruments to further the mix of socialist and welfare liberal policies it favoured — in provincial societies which themselves have a collective identity and legitimacy.

Controversy over Meech Lake arose again with renewed vigour after the 1988 election when, in December of 1988, the Supreme Court of Canada struck down certain provisions of Quebec's *Bill 101* — the Charter of the French Language — dealing with the use of English in commercial signs as inconsistent with the Charter. The response of the Bourassa Government was to enact new legislation restricting the use of English to signs that could not be seen from the outside of the store. This was clearly contrary to the Charter's free speech provisions, as discussed in the Supreme Court judgement, and the Quebec legislation invoked the "notwithstanding" clause in section 33 of the Charter to override those provisions. The use of collective power in this manner to override individual rights gave added weight to critics of the Accord who either argued that the "distinct society" clause in the Accord would be used to justify similar actions, without recourse to the "notwithstanding" clause, or that it was wrong to make concessions to Quebec when Quebec was not treating its English-language minority fairly.

The most immediate political consequence from the controversy was the decision in January of 1989 by the Conservative Government of Gary Filmon in Manitoba to withdraw its support for the Accord. At the same time, the new Liberal and New Democratic Party caucusses in parliament showed increasing restiveness with their parties' support for the Accord. In the case of the Liberals, most of their new members were from Southern Ontario and included a number of persons who clearly had supported Pierre Trudeau's opposition to the Accord. After the election, the pragmatic argument that support of the Accord was required to gain votes in Quebec had lost its force, particularly given the disastrous Liberal showing in Quebec (thirteen of seventy-five seats). Similarly, in the New Democratic Party, the failure of Ed Broadbent's attempt to increase NDP support in Quebec (including, as a major component, support of the Accord) removed a consideration that had formerly restrained New Democrats unhappy with the Accord.

The apparent contradiction between a Liberal Government of Quebec pursuing nationalist and collectivist policies apparently at odds with liberal principles and Liberal Members of Parliament in Ottawa increasingly restive with the Accord both illustrates the continuing power of French-Canadian nationalism and the way in which different ideologies interact with each other and with a single poitical party in Canada.

The Free Trade Agreement was similarly troubling for the Liberals. The main features of the Agreement[114] included:

- elimination of all tariffs on goods passing between Canada and the United States over a ten-year period.

- elimination of restrictions on trade in many services between the two countries.

- a mechanism for resolving trade disputes.

- easing of restrictions on U.S. investment in Canada (with exceptions for cultural industries and certain energy-related investments).

- restrictions on Canada's ability to give Canadian consumers energy prices lower than those charged on Canadian energy exported to U.S. consumers.

The Agreement was clearly responsive to demands of the Canadian business community for market-based economic policies and it was no surprise that the Agreement received overwhelming support from this group. Business opposition, in general, came only from groups such as grape growers and wine producers who were affected adversely by the Agreement, and was not based on broad questions of principle. As we discuss in Chapter IV, the Agreement reflected the growing strength of business liberalism in the Progressive Conservative Party. It equally appealed to the business liberals in the Liberal Party and, indeed, had its origins in the 1985 report of the Royal Commission headed by Donald Macdonald, a former Trudeau cabinet minister, which strongly endorsed the idea of Canada-United States free trade. The Agreement also appealed to the Liberal past — Laurier's unsuccessful campaigns for free trade in 1891 and 1911, and the continued and largely successful efforts of the King, St. Laurent and Pearson governments to integrate Canada economically with the United States and to generally remove trade barriers with the United States.

The dominant welfare-liberal wing of the party viewed the Agreement very differently, though the idea of such an agreement in theory was not rejected. Indeed, the notion of freer trade — removing external restraints from individual economic liberty and with connotations of internationalism and the rejection of national particularity — made it difficult for welfare liberals to dismiss the concept outright. In a speech on the free trade issue delivered in 1986, Turner stated that:

We stand where we have always stood as a Party. The Liberal Party has always favoured widening trade. We have always favoured liberalized trade... We would never
oppose discussions with the United States in an attempt to enlarge our mutual access
to each other's respective markets.[115]

Instead, Liberals opposed to the Agreement, such as John Turner, generally
took the position that there was nothing wrong with freer trade with the United
States in the abstract, but the Agreement the Mulroney government formulated
was found wanting.

In practice, the Liberal Party welfare liberals' criticisms of the Agreement were
very similar to those of the New Democrats, which is not surprising, given the
growing strength of the welfare-liberal wing in the New Democratic Party under
Ed Broadbent. The principal criticism of the Agreement, apart from noting the
possible effects on specific industries or specific areas (which was as much for
immediate and tactical political gain as anything else), was that directly and indirectly it would limit the ability of Canadian governments to intervene in social and
economic matters.

First, it was argued, the provisions of the Agreement dealing with energy policy and pricing and with restrictions on United States investment in Canada, directly limited the federal government's ability to act in these areas. Indeed, some
business liberals opposed to previous actions of the Trudeau government, such as
the NEP and FIRA, claimed this to be one of the merits of the Agreement.

Second, it was argued that in an indirect way closer integration of the Canadian
and American economies and more unrestricted competition from American goods
and services would create strong pressures to conform Canadian social policies,
such as medicare, unemployment insurance, welfare and environmental protection,
to American standards which were thought to be lower. Such Canadian social
policies might be viewed either as forms of subsidies, which would entitle the
United States to take countervailing action, or would be attacked by Canadian
business as a threat to its ability to compete. On this argument, under free trade,
Canadian and American business were to be allowed to compete on a "level playing field," and the costs of supporting Canadian welfare programs would hinder
Canadian business in doing so. Canadian business would therefore press for reducing benefits in those programs to American levels. In turn, these social policies
were seen to be a vital part of a Canadian national identity, which would therefore
itself be threatened by the Agreement. Although "cultural" industries were specifically excepted from the Agreement, it was also suggested that offsetting benefits
would be required for Americans, which would also place strong, if indirect, pressure on Canadian governments to limit policies protecting Canadian culture. This,
it was argued, posed an even more serious threat to Canadian identity. The result
was a conclusion similar to that drawn by Sir John A. Macdonald in 1891 or Sir

Robert Borden in 1911: free trade with the United States ultimately threatened Canada's separate existence as a nation.

The opposition of welfare liberals to the Free Trade Agreement reflects, in part, the instrumental rather than substantial nature of welfare-liberal nationalism. The principal criticism of the Agreement was that it would restrict the ability of Canadian governments, and particularly the federal government, to provide certain services and benefits to Canadians, primarily of a welfare nature such as medicare or unemployment insurance. This reflects the attraction of nationalism to welfare liberals as a means of protecting the ability of the state to provide these benefits, so central to welfare liberalism, to its citizens. Nationalism is, therefore, an instrument to obtain certain welfare liberal ends rather than the pursuit of the substance of national interest or identity itself. In the leaders' debate in the 1988 election campaign, for example, Broadbent defended the difference in identity between Canada and the United States in these terms:

> I think, unlike the United States — and this is a crucial social point about this country that makes us so different... — we have universal programs.[116]

This is not to suggest welfare liberals were not motivated by genuine patriotism in their attack on free trade, for as was argued in Chapter VI, patriotism does not respect ideological borders. John Turner's passionate outburst against free trade, in the English-language leaders debate in the 1988 election campaign is proof enough of this:

> We are just as Canadian as you are, Mr. Mulroney, but I will tell you this: You mentioned 120 years of history. We built a country east and west and north. We built it on an infrastructure that deliberately resisted the continental pressure of the United States. For 120 years we have done it. With one signature of a pen, you have reversed that, thrown us into the north-south influence of the United States... and will reduce us, I am sure, to a colony of the United States, because when the economic levers go, the political independence is sure to follow.[117]

Our point is that welfare liberalism and nationalism have found points of contact in recent years in Canada, and the free trade issue is one of them. As we argue in Chapter VI, that point of contact is the identification of the nationalist goal of national independence and freedom with the liberal goal of individual liberty — national independence, up to a point, is a condition of individual freedom and independence. Turner attacked the Free Trade Agreement in Parliament on the grounds that it threatened Canadian freedom to pursue its own way which, in the context of other remarks of Turner discussed below, meant freedom to pursue welfare liberal goals:

> The price is our sovereignty, our freedom to make our own choices, to decide what is right for us, to go on building the kind of country we want... that is what the Government wants to give away, our freedom to be different, our freedom to be ourselves, to do things our own way, not the American way.[118]

This was reinforced by perceived ideological differences between the societies of Canada and the United States. We argue in Chapter VI that Canadian nationalism has often been influenced by the degree of "foreign-ness" of the United States from an ideological perspective. Nineteenth-century tories saw it as a liberal society of the worst sort. Canadian liberals in the early 1960s saw the United States in the Kennedy era as a beacon of welfare liberalism and, therefore, attractive. Canadian liberals in the 1980s, even more committed to welfare liberalism, saw the United States under Reagan and Bush as a stronghold of business liberalism, a contradiction of values held by many Canadians and incompatible with Canadian society's dominant welfare liberalism heavily tinged with tory-socialist collectivism. Those views were strengthened by the numbing social problems of urban and societal decay in American society and the general decline in American power and prestige. At the same time, many Canadians would attribute those problems to a different and less attractive ideological climate in the United States. In the final debate on free trade in the House of Commons in August of 1988, Turner implicitly set out this criticism of business liberalism and of contemporary American society:

> Free market forces alone would not have given us public housing, or a public transportation network, or the best medical care system in the world, the Canadian Wheat Board, or a very comprehensive support system for the weaker elements in Canadian society. What I am saying is not anti-American; it is pro-Canadian.[119]

Turner's views clearly reflected the perception of Canadian welfare liberals (among others) of the United States as a society dominated by business liberalism:

> The Americans put all their faith in market forces. Yes, we believe in enterprise and we believe in rewarding success, but as Canadians we have the ultimate goals of fairness and sharing. We feel that these purposes have been accomplished better in a mixed economy.[120]

For business liberals it was also possible to rationalize support of the Agreement with love of country. In the late 1960s, Eric Kierans, then a minister in the Trudeau government, had called for market-based nationalist policies, which, he believed, would strengthen Canadian private enterprise and enable it to compete more effectively with foreign business. Included in Kierans's prescription was a removal of all tariffs to promote greater efficiency in Canadian manufacturing. While most nationalists rejected reliance on private enterprise to protect Canadian interests and identity in this manner, it was not illegitimate for patriotic business liberals to argue that, by the 1980s, many Canadian business enterprises were equal to, or better than, their foreign competitors and that the greater efficiencies allowed under free trade would enable them to develop as world-class institutions. On this argument, Canadian entrepreneurs, given the necessary encouragement, did not need government protection, but greater access to foreign markets.

During the 1988 election campaign, many voters were apparently confused by the free trade issue because of the claims by the Liberal and New Democratic Parties that the most fundamental Canadian interests were being threatened by the Agreement. How, such voters asked, could this be when so many obviously decent and loyal Canadians (inside and outside the Conservative Party) supported the Agreement? This argument was, in fact, used by the Conservative Party during the election campaign. The answer is that both sides believed that they were best pro-tecting Canadian national interests. The fact that they adhered to different politi-cal ideologies, whether business liberalism, welfare liberalism or socialism, meant that they found the national interest embodied in different policies and different goals. For the Conservative Party, in power and dominated by its business liberal wing, any contradiction between the business liberal and tory analyses of the issue caused no more than a few ripples. In the Liberal Party, out of power with an unpopular leader and dominated by the welfare liberal wing opposing the Agree-ment, it is not surprising that there was open disagreement between Liberals on the free trade issue. For some like Donald Johnston, disagreements with Turner on free trade coincided with disagreements on the Meech Lake Accord, and it is not sur-prising that Johnston left active Liberal politics shortly before the 1988 election. For John Roberts, John Munro and others who opposed the Free Trade Agreement and the Meech Lake Accord, it was possible to participate actively in the campaign (albeit, Roberts and Munro, unsuccessfully) on the strength of Turner's approach to free trade and his commitment to seek amendments to the Accord after it had been enacted. As Roberts stated:

> I would not be running in this campaign if I did not think I could support Mr. Turner's leadership, and I can on Meech Lake because I believe in the kinds of amendments which he has brought forward.[121]

In a wider sense, the Free Trade Agreement was but one product of the tendency of the Mulroney government to allow market forces a freer reign in Canadian society. The provisions of the agreement, which purported to prevent any re-im-position of the NEP or of the old FIRA-type restrictions on American invest-ment in Canada, were not viewed by proponents of the agreement merely as a necessary price to be paid, but as positively beneficial in themselves in so far as they restricted the ability of future Canadian governments to ignore or suppress market forces. As we have argued, this was fully consistent with the dominant business liberalism of the Mulroney government and was clearly ideologically motivated. However, it clashed directly with the growing interventionist tenden-cies in the Liberal Party, whose development during the Trudeau years we have discussed previously and which were justified on the basis of the welfare liberal goal of maximizing the positive liberty of individual Canadians. Fears that the agreement would ultimately force a scaling down of the Canadian social-welfare system not only stirred nationalist objections in Liberals but objections from a perspective of welfare liberalism, which had long supported the development of those programs. While business and welfare liberals clashed on other fronts in the 1988 election campaign, the free trade issue became in many ways the symbol of the clash of ideologies.

Many advocates of welfare liberalism, such as John Roberts, also connected the Meech Lake Accord with this assault on welfare-liberal values as threatening the ability of the federal government to pursue welfare-liberal goals. This division, however, was not so clear because the Accord did not place any obstacles before the provincial governments pursuing such policies (so that the Accord was acceptable to welfare liberals in Quebec who were also attracted to French-Canadian nationalism). Conversely, opposition to the Accord on the basis of a rejection of French-Canadian nationalism was not incompatible with business-liberal views, witness Donald Johnston's position.

Beyond the pivotal issues of the Meech Lake Accord and free trade, the Liberal platform in the 1988 election further accentuated the dominance of welfare liberalism in the party. Gone was Turner's emphasis on deficit reduction and fiscal rectitude from his 1984 leadership campaign and the modest steps towards privatization taken in the closing year or two of the Trudeau government. The Liberals adopted a number of policies: they opposed any further privatization, including a promise to re-nationalize the shares of Air Canada sold to the public shortly before the election; they condemned any introduction of a value-added type of national sales tax as regressive and generally promised greater government intervention in the economy, including a $1.5 billion increase in regional development spending; they promised a reintroduction of the registered home ownership savings plan, government assistance for profit sharing by companies, more tax incentives for regional development and an interest and dividend tax deduction for senior citizens.

The issue of the polarization of Canadian political parties along ideological lines was explicitly raised in the 1988 election campaign by NDP leader Ed Broadbent, commenting early in the campaign on polls indicating the New Democrats might replace the Liberals as the official opposition. Mr. Broadbent justified his hope on the grounds that polarization on ideological grounds would give the Canadian public a clearer choice and generally make the electoral process more meaningful. While the Liberal Party would have been, in Broadbent's view, the chief casualty of such a development, it has itself contributed to whatever polarizing developments have occurred in recent years in Canada. The eclipse of the business-liberal wing of the party has not only driven individuals such as Donald Johnston and Donald Macdonald from active involvement in the party but has made the Conservative Party the unquestioned champion of the Canadian business establishment. This development has arguably been under way for the last twenty years and is certainly not the work of the Liberal Party under Turner alone. Turner, however, has been either unwilling or, more likely, unable to reverse the trend which, in the longer term, represents a major change in the party from its identification with Canadian business in the 1950s, which in its turn was the end of a long process of convergence between the interests of Canadian business and the Liberal Party dating back to the time of Mackenzie King.

By relegating business liberalism to a secondary position in the party at the same time as business-liberal support was increasingly concentrating in the Conservative Party, the Liberals have contributed to an increasing polarization of Liberal and Conservative support in Canada and have reduced the differences between the Liberal Party and the New Democrats. Indeed, on many issues, the Liberals and New Democrats have become, personalities aside, indistinguishable, which is not surprising given the way in which welfare liberalism predominates in both parties. Paradoxically, the description of Liberals and Conservatives as the Tweedledum and Tweedledee of Canadian politics, so long loved and used by New Democrats, may have become as true of the Liberals and New Democrats, as of the Liberals and the Conservatives. As Sheila Copps, a Liberal M.P. and member of the "rat pack" admitted: "When I first joined the Liberal Party I wondered secretly whether I was not really a closet New Democrat since some of their views seemed to fit... my concerns."[122]

We first argued that in 1974 there were significant ideological differences within the Liberal Party and that these differences contributed to real ideological divergence between the Liberal and Conservative Parties. Martin Goldfarb and Thomas Axworthy's analysis of opinion surveys of party convention delegates between 1968 and 1984 gives substantial empirical support for this conclusion:

> William Christian and Colin Campbell have identified property, or business liberalism, versus social democratic, or welfare liberalism, as one of the critical cleavage of the party, and the 1984 data confirms that this policy debate continues. Of the 10 issues that most divide the party, six related to this business-welfare dimension.[123]

Goldfarb's and Axworthy's thesis is that Liberals and Conservatives have become more ideologically distinct since the 1960s:

> Twenty years ago, it was popularly understood that the two major parties were ideologically quite similar. Today, the Liberals and Conservatives are ideologically distinctive. The Liberals have become more liberal and the Conservatives have become more conservative.[124]

What Goldfarb and Axworthy mean by "liberal" and "conservative" is clearly, in light of their overall analysis, what we call welfare liberal and business liberal, respectively. This conclusion is well justified, certainly as it applies to the Liberal Party, as we have detailed the shift to welfare liberalism. It is interesting that they do not believe the proportion of welfare liberals among party activists has changed much since 1968 (at from two-thirds to three-quarters). One might speculate that since the 1960s the welfare-liberal majority among party activists has used its majority position to alter the policy mix inherited from King and St. Laurent so that the party's posture now more accurately reflects its membership's views. John Turner's "conversion" to welfare-liberal views since 1984, particularly on free trade, is a good index of the power of the welfare-liberal majority.

Goldfarb and Axworthy also conclude that the voters, in general, appreciate these differences.

> Despite assertions to the contrary, the electorate does, in fact, distinguish between the political ideology of the Liberal and Conservative parties. There is a sense that the Liberal and Conservative parties do differ in their political orientation and ideology.[125]

This suggests that the polarization of electoral support may be accompanying ideological polarization. For the Liberal Party, following its defeat in the 1988 election, the practical question is whether the abandonment of business liberalism, and the loss of the support of the powerful elites who espouse it, will be offset by the support of welfare liberals who formerly supported the Conservative or New Democratic Parties. The answer is beyond the scope of this book, but will play an important role in determining the Liberal Party's future in the 1990s under the stewardship of John Turner's successor as Liberal leader.

LIBERALISM AND THE END OF IDEOLOGY

It has been a common liberal argument, most clearly restated by Pierre Trudeau, that liberalism is the enemy of ideology. Liberals have tended to think of ideologies as collections of abstract and complicated systems of ideas, and consequently have placed them in opposition to their own rather simplistic view of society as a collection of atomistic individuals governed by a calculating rationality, which they call pragmatism, empiricism or, in a phrase Trudeau used, common sense. Hence, Trudeau's boast that he was not tied down or restricted by any ideological superstructure: "The only constant factor to be found in my thinking over the years has been opposition to accepted opinions." Indeed, such "ideological systems are the true enemies of freedom."[126]

John Turner expressed the same conviction, albeit less elegantly, in a speech to a Liberal policy conference in Halifax in 1985:

> We are not doctrinaire, we are not ideological, we are not rigid, we are not static...[127]

This common-sense attitude delivers liberals from some ideological ways of thinking, since the liberal mind is trained on the low but solid ground of furthering individual interests by the use of reason limited to discovering techniques rather than ends. Not only does it escape the lure of more speculative or less popular systems; it does not even, except when forced by electoral considerations, pay them the compliment of listening to what they have to say. It is however, this very simplicity or common-sensical aspect of liberalism, that justifies our calling it an ideology, for it presents a very partial or limited view of the world. The liberal preoccupation with the individual and the consequent shallow analysis of the social and collective aspects of human existence is an excellent example of this limited nature, and in itself a sufficient refutation of the argument that liberalism heralds the "end of ideology." The incompleteness of the liberal account of the nature of political and social life contributes to the continued strength of the other ideologies, to which we now turn.

---

1. *The Report and Despatches of the Earl of Durham* (London: Ridgways, 1839). Reprinted London, Methuen Publications, 1902, p. 8.

2. *Ibid.*, p. 12.

3. *Ibid.*, p. 16.

4. *Ibid.*, p. 16.

5. *Ibid.*, p. 22; this belies the popular misconception that economic individualism meant an automatic decrease in governmental activity. In fact, individuals who wished to exercise their economic liberties more fully were quickly led, on both sides of the Atlantic, to demand certain kinds of government action to support this provision; for example, of transportation facilities and enforcement of common standards. They also required, to match the new technological advances, a greater degree of technical sophistication in such government actions. The result was, in real terms, a net growth in governmental activities and expertise, despite the government's retreat from other areas.

6. *Ibid.*, p. 31.

7. *Ibid.*, p. 31.

8. *Ibid.*, p. 33.

9. *Ibid.*, p. 105.

10. *Ibid.*, p. 117.

11. *Ibid.*, p. 111.

12. Samuel Thompson, *Reminiscences of a Canadian Pioneer*, Vol. 1. (Toronto: Hunter Rose, 1884), p. 215. Reprinted by McClelland & Stewart, Toronto, 1968.

13. The anti-clericalism they acquired from continental European liberalism, however, was a good deal more secularist than the voluntarism of the Clear Grits, which was derived more from a concern for the vitality of religion than from any coolness or scepticism about it.

14. Sir Allan MacNab, an arch-Tory, declared on his appointment to the presidency of the Grand Trunk: "my politics are railroads."

15. See J.M.S. Careless, *Brown of the Globe* (Toronto: Macmillan), Vol. 1, p. 295.

16. "Resolutions of Reform Convention, Toronto June 27, 1967," Toronto *Globe* June 28, 1867 in D.O. Carrigan, *Canadian Party Platforms 1867-1968.* (Toronto: Copp Clark, 1968), p. 6.

17. Their reasoning was put succinctly by Alexander Mackenzie in a speech of 1865: "The French people felt it necessary to maintain a strong national spirit, and to resist all attempts to procure justice by the people of the west, lest that national existence should be broken down....mere representation by population, under such circumstances, would perhaps scarcely meet the expectations formed of it, because although Upper Canada would have seventeen more members than Lower Canada (in the proposed Dominion House), it would be an easy thing for the fifty or fifty-five members representing French constituencies to unite with a minority from Upper Canada and thus secure an Administration subservient to their views." p. 423. *Parliamentary Debates on the Subject of the Confederation of the British North American Provinces* (Quebec: 1865).

18. J.M.S. Careless, *Brown of the Globe*, Vol. II, *Statesman of Confederation* (Toronto: Macmillan, 1963), p. 19.

19. *The Address of the Liberal Leader* (Toronto: 1882), in Carrigan, *Canadian Party Platforms*, pp. 18–19.

20. Joseph Wearing, *The L-Shaped Party: The Liberal Party of Canada 1958-1980* (Toronto, 1981), p. 4.

21. *Parliamentary Debates:* Vol. VI, No. 1. 14 March 1879, p.p. 468, 473, revised.

22. *A National Sentiment* (Ottawa), in Vol. II., p. 325.

23. Goldwin Smith, *Canada and the Canadian Question* (London: Macmillan, 1891), p. 45. Reprinted Toronto © University of Toronto Press 1971.

24. *Ibid.*, p. 279.

25. *Ibid.*, p. 30.

26. *Ibid.*, p. 284.

27. *Ibid.*, p. 56.

28. *Ibid.*, p. 39.

29. *The Address of the Liberal Leader* in Carrigan, *Canadian Party Platforms*, p. 20.

30. *Ibid.*, p. 24, Toronto *Mail*, Feb. 1, 1887, Campaign Speech by Edward Blake.

31. Wilfrid Laurier, Lecture delivered at the Academy of Music, Quebec, on the invitation of the Club Canadien, June 26, 1877, p. 67.

32. *Ibid.*, pp. 69–71.

33. *Ibid.*, pp. 61–62.

34. *Ibid.*, p. 472.

35. Regulation 17 was intended to forbid French-language schools in Ontario.

36. Skelton, Vol. II, p. 479.

37. Carrigan, *The Address of the Liberal Leader in Canadian Party Platforms*, p. 19.

38. Campaign Speech by Blake, *ibid.*, p. 24.

39. Skelton, Vol. 1, pp. 376–377.

40. *Ibid.*, pp. 380–381.

41. The reluctance or refusal of Liberals like Brown, Mackenzie and Laurier to take titles was one manifestation of this.

42. In 1897, he apparently approved the seating of colonial representatives in the Imperial Parliament, saying, "it would be the proudest moment of my life if I could see a Canadian of French descent affirming the principles of freedom in the parliament of Great Britain." This, however, seems to have been an aberration produced by the intoxicating display of imperial might in the Diamond Jubilee celebrations. Skelton, II, p. 72.

43. *Ibid.*, p. 105.

44. *Ibid.*, p. 293.

45. Dafoe to George Iles, 27 September 1911. W.L. Morton in *The Progressive Party in Canada* Copyright Canada, 1950 by University of Toronto Press, Toronto, p. 26.

46. *Ibid.*, p. 26.

47. *Ibid.*, p. 15

48. *The Grain Growers' Guide*, 7 February 1912, in Morton, *op. cit.*, p. 25.

49. Morton, *op. cit.*, p. 16.

50. The United Farmer's Platform, 1919, *The National Liberal and Conservative Handbook*, 1, pp. 74–77, in *Canadian Party Platforms 1867-1968*, p. 91.

51. See Morton, *op. cit.*, p. 130.

52. *Ibid.*, p. 164.

53. Statement on Progressive Policies, Issued by Robert Forke, Progressive Leader, *The Grain Grower's Guide in Canadian Party Platforms 1867-1968*, pp. 99, 102.

54. Quoted in H.B. Neatby, "The Political Ideas of William Lyon Mackenzie King" in *The Political Ideas of the Prime Ministers of Canada* (Ottawa: University of Ottawa, 1968), p. 125.

55. William Lyon Mackenzie King, *Industry and Humanity* (New York: Houghton Mifflin, 1918), p. 336.

56. *National Liberal and Conservative Handbook*, I, pp. 55-62 (Ottawa: 1921) in *Canadian Party Platforms*, p. 82.

57. "Every dispute and every controversy of which I have had any intimate knowledge has owed its origin, and the difficulties pertaining to its settlement, not so much to the economic questions involved as to 'this certain blindness in human beings' to matters of real significance to other lives, and to an unwillingness to approach an issue with any attempt at appreciation of the fundamental sameness of feelings and aspirations in human beings." King, *Industry and Humanity*, p. 7.

58. Mackenzie King to Charles Dunlop, 8 July 1933, in Neatby, *op. cit.*, p. 128.

59. *National Liberal and Conservative Handbook*, in Carrigan, p. 82.

60. "A Campaign Statement of the Liberal Party," *Sydney Post Record*, March 8, 1940, in *ibid.*, p. 140.

61. We as "Liberals again place on record our appreciation of the object of the said Agreement and our faith in the principles of friendly international relations underly-

ing it, and we express our earnest hope that in both countries such principles will be upheld, and that a favourable moment may come when there will be a renewed manifestation by the two Governments of a desire to make some similar arrangements." *National Liberal and Conservative Handbook* in Carrigan, p. 81.

62. Mackenzie King, *The Liberal Party's Position* (Ottawa: 1935), in *ibid.*, p. 128. Reprinted by permission of The National Liberal Federation of Canada.

63. "Resolution Adopted by the Third National Liberal Convention," Ottawa, 1948. *The Liberal Party of Canada* (Ottawa: 1957), in *ibid.*, p. 181. Reprinted by permission of the National Liberal Federation of Canada.

64. From "Introduction" by Lester B. Pearson to *The Liberal Party* by J.W. Pickersgill (1962, p. ix) reprinted by permission of the Canadian publishers, McClelland & Stewart Limited, Toronto, p. ix.

65. "Liberalism, also, while insisting on equality of opportunity, rejects any imposed equality which would discourage and destroy a man's initiative and enterprise. It sees no value in the equality, or conformity, which comes from lopping off the tallest ears of corn....Liberalism accepts social security, but rejects socialism; it accepts free enterprise but rejects economic anarchy."

66. P.E. Trudeau, *Federalism and the French Canadians* (Toronto: Macmillan, 1968), p. xxi.

67. See P.E. Trudeau: *Conversations with Canadians*, p. 86 © this selection University of Toronto Press 1972, Toronto.

68. *Ibid.*

69. *Ibid.*, p. 87.

70. See R. Joy, *Languages in Conflict* (Toronto: McClelland & Stewart, 1972).

71. Trudeau, *Federalism and the French Canadians*, p. 18.

72. *Ibid.*, p. 4.

73. *Ibid.*, p.p. 157–158.

74. *Ibid.*, p. 158.

75. *Ibid.*, p. 159.

76. *Ibid.*, p. 177.

77. P.E. Trudeau, "Federalism, Nationalism and Reason" in P.A. Crepeau and C.B. Macpherson, eds. *The Future of Canadian Federalism*, p. 26, © University of Toronto Press, 1965.

78. *Ibid.*, p. 26.

79. *Ibid.*, p. 27.

80. *Ibid.*, p. 28.

81. *Ibid.*, p. 34.

82. Trudeau, *Federalism and the French Canadians*, p. 13.

83. Trudeau, "Federalism, Nationalism and Reason," p. 34.

84. Trudeau, *Federalism and the French Canadians*, pp. 33–34.

85. See *ibid.*, pp. 79-102, criticizing federal grants to universities.

86. "It was because of the federal government's weakness that I allowed myself to be catapulted into it," *ibid.*, p. xxiii.

87. *Globe and Mail*, May 28, 1987.

88. *Ibid.*, p. 36.

89. Martin Goldfarb and Thomas Axworthy, *Marching to a Different Drummer*, (Toronto: Stoddart, 1988), p.57

90. Polling of the convention delegates indicated that Turner was perceived as the most "right wing" of all the leadership candidates: Goldfarb and Axworthy, *op. cit.*, p.54

91. See Goldfarb and Axworthy, *op. cit.*, p.p. 61–62, and 67:..."above all, [Liberal delegates] saw John Turner as a man who could win."

92. *Globe & Mail*, March 17, 1984.

93. *Globe & Mail*, April 27, 1984.

94. *Globe & Mail*, March 17, 1984.

95. *Globe & Mail*, April 30, 1984.

96. *Globe & Mail*, May 10, 1984.

97. *Globe & Mail*, March 20, 1984.

98. *Globe & Mail*, May 14, 1984.

99. *Globe & Mail*, April 12, 1984.

100. Speech to Liberal Party Reform Conference, Halifax, November 9, 1985, mimeo, pp.8–9.

101. *op. cit.* p.9.

102. *Globe and Mail*, May 14, 1984.

103. *Montreal Gazette*, March 22, 1984.

104. *Globe & Mail*, March 12, 1984.

105. *Globe & Mail*, April 26, 1984.

106. *Globe & Mail*, March 21, 1984.

107. *Globe & Mail*, April 18, 1984.

108. *Globe & Mail*, April 18, 1984.

109. *Globe & Mail*, March 20, 1984.

110. *Globe & Mail*, May 7, 1984.

111. *Globe & Mail*, May 18, 1984.

112. *Globe & Mail*, March 20, 1984.

113. *Globe & Mail*, May 14, 1984.

114. See *The Canada-United States Free Trade Agreement*, Toronto: CCH, 1988.

115. Speech to the Ottawa-Carleton Board of Trade, Ottawa, June 19, 1986, mimeo, p.3.

116. *Encounter 88*, October 25, 1988, mimeo, p.36.

117. *Encounter 88*, October 25, 1988, mimeo, p.43.

118. *House of Commons Debates*, August 30, 1988, p.19059.

119. *House of Commons Debates*, August 30, 1988, p.19064.

120. *House of Commons Debates*, August 30, 1988, p.19059.

121. *Globe & Mail*, October 24, 1988.

122. Sheila Copps, *Nobody's Baby* (Toronto: Deneau, 1986), p.122.

123. Goldfarb and Axworthy, *op. cit.*, p.53.

124. Goldfarb and Axworthy, *op. cit.*, p.ix.

125. Goldfarb & Axworthy, *op. cit.*, p.104.

126. Trudeau, *Federalism and the French Canadians*, p. xxi.

127. Speech to Liberal Party Reform Conference, Halifax, November 9, 1985, mimeo p.9.

CHAPTER IV

Δ

CANADIAN CONSERVATISM

THE CONSERVATIVE CONUNDRUM

Following the first election in the newly formed Dominion of Canada, the Governor-General selected the foremost politician in the new confederation as its first Prime Minister. John A. Macdonald had been the leading instigator of the plan to unite the British North American colonies into a single political unit, and his vision and determination more than anything else had secured the passage in the Imperial Parliament in 1867 of the *British North America Act*. Although party lines had not been clearly drawn in the election, his supporters predominated in the new parliament.

The opposition was so fragmented that its members could not even agree among themselves what it was that they particularly opposed. Some, like the contingent from Nova Scotia, took a very dim view of Confederation itself, as did a less united group from Quebec. Others had reservations about the character and personality of the new prime minister, whom they considered, on the basis of his previous record in colonial politics, an unscrupulous and, possibly, venal manipulator. Opponents like Brown and Mackenzie favoured different domestic policies than Macdonald; and a few, holding to a tradition that was already declining, prided themselves on their independence. Although they sat on the opposition side of the Commons, they were prepared to vote for any measures from the government side that appealed to them. They were sufficiently disunited that Macdonald himself chose the first leader of the opposition.

Yet from such an inauspicious beginning the Liberal Party rose as a political organization that was to dominate federal politics in the twentieth century, disliked for its success and arrogance, but at the same time, admired for its skill and, after a while, for its experience. When times were good, vote Liberal and preserve them; in an economic or military crisis, go with those who exude confidence in their ability to handle it. Although the Conservatives dominated the electoral contests of the nineteenth century, the twentieth century, if it has not belonged to Canada as Laurier predicted, has been dominated by the Liberal Party. Of the twenty-six elections this century, Liberals have formed the government after seventeen, while the Conservatives, running under the names of Liberal-Conservative, Union Government and Progressive Conservative, have found themselves in office after only nine. All told, the Liberals have held office for sixty-four years in this century. Since 1935, Conservatives have formed the national government for about thirteen years.

In spite of this record of victories, the Conservatives have not done as poorly as it might appear at first glance. Only once since 1921, during wartime in 1940, have the Liberals secured a majority of the popular vote in a general election, a feat the Conservatives achieved twice, in 1958 and 1984. For many Canadians, the Conservative Party was the one for which they hoped and voted, and as the size of the undecided category in any public opinion poll indicates, 20 percent and more of the electorate keeps its options open, perhaps even up to the moment of truth in the polling booth.

In 1911, Henri Bourassa's Nationalists intruded into the cozy rivalry for office between the Liberals and the Conservatives. Subsequently, in 1921, the Progressives elected more MPs than the Conservatives; and with that election Canadian federal politics became a contest between at least three, and sometimes four or five parties, each with a reasonable chance of returning members to the federal house. Members have been elected to the federal house under the banner of more than twenty different party names. More than a hundred other parties have run candidates unsuccessfully in federal elections. Their programs have been varied and their success usually poor, but most have agreed on one thing: Liberals and Conservatives, they have maintained, are virtually indistinguishable, as alike as Tweedledum and Tweedledee, and if it were not for the fact that at any given time, one is In and the other is Out, it would be impossible to tell them apart. Most Canadians who sense significant differences between them would be hard pressed to spell out in any detail exactly how they differ. Yet differences exist. In this chapter we will argue that Canadian Conservatism has a tradition and a character distinct from Canadian Liberalism, though we will also point out some reasons why the two parties at times bear a striking similarity to each other.

We have seen in the preceding chapter that Canadian Liberalism is an alliance between the two major strains of liberal ideology, welfare liberalism and business liberalism. It has been affected at times by other doctrines such as nationalism, as we will note further in Chapter VI, but never in such a way as to challenge the

Liberal Party's basic commitment to individualism and liberty. Canadian Conservatism has also shown a deep and abiding care for individual liberty; one of its major strands has been business liberalism. But, as Gad Horowitz argued, there was also a tory element in Canada, collectivist and hierarchical, that was brought both by the earliest settlers from France and later by the United Empire Loyalists, and subsequently reinforced in English Canada by the continuing British immigration of the nineteenth and twentieth centuries. This toryism, whose significance within the party has waxed and waned through time, is still a force in the contemporary Progressive Conservative Party and remains an important factor that distinguishes it from the Liberals.

It should be obvious that these two sets of ideas are not easily reconciled; a large part of the history of Canadian Conservatism has consisted of the shifting balance between the business liberal and the tory elements within the party. In partnership since the 1850s, each has been influenced by the compromises it has had to make with the other for the sake of party unity. As well, nationalism and, to a lesser extent, welfare liberalism have had followers within the Conservative Party, although the latter is much less prominent than it appears, since often what seems to be a manifestation of this version of liberalism is in fact the consequence of toryism.

It would be convenient if the word "conservatism" meant only this association of ideologies in the Canadian Conservative Party, but "conservative" has a variety of additional meanings in ordinary speech. It would be tempting to ignore them were it not for the fact that these alternative meanings also shed light on the phenomena we are exploring.

One use of "conservative" is to describe those who are hostile to change, and who prefer things just as they are. This is not, in itself, a political doctrine, but a disposition which dislikes rapid changes; which prefers change to be slow and cautious; which regrets any alteration in the state of affairs that destroys what is known and loved, regardless of the advantages to be gained by the change. It is the bane of banks wanting to raze historic buildings, of highway planners whose road-widening schemes would imperil a stand of oak trees, of developers who want to develop recreational opportunities in an isolated wilderness area. It is sadness when a neighbour moves away, disappointment when a favourite hockey player retires, even mingled regret as a child grows up.

Those with this preference for the familiar can easily fall into nostalgia for the immediate or distant past. If society or politics changes rapidly, some people will look with longing on the world they lost and will seek to restore the old order rather than accept the altered circumstances. All parties, but especially the Conservatives, have at times in their history become the preserve of those who, sometimes rightly, saw the past as superior to the present. Such a sentimental yearning affected Arthur Meighen's understanding of imperial affairs, limited George Drew's electoral appeal and encouraged John Diefenbaker to fight for the Red Ensign and the monarchy. Nor is nostalgia limited to particular items: it can encompass an entire age or state of affairs, a golden past to be recaptured.

This disposition and this sentiment are human, not merely political, phenomena. However, people still expect words to mean something certain and simple; they expect a party that calls itself Conservative to be conservative in its approach, and to hanker after the past, or at least to try and preserve the status quo. Consequently, there is a natural gravitation of activists and supporters who are inclined to these values towards such a party and this very movement helps to fulfil their expectations. Although these dispositional elements can be identified, and are undoubtedly significant for Canadian Conservatism, it is the combination of business liberalism and democratic toryism that, in our opinion, gives the party its distinctiveness.

There is a final complicating factor. We noted in the first chapter that Canadian political parties have remained open to external ideological influences. In the nineteenth century, the overwhelming source of new ideas for the Canadian Conservative Party was the Conservative Party of the United Kingdom, and especially its great leader, Benjamin Disraeli, later Lord Beaconsfield. Although the tradition of this legacy is still important, as we shall see in our examination of John Diefenbaker and Robert Stanfield, it has largely been superseded by an openness to ideological developments in the United States.

Canadian Prime Minister R.B. Bennett felt the impact of U.S. President Roosevelt's New Deal in the 1930s, but more recently there have been two major eruptions that sent waves into Canadian Conservatism and threatened to destroy the historic ideological compromises on which it rests. The first occurred in the early 1960s when, for the first time since the 1930s, in the United States a serious challenge was raised to the welfare liberalism that had dominated its national policies from Roosevelt to Kennedy and Johnson. Proponents of an older tradition in American politics, concerned with the proper role of the state, won control of the Republican Party and chose Senator Barry Goldwater as their party's presidential candidate in 1964. Although he was convincingly defeated by Democratic President Johnson, many Republicans and some Democrats continued to argue that a major shift in American domestic policy was essential.

More recently the pressures have come from the electoral successes of neoconservatism in the two major English-speaking democracies. Margaret Thatcher's three consecutive victories in Great Britain have convinced some Canadian Conservatives that imitation of her domestic policies, especially privatization, would prove equally popular here. Similarly, Ronald Reagan's two terms as president advocating policies roughly similar to Thatcher's have lent additional support to the argument that these programs would prove successful in a North American setting. In the terms we have been using in this book, these

Americans could be described as radical business liberals; but the conventional American term for them is conservative, and of course, Thatcher heads an avowedly Conservative government.

Seen in this context, it is easier to understand why leading Conservative theorists such as Heath Macquarrie and George Hogan, who faced the first onslaught of these ideas in the 1960s, were anxious to deny that there were "deep philosophical differences" between their party and the Liberals;[1] or why a research director of the party would repudiate, in the strongest possible language, the notion that either party had a consistent ideology in the twentieth century: "The names Liberal and Conservative do not have ideological meanings vis-a-vis their parties."[2]

These arguments were developed to impede, as best they could, the influence of American conservatism on Canadian politics. Their fear was by no means groundless. The former Social Credit premier of Alberta, Senator E.C. Manning, published a book in 1967 entitled *Political Realignment* in which he proposed to "rationalize federal party politics," and he selected the Conservative Party as the agency to polarize Canadian politics "over fundamental values and principles of life, government and nationhood."[3]

The ascension of Ronald Reagan to the American presidency in 1980 gave renewed impetus to those business liberals within the Conservative Party who were becoming tired of the necessity of continued compromise with democratic toryism, and who felt that the time had come to make a determined assault on welfare liberalism in Canada. Heartened by the electoral successes won by American conservatives, the business liberals urged that a version of Reaganomics — monetarism, reduction of the federal deficit, a decreased role of the national government in economic matters generally — be adopted as party policy in Canada. They argued that the party should take a determined and clear stand on these issues. As Robert Stanfield described them in his address to the Progressive Conservative National Policy Conference in May, 1982:

> Some Conservatives today assert that the dominant principle of Conservatism is individual freedom in the form of free enterprise. They assert that a free market, with free competition and free enterprise, produces the greatest growth, employment, opportunity, freedom and stability. To them government enterprise or government regulation is an abomination. These Conservatives wish to identify the Conservative Party with this doctrine. Any deviant is a heretic. I do not believe that makes sense, historically or politically. This exaggerated claim for the marketplace, and this denigration of government, were 19th-century Liberalism. They are not in the Conservative tradition we have inherited.[4]

In his last reference to the Conservative tradition Stanfield hit on something profoundly important. There can be little doubt that Senator Manning believed himself to be a man of sound conservative principles, and that he was widely acknowledged to be one. Yet there also seems to be something that links

Macdonald, Borden, Meighen, Bennett, Bracken, Diefenbaker, Stanfield, Clark and Mulroney, something that gives more than merely a nominal unity to their claims to be Conservatives. Let us, therefore, see if we can unravel some of the factors that lie at the root of the differing opinions about the nature of Canadian Conservatism, and that cause the Conservative Party to appear, at times, to spend as much of its energy on internecine warfare as it does on attacking its major rivals for electoral office.

This riddle is not a particularly difficult one, nor is the problem itself new. Lord Durham, in his famous *Report* of 1839, drew to the attention of his readers what he took to be a perplexing feature of Canadian politics:

> Thus the French have been viewed as a democratic party, contending for reform; and the English as a conservative minority, protecting the menaced connexion with the British Crown, and the supreme authority of the Empire....But when we look to the objects of each party, the analogy to our own politics seems to be lost, if not actually reversed; the French appear to have used their democratic aims for conservative purposes, rather than those of liberal and enlightened movement; and the sympathies of the friends of reform are naturally enlisted on the side of sound amelioration which the English minority in vain attempted to introduce into the antiquated laws of the Province....[5]

Durham's observations are important for two reasons. First, they lend credence to the Horowitz thesis that there has long been in Canada an indigenous conservative tradition with strong local roots — more pervasive in French Canada than English Canada — though at the time Durham wrote it was still dominant in English Canada through the political control of the Family Compact. Second, he highlights the difficult nature of conservatism, for he notes that the word could correctly be used to refer either to the substance of a particular political position which at that particular time involved the continuation of Canada as a monarchy within the Empire; or it could more generally refer to a disposition. The French Canadians wanted to preserve a particular state of affairs to which they were, for various reasons, attached. Now this disposition is most often found in those who are, in the words of Professor Michael Oakeshott, "acutely aware of having something to lose."[6] As a consequence, it is more often the businessman or the farmer than the property-poor wage earner who is disposed to be hostile to change, since he has a stake in the status quo, which an alteration might imperil. As nations become richer, however, even the labourer begins to have a consideration in things as they are, and in turn begins to resist change.

Material goods are only one, albeit an important, type of possession, and the conservative disposition can appear in any class of society and in any age group. It is in this sense, as Durham understood, that the *Canadiens* were profoundly conservative. They had been threatened, first by the Conquest, and then by the subsequent drying up of immigrants from France. The flood of immigration, initially by the United Empire Loyalists and then from Britain, placed their language, their customs, their culture and their faith in jeopardy; indeed, everything was put at risk, and *la survivance* became the rallying cry for those with a consciousness that they had something valuable to lose. Again, in Oakeshott's words: "With some people this is itself a choice; in others it is a disposition which appears, frequently or less frequently, in their preferences and aversions, and is not itself chosen or specifically cultivated."[7] It was in both these senses that Lord Durham believed that the French Canadians were conservative: "They clung to ancient prejudices, ancient customs and ancient laws, not from any strong sense of their beneficial effects, but with the unreasoning tenacity of an uneducated and unprogressive people."[8]

MACDONALD'S PARTY

Conservatism began to take its shape as a powerful political belief in Canada under the influence of John A. Macdonald, who sought, he said, to "enlarge the bounds of our party so as to embrace every person desirous of being counted a progressive Conservative."[9] He was, however, anxious to claim that "while I have always been a member of what is called the Conservative party, I could never have been called a Tory."[10] Macdonald's desire to disembarrass himself of this description and the connotations it bore in the Canada of his day is understandable. What we might describe as the High Tory ideology consisted of a doctrine centred exclusively around collectivism and privilege; but as Durham had argued in his *Report*, those beliefs were becoming increasingly less adequate as an explanation of contemporary political and social realities.

Macdonald cast his net more widely and developed a party with a doctrine of wider appeal to the increasingly liberally-minded populace of the Canadas. The historian, W.L. Morton, distinguished in this ideological coalition three important strains that Macdonald was attempting to construct: the French-Canadian tradition of the *Bleus*, the United Empire Loyalists, influenced by the principles of the Whig Settlement in England in 1688, and the second Tory party in the United Kingdom, whose desire it was to give Canada "the British Constitution in all its balanced perfection, confident that the liberty it conferred would ensure the loyalty of those who enjoyed that liberty."[11] The consequent melding of these different traditions, Morton believed, led to the conclusion that although Canadian Conservatism took its intellectual source from England, it developed in Canada a unique character of its own.[12]

Although historians normally link the origin of the party with the MacNab ministry of 1854, it was not until the Confederation controversy of 1864 to 1867 that Macdonald's group in the legislature had an issue of sufficient importance to transform its organization from an electoral faction to a party. It was at this time that many of the ideas that were to become important in Canadian Conservative thought were first given expression in an institutional setting. Confederation itself, as a scheme, was scarcely a novelty in the politics of British North America. The idea had first been mooted as early as 1754 as a system of defence against the French and Indians; by 1858, when Alexander Galt moved the last of his three resolutions favouring the possibility of a union of all British North America, little interest was shown "in the grandiose scheme of a young man; they had heard it all before. Theirs was not the indifference of hostility but of overfamiliarity."[13]

It would be contentious, however, to suggest that merely because an idea has a long history, it thereby acquires a conservative character. At least one anti-confederate took his stand on such grounds. Luther Houlton suggested in the Canadian Confederation debates that Macdonald's faction had not established the need for this measure. "They are proposing revolution, and it was incumbent upon them to establish a necessity for revolution."[14]

In spite of opposition of this sort, which could be characterized as Tory in the terms Macdonald used, the Confederation package contained certain key elements, which were to become central features of the Conservative ideology in Canada. First, there was the question of loyalty to the Crown and membership in the Empire. In Sir Etienne Taché's words: "if [we] were anxious to continue our connection with the British Empire, and to preserve intact our institutions, our laws, and even our remembrances of things past, we must sustain the measure."[15] The alternative to preserving the distinct British identity in North America was absorption by the United States: "We would be forced into the American Union by violence, and if not by violence, would be placed upon an inclined plane which would carry us there insensibly."[16] Macdonald shared this attitude. In the words of an historian, "his dominant concern was to keep the British connection unbroken, to follow British institutions, to preserve the spirit of the British constitution, and to save Canada for a British civilization. Canadians must be either English or American, said Macdonald, and he was determined to be English."[17] Cartier also shared a love for British institutions, and even more than Macdonald, a dislike and distrust of the Republic to the south. "To Cartier the United States was a menace or, at best, an example of what not to do."[18] Nor was Cartier untypical of French-Canadian sentiment at the time.[19]

This attitude can be understood if we examine the fundamental premise upon which it was based. The assumption was that a shared loyalty to a common Crown was a bond between diverse subjects. Considered together with economic interests and potential future development, as well as geographic proximity, this shared allegiance was enough to constitute a nation. Thus, Cartier said: "Now, when we were united together, if union were attained, we would form a political nationality with which neither the national origin, nor the religion of any individual, would interfere."[20] The desire to form such a union and the belief that it was possible to do so evidenced an attitude to the whole, which we will call collectivism.

Liberalism has to devise an explanation for the coherence found in society. How is it that these individuals hold together, in spite of their cultural, educational, linguistic, religious, and economic differences? That it is difficult for them to do so is one conclusion liberalism can draw, and that policy should attempt to minimize these differences. A greater similarity between the constituent units in the state makes the development of a consensus easier and the difficulties of governing, fewer. For the conservative, this problem is less pressing, since he is more willing than the liberal to assume unity, and, indeed, is disturbed by disruptions indicating anomalies in the presumed order. Hence, Cartier observed:

> It was lamented by some that we had this diversity of races. Distinctions of this kind would always exist. Dissimilarity, in fact, appeared to be the order of the physical and of the moral world, as well as of the political world.[21]

And Taché, also thinking in the context of an ordered social and political system, was convinced that

> the French Canadians would do all in their power to render justice to their fellow-subjects of English origin, and it should not be forgotten that if the former were in a majority in Lower Canada, the English would be in a majority in the General Government.[22]

A second important feature of Canadian Conservatism as it developed at this time was a belief in the importance of privilege, as we noted in the first two chapters. This applies to Macdonald, and this observation doubtless would hold about most of Victorian British North America, that they "accepted and approved of class, rank, and distinctions."[23] This same attitude comes out strongly in Cartier. He described some of the opponents of Confederation as the "extreme men, the socialists, democrats and annexationists,"[24] and went on to say that he "was opposed, he might as well state most distinctly, to the democratic system which obtained in the United States."[25]

This ready acceptance of society as constituted by a graded series of social classes could easily be seen in the creation of the Canadian Senate. Although a few contemporary radicals preferred a more democratic legislative body consisting only of an elected house, Macdonald sought to create a bicameral legislature, with a popularly chosen lower house balanced by an upper chamber not chosen democratically. Senators were to be men at least thirty years old, substantial property holders and representatives of the regions without regard to the relative populations of those areas. To give them greater independence from popular pressure, Senators were appointed rather than elected, and their appointment was for life.

The Senate today strikes us as a profoundly undemocratic body; and it was exactly Macdonald's intention that it should be. Indeed the general agreement on the appropriateness of privilege is indicated by the fact that the only serious alternative to the body he constructed was an hereditary upper chamber. As early as 1790 in a debate on the Constitution Act in the British Parliament, Charles James Fox and Edmund Burke had clashed on this issue. Burke had favoured developing a local aristocracy in Canada on the grounds that the colonies would then have a faithful copy of the British constitution. Fox objected that it was unnecessary and undesirable to attempt to export marks of hereditary distinction to a new country that did not know them.

Macdonald's own position in the 1860s was probably influenced by the colonial experience with Executive Councils, which tended to be dominated by a wealthy few who sought to promote their own interests. The fight to limit their control had then only recently been won in the British North American colonies, and although Macdonald did not suggest that there was anything intrinsically wrong with the principle of heredity, he proposed that such a scheme would be "impractical in this young country." His analysis revealed an approach similar to Burke's general attitude to such questions: namely, that the test of the appropriateness of constitutional arrangements was whether they were in harmony with the social structure of the country. In Canada's case, Macdonald was worried because there was no large landed interest comprising a distinct and identifiable social class, and therefore there was no stable group of prominent families from whom the leaders of the community could be chosen. "An hereditary body is altogether unsuited to our state of society, and would soon dwindle into nothing."[26]

Macdonald, then, accepted privilege as a possible guide in the construction of the new country's government; this willingness to use such a principle is surely part of the tory inheritance forming part of the Canadian ideological structure. But Macdonald could not escape the influence of liberal ideas,[27] even if he had wanted to do so. Part of the ideological coalition from which he fashioned his Liberal-Conservative party consisted of the descendants of the United Empire Loyalists, who, although they had too much of the tory in them to accept the doctrinaire liberal society of the United States, were also strongly influenced by the Whig settlement in England consequent to the Revolution of 1688. The ideas of Locke, who was the foremost philosopher for the winners in that controversy, were a pervasive influence throughout Anglo-American political thought from which few, if any, of the major thinkers of the eighteenth or nineteenth century escaped.

This Lockean liberalism, with its concern for the rights of property, had been raised to the status of doctrinal orthodoxy by subsequent thinkers in Britain, especially Jeremy Bentham. No political thinker in mid-nineteenth-century

Canada could have hoped to make a successful electoral appeal to the vast majority of those who heard him, without incorporating substantial liberal elements into his message.[28]

Although Macdonald was undoubtedly concerned with enhancing liberty and promoting individualism, his toryism kept him from pursuing these ideas to the conclusions reached by men such as Mackenzie and Goldwin Smith. He was not convinced by the arguments of such men as John Simpson, who objected to the construction of the Intercolonial Railway on the grounds that it would be a political interference that would "divert trade and commerce from their natural channels [i.e. New York and Boston]."[29]

As Robert Stanfield explains this tradition: "In Canada, it was natural for Conservatives to put rather more emphasis on the individual and less on society and social order than in the U.K., because opportunity was the thing here in a relatively new country."[30] However, Stanfield went on to note the Conservative belief in "strong government, but government limited in scope."[31] This was surely Macdonald's position, too. His business liberalism disposed him sympathetically to the problems of the commercial and manufacturing interests in Canada, even if that might point in the direction of increased trade relations with the United States. But his toryism made considerations of national political interest of primary importance, and this belief in the primacy of politics over economics drew him back from any continentalist measures that threatened to extinguish a separate Canadian political identity.

The tradition of economic liberalism in Britain, from Adam Smith through the Manchester School and Herbert Spencer, was to curb the power of the state over the organization and conduct of both industrial and commercial enterprises. It enthusiastically canvassed the possibility that the demands of the economy should, in most instances, predominate over merely political problems and arrangements. Macdonald clearly did not accept this approach. It is a commonplace that the *British North America Act* did not make provision for the extensive range of social services the state is now expected to provide for its citizens. It is also an accepted interpretation that Macdonald, whatever some of the other Fathers of Confederation might have envisaged, preferred a strong central government, if possible, a legislative union, in order to avoid both what he had analyzed to be the major weaknesses in the American federal system, and to endow the Canadian general government with sufficient powers to engage in the important task of building a transcontinental political unit in British North America.

Macdonald set out on this task by acquiring the lands of the Hudson's Bay Company. To prevent the Americans from annexing the land by settlement and to entice British Columbia into Confederation, he sought to construct the railway that eventually became known as the CPR. The brunt of the Liberal criticism of the railway was that it was too expensive for the young country and that it was unnecessary, since a more economical system could be devised that would utilize the existing American rail lines.[32] In 1874 Macdonald had objected to the proposed Liberal scheme on two grounds. First, such a proposal as Mackenzie had made would violate the terms of the agreement made with both British Columbia and with the Imperial Government. Second, "[w]e would build no railway for the United States as Mr. Mackenzie wanted, and we would have no hermaphrodite system of transport, carrying away the great products of the West from Canada."[33]

As Macdonald saw it, the choice of a tariff strategy was political, a conscious attempt to control economic forces, which would otherwise operate to the detriment of the country:

> The time has come, gentlemen, when the people of this Dominion have to declare whether Canada is for the Canadians, or whether it is to be a pasture for cows to be sent to England. It is for the electors to say whether every appliance of civilization shall be manufactured within her bounds for our own use, or whether we shall remain hewers of wood and drawers of water to the United States.[34]

The issue was joined again in 1891 when the Liberals put forth the suggestion of Unrestricted Reciprocity with the United States as an alternative to the National Policy of the Conservatives. Macdonald was quick to note that the political consequences of this economic suggestion were what he feared: "I have of course pointed out that U.R. meant annexation."[35]

Intimately connected with this approach to the relationship between politics and economics was an aspect of nationalism. Conservatism, concerned as it is with a desire to preserve what is "our own," and with a disposition to maintain the existing state of affairs in most essentials, is necessarily more sensitive to new foreign infusions of ideas or capital than are either liberalism or socialism. This hostility, though, took the form of an irritated annoyance at being disturbed, and a suspicion of the foreigner, rather than a systematic doctrine. Macdonald, for example, in the letter mentioned above, went on to say "the movements of Cartwright, Farrer & Wiman enabled us to raise the loyalty cry, which had considerable effect." This sounds cynical, but there can be little doubt that Macdonald had a dislike and distrust of Americans, which ran deep:

> If left to ourselves, I have no doubt of a decision in our favour, but I have serious apprehensions which are shared by all our friends here, that a large amount of Yankee money will be expended to corrupt our people....Sir C. Tupper will tell you that every American statesman (and he saw them all in 88), covets Canada. The greed for its acquisition is still on the increase, and God knows where it will end.[36]

This fear of American invasion or annexation, which had been one of the lodestars of Macdonald's political conduct, was not surprising in a man who was one of the founders of a political approach with a distinctively national character.

What is more curious is the observation Macdonald makes in the sentence following the passage quoted above. "If Gladstone succeeds, he will sacrifice Canada without scruple."

Here, then, is no blind and dogmatic devotion to Britain, no willingness to be subordinate to the imperial design for its own sake. Was the man who spoke about raising "the loyalty cry" merely a cynic, willing to use whatever rhetoric would prove effective, within the limiting constraints imposed by the established traditions of his party's doctrine? We think not. Macdonald's attitude to Britain here has all the hallmarks of ideological politics. He was undoubtedly committed to a belief in the importance of the Empire and the value of the British example. Because he would not follow every twist and turn of imperial policy, he adopted a simplified image of what Britain stood for. Britishness was an ideal to be imposed not only on Canada, but on Britain itself; and Canada was justified in charting an independent course whenever Britain deviated from the true British policy. To approach the point from a slightly different angle, one could suggest that Britain, from a Canadian viewpoint, had a divided self. On the one hand, she was the centre of the Empire, seat of the Imperial Parliament, presiding over a colonial assembly of free men. On the other hand, she was the home of traditional European intrigues, pursuing a national interest at the expense of the Empire. It was only the former to which Macdonald thought Canadians owed strong allegiance.

Macdonald's Conservative ideology was a skilful blend of toryism and liberalism. It was never thoroughly consistent, but Macdonald succeeded well in keeping the different elements in an harmonious balance. This allowed him to win every election he fought from Confederation to his death, with the exception of 1872, when his government was embroiled in a major scandal. Macdonald's success should not be surprising since his ideological appeal was broader than the more limited ideological range of the Liberals in the early years of Confederation. Even the execution of Louis Riel might not have hurt the Conservative predominance in Canadian politics were it not for the rise of Laurier to the leadership of the Liberal Party. We traced in the last chapter Laurier's modification of Canadian Liberalism, and his truce with the nationalist and collectivist sentiments in Quebec through the doctrine of provincial rights. Canadian Conservatism had to await John Diefenbaker before it was again to have as wide an appeal as it had under Macdonald.

ROBERT BORDEN: FREE TRADE AND THE GREAT WAR

When Laurier deprived the Conservatives of Quebec support, he cut them off from the collectivism and hierarchy of the *Bleu* tradition. The tory elements within the Conservative Party were thereby isolated from precisely that society for which their ideology had the greatest appeal and the greatest explanatory power. Under Borden and Meighen the liberal elements in the party took on an increased prominence, implied in a reminiscence of Borden, written in 1935. In the Imperial War Cabinet during the Great War, when Lord Curzon of Kedleston asked him what he thought of the English social system, Borden replied: "If you wish me to speak frankly, we regard your social order as little more than a glorified feudal system."[37] This liberal hostility to privilege was also reflected in Borden's unwillingness to allow Canadians to receive peerages or other British marks of social distinction.[38] As biographer R.C. Brown explained: "Borden concluded that (hereditary titles) 'are very unpopular and entirely incompatible with our institutions.'"[39] Arthur Meighen, Borden's successor as party leader and prime minister, had showed a similar resentment of privilege earlier in 1911 when he attacked the Liberals as "the slaves of those who helped them into power and who now maintain them there behind ramparts of gold."[40]

These attacks on privilege might suggest that by the beginning of the twentieth century, Canadian Conservatism had already abandoned the toryism that we have identified as the major feature differentiating it from Canadian Liberalism. Such an interpretation would be mistaken. Borden had, in historian John English's words, "the opportunity to reconstruct the party in his own image."[41] He responded by seeking to attract those who were disaffected with Laurier's Liberalism by developing a "new public philosophy,"[42] most notably in his celebrated Halifax Platform of 1907, which he described as "an effective and honest rallying cry which will appeal to the more progressive spirits and communities."[43]

Although business liberalism took on an increased significance in Borden's Conservative Party, the form it took was powerfully affected by the traditional tory elements within the party. Equality of opportunity was an idea to which Borden appealed, but he made it clear that his interpretation of this liberal concept was tinged with tory overtones. As he observed in 1913, "All men are not born equal in their capacity and energy, and in an individualistic world there can be no expectation of equality of results."[44] In the words of his biographer,

> Who would determine when the public desired policies to enhance the equality of opportunity in society? The answer, in Borden's mind, varied from situation to situation;...equality of opportunity was not going to be forced by the enactment of a radical legislative program by Borden's government. To do so would have challenged the basic assumptions of the "individualistic world" in which Borden lived. Instead, his government would proceed slowly, cautiously in step with accepted public attitudes and public opinion. Borden and his colleagues would try to correct the worst abuses of modern Canadian industrial society: they were not about to overturn it.[45]

This ready acceptance of an equality of opportunity, which necessarily led to considerable social inequality, and an unwillingness to use government to do more than mitigate the most serious manifestations are perfectly compatible with both toryism and business liberalism. Moreover, Borden was no "Benthamite, confident of the rightness of public choice. He had an inherent distrust of the irrational and emotional in politics."[46]

Neither was Borden insensitive to the collectivist aspects of toryism, which came out most clearly in his hostility to Liberal proposals for a reciprocity treaty with the United States. The Conservative belief in the primacy of politics over economics was a derivation from the principles of collectivism — the nation had a right and a responsibility to ensure that the interests of the whole took precedence over the liberty of the business interests to pursue their economic advantage unchecked. It is therefore worth looking at Borden's objections to Laurier's proposed reciprocity treaty with the United States for the light it sheds on the nature of post-Macdonald Canadian Conservatism.

Reciprocity was a policy that drew little support from Canadian Conservatism. It flew in the face of Macdonald's National Policy by segregating "the provinces which confederation aimed to unite." It stood in the way of improving co-operation within the Empire: "The President of the United States had avowed that the main purpose with which he sought the treaty was to prevent consolidation of the British Empire." Finally, it abandoned the attempt on the part of the Canadian nation to control economic forces: it "virtually surrenders control of [Canada's] destinies." Although this would have been sufficient reason in itself to lead Canadian Conservatives to oppose the measure, they also continued to worry about the same fear that had haunted Macdonald and Taché, that without firm control over economic forces, the nation's political sovereignty would be eroded: "if Canada places itself under the commercial control of the United States its political independence, if retained, will be a shadow and not a substantial reality."[47]

Although Borden did not get much sympathy from "certain leading British statesmen," whom he claimed did not understand the basis upon which Canadian economy, and especially the protected industries in this country, stood, he did get unintended assistance from American politicians:

> President Taft's indiscreet reference to Canada as being "at the parting of the ways" was useful to us during the campaign. Mr. Champ Clark was even more indiscreet in his declaration that he favoured Reciprocity because: I hope to see the day when the American flag will float over every square foot of the British North American possessions, clear to the North Pole.[48]

As far as Borden was concerned, the very survival of Canada as an independent political unit in North America was at stake in this election; and here the Conservative Party's collectivism triumphed over the free trade doctrines of Laurier's Liberals. It would be perverse in the extreme to try to fit the events of 1911 into a brokerage theory of politics. If there ever was a difference between the parties over an issue fundamental to the nature of the Canadian polity, this was it; and Borden was consciously aware of the fact:

> the Conservatives quickly identified the election as a struggle between those who would preserve nation and Empire and those who would not. "We are face to face with the fight of 1891 but under the circumstances of greater difficulty," Borden wrote. As he put it in his final campaign speech, the issue was quite simple: "We must decide whether the spirit of Canadianism or of Continentalism shall prevail on the northern half of this continent."[49]

Borden's nationalist collectivism was received sympathetically by the electorate. Borden became prime minister after the 1911 election and with the subsequent outbreak of hostilities in Europe in 1914, Canada's war leader. Throughout the Great War, the tory aspects of Borden's Conservatism were primary elements in his approach to imperial relations and to the domestic crises the war occasioned. In both cases, Borden took for granted the importance of the Canadian nation. With regard to the Empire, he consistently emphasized the importance of recognizing the significance of the nation within the larger unit. Domestically, he welcomed the influx of pro-conscriptionist Liberals into his government, and ran in the 1917 election not as a Liberal-Conservative, but as the leader of the Union Government party. His colleague, Sir George Foster, had hoped that it would "cement east and west, show Quebec the need of restraint and the danger of trying to dominate, and prove the strength of Canada for war to victory."[50] Borden himself anticipated that "New party alignments, reconstruction of past political formulas and a new political outlook will result from the intensely critical conditions through which our country is passing and from the broader outlook which the overseas Canadians must acquire in this war."[51]

However, the advent of such a substantial Liberal element into the Conservative Party did not sit well with the more traditional elements. During the strain of the conscription crisis, those Conservatives who had been desperate to seek support for compulsory military service wherever it could be found had been willing to tolerate their new colleagues; but after the crisis had passed, and the war had been brought to a successful conclusion, the ideological divisions within the Union Government became intense. The collision came on Sir Thomas White's budget of 1919, and led to free-trader Thomas Crerar's resignation from the cabinet. As Crerar explained his decision: "The break with the Government has, I think, been definite. The plain fact is that the Administration is entirely dominated by the Tory element in it and I see no prospect of any change in this regard."[52]

As we have seen in the last chapter, Crerar left the Union Government, and later became one of the leaders of the Progressive movement. Borden himself was soon to retire, and since Sir Thomas White felt that his wealth was not adequate to the strain, Arthur Meighen succeeded Borden as prime minister and party leader.

With Meighen, the atrophy of the tory element in Canadian Conservatism, begun under Borden, continued. This development had particularly serious electoral consequences, since, as we have seen in the last chapter, it coincided with Mackenzie King's selection as leader of the Liberal Party and with the adoption in the Liberals' 1919 program of policies that originated in a genuine, though reserved, commitment to a relatively new form of liberalism: welfare liberalism. Consequently, the ideological scope of the Conservative Party slowly narrowed, while the ideological breadth of the Liberal Party was expanding.

This shift was portentous for Canada. Toryism and welfare liberalism do not reflect common principles, although in Canadian politics they have often played similar roles, and for that reason have just as frequently been confused. Both, for example, envisage an important role for the state. The welfare liberal argues for the necessity of expanding state activity with a view to enhancing the freedom of individual in the society, and sees the state as a necessary instrument in the redistribution of wealth. The tory, in Robert Stanfield's words, believes in "strong government, but government limited in scope." His concern is not individual freedom, at least not as the prime focus, but rather the maintenance of social order. The consequences of both sets of beliefs are similar: both the tory and the welfare liberal affirm the value of state involvement in the economy and in society.

Their positions also overlap on such questions as the provision of services to the poor and needy. Here the welfare liberal is motivated by his concern that the actual realization as well as the formal extent of freedom should be taken into account, and that society has a responsibility to strive, as much as circumstances allow, to ensure that all human beings are able to live a decent life and achieve their human potential. The tory comes to comparable conclusions, but for different reasons. He has accepted that people are endowed with different natural attributes, and are born into different social positions, which means that some will have more social goods than others. However, the tory sees the privileges of the better-off as involving commensurate responsibilities. There is a strong, but not sentimental, element of compassion in democratic toryism, which takes for granted that those who are wealthier, better educated and more esteemed ought to care for the poor, the sick and the elderly. In modern terms, both the welfare liberal and the tory will often support the same goals, but will frequently differ about appropriate means. On balance, the welfare liberal will support the principle of universality in social-welfare programs, whereas the tory will look more favorably on selective devices such as eligibility based on income. However, since politicians generally prefer to talk in terms of policies rather than principles, such differences are often overlooked and confused by journalists and the general public who conclude, falsely, that nothing distinguishes parties that seem to be making similar campaign promises. It was precisely this general inability to distinguish between democratic toryism and welfare liberalism that allowed the latter to make substantial gains at the expense of the former.

ARTHUR MEIGHEN AND THE RISE OF WELFARE LIBERALISM

Our general treatment of the ideological composition of Canada in Chapter II, although it differentiated English and French Canada, did not attempt to make fine distinctions. We treated English Canada as a unit, and made general observations regarding it. Ultimately, of course, this broad approach is unsatisfactory, since it is clear that the immigration and settlement patterns in English Canada vary dramatically, both between regions and provinces, and even within provinces. Any comprehensive treatment of Canadian ideologies, especially one dealing with provincial as well as national politics, would have to take these very considerable differences into account. Here, we introduce this problem only to help explain the stronger liberal strain in Meighen's thought. The Maritimes from which Borden hailed had a strong loyalist and tory aura. Its immigration was earlier than the Canadian West's, and it drew a substantial number of United Empire Loyalists who brought with them a view of politics in which the tory element had been highlighted by the conflicts of the American revolution. Meighen had grown up in the West. There were considerable differences in the ideological composition in that vast area, which continue to be reflected in the different natures of the provincial politics of the four western provinces. Alberta, heavily settled in the late nineteenth and early twentieth centuries by Americans, was the most purely liberal of all Canadian provinces. The frontier spirit, the rough equality of the settlers and the absence of a deep local history all gave ample opportunity for the development of an increasingly powerful liberal strain. Meighen's approach to politics reflected this background.[53]

Meighen was, of course, one of the major architects of the Canadian National Railways system, a policy that earned him the implacable hatred of the Montreal business community and especially the Canadian Pacific interests, who would have preferred to be given control of their bankrupt competitors. Moreover, Meighen did not follow the course of nationalizing the railways out of mere expediency, for he believed in the state control or certain important natural resources. As he said in London in 1918: "Dictates of wise policy have suggested that our invaluable waterpower — an asset of a clearly distinctive character — should be to the utmost possible extent not only state-owned and controlled, but state developed and operated. All arguments that go anywhere to support Government monopoly apply with peculiar force to water power."[54] This was, after all, traditional Conservative policy.

The tory strains in Meighen's thought precluded a belief in equality. Meighen, in the year after this speech, in 1919, took firm and vigorous action to repress what he considered to be the dangerous edition of the Winnipeg General Strike. State ownership was as far as he was willing to go. In his 1918 speech, he was quick to point out to his listeners that, although the Conservative government was willing to undertake the regulation and operation of what economists know as natural monopolies, "there is no spirit of rampant or headlong socialism in possession of the Canadian mind." And he assured his audience that: "Capital is as safe as in any country on earth."[55] This defence of business and capital, as we will see later when we come to consider Meighen's position in the 1940s, was a preoccupation with him. But it is not this aspect of Meighen's political approach to which we wish to draw immediate attention. We noted earlier that conservatism stands in constant danger of being overtaken by events, and that it easily becomes transformed into nostalgia.

The Great War and the peace negotiations that led, among other things, to full Canadian membership in the League of Nations, effectively raised Canada to the status of a fully independent nation. This, and the declining position of Britain in the world, changed the nature of the imperial tie. In Borden's address to the caucus in 1920 on his retirement, he mentioned "our relations with the Mother Country and the other nations of the Empire" first in the list of "the most immediate and urgent problems" the new government faced.[56] Of what was this new bond to consist?

This question was to arise for Meighen in an unexpected way in the famous King-Byng constitutional controversy of 1926. For reasons we touch on more fully in the last chapter, Canadian Liberalism was prone to identify the cause of Canadian independence with a breaking of ties with Britain and the Empire, and to see the Crown as the central link in the chain binding Canada to a colonial dependence. There can be little doubt, especially after the analysis of the crisis by both Forsey[57] and Graham,[58] that Meighen and Lord Byng acted on correct constitutional principles, as they were then understood. King's attempt to escape from the vote of censure on corruption in the Customs Department had been an audacious manoeuvre, which, thanks to Meighen's actions, led to King's victory in the 1926 election.

Meighen took the fateful step of assuming office with a very thin majority in a confused constitutional situation because he felt that he owed a debt of honour to the Governor-General, and because he thought that it was constitutionally proper for him to do so. Clearly, this was an ideologically motivated move, and not one induced by consideration of electoral advantage, although some of the latter could reasonably be expected to accrue to an incumbent prime minister. Canada's changing relationship within the Empire was at stake here. A

Conservative apologist such as Heath Macquarrie might call the whole issue falla-
cious,[59] but Mackenzie King was probably closer to the truth when he described it
as "a constitutional issue greater than any that has been raised in Canada since the
founding of this Dominion."[60]

The Imperial Conference of 1926 and the *Statute of Westminster* in 1931
brought about a constitutional revolution, however peaceful, which permanently
altered the imperial relationship. Meighen's attachment to the Crown, real as it
was, and expressive of traditional Conservative policy, blinded him (as we argued in Chapter I that ideologies sometimes do) to the important changes that
were taking place in both world and nation. King's anti-imperial ideology was a
handier instrument in this crisis for understanding the changing nature of this relationship, and this greater clarity partly accounts for King's electoral success in
the succeeding election.

Meighen, for all his intellectual penetration and brilliance, spoke more truly
than he knew when he entitled his collection of speeches, *Unrevised and Unrepented*. His greatest weakness was that he knew too well what were the traditional policies of his party, and his disposition was to hold fast to them. His nostalgia for the Empire came out in the "Ready, aye, ready" of the Chanak crisis, and
his belief in the tariff and in class stability made him unsuited for dealing with the
turmoil of the West. He could, and did, write powerfully and evocatively in defence of this conservative disposition of his character. During the debate over
Church Union in 1924, he said that his "inclinations lead me naturally to cling to
the Church with which my family for many generations has been associated,"[61]
though uncharacteristically he subsequently supported the reform forces that led
to the creation of the United Church. In an address in the next year, 1925, in commemoration of D'Arcy McGee, he expressed the belief that it "will be a good thing
for the national personality when we can all join in veneration of the great deeds
of the fathers of our country."[62] And in 1927, when he addressed the convention
that chose R.B. Bennett as his successor, he gave a powerful and moving address
in defence of his controversial Hamilton speech, but the mode he chose here was
also retrospective:

> The chords of memory unite us with the past, and this is the time and this is the place
> when all of us...should catch the spirit and hear the voice of the noble founders of
> our political faith....They would urge us to be conscious of our mighty heritage, proud
> of the Imperial Fountain of our freedom and the flag that floats above us, worthy of
> those British ideals of liberty and justice which have sent their light forth and their
> truth among all races of men. To our history, our principles, our traditions let us be
> faithful to the end.[63]

This aspect of Meighen's conservatism has not passed without notice. George
Hogan described Meighen's economic policies as almost "a reversion to the

mercantilist theories of colonial Toryism,"[64] and accused Meighen and Bennett of letting the Conservative Party drift "away from the positive nation-building concepts upon which its earlier greatness was based."[65] Hogan's description is not fair. Meighen could not be called a reactionary in the way that Hogan's argument implies. His nostalgia was for continuation of the traditional policies of the party, not for a return to a state of affairs long since outmoded. Meighen's politics were ideological, and probably outdated, but they did not represent an attempt to turn back the clock. Neither were they a repudiation of the nation-building principles of Canadian Conservatism. As we have just seen, Meighen was not a man to make such a repudiation. His guilt, if any, was one of omission, rather than of commission; his treason was a failure to adapt.

Soon after the 1926 election Meighen resigned as party leader, and the Conservatives adopted a device pioneered in Canada by the Liberals: the use of a leadership convention rather than the parliamentary caucus to select the party's leader. There have been several consequences of this change in procedure, such as the tendency to choose leaders with less rather than more parliamentary experience, but the one that interests us most is the opening up of the party to a wider and more comprehensive range of ideological opinion than might at any time exist within the parliamentary party. Indeed, the sometimes unrepresentative nature of the party's parliamentary representation was a major consideration in moving to leadership conventions and in retaining them.

R.B.BENNETT AND THE NEW DEAL

There appears to have been little dissension or controversy within the convention that met in October 1927 to select a new leader for the party.[66] Six candidates presented themselves: Hugh Guthrie, R.B. Bennett, C.H. Cahan, R.J. Manion, Robert Rogers and Sir Henry Drayton. Bennett, who had been born in New Brunswick but had followed a legal career in the West, was the choice of the convention on the second ballot. Although the retiring leader, Meighen, was the most controversial figure at the convention, Bennett's success in winning the support of a majority of delegates gave an important new lease on life to the tory element within the Canadian Conservative Party. His convincing victory in the 1930 general election gave Canadian Conservatism the opportunity to show how it could respond to the developing economic crisis.

The Great Depression presented the two leading ideologies with a set of problems to which Canadian Conservatism was able to respond more creatively than Canadian Liberalism. Most economists now agree that extensive and vigorous state action was required to alleviate or moderate the ravages of the economic decline of the 1930s. The Conservatives believed in the importance of using the state to control economic events.[67] Bennett's ill-fated tariff policy of 1930 is a case in point. Bennett spoke in his Winnipeg speech of how we would use tariffs to sell Western agricultural products.

> You have been taught to mock at tariff and applaud free trade. Tell me, when did free trade fight for you? You say our tariffs are only for the manufacturers; I will make them fight for you as well. *I will use them to blast a way into the markets that have been closed to you.*[68]

This policy of protection was not the only instance of this cast of mind that Bennett evidenced in 1930. He also spoke vigorously in favour of the Canadian National Railway: "I love my country and what it has done, and one of its greatest achievements, has been the development of this great national transportation system of which I believe every Canadian is proud. Amalgamation? Never! Competition? Ever! That is the policy for which I stand."[69] This short passage reveals the mix of principles to which we have drawn attention several times before. Although Bennett here showed a strong belief in the importance of continuing this state activity ("And more, I say, that if you see any attempt on my part at any time to violate that pledge I give you here and now, then ask for my resignation — insist upon it."),[70] and indignantly refused, as Meighen had done before him, to hand the CNR over to CPR interests, he justified his stand by appeals to patriotism ("I love my country") and to the capitalist aspects of liberalism ("Competition Ever!").

These liberal aspects of Bennett's Conservatism impeded his adoption of a more vigorous program of state action in the early days of the Depression. W.D. Herridge, Bennett's brother-in-law and then Canadian Ambassador to Washington, early on had been impressed by the success of Franklin Roosevelt's New Deal. In September 1933 he wrote a secret memorandum to Bennett, counselling him to abandon *laissez-faire*, at least for the duration of the Depression.[71] By June 1934 Herridge was pressing the idea on Bennett with increased vigour. He argued that the time had come to rid the party's ideology of the increasingly burdensome legacy of the past, a task, we have argued, for which Meighen was unsuited, although the events of the 1920s necessitated it in imperial relations as much as those of the 1930s did in economics.[72] As long as the party held to its old ideological vision, it would encounter difficulties because it would prove unable to devise any effective solutions to the problem. It had to be willing to repudiate those aspects of its thought, which we have called nostalgic.[73]

To this end Herridge put forward two initial suggestions. First, it was critical for Bennett to understand the importance of ideological thought and to guide his actions by an underlying philosophy.[74] Second, the ideology that Bennett adopted should be as free as possible from liberal elements. In Herridge's view liberalism was an outmoded doctrine that had to be superseded.[75]

Herridge was proposing an ideological purification of Canadian Conservatism, ridding it of liberal elements, and adding to its traditional policy of state action and political control over economic forces. But Herridge went dangerously beyond this; he advanced a dramatically exaggerated notion derived from another constituent element in Canadian conservatism: the belief in inequality or privilege. In April 1934 he wrote of the American New Deal as a Pandora's box, and argued that the American President had been successful precisely because he had mystified the American people; Roosevelt had created an illusion that he was their saviour. Whether he had any practical solutions was of less immediate importance.[76]

Canada, too, needed a Pandora's box, a program or slogan to persuade the people that a better life was in the offing for them as well.[77] To achieve what he called a new order of prosperity,[78] Herridge went wildly beyond anything that the Conservative Party had contemplated before this time. He was influenced by the American New Deal, but his eyes were on Europe as well. He drew Bennett's attention to the success of Stalin, Mussolini and Hitler and urged him to imitate their success by imitating the motor spring of their greatness: a new and coherent ideological vision.[79]

Herridge's analysis of the problems Canada faced bore an affinity to some of the doctrines of European fascism. In an important letter to Bennett in June 1934, Herridge argued that the Depression had led to a serious crisis of confidence. Worse, the people of the country had begun to despair that prosperity would not return under the old regime. Herridge urged Bennett to harness the discontent that had been created and seize the opportunity that events were affording him to take a commanding control of the situation.

The Liberals might suggest, as they did in 1935, that the choice was between King and chaos, but they did not have the inherent disposition in favour of privilege to take them as far as Herridge. Herridge here showed no confidence in the judgement of the democratic process or in the people of the country. He argued that they were incapable of judging their own best interests. This was not the time to consider the "present whims of the electors," the "non-combatants in this battle."[80]

It is impossible in the light of this analysis to agree with Gad Horowitz that Bennett was a "red tory," a man who might prefer the CCF-NDP to the Liberals. Nor can we accept the argument that the Bennett New Deal was, as Horowitz claims, a manifestation of "leftism" derived from tory democracy. This latter might have been true for Bennett's minister of Trade and Commerce, H.H. Stevens, who created a sensation in 1934 by attacking the large retailers and accusing them of pricing practices that led to the exploitation of workers in the manufacturing sector. Unable to gain satisfaction within the party, Stevens left the Conservatives and in July 1935 formed his own Reconstruction Party, which, although it elected only Stevens, drew 9 percent of the popular vote and severely damaged Conservative hopes of victory in the 1935 general election.[81]

Bennett himself did not follow this tory populist route. We touched briefly in Chapter I on a doctrine called corporatism, which some writers have seen as an important factor in the Canadian ideological conservation. This doctrine holds, among other things, that society can remain stable and provide goods and services to its citizens if the major elements in society — workers, manufacturers and government — are organized into co-operative groups. This idea had wide appeal in Europe in the 1920s and 1930s. It is our contention that in Canada, Bennett was the only major political figure who was strongly attracted to a Canadian variant of it; and that, for Bennett, this appeal was stimulated by the tory elements in this ideological outlook.

Herridge and Bennett were locked into an ideological understanding of Canadian society that placed great emphasis on privilege. Bennett's program, which he brought forward late in his term of office, certainly contained collectivist elements, but these were enduring features of Canadian Conservatism. Although it was this which he shared with the socialists, we will see in the next chapter that one of the abiding concerns of Canadian socialism was precisely the elimination of that privilege for which the Conservatives stood. The traditional picture has painted Bennett as a man who was an autocrat when it came to dealing with his cabinet colleagues. Neither did he have great faith in democracy.

> It is almost incomprehensible that the vital issues of life and death to nations, peace or war, bankruptcy or solvency, should be determined by the counting of heads and knowing as we do that the majority under modern conditions — happily the majority becoming smaller — are untrained and unskilled in dealing with the problems which they have to determine.[82]

Bennett announced his New Deal in a series of surprise radio addresses, which look in retrospect like a mild *coup de main* against his cabinet. Borden noted at the time that they were undertaken "without previous consultation with any of his colleagues" and went on to observe, perhaps with some understatement, that several "were extremely disturbed by his course."[83] More significantly, though, Borden realized that a change of some significance was in the air. "Undoubtedly, the Prime Minister has entirely changed the current of political thought in Canada by his enunciation of these policies."[84]

Bennett was, however, no Canadian Mussolini or Hitler. He did not wish, nor did he intend, to subvert the democratic basis of the Canadian government, however sceptical he may have been about certain of its features. He had no wish to work a revolution; in his own words, "I am for reform."[85] Bennett was attempting in the five radio broadcasts to reassess and modify Conservative thought in Canada, a body of doctrine which, we have argued, had become increasing rigid and nostalgic. Bennett's very language signals an awareness of the need for an ideological alteration of perspective, a change at least in emphasis among the conceptual categories in which Canadian Conservatism thought. "In the last five years, great changes have taken place in the world. The old order is gone. It will not return."[86]

Bennett had to face squarely this question: in what direction would Canadian Conservatism move? Would it emphasize the liberal, *laissez-faire* aspects Meighen seemed to favour, or would it look back to the past? Meighen himself seemed to think it should. In 1935, he confessed that he did not "believe the thinking of today is nearly as careful or as well-informed or as thoroughly guided by moral principles as the thinking of forty years ago."[87] Or, would he pursue the exaggerated elitism that Herridge was pressing on him from Washington?

Bennett took neither of these courses. The strains of the party's past on which he tried to build the new Conservatism were its collectivism, especially the belief in the value of political action to control economic forces. Conservative unwillingness to participate in a class war, to set one section of the country against another, finds it intellectual ancestry in England, in Burke and in the doctrines of Disraeli's second Tory Party. In the second address, Bennett announced this choice: "I hold the view that if we are to have equality of social and political conditions throughout this land, we must have equality in economic conditions as well."[88] It is only on the assumption that Canadian Conservatism is nothing but a business doctrine that this position sounds implausible or hypocritical. But within the collectivist assumptions of Canadian Conservatism — sometimes very misleadingly described as organicism — the belief that the government should attempt to serve the interests of all is an entirely possible one. To understand this position correctly, we have to grant the assumption, which we have previously argued that Canadian Conservatism makes, that there is a fundamental unity of the whole that needs to be neither explained nor justified.

Second, Bennett did as Herridge urged; he repudiated *laissez-faire*. "Reform heralds certain recovery. There can be no permanent recovery without reform. Reform or no reform! I raise that issue squarely. I nail the flag of progress to the masthead. I summon the power of the State to its support."[89] This was brave, but it could not be expected to work an ideological miracle overnight. After all, the majority of Canadians still held liberal notions, and they were all the less liable to be persuaded to what they would have taken to be socialism. Although some of Herridge's dangerous rhetoric found its way into the speeches (Bennett spoke of "the corporate strength of the State" in the third address), the legislation following these addresses was considerably less radical. The party's elder statesman, Robert Borden, thought that "Mr. Bennett has conducted the Conservative Party into extreme, even radical, paths."[90] However, Meighen was probably closer to the mark as he put it in a curiously ambivalent farewell to Bennett in 1939: "Our guest will not be offended when I say that what a lot of people have still in their minds like a nightmare is not the legislation, which was enlightened, but the speeches, which frightened."[91]

The election of 1935 returned Mackenzie King to power, and by putting Bennett into opposition ended his chance of transforming Canadian Conservatism along the lines set out in the New Deal addresses. Bennett's successor, R.J. "Fighting Bob" Manion, was not a man for the times. In retrospect, he does not appear to have had a wide ideological vision; and when the war intervened, he attempted to stand against King's administration in the election of 1940, exclusively on a modified version of Conservative collectivism: National Government. The National Government policy, like the Union Government before it in 1917, can be explained partly, of course, by the dictates of electoral expediency. But the reasons why the Conservatives, both in and out of office, proposed it, and the Liberals, both in opposition and government, refused it, must include a reference to this ideological difference between the two parties in Canada.

THE CONSERVATIVE NADIR

Disregarding Manion, Canadian Conservatism had three clear choices, though none would guarantee success. First, Herridge, like H.H. Stevens before him in the 1935 election, left the Conservative Party and led his anti-financialist New Democracy Party to ten seats in Social Credit Alberta. But Herridge, as we have suggested before, was too extreme in the implications he drew from certain intimations of Canadian Conservatism, and it is not surprising that he met with little electoral success, except where Social Crediters supported him. Second, Canadian Conservatism could have attempted to return to its more rigid, nostalgic beliefs. It indicated that it might move in this direction when it again chose the redoubtable Meighen as leader.

It could be said that Meighen, like the Bourbons, forgot nothing and learned nothing. His ideas had changed very little since he had given up the leadership of the party. The question of the imperial relationship was not the pressing issue that it had been in the 1920s, though Meighen still was an Anglophile as much as ever.[92] In the early 1940s, Meighen was faced with another challenge to his ideological presuppositions: the rise of Canadian socialism through the CCF. Meighen objected to this ideology on two grounds. First, it conflicted with his tory ideas of collectivism, to the extent that he believed that the CCF demanded that "the nation be split in twain on a class basis."[93] Second, it also contradicted his individualist assumptions. Meighen rejected the ideal of the co-operative commonwealth. We argued in Chapter I that one important function of ideology was to settle the question of the nature of the relations between those who compose society. Meighen's clear choice was that people were competitors: "Rivalry and struggle under equitable laws are the glory of living."[94]

Meighen's 1942 by-election defeat at the hands of a CCF candidate settled his fate politically, but it also probably settled the fate of the conservative blend of nostalgia and liberalism for which he stood. He was succeeded as leader in 1942 by John Bracken, the former Progressive Premier of Manitoba. Prior to the convention, influential Conservatives had met at Port Hope in Ontario to reassess the political principles of the party. A contemporary journalist described the condition of the Conservative Party as follows:

> at the lowest ebb of its fortunes since Sir John A. Macdonald created it....Orphaned of leadership, unrecovered from shattering defeat in two successive elections, holding power in no single province, nudged into oblivion...its decline and fall from its once proud eminence...is one of the strange tales of politics.[95]

It was the aim of those who met at Port Hope "to formulate a present-day political philosophy in terms of modern needs and the best traditions of the Conservative Party."[96] In the opinion of a writer in *Saturday Night*, they had succeeded, and the conference was

> an event likely to have lasting influence on Canadian politics. Whether or not it has the result of improving the fortunes of the Conservative Party, it produced a document which gives political thinkers something upon which to chew.[97]

The choice of Bracken, and the addition of "Progressive" to the name of the party, were indications that, for the time being, the Conservatives were attempting to chart a course different from that on which Meighen would have guided them. The important choice made at this time, however, was not in favour of a more distinctive style of Canadian Conservatism, as Bennett, Herridge and Meighen had successfully attempted. The party decided to minimize the differences between the Conservative and the Liberal Parties. Here is ample testimony, if proof of this really be needed, of the power at this time of Mackenzie King's ideological vision.

The post-Port Hope party reversed a number of historic stands. First, it adopted the Progressive hostility to tariffs, and proposed that "as far as may be practicable, those barriers to trade must be taken away."[98] This was a momentous step, because, as we have argued, time and again, Canadian Conservatism had affirmed the importance of state intervention and control over economic forces in the interests of the nation. But now, Bracken was repudiating this position. A corollary of this new emphasis was the diminished importance of state initiatives. Previously, Conservatives had sought to harness the state's power in the national interest; Bracken, on the other hand, believed that "government must be decentralised." And more, in place of the traditional assumptions of privilege displayed by the party's leaders, Bracken was a more thorough-going democrat: "All organized elements in the community should be given an opportunity to participate in the determination of policy."[99]

Perhaps the most significant change that Bracken introduced in the party's ideology was on the issue mentioned above in connection with Meighen: the nature of social relationships. Meighen had favoured a policy of individualism, of competition in business matters, but that individualism had been little more than economic. His views did not trench on a doctrine that had been fundamental in

Canadian Conservatism from the time of Cartier: a belief in the importance of diversity. The liberal elements in Bracken's thought denied this value; Bracken believed not only in the advantages of economic individualism, but also in social individualism. However, his was an individualism that led in the direction of greater conformity. "Let us have less of hyphenated Canadianism."[100] To solve the problem this new emphasis created — how does a society of competitors hold together — Bracken was driven to assume away major divisions and differences. This done, it was possible to take the next step, and affirm that it "is a most ironical paradox that the Party which I lead is striving to create a co-operative Commonwealth, while most of those who parade under the banner of the Co-operative Commonwealth Federation are advocating state socialism."[101] Since the men he observed in his contemporary society were manifestly not co-operators, Bracken had to make one final move.

Canadian Conservatism before Bracken had consistently displayed what we have called the conservative disposition. For example, in 1933, Bennett had mused (and his reflections were in no way untypical of a widespread spirit among Canadian Conservatives): "I begin to realize how slow indeed has been the progress of mankind."[102] This scepticism about the possibility of making radical and dramatic improvements in the condition of mankind is referred to as conservative. Bracken's new Conservatism would have none of that. More satisfactory, Bracken preached, was the liberal ideal of progress. His party, he said, believed "that our economy is man-made — and, therefore, not necessarily perfect, and that our duty is to work toward its perfection."[103]

In the last chapter we argued that the Progressive Party to which Bracken belonged advocated a more radical form of liberalism than that which found a home in the mainstream of the Liberal Party. Therefore, the change in the Conservative Party's name in 1942 was significant. From the time of Macdonald, with a few deviations, it had been known officially as the Liberal-Conservative Party. This name, as our discussions to date indicate, was singularly appropriate. The substitution of Progressive for Liberal signalled the infusion of a more powerful and more radical strain of liberalism into the party.

Although Bracken proved to be an electorally more satisfying leader than Manion, the Progressive Conservatism he confidently offered the party and the country did not appeal to the voters as strongly as King's Liberalism. Bracken's successor, the former Conservative Premier of Ontario George Drew, also had little to offer in the way of ideological differences between the parties. Under Drew, the party continued on the path charted by Bracken, repudiating many of the historic principles that had comprised Canadian Conservatism before that time. Drew signalled this by quoting, in the 1949 election campaign, from the party's Declaration of Policy: "Economic freedom is the essence of competitive enterprise, and competitive enterprise is the foundation of our democratic system."[104]

Although he spoke of the "vast areas of the North [which] challenge our vision and our courage,"[105] he did not pursue the plan with much enthusiasm. It was left for John Diefenbaker to recapture the historic Conservative attitude to the use of government for nation-building purposes. Drew's views in other areas were narrowly individualist in orientation as well. He was concerned about what he considered were the infringements on liberty under the Liberals and pledged his party to end them: "We believe in the widest possible measure of personal liberty consistent with law, order and the general national welfare."[106] Beyond any doubt, then, Drew narrowed the ideological breadth of Canadian Conservatism. It is not surprising that, lacking even the sense of transformation and novelty that Bracken enjoyed, the Conservatives under Drew won fewer seats in both 1949 and 1953 than had his predecessor.

JOHN DIEFENBAKER AND THE TRIUMPH OF DEMOCRATIC TORYISM

The convention that met in 1956 on the resignation of the ailing George Drew was presented with an intriguing ideological choice. John Diefenbaker, Donald Fleming and Davie Fulton were the candidates for the leadership of the party, and each can be seen as representing distinctly different mixes of conservative principles. The weakest candidate, securing fewer than 10 percent of the votes, was the one who represented the clearest, and in some ways, the most radical ideological choice: Davie Fulton. Fulton relied heavily on one strand of traditional Canadian Conservatism: the tory element of British inspiration. Early in 1957 he contributed an introduction to John Farthing's book with the revealing title *Freedom Wears a Crown*. Farthing was a man of strong attachment to the British monarchical tradition in Canada, one he emphasized virtually to the exclusion of all others.

Fulton subscribed completely to Farthing's argument that the Crown in Parliament was the considered choice of the "two main elements of the population of Canada.[107] On this proposition hangs the Farthing-Fulton defence of the British tradition in Canada. By "British," it must be pointed out, Fulton is referring to an ideal, one which "must be given local habitation."[108] He does not mean the anglicization of the Canadian nation. Rather, he believed that this tradition was of value to French as well as English.

> I have never found any thoughtful French Canadian who did not agree that the British tradition on which our constitutional processes are based, and particularly the preservation of the proper position of the Crown, is, by its protection of the rights of Parliament, in itself the surest protection of those rights—personal, cultural and religious freedom — which they hold dear.[109]

Here Fulton was on firm ground, expressing a line of thought that stretched back to Cartier, Taché and Macdonald. There can be no doubt that most, if not all, leading Canadian Conservative thinkers have been firmly convinced that the Crown and the British connection is a thing of value to all Canadians, English, French and others, as well as to the Canadian polity as a whole.

However, Fulton was also in agreement with "the belief of the author that all life, in its fullest sense, and certainly all political conduct, must be conducive to the realization of, as well as answerable to, some higher moral concept...."[110] This emphasis puts both Fulton and Farthing in a very small group of English-Canadian political thinkers, of whom the most notable is George Parkin Grant, who have attempted to introduce an element of natural law philosophy into a consideration of Canadian political life. In Canada, this element derived, at least in Fulton's case, from Catholic doctrine and the works of the eighteenth-century statesman, Edmund Burke. Such providential and religious assumptions were unpalatable in the market place of secular Canadian Conservatism.

To these principles, Fulton added others borrowed from the writings of Burke and Disraeli: "The reverence of our ancestors, the soundness of those past institutions and laws suitable to changing conditions, and the proposition that conservatism is not a class position, but an attitude of mind which aims at the general benefit of all classes and occupations in society."[111] However, Fulton did not pursue the implications of his doctrines rigorously to their conclusions. The fact that he, too, was captivated by the importance of "private property and a system of free enterprise," and that he strongly affirmed individualism was "so much a part of Conservative philosophy" is dramatic evidence of the power of the business liberal element in Canadian political thought.[112] Underlying Fulton's ideas, however, was the basic caution that we have called a conservative disposition. This preference for slow, incremental change, for the familiar rather than the novel, has usually been justified by reference to utilitarian standards, by fears of palpable harm. Fulton preferred other grounds. He suggested that the disposition was one of "humility, because he [the Conservative] is conscious of the degree to which his conduct falls short of the ideal, and indeed of the limitations of his very horizon as compared to the concept of the Universe that is there if we had the capacity to grasp the vision."[113]

Donald Fleming, who attracted the support of about 30 percent of the delegates, had ideas different from Fulton's in a number of important ways. He was the candidate whose thoughts most closely resembled Drew's. Fleming shared with Fulton the belief that the Conservative Party stood for the continuation of the monarchy in Canada,[114] and feared the influence of the United States[115] perhaps even more than Fulton. But the important difference between the two men can be seen in their attitudes to the past and to change. Fulton was sceptical about the future, and emphasized the importance of preserving traditions and opposing inroads on the cherished institutions of the past. Fleming had a much more forward-looking approach, but since Fleming offered little in addition to the ideas Drew already had put forward, his appeal was limited to those with a strong commitment to Drew's liberal, business-oriented Conservatism.

The convention's choice turned out to be a man who had twice before contested the leadership: John Diefenbaker. The decision gave it and the country perhaps the most enigmatic and controversial prime minister since Confederation. Diefenbaker has perplexed such serious writers on Canadian affairs as Peter Newman and George Grant. The latter wrote in 1965 that in "studying his government, one becomes aware of a series of mutually conflicting conceptions,"[116] of which populism, nationalism and small-town free enterprise were the most prominent.

Although Newman in his highly critical contemporary portrait argued that Diefenbaker had obscured the ideological differences between the Liberals and the Conservatives,[117] he himself had little doubt concerning the fundamentally ideological character of Diefenbaker's politics. Diefenbaker, Newman observed, "behaved as if he were the sacrosanct head of a people's government and tended to view events at home and abroad in black and white terms, depending on their appropriateness to his scheme of things."[118] In so doing, Diefenbaker displayed the hallmark of ideological thinking: he "tried to reduce complicated national issues to memorable slogans — the Vision, the National Development Policy, Unhyphenated Canadianism, the Confederation Platform, the Five-Year Plan, the *Bill of Rights*, pro-Canadianism."[119]

Diefenbaker was a frustrating and elusive figure for his contemporaries, and he is no less exasperating for those of us who try to understand his principles. Consider, for example, the following passage in which he reflected on the period of 1956-1957:

> In emphasizing the question of northern development and northern vision, I advocated a 20th-century equivalent to Sir John Macdonald's national policy, a uniquely Canadian economic dream. The Liberals were coming to believe that what was good for General Motors was not only good for the United States but good for Canada. My advocacy of a northern development policy was not suddenly produced. Indeed, in July of 1956, I spoke in the House of the need for a national vision to equalize economic opportunities everywhere in Canada.[120]

In the space of less than a paragraph, Diefenbaker appealed to nostalgia and a sense of history ("a 20th-century equivalent to Sir John Macdonald's national policy"); pro-Canadianism ("uniquely Canadian"); hostility to continentalism ("The Liberals were coming to believe"); conservatism as caution ("not suddenly produced"); toryism ("a national vision"); and an ambiguous liberalism ("equalize economic opportunities"). As David Lewis commented perceptively, "I don't think he ever recognized the line between campaigning for votes and running the country, but he was a spellbinder on the platform, mixing indignation, vision, and wit into a powerful brew."[121] To the themes mentioned above, at least two others of importance can be added, namely his concern for civil liberties and his self-understanding as a friend and advocate of the weak and oppressed.

Let us then try to impose some order on Diefenbaker's thought. We have seen that the Conservative Party has been, throughout its history, a coalition primarily of tory and business liberal elements, and that in the first half of the twentieth century the latter had gained in strength and had become the dominant, though not the exclusive, strain of Canadian Conservatism. With Diefenbaker, toryism was resuscitated, but in a form with important differences. We have previously made reference to democratic toryism as an important derivation from the classic toryism of the early settlers.

Democratic toryism was pioneered in the United Kingdom in the late nineteenth century by politicians such as Lord Shaftesbury. There were even some intimations of it in some of the policies of Macdonald, such as the broadening of the franchise and the legalization of the trade union movement. Its original impulse can perhaps be traced to Disraeli and his view that the state must overcome the divisions within the nation between rich and poor.

What distinguishes the democratic tory is his concern for the well-being of the poor, and his belief that those who enjoy the benefits and privileges of society have a responsibility to care for those who are less well-off. However, unlike the welfare liberal with whom the democratic tory is often confused, the programs they advocate do not have as their goal the enhanced freedom of the recipient. Instead they are aimed at increasing his security. And unlike the socialist who sees the state as the agency for generating greater equality, the democratic tory sees nothing wrong with the wealthy retaining their privileges, provided that their advantages also yield subsidiary benefits to those at the bottom of the social scale. The democratic tory, therefore, can accept progressive taxation to the extent that it reflects the fact that the rich ought to bear a greater burden of responsibility commensurate with their greater wealth; but he does not see higher marginal rates for the rich as desirable in themselves.

There can be little doubt that Diefenbaker had a deep sense of the history and roots of his party. In the first volume of *One Canada*, he described his early days in politics: "To those who have labelled me as some kind of Party maverick, and have claimed that I have been untrue to the great principles of the Conservative Party, I can only reply that they have forgotten the traditions of Disraeli and Shaftesbury in Britain and Macdonald in Canada."[122] And in his great speech to the 1967 leadership convention, which he described as "the testament, the sum, of my experience in public life," he said:

> We are a party with a great tradition, a party of great principles. In this convention, we must hold communion with those who have gone before. We change not principles, we change programs to meet modern conditions, using as a basis principles

which brought this party into existence. These principles have served our country before and since confederation. Our purpose must be to leave a memorial of greatness to future generations....[123]

This sense of the past and of the traditions of this party and country, which at times slipped into nostalgia, and his instinctive caution (seen frequently by contemporary journalists as dithering and an inability to make up his mind) are aspects we have already identified as conservative.

Although he was at heart a democratic tory, classic toryism was also present in Diefenbaker's thought. His devotion to the monarchy was legendary, and his sense of the importance of the British Commonwealth as the inheritor of the civilizing values of the British Empire was powerful as well. Yet his understanding of Canadian toryism was deeper than this loyalty to such institutions as the monarchy, the commonwealth and parliament. His frequent references to his vision of Canada was another aspect. To some extent the notion of the Vision is a weakened version of the higher law in which Fulton believed. It is an affirmation that there are leaders who see further and more truly than the general public. "...I believe that no political party worth its salt would determine its course on the basis of (public opinion) polls. If it does, out goes principle and in come the temporary views of the population as a whole. Leadership does not consist in finding out in which direction the people are going or want to go and then running to the front of the parade to announce: I'm your leader."[124] Such an approach does not sit comfortably with the classical democratic idea of a society of reasonable, deliberating individuals deciding their own fate. As Diefenbaker wrote, he was "aware of man's inherent limitations, and aware that the majority is not always right in the short run, and is sometimes prone to trample on the rights of minorities...."[125] This suspicion of popular sentiment appeared even when he was fulminating in his most populist rhetoric. "There was no question that everyone was against me but the people....I have an unwavering conviction that if given a chance the people are not easily misled."[126]

In general, Diefenbaker's attitude strikes us as comparable to that of Bennett and Herridge in the thirties—but nothing about John Diefenbaker was simple and uncomplicated. In his hostility to the "few and the powerful,"[127] an aversion that struck even a socialist such as David Lewis as sincere,[128] Diefenbaker was simultaneously appealing to the strain of toryism that Bennett's nemesis, H.H. Stevens, articulated in the middle 1930s. Of his early life he said that he was "an unsworn enemy of injustice, particularly against the weak. I have spent my years on the side of the individual against the powerful establishments of our nation, whether public or private."[129] As usual, Diefenbaker brought the two strains together, his rhetoric and passion masking the philosophical difficulties:

In discussing our 1957 election platform, I have left until last our program of social justice. This was an essential part of my national vision. To me government not only had to be *of* and by the people, but most positively *for* the people. Unless government concerned itself with the problems of the individual working man and farmer, unless government was cognizant of the problems of the small businessman and not just the corporate giants, unless government acted in the interests of our senior citizens, our veterans, our blind and disabled, unless government sought a basic equality of citizenship, of opportunity, and of well-being for all our peoples, then government had lost sight of its true purpose.[130]

However, like Bennett, Diefenbaker was no ruthless demagogue. His Vision was closely associated with another slogan, the National Development Policy. The platform of 1957 was called "A New National Policy" and the title was revealing. The recurrent references to the maintenance "as a sacred trust [of] the vision of Macdonald and Cartier...."[131] was an indication more of Diefenbaker's awareness of the extent to which the country had deviated from that original conception. It represented a determined attempt to overhaul the economy after twenty-two years of Liberal rule. Devised in large part by Saskatchewan colleague Alvin Hamilton, the National Development Policy revealed a return to the traditions of Conservative collectivist control over economics. The Five Year Plan was evidence of this. There can be little doubt that Diefenbaker saw the national government as a powerful agent that could be used, in the northern development program for example, to create a sense of national urgency and importance by expanding and exploring a vast, undeveloped area of the country. This development was to take place for political, more than economic, reasons.

Diefenbaker's tory sense of the nation as the most important collectivity had kept him from joining the Progressive Party.[132] In addition, this same sense of the nation as a whole allowed him to attach a high value to the importance of diversity within the nation, as had Conservatives before him such as Cartier. "For I see Canada," Diefenbaker wrote, "not as a mosaic but rather as a peopled garden in which the flowers of different lands lend richness and beauty and the strength of their diversity to our body politic."[133] The same sentiment led him to attempt to "preserve and strengthen our Canadian inheritance" and he took exception to "'Canadianization' in the Liberal sense," which he thought "meant the neutralization — perhaps better, 'neutering' — of our history."[134]

Strong as Diefenbaker's toryism was, it in no way overshadowed his liberalism. The modern Conservative Party has enjoyed more than its share of civil libertarians, such as Gordon Fairweather, David MacDonald, Ged Baldwin, and Perrin Beatty; but none has excelled him in eloquence or in the determination to pursue the liberal goal of the protection and enhancement of individual liberty. In 1947, Diefenbaker argued for a *Bill of Rights* on the grounds that it "would assert the right of the individual; it would assert the right of the minority to be protected in the exercise of its rights against the majority." Again, in 1952, he proposed such a bill on the grounds that it would make parliament "freedom-conscious." A Canadian *Bill of Rights*, he wrote, was "fundamental to my philosophy of social justice and national development."[135]

However, the Chief did not just share the business liberal's concern for the rule of law and for procedural safeguards for formal liberty. Diefenbaker also joined with the welfare liberals in seeking to achieve a minimum degree of "positive" liberty for all Canadians. He spoke of his attempt "to equalize opportunities for all Canadians wherever they lived."[136] And he declared, in reflecting on his administration, that it had been motivated by the thought that "government had a responsibility to bring about a higher standard of welfare for all Canadians, and in particular for those who because of age, disability, unemployment, or other causes would not normally enjoy a reasonable share of the good life."[137]

It was in the critical area of state-business relations that the traditional conflict between toryism and business liberalism within the Conservative Party showed the most disastrous confusion in Diefenbaker's thought. In talking about his new national policy, he claimed to have offered "a policy of positive government, although not unnecessary government," and he praised Macdonald for knowing "instinctively that the goals of an economically independent and viable Canada could not be realized except by positive, even heroic government action...."[138] This observation undoubtedly rings true for Macdonald and for the concern he consistently showed in asserting the primacy of politics over economics. Yet Diefenbaker reports a speech in the 1965 election campaign, during which "the crowd broke into applause forty-two times" when he had thundered "that the time had come for Canadians to declare whether they believed in a socialist state or in the principles of private enterprise, tempered to assure the public interest."[139] Even in his calmer moments, the position Diefenbaker took was that "the role of public or government enterprise (was) a necessary catalyst for the fullest functioning of our system of private enterprise."[140]

It is difficult to come to any conclusion other than that Diefenbaker simply had little clear idea of the nature of the structure of the Canadian economy. There can be little doubt that his sympathies were with the small businessman and the farmer, each with little or no control over the market, and against the large corporations, whether national or multinational. Here the blinkers of ideology worked to Diefenbaker's detriment. The Canadian economy had changed dramatically since the days of his youth; he railed against subsequent developments but he was unable to develop any effective policies that would shatter the concentrations of economic power and restore the competitive market. Because he could not fully accept the legitimacy of the large corporations, he alternated between assuming them away and treating them as enemies to be bested. Consequently, he was ready to draw on the tory readiness to use government to order national priorities, in programs such as northern development, ARDA, Resources for Tomorrow, the South Saskatchewan River Dam and the Columbia River Treaty.

Associated with this preference for economic individualism was, just as with Bracken, a strong feeling for social individualism. As Diefenbaker did in every other idea he developed, he drew on several incompatible strains, often at the same time. In his speech to the 1967 convention, he lauded equality, but also praised the "diversity of our national origin" and urged Canadians to "realize the richness of its [sic] many cultures."[141] The very title of his memoirs, *One Canada,* and his decision to contest the 1967 leadership convention on the grounds that the party was tempted to adopt a *deux nations* theory of Canada bore telling witness to the depth of his feelings about social individualism. Although he had no desire to undermine the basis of French-Canadian culture, it is small wonder that French Canadians, attached as they have been to their distinctive collectivity, saw the objective consequences of his policies as hostile to their hopes of maintaining cultural and linguistic identity.

Finally, we come to pro-Canadianism. In George Grant's view, this was the area in which Diefenbaker's greatest and most tragic failure lay. His attempts to preserve Canadian independence, or to prevent an increasing dependence on the United States, by, among other things, diverting trade from that country to the Commonwealth met with failure. That he made the attempt at all is an important indication of the continuing hold of the pro-British element in Canadian Conservatism. Pro-Canadianism is an appropriate Conservative phrase; it is neither aggressively internationalist nor nationalist in approach. It expresses most acutely exactly what it is that the Canadian Conservative is interested in: namely, the preservation of an identity distinct from all others. To the extent that it concerns itself with identity, and indulges itself in merely a suspicious hostility of foreign elements, it is probably the mildest and safest form of nationalism. Grant's charge was that it was insufficient; lamentably, it probably was.

There can be no doubt at all, if our argument is correct, that Diefenbaker expressed a complex ideological vision of Canada. His appeal, so widely successful in 1958, was dissipated by 1962. The reasons for this are not as difficult to understand as some commentators have made out. In the campaigns of 1957 and 1958, Diefenbaker's ideological appeal, containing as it did such powerful liberal and tory elements, attracted wide support. The liberal elements in the doctrine added a reassuring ring to a basically liberal population; yet there were sufficient traditional conservative elements to preserve the support of the smaller conservative section of the country. Diefenbaker's failure arose from the very success he originally enjoyed. He had evoked a heightened awareness of the divergent strains in Canadian Conservatism; he had used the different elements to appeal to different segments of the community. But he never succeeded in reconciling them, of resolving them into a new synthesis that would preserve him from mere inconsistency on the ideological level, and he confused directions when fundamental policy choices had to be made. It is one of the merits of Grant's argument in *Lament for a Nation* that he realized that Diefenbaker's problem was not that he promised things that he could not provide, but that he promised things no man could provide. His personal appeal had succeeded, for a brief period, in masking the ideological divisions in the nation, but when it came to the task of governing, it was no longer possible to avoid specific decisions. Had he made a clear choice, or had he, more significantly, succeeded in achieving a new synthesis of Canadian Conservatism, he might easily have become the national hero he aspired to be. His tragedy is that there is no evidence he even tried.

In the early 1960s, Canadian Conservatism, as a consequence of Diefenbaker's ideological incoherence, was confused and vulnerable. We have argued that all Canadian ideologies have shown an openness to influences from outside the country, and during this period, American Senator Barry Goldwater and his followers in the Republican party were aggressively propounding a radical version of individualist liberalism, which in the United States was normally called conservatism. Because of the similarity in names, and because American conservatism overlapped to a considerable extent with many of the central concerns of Canadian business liberalism, some Conservatives urged this doctrine on their party. Writers such as George Hogan, Heath Macquarrie and George Grant responded, marshalling evidence to show that Canadian Conservatism had a distinctive identity, and that it was not merely a failed and sullied version of the American variety. Their books showed that Canadian Conservatism possessed an identifiable past, although Goldwater's conservatism had temporarily placed that past in doubt. To that extent they were successful; however they did not know any more than Diefenbaker did whether it had a future, or what the future should be. At the same time, George Grant reflected that perhaps it did not much matter in any event, since the very possibility of an independent Canadian nation had been eroded.

Grant had made this point as early as 1959 when he wrote: "To express conservatism in Canada means *de facto* to justify the continuing rule of the businessman and the right of the greedy to turn all activities into sources of personal gain."[142] He followed up this argument more systematically in *Lament for a Nation*. There he spoke of:

> ...the impossibility of conservatism as a viable political ideology in our era. The practical men who call themselves conservatives must commit themselves to a science that leads to the conquest of nature. This science produces such a dynamic society that it is impossible to conserve anything for long. In such an environment, all institutions and standards are constantly changing. Conservatives who attempt to be practical face a dilemma. If they are not committed to a dynamic technology, they cannot hope to make any popular appeal. If they are so committed, they cannot hope to be conservatives.[143]

Grant's pessimistic conclusion is open to two major objections: that he has overestimated the force and power of the technological society, or underestimated the strength of substantive conservatism in Canada, or both. Grant himself admitted in the introduction to the Carleton Library edition of *Lament for a Nation* (1970) that the situation was not one of unrelieved gloom, noting the resurgence of nationalism in the young, and even "traces of care about Canada" in the Trudeau government.

Grant's estimation of the dissolvent effects of technology was based on a powerful and compelling argument that cannot be discounted. Nevertheless, the survival of non-liberal values in the public realm, which we have examined in this chapter and shall consider further with respect to socialism and nationalism in Canada, and their resurgence in the present time, clearly tempers the full force of Grant's argument.

THE GREATEST PRIME MINISTER CANADA NEVER HAD

The 1967 leadership convention revealed the extent to which the party had been fragmented. Eleven candidates presented themselves, of whom nine were men of substance: the former prime minister, six of his former cabinet ministers, and two provincial premiers. The results of the balloting further revealed the divisions within the party. No candidate secured more than 25 percent of the votes on the first ballot, and five received the support of at least 10 percent of the delegates. The succeeding ballots eliminated the more extreme or ideologically limited candidates — Fulton, Hees, McCutcheon and Fleming — as well as Diefenbaker himself. On the fifth ballot the choice lay between two provincial premiers: Roblin of Manitoba and Stanfield of Nova Scotia. Victory went to Stanfield who won majority support from delegates from Atlantic Canada, Ontario, Alberta and British Columbia. However, his victory was by no means either decisive or a healing experience for the party; his main rival, Roblin, secured the support of 969 delegates out of the 2119 who voted in the fifth ballot.[144]

Stanfield, although not an exciting speaker like his predecessor, was a reflective, thoughtful man. As an undergraduate at Dalhousie University, he had briefly flirted with socialism,[145] though by the time his political ideas had matured, he was, in the words of a Nova Scotian colleague, "Conservative in the best sense of the word, by temperament and by reasoned judgement, as well as tradition....His brand of Conservatism finds the word 'Progressive' quite compatible with Conservatism. Of course if the name had been changed, Stanfield's brand of Conservatism would still be progressive, in the sense that it was, and is, a philosophy of political thought and behaviour, which is fluid, alive, questing and constructive."[146]

Stanfield's government in Nova Scotia had been consistently but moderately reform-minded. He brought the same concerns to federal politics. In Geoffrey Stevens's words, he tried to develop policies "that would move his party well away from the curious blend of prairie populism and traditional conservatism that it had embraced under Diefenbaker" in favour of "contemporary policies that would be attractive to the young and to the city dweller."[147] This desire, however, by no means meant that he intended a purge of the business liberal or other elements within the party. As he hastened to assure the convention: "The Progressive Conservative Party is big enough, and great enough, to accommodate all of us...."[148]

Nonetheless, important changes in party doctrine could be seen in the leader's subsequent pronouncements and in the party's platform. Perhaps the most significant of these is a decline in the importance of the individualist element the western members of the party had encouraged. The 1968 platform, while acknowledging that "Canada is, and should be, one country" took pains to emphasize the bi-national nature of the country: "Canada is composed of the original [sic] inhabitants of this land and the two founding peoples with historic rights to maintain their language and culture, who have been joined and continue to be joined by people from many lands who have a right to play a full part in Canadian life."[149] Stanfield returned to this theme in a speech delivered in April 1972 in Toronto. There he rejected the beliefs the slogan of Unhyphenated Canadianism implied. "[T]his is not a country that believes in the philosophy of the melting pot. This is not a country where it is necessary to submerge your national or ethnic origins, nor forget the language of the country of your birth in order to function as a good citizen."[150] In rejecting rigorous individualism, Stanfield went even further. He affirmed that the "kind of society I am talking about involves a number of groups, each of which has a rich and cohesive interior life, but each of which also has a desire to reach outward to others."[151] This style of pluralism, whether applied to the French-Canadian nation, or to the immigrant communities much more recently formed in Canada, represents a renewed belief in the importance of Conservative collectivism, and a willingness to assume that unity rather than division is present: "What we feel for Canada is our common bond. What we do about it is our common purpose."[152]

It was therefore significant when Stanfield selected Marcel Faribault as his Quebec lieutenant in 1968. Such a move did more than indicate an appreciation of the electoral importance of the province of Quebec. It also was a manifestation of this new direction in Canadian Conservatism. The party had seemed in danger of splitting over the *deux nations* concept in the 1967 convention. Yet his Quebec lieutenant was a man who affirmed that this idea was "a good notion"[153] and who believed that: "When one speaks...of the two founding peoples, their differences in approach and the actual clash of their national traits should always be remembered, the more so for being so often ignored in the past."[154] The corollary of this larger concept was a rejection of Unhyphenated Canadianism. "For we are, after all, all hyphenated to a certain degree....Has not your own Conservative party been called for many decades Liberal-Conservative or Progressive Conservative?"[155]

Although French-English relations had been a volatile subject at the leadership convention itself and, subsequently, as in 1969 when seventeen Conservative MPs voted against the *Official Languages Act*, Stanfield's democratic toryism extended much further. Throughout his national political career he was deeply concerned with questions of social justice. In 1968, he told the House that he had "long felt that the extent of poverty in Canada is a national disgrace. I have said here that I have dedicated this party to fighting it now."[156] He reaffirmed this position in 1974: "It is a fundamental article of faith to our contemporary philosophy to see social justice fulfilled. We want to see social justice fulfilled as it can only realistically be fulfilled in an environment of national order and national purpose."[157]

The 1968 election saw Stanfield, his popularity already declining before the Liberals chose their new leader, overwhelmed by Pierre Trudeau. The 1968 platform reflected many of Stanfield's concerns: the desire for constitutional renewal, fairness for aboriginals, a decent life for all Canadians supported by a Guaranteed Annual Income and extensive proposals for pollution control, among other items. By 1972 popular support for the Liberal administration had declined, and Stanfield ran a very close second, leading his party to 107 seats, compared with 109 for the Liberals. In this election, Stanfield had concentrated on issues such as unemployment and the cost of living, matters that fell into the area of ideological agreement among all of the major parties in Canada. His selection of the former Liberal, Claude Wagner, as his Quebec lieutenant was a further indication that, for the time being, he was emphasizing his party's liberal aspects in the hope that dislike of Pierre Trudeau would prove the decisive factor if ideological and policy differences were not emphasized.

The tactic almost succeeded, but subsequent developments revealed its limitations. By accentuating to such an extent the liberal elements, or elements which may be mistaken for them in the Conservative ideology, Stanfield made it easier for the Liberal minority government to construct a Throne Speech in January 1973 that included a number of the more prominent suggestions that the Conservatives made during the campaign. The leader of the opposition was reduced at one point early in the session to the charge that "we have a lame-duck Liberal government, bargaining with the New Democratic Party to keep it in office so that it may attempt to implement some Progressive Conservative policy."[158]

Although the liberal elements in Canadian Conservatism, under Stanfield's cautious and restraining hand, had been temporarily pushed to the forefront, his deep commitment to the tory tradition in his party's ideological make-up was by no means forgotten. The idea of the primacy of politics over economics, which we have argued was probably Canadian Conservatism's noblest contribution to the country's ideological conversation, was clearly restated. In a speech delivered in Winnipeg in April 1972, Stanfield declared: "Canada must have and must have quickly a national development strategy that will enable us to decide our industrial, environmental, social and human priorities for the years and decades to come." He went on to say that "such a plan involves a close look at our economic and trading regulations with other countries, and especially the United States. It involves planning for our industrial and agricultural future. It involves the quality of life and environment and *it involves a choice of the way in which we want to organize our economy and our whole society.*"[159] A Conservative position paper on the Canadian identity speaks in the same vein: "The threats to the survival of Canada as a nation can be met only by a comprehensive policy embracing all aspects of the question — cultural, economic, and political."[160]

This principle led to the development of an issue during 1973, wage and price controls, which some observers think cost Stanfield the 1974 election and the Conservative leadership. Speaking in the House of Commons in September 1973, he described the inflationary psychology as a "disease," and went on: "But you must also make a massive public assault on halting the spread of the disease."[161] And in May 1974 he reaffirmed his support for temporary controls "to restore some sense of order, stability and purpose."[162]

The party was by no means united on this issue in the 1974 election campaign. John Diefenbaker, on a national speaking tour, was almost openly hostile and many other Conservative candidates either repudiated the policy directly or, more commonly, explained it away. The business liberals were especially critical. They feared the intrusion of government into private enterprise, worried about the short-term distortions of the market place and had an abiding worry lest controls that were meant to be temporary prove permanent. Although the business liberals had been relatively quiet in the party since Stanfield's accession to the leadership, they began to struggle for pre-eminence again when Stanfield announced, soon after his 1974 election loss, that he would step down as party leader before the next election.

Stanfield, however, was not prepared to abandon the party or the principles for which he had fought so long and so hard. In November 1974 he initiated a discussion of Conservative principles within the parliamentary caucus, to which he himself contributed "Some Comments on Conservative Principles and Philosophy."Although his paper contains, as he freely admitted, "rough edges," it was probably the single most important contribution to Canadian Conservatism since the Port Hope Conference of 1942.

As Stanfield pointed out to his colleagues, he was discussing principles, "what we do or should stand for through the years, rather than a set of proposals designed to deal with the problems and issues of the moment," though any platform the party presented to the public "should be consistent with our principles."

He opposed what he described as the Manning thesis, which we have discussed earlier, which "urges polarization of political viewpoints in this country"[163] on the grounds that our political parties are not doctrinaire and that "some acceptance of common ground among the major parties is essential to an effective and stable democracy."[164] Drawing repeatedly on British Conservatism as his inspiration, he argued that Conservatism favours individual freedom, tempered by the belief that "a decent civilized life requires a framework of order." This order was not to be taken for granted, but rather was "quite rare in the world and therefore quite precious."[165]

Most particularly, Stanfield emphasized traditional British Conservatism's rejection of "the supreme importance of private enterprise," a view he associated with the liberalism of Adam Smith, Cobden and Bright. In contrast, he recalled Wilberforce's factory legislation, which he described as a logical measure "to protect the weak against the excesses of private enterprise and greed."[166] The Conservative attachment to order "favoured strong and effective government, but on the other hand they [Conservatives] saw a limited or restricted role for government." Limited government held a special appeal for three reasons. First, decentralization of power limits the possibility of effective revolution. In Canada the provinces, trade unions, farm organizations, trade associations and the press were the leading agents of countervailing power and influence, balancing the claims of the government. Second, Conservatives were sceptical that government could, in any event, work much good, because of human imperfection. Third, Conservatives had doubts about human capacities to grasp fully the fundamental features of their society, and "consequently have recognized that success in planning the lives of other people or the life of the nation is likely to be limited."[167]

Stanfield then turned to address directly the tory sense of collectivism:

> Conservatism is national in scope and purpose. This implies a strong feeling for the country, its institutions and its symbols; but also a feeling for all the country and for all the people in the country. The Conservative Party serves the whole country and all the people, not simply part of the country and certain categories of people.[168]

Following from this, Stanfield drew attention to what we have called the primacy of politics over economics. "Economic policy," he wrote, "was and is subservient to national objectives in this full sense of the word national." By contrast, he alleged that "Liberalism traditionally emphasized the individual and opposed the subservience of the economy to national political objectives and purposes."[169]

In an attack on those who sought to make business liberalism the sole orthodoxy within the party, he denied that "any particular economic dogma" is a "principle of our party." Although he contrasted "traditional Liberalism" — with its belief in the individual, in liberty and "calling for a minimum of government interference with the individual" — with Conservatism, which "emphasized the nation, society, stability and order,"[170] he did not set the two parties at war. As we have argued throughout this chapter, Canadian Conservatism has always been a coalition between business liberalism and toryism, and Stanfield believed that this condition had to continue if the party were to hope for future electoral success. So Stanfield offered a position that attempted a reconciliation of the two views. "The Conservative tradition has been to interfere only where necessary, but to interfere where necessary to achieve social and national objectives. Conservatives favour incentives, where appropriate, rather than the big stick."[171]

Although he acknowledged, as we have also argued, that "resistance to changes and the support of privilege has been part of the behaviour of Conservatives from time to time," he denied that they should be principles upon which the party was based. Instead, he proposed to emphasize the "nation as a whole" and suggested that "this is a period when true Conservative principles of order and stability should be most appealing."[172] It would certainly be appropriate for a Conservative to suggest that we must achieve some kind of order if we are to avoid chaos; an order which is stable, but not static; an order, therefore, which is reasonably acceptable and which among other things provides a framework in which enterprise can flourish. That would be in the Conservative tradition.[173]

Reactions within the Conservative caucus to Stanfield's arguments were mixed. Many probably sympathized with the MP who is reported to have said: "What's all this talk about ideology. I thought we were Tories because we hate Grits." Others responded more thoughtfully. Perrin Beatty, then a young Ontario MP first elected in 1972, replied with an elegant and articulate statement of the business liberal position. Beatty complained that even if Stanfield's observations about the history of Canadian Conservatism and Liberalism were true, there were no longer significant differences between the parties. "The sad fact about Canadian politics is that the real difference between the three national parties is one of degree and not one of kind."[174] It was Beatty's belief, one which lay at the heart of his deep commitment to civil liberties, that "the primary function of government is to ensure that the individual can live his life in his own way, free from unwarranted intrusion and in a climate of sufficient order essential to freedom within society."[175] Beatty was less enthusiastic than Stanfield about the tory appeal to collectivism and to the role of the state. He thought that "except in very limited areas where the state must intervene because the private sector is incapable of acting, government activity should be negative activity designed to prevent the loss of something we possess."[176]

This desire to limit the state is frequently advanced by business liberals within both the Conservative and Liberal Parties in defence of crass materialism or in callous indifference to the suffering of the needy in society. However, Beatty showed that business liberalism can be applied to more noble purposes. "Perhaps the most significant domestic activity of government is to break up or control concentrations of power that victimize the individual, or reduce his suffering."[177] Probably Beatty's most creative suggestion for the future development of Canadian Conservatism was that business liberalism should be combined with the democratic toryism, which we noted as a minor strain within the party of which H.H. Stevens in the 1930s and John Diefenbaker were the most notable earlier exponents.

> I believe that the Progressive Conservative Party should be the voice of the Canadian who does not belong to powerful organized groups—the small businessman, the senior citizen, the family farmer, the housewife, the young, and the unorganized worker. Both in terms of numbers and of their contributions to our country, these people are the mainstay of our society. They are also the people who are increasingly losing their confidence that there is room in the political system for them. The rich and the powerful can look after themselves. They already have their friends in court and do not need us, but the middle-class Canadian does need our help.[178]

JOE WHO AND DEMOCRATIC TORYISM

Stanfield's announcement that he would step down from the party leadership obviated the need for any attempt to drive him out. Although in 1975 a faction in caucus formed itself into a group called the Chateau Cabinet, the main focus of disagreement within the party was on the leadership convention, which was called for 1976. There were fully eleven candidates, none of whom was an obvious front runner, as Diefenbaker had been in 1956 or Stanfield and Roblin in 1967. Indeed, the eventual victory of Joe Clark, thirty-six years old, and an MP for only four years, provoked "Joe Who?" headlines on newspapers and magazines across the country.

Although, as George Perlin explains in *The Tory Syndrome,* there are many factors that must be taken into account to explain why a delegate votes for one candidate rather than another (considerations such as personal loyalty, regional ties, hopes for party patronage, and the like), ideology was generally seen by candidates, the press and popular opinion as a significant factor. Jim Gillies, one of the leadership candidates, noted: "Red Tory. Blue Tory. Nobody has to tell you about these divisions. They're real. And they've hurt us at the polls. And in part, this leadership contest is a contest for control of the party being waged between different groups."[179]

One of the groups, and the most clearly identifiable, consisted of those whom we have called the business liberals. Although Paul Hellyer, Jack Horner, Sinclair Stevens and Claude Wagner differed among themselves on some issues, all held ideologically comparable positions. The seven others varied considerably, with Flora MacDonald and Heward Grafftey perhaps most closely aligned as welfare liberals, and the others showing various ideological compromises in which democratic toryism and business liberalism predominated.

Although Perlin himself does not think that ideology was a major contributing factor to the overall outcome,[180] he does report survey data that 19 percent of the delegates considered themselves on the left of the party, 37 percent in the centre and 42 percent on the right. As well, he reports that 47 percent of the delegates thought that there were big ideological differences between left and right within the party, and that 7 percent thought these disagreements so great as to be irreconcilable.[181]

The delegates were eventually presented with a choice between Joe Clark and Claude Wagner. Wagner, a former Quebec provincial Liberal cabinet minister and a tough "law and order" judge, had been induced by Stanfield to enter federal politics as a Conservative. Although Wagner was eventually supported by most of the business liberals within the party as well as by former leader John Diefenbaker, who found the prospect of a French-Canadian Conservative leader attractive, many delegates were sceptical of Wagner, since he was a former Liberal. In addition, it was revealed at the time of the convention that when Wagner left the bench to return to politics, a substantial trust fund had been established to provide him with financial security. This fact alone disturbed many who might otherwise have found Wagner attractive and it also raised serious doubts as to the sincerity of his endorsement of the Progressive Conservative Party.

Clark was seen as being on the democratic tory wing of the party, but this category has increasingly become a catch-all to describe those Conservatives who are not clearly committed to business liberalism as a relatively pure doctrine. Like his predecessor, Clark opposed the adoption by the party of a striking and different doctrinaire ideology, although as we have seen in this chapter, the refusal of a Conservative leader to accept ideological polarization does not mean he is without principles or ideology.

This conclusion was endorsed by Sinclair Stevens, who withdrew his name from the ballot at the leadership convention, and then supported Clark rather than Wagner, to whom he was ideologically much closer. As Stevens explained: "In the Conservative party there is certainly a great body of true blue. But it is unrealistic to think that they represent a majority of voters in Canada. It is wrong to think that we can mould a party that will appeal mainly to the true blues and win."[182]

Jim Gillies, a rival for the leadership and subsequently Clark's chief policy advisor, described him as "philosophically pretty close to neo-conservatism," believing that the federal government should withdraw from some social services, and that there should be less government intervention in general, and a lowering of trade barriers.[183] However, his cabinet colleague, David MacDonald, described Clark as "pink with blue tinges," meaning that he usually took a democratic tory position on human rights issues, but sided with the business liberals on economic policy.[184]

The difficulty in establishing Clark's exact stance stems from two factors. First, there was his clear awareness of the strength and confidence of the business-liberal element within the party, and his desire to avoid a split or even a confrontation with a powerful faction that did not look to him as its leader. Second, he had a firm belief in the value of pragmatism. In his first speech as Prime Minister in the House of Commons, he praised Macdonald as a "practical, pragmatic man. He wanted to make the nation work. He was more interested in having a nation that worked than having a nation which accorded to his theories."[185]

Nonetheless, it is possible to discern both democratic tory and business liberal strains in Clark's political thinking, principles that place him clearly in the tradition of the mainstream of Canadian Conservatives. Let us consider the democratic tory strains first. His biographer writes: "If one word had to describe Joe Clark's own campaign for the leadership, or even his own political principles, diversity would have served well. For his entire purpose had been to establish a genuine respect in Ottawa for the Nation's diversities."[186] Clark returned to this theme again and again. As he said in a speech during the leadership race, "Canada is too big for any one identity or ideology, and the attempts to make us all the same serve only to frustrate and divide. We should recognize that a respect for diversity is itself a form of Canadian identity."[187] He reiterated the same ideas as Prime Minister:

> If the House accepts the challenge that we are placing before it, I believe that we can make this again an instrument which is strong enough and respected enough to reflect the diversity of an exciting country....The lesson is that this nation cannot be ordered together. This nation must be brought together, and the starting step must be to establish a basis of mutual trust, of goals that emerge from the community of Canada rather than being imposed upon the community of Canada.[188]

And with the tory sense of the importance of collectivism, he even ventured a reference to the concept that had caused Stanfield so much grief in the 1967 convention: he alluded in the House to "the relations between the two founding nations."[189]

However, his scepticism about the extent of government involvement in the economy revealed business liberal aspects as well. The Edmonton *Journal* reported him during his campaign for the leadership as blasting "the notion that big business and big labour be counterbalanced by big government. Big government...is more dangerous than the other giants....The Liberals may support labour, but the Conservatives are not the voice of unregulated big business. Rather, the Conservatives have a wider mandate, a mandate to all Canadians. We must pay attention to Canadians whom other parties, other groups ignore."[190] In the House of Commons, he spoke of his government's determination "to place much greater reliance on the private sector" and to "reduce the burden of government on the economy and offer practical incentives to individual Canadians to build a stake in our country."[191]

Yet the government was not simply to be dismantled; as with Stanfield, Diefenbaker, and Macdonald, Clark intended to use it as an agent of national purpose. He brought the divergent strains within the party together when he said that "all of us, coming from every corner that is represented here in this House of Commons, have in our heritage, in our past and as part of our being, a different sense of what this country can become, and a different identity that, woven together, can create a vibrant and strong national identity."[192]

In spite of these democratic tory elements in his political thought, Clark's short period as prime minister appeared to the Canadian public to lean heavily towards business liberalism. It is probably true, as Jeffrey Simpson argues, that the Canadian public had not voted on balance for Clark as an alternative approach to government. Dissident Liberals and New Democrats, who had cast their ballots for the Conservatives in 1979 as a means of getting rid of Pierre Trudeau, became worried that they had unleashed an unattractive force. As Simpson concludes:

> The Conservative Party has prospered in the past by reaching out to these groups with imaginative policies in which the state played an indispensable role. The belief in the utility of state intervention in the economy is an honourable part of the Conservative tradition in Canada and the prerequisite for a Conservative Government to sustain itself in power....Privatization of Petro-Canada, mortgage interest and property-tax giveaways, cutbacks, and slogans such as "real change," "tough times," and "short-term pain for long-term gain" were all offensive to this Conservative tradition and disastrous politically for the Clark Government.[193]

Many rank-and-file Conservatives, however, would not agree with Simpson's judgement. Turning their attention to the electoral success of Margaret Thatcher's Conservatives in the United Kingdom and to Ronald Reagan's election victory in the United States, they have concluded that it was not Clark's attachment to business liberal policies while in office, but rather his moderation, his "toryness," that brought his government to grief. Although much of the dissatisfaction with his leadership was obviously a consequence of doubts concerning his personal effectiveness, there was also clearly considerable concern about Clark's intention to pursue Reaganite-style policies, should he retain office. Aileen McCabe, writing in the Ottawa *Citizen* about the Conservative convention in February 1981, observed: "After a weekend of meetings, discussions and socializing, the two ideologies which make up the Progressive Conservative Party do not seem any closer together. In fact, the division in the party looks worse than ever since both sides have had the opportunity to hear first hand what the other is really saying."[194]

The growing determination of the business liberals to impose their ideology on the party as its sole doctrine was evident in May 1982 when the Conservative policy conference convened in Toronto. It was to warn the party against doing so that Robert Stanfield delivered a forceful address, on a panel with journalists from the London *Economist* and the American *National Review*. Stanfield attacked those Conservatives whom he felt were naively celebrating free market values that did not exist, and he drew their attention to the problem that "we hold values that the market, even where it is free, will not protect or uphold. The market is not likely to emphasize enhancement of our environment, be this control of pollution, decent urban planning, or the protection of a valuable heritage."[195] Nor, he said, was it especially good at protecting all freedoms. Freedom of discussion, civil liberties and human rights were not values the market was suited to protect and promote. Acknowledging that over the past forty years or so there had been constant pressure for government's role in society to increase, Stanfield reflected that it was not surprising that governments had overreached themselves. His counsel to his party, however, was not to react violently and dogmatically to these developments, and especially not to propose "economic solutions which are likely to weaken important Conservative values"[196] such as a "sense of fairness, fulfilment, social order and the quality of national life.[197] And he concluded:

> The challenge facing Conservatives today is not how to get back to the free-wheeling twenties, followed by the terrible thirties, any more than to get back to the halcyon sixties, followed by the unfortunate present. The challenge is to find a new and more satisfactory balance that curbs the excessive claims of government to both competence and resources, but recognizes the necessary role of government in serving human values in modern society.[198]

Stanfield's fears that the ideological compromises within the Conservative Party might be imperilled were to a considerable extent borne out by the sustained campaign within both the parliamentary party and the party-at-large to force a leadership convention; these efforts eventually proved successful. At the Conservative General Meeting held in Winnipeg in January 1983, one-third of the delegates voted for a leadership review. Although Clark was legally in a position to retain his office as national party leader, the attacks of his opponents and the lingering doubts even of many of his supporters apparently convinced him that he no longer had sufficient support to maintain party unity. The danger existed that the more radical business liberals, as well as the more impatient ones, would continue their campaign within the party, or, at the worst, would leave and found a new political movement.

As we can conclude from the analysis throughout this chapter, Clark's quandary was similar to that faced by almost all leaders of the Progressive Conservative Party. Democratic toryism does not command majority support within the party, let alone the country as a whole. Any leader with a strong belief in tory values must make compromises with business liberalism. Yet it seems that there are some members of the party, libertarians and the more aggressive business liberals, who are no longer willing to make concessions to democratic toryism.

Like the New Democratic Party, whose alliance between socialism and welfare liberalism we analyze in the next chapter, the Conservative Party has, in the past, proved more ideologically fractious than the Liberal Party. The Liberal Party, as we have argued, consists primarily of proponents of a single ideology, although that ideology, liberalism, appears in both welfare and business variants. Not surprisingly, the Liberals normally appeared the most unified of the major Canadian parties. The leader of the Conservative Party, however, must find some way of handling the often conflicting ideological demands that arise from the followers.

Joe Clark clearly failed to develop a coherent ideological synthesis that would provide the basis for a long-term reconciliation. Neither were his personality nor rhetoric sufficiently captivating that he could charm, cajole and bully his way to ideological peace. Only on some policy issues, such as the constitution debate of 1981, was he able to submerge the ideological divergences in a common determination to attain a goal on which both tories and business liberals could agree. However, these occasions were rare, and, for the most part, they arose in response to initiatives of the Liberal government. Clark, in the period from 1976 to 1983, failed to develop policies that persuaded both tories and business liberals that, under his leadership, important steps would be taken by a Conservative government to realize the social values each group held.

Yet much of the dynamism and vitality of Canadian politics stems from the antitheses both between but also within our parties. As Robert Stanfield reminded the Ontario Conservatives in September 1983:

> More than one stream from the past has fed into our party. The same applies to the Liberals, and to the NDP, although they might not admit it. The N.D.P. is in fact a coalition like the Liberals and ourselves. Is this difficulty — or impossibility — in getting agreement on principles something to be ashamed of?
>
> What it means, I suggest, is that parties are complex. Certainly the old line parties have not been doctrinaire. They differ in their traditions and in their emphasis. They consist of men and women who will not all have the same reasons for supporting the same party in a province as large and diverse as Ontario or a country like Canada.[199]

Stanfield clearly realized, as some academic commentators have not, that there is an important distinction between being indifferent to values and principles, and not taking ideological commitment to divisive extremes.

> I don't wish to be misunderstood. I am a policy bug myself. I want my party to have intelligent policies and to have courage. That is quite different from being rigid or doctrinaire.[200]

The reason, in Stanfield's view, why politicians cannot afford the luxury of pursuing their own principles without attention to their circumstances is that they must always find a point of close contact between their values and the views of the electorate whom they must convince. Canada has survived as a stable and democratic country in large part "because we have not been doctrinaire in politics and generally we have been able to compromise and find solutions to differences rather than mounting our ideological high-horses and galloping off in all directions, incapable of the compromises necessary for effective government and undermining the foundations of democracy with the bitterness of our struggles."[201]

Political parties are, in our analysis, necessarily fragments of the national political consciousness, the understanding of social, economic and political life, which originated in Europe but has subsequently been adapted to Canadian conditions. Although all our successful political parties accept that the free individual is a fundamental value in any decent and sane society, none by itself contains all the elements that constitute the complete ideological inheritance. Consequently, parties and their leaders must be prepared to make compromises with the beliefs of others. In Stanfield's words, "Parties must take positions, especially when in government, and these positions must be workable and not just pleasant; but these positions must have acceptance that is broadly based."[202]

Not everyone, even in the Conservative Party, would agree with Stanfield's analysis or conclusion. There were many in the Conservative Party who thought that the country would be better served by sharp divisions between the parties. To promote such incisiveness they advocated that the Conservative Party should align itself closely with such policy goals as those pursued by Ronald Reagan in the United States and Margaret Thatcher in the United Kingdom.[203]

We pointed out that Joe Clark had won the leadership of his party in 1976 by effecting a coalition between the democratic tories within the Conservative Party and the more moderate of the business liberals who believed that the Conservatives could achieve a national government only if they maintained their historic compromise between the ideologies upon which their party was founded. Nonetheless a substantial majority in 1976 believed that an aggressive business liberal such as Claude Wagner would make a better leader for the party, and many continued to be dissatisfied when Clark persisted in the kind of policy compromises his predecessor, Robert Stanfield, praised.

Even the brief period of minority government did not quell all dissatisfaction with Clark's moderation, and the more radical of the business liberals pressed with all the greater urgency for his replacement after his minority government fell. Clark himself, in his speech to the Winnipeg meeting that in effect deprived him of his leadership, had taken the consistent view that the Conservative Party could never be electorally successful if it restricted itself to those who found unalloyed business liberalism attractive. Thus, he explained Diefenbaker's 1958 victory as the result of having made "this the party of all Canadians, all regions, all backgrounds, all legitimate points of view. We were a party of the whole country, open to everyone in Canada."[204] Electoral failure, however, arose from two factors. First, the party had too rarely succeeded in containing and also controlling the ideological divisions within it. Second, the party had forgotten the necessity of making compromises not only within itself but also between its own views and those of a majority of the electorate. "Too often," Clark said, "at other times, this party looked inward on itself instead of reaching out to the whole broad Canadian community."[205]

WHO CAN BEAT JOHN TURNER?

No one represented more clearly than John Gamble the kind of ideologue whom both Stanfield and Clark fought within the parliamentary caucus and among the activists of the party. Gamble was one of the eight declared candidates to succeed Clark, and although he received a derisory number of votes on the first ballot and subsequently lost his seat to an Independent in the 1984 election, he spoke for many more sensible business liberals when he declared:

> But there is really no point in simply taking office if it is to do so without some per-
> spective, without some guidelines and without some principles. I refute any comment
> by anyone that this Party is not the party of principles, that it is not the Party that
> should establish standards but should rely on the rejection by the public of a Liberal
> administration.[206]

He went on to propose a smaller role for government, lower taxes, the virtual elimination of the foreign aid budget, the drastic reduction of government subsidies for the CBC and Petro-Canada and the reintroduction of capital punishment. Although Gamble had been one of Clark's earliest and most vocal critics, those who shared his general views were not likely to find so crude an exponent appealing. They were prepared to support, as we shall see, a much more substantial figure.

A similar problem faced David Crombie, former mayor of Toronto. Extremely well liked except perhaps within caucus, elegantly articulate and a powerful orator, Crombie's campaign suffered from appalling organization, his inability to speak French and, most decisively, from the presence of Joe Clark who espoused many of the same values. Those who deny the existence of tory values with their compassion for the suffering and concern for the underprivileged overlook figures like Crombie within the party. Less skillfully but more articulate than either Stanfield or Clark, he reminded the delegates of the Conservative Party's historic attachment to social programs:

> Don't forget what John Diefenbaker did for this country — he gave voice to the
> voiceless and power to the powerless. Remember what John Diefenbaker did and
> show Canada we do not want power for power's sake. We want power to free the
> enterprises and help the helpless. I hear foolish talk about solving the nation's so-
> called problems by gouging and scrimping on the programmes of simple, social jus-
> tice that care for our old people — our sick people — our newborn — our disadvan-
> taged and disenfranchised.[207]

This powerful appeal for social justice, a love of the land, a sense of the past, a mild but firm hostility to the United States — indeed, all of the features Charles Taylor identified in his book *Radical Tories* — featured in Crombie's speech. Crombie summed up his beliefs succinctly and beautifully:

> The broad mainstream of Canadian life is carved out by these three great forces: hope, economic freedom and social justice. And so we must chart the broad mainstream of the Conservative policies in exactly the same way. And so we must remember what being a Tory is all about: It's about remembering the incredible hunger Canadians have for a sense of community. It is our sense of community that has conquered our geography, swept aside our weather and pierced our solitudes to forge us into a strong nation....
> I am a Tory.
> I glory in the individual. I cherish community. I seek liberty. I neither trim nor tack to every social whim. I honour tradition and experience. I exalt faith, hope and fairness. I want a peaceful, ordered, well-governed Canada.
> I am a Tory.[208]

This appeal to the delegates failed in part because of its strengths. Crombie was too closely identified with the democratic tory element of the ideological coalition, and consequently he failed to convince the business liberals that he could be trusted to take sympathetic account of their concerns. Although he did address in his speech some of the themes that they valued, the overwhelming impression was that he was attacking rather than compromising. And the business liberals, sensing a victory, were in no mood to capitulate, no matter how sweet the rhetoric.

Both Michael Wilson and John Crosbie cut their cloth more closely to the business liberal seam, but each acknowledged the need for the party to be moderate in its ideological position. Wilson aimed "to provide the kind of leadership that will attract the competent, compassionate people we need in public life...."[209] And Crosbie announced firmly that "to be Conservative today is to be in the middle of the political road."[210] Both revealed the inherently business liberal concerns for individual freedom, especially in the realm of commerce and industry. Wilson claimed that "we know that the source of creativity and initiative in our society is the individual. We know our economy grows—not as a result of government—but through the enterprise of people who are willing to work, to take risk, to transform ideas into industry and jobs for Canadians."[211] Crosbie underlined similar points when he argued:

> Unless we have an economic system that permits the free flow of capital, the acquiring of profits, the right to private property, the right to competition in the market place, our society will not protect the freedom we value so greatly. It is only with a privately-owned sector that we can, or may as a society, provide and protect human civil liberties. There is no society that has no privately-owned economic sector that has any human or civil liberties enshrined therein.[212]

These ideological predispositions, especially in the case of Crosbie who was personally very popular within the party and who had been cultivating delegates for some time before the convention was called, secured him a strong third place. However, the two front runners when the delegates met were the same who were leading when the convention was called, the former Prime Minister, Joe Clark, and his rival from the 1976 leadership campaign, former Iron Ore of Canada president, Brian Mulroney.

For many in the party Clark represented its best traditions, a realistic and electorally appealing balance between the desire to promote individual freedom, especially in the field of business activity and the more tory concerns of the sort that Crombie had articulated. Throughout his leadership Clark had tried to moderate the ideological divisions within the party, partly, of course, because the more radical business liberals were resolutely opposed to his continued leadership. It was a theme he continued throughout his leadership campaign. As he said in Toronto in February 1983: "...there is the danger of panic, there is a danger in extreme solutions being imposed....The principle is that the answer to our problems in Canada is common sense, pragmatism, realism — not some magic words or radical ideology."[213]

In his recognition of the value of diversity, and in his assessment of the role of the state in society, Clark showed himself solidly in the Canadian tory tradition as it has been molded by its long historical association with business liberalism. Stanfield has described the tory view of the role of the state as strong government, but government limited in extent. Clark agreed.

> We have some challenging opportunities. One is to redefine what governments should do, and what can be better done by individuals, and by voluntary agencies, or by private enterprise, or by other forces outside government. Of course, the modern world needs active government. But...we need more than governments. We need people who care for their neighbours. We need communities that work together because they want to.[214]

His speech to the delegates addressed the same themes. There he spoke of the "tradition of diversity which allowed many cultures to flourish here." And he continued:

> In a world becoming the same, we Canadians are free to be ourselves. That is why we celebrate a distinctive Newfoundland, a distinctive Quebec, a distinctive British Columbia. That is why we encourage the creative individual in business, in the arts, in life.[215]

There can be little doubt that most delegates understood that Clark stood for ideological moderation and for maintaining the Conservative party as an alliance between business liberals with their concerns of fiscal probity, economic efficiency and individual liberty and the tories' sense of tradition, love of the land, desire for community and active compassion for the weak and underprivileged. However, in spite of the publication of a collection of speeches titled *Where I Stand,* few among either the delegates, journalists or the general public were entirely confident about Brian Mulroney's predilections.

Although he had run for the leadership previously, in 1976, and had finished third behind Clark and Wagner, his subsequent career took him, not into electoral politics, but into the world of business as the successful president of a mining company. He declined to run for a seat in either the 1979 or 1980 general elections, later explaining that he had given firm undertakings to his employers that he would stay for a minimum period in the presidency of the company. However, for many within the party, he still had enormous allure. They objected to Clark for three main reasons. First, they believed that his principles and policies were not sufficiently distinctive from the Liberals, or as the more extreme among his opponents described it, the Liberal-Socialists. The consequence of this, they believed, was that Clark had surrounded himself with unprincipled power-hungry compromisers and had left the "genuine conservatives" to languish on the back benches. Although Sinclair Stevens exercised considerable influence during the period of Clark's leadership, most of the other more extreme business liberals did not.

Second, many in the party, regardless of ideological position, could not forgive Clark for having lost power after such a brief period in government. For them Clark remained a vacillating nonentity, the ultimate manifestation of the Peter principle, the inheritor of the Stanfield disposition to fumble footballs at awkward moments, in short, the definitive Wimp. However untrue all this was, there can be little doubt that it deeply hampered Clark's political effectiveness. Could such a man — and this was the third factor that weighed heavily with many delegates — ever beat John Turner?

Turner's presence was almost as significant a factor at the Conservative leadership convention of 1983 as it was to prove at the Liberals' own the next year. It was generally thought that, given the general unpopularity of the Trudeau Liberals, even Joe Clark could win an election against anyone other than Turner. But many Conservatives, with an exaggerated sense of the Liberals' shrewdness and guile, believed that the Conservatives had to field a candidate who could beat the silver haired ex-finance minister. So it was to Mulroney, who had been playing the game of successor-in-waiting with as much skill as Turner, that they turned.

However, those who favoured him for ideological reasons were to be disappointed. Mulroney, it appeared, agreed with his predecessors that the Conservative Party's electoral strength lay in its character as an ideological coalition. As he told the delegates in his speech:

> There shall be honest differences among us but there shall be no incivility because of divergent views. This sense of generosity will quickly be discerned by the

Canadian public and will be translated into electoral support and confidence at the right time....There are going to be no ideological tests of purity, absolutely none. It matters not, as Conservatives, whom you support tonight; it matters only that you care about Canada and that you care about this Party, and that is absolutely good enough.[216]

His address to the delegates naturally enough played on the themes of Clark's electoral failures and their fears about the future should Clark continue in charge. When he spoke about the kinds of policies his government would favour, he appealed to both of the major strains within the party. First, for the business liberals, he declared:

We've got to send signals around the world that investment capital is welcome here and this is a good, an honourable, and a decent place to do business again. We have got to state clearly, and act decisively, that the private sector is the only motor whereby new wealth and new jobs and new opportunity can be created for Canadians.[217]

Yet, despite this desire to diminish the role of government in Canadian society and in the economy, Mulroney also affirmed his belief in the continuation of those programs for the worst-off in society, which had always been a component of Canadian democratic toryism.

...we must always honour that vital responsibility of government to demonstrate compassion for the needy and assistance for the disadvantaged, the equalization of opportunity for all, with an elevated sense of social compassion. Of all the challenges of government, none is more sacred, none binds us more as Conservatives, than to care for those who are unable to care for themselves. That is our commitment to Canada.[218]

Mulroney's successful blend of ideological moderation and electoral appeal were successful on the final ballot to overcome Clark's advantages of incumbency. Those who saw in Mulroney a man who would transform Canadian Conservatism into an instant imitation of Reaganite Republicanism were to experience considerable disappointment. Indeed, it could well be argued that he did not have the support within the party to make dramatic changes in its direction. He had defeated Clark by 259 votes out of nearly 3000. The final count turned out to be: Mulroney 1584, Clark 1325. Not only was Clark not driven from the inner counsels of the party as the former British Prime Minister Edward Heath had been when Margaret Thatcher wrenched the leadership from him, but after the 1984 election, Clark was given the prestigious and influential post of Secretary of State for External Affairs.

BRIAN MULRONEY AND THE CONSERVATIVE SWEEP OF 1984

We suggested above that at the Conservative Convention both Clark and Mulroney had indicated that they were prepared to compromise with the different ideological elements within their party's coalition and that they rejected the idea of abandoning their party's tory inheritance in favour of an uncompromising business liberalism. There can be little doubt, however, that the general public saw Mulroney's inclinations as predominantly business liberal. Much of the initiative for policy change that he spelled out both before and after the general election had been called revolved around economic questions. Moreover, the bulk of those initiatives were intended as reforms that would aid the business community in the production of wealth. The important policy statements that Mulroney made at Prince Albert on July 5, 1984, at Sherbrooke on July 26, and at Halifax on August 2 all addressed predominantly economic concerns that affected the region in question. Although the Quebec statement dealt as well with women's issues and policy that concerned old age pensioners, the focus again was primarily economic. Nevertheless it would be fair to say that the proposals were laudably precise and reasonably fully developed. However, there was a reasonable concern voiced by the press and felt by much of the general public that Mulroney had been less than candid throughout the campaign as to the likelihood of his proposals being implemented in the foreseeable future, given the size of the federal government's budget deficit and the slow state of the Canadian economic recovery.

Other themes that Mulroney developed during the campaign had to do with areas that had been of concern to Clark's 1979 government. These included reform of the civil service and of parliamentary procedures and Crown corporation accountability. As well, a party-sponsored task force led by Perrin Beatty had levied substantial criticism against Revenue Canada for procedural and other abuses, and this also became a theme that played a major role in the 1984 campaign, as it drew on the business liberal's concern lest governmental activity needlessly and dangerously infringe on the liberty of the individual.

However, in spite of the Liberals' and New Democrats' best efforts to paint Mulroney as a Reaganite or a Thatcherite with their public images of indifference to the well-being of the disadvantaged, Mulroney carefully avoided any suggestion that the cherished programs of the welfare state might be threatened under his administration. For example, although the Liberals attempted to manoeuvre the Conservatives into opposition to health-care programs, Mulroney countered in the House of Commons:

> There must be certain things that are above politics—there are certain things in Canada which must be safeguarded against any partisan attack—and Medicare has to be one of them at all times.[219]

Even more uncompromising was Mulroney's firm rejection of means tests and his "acceptance of universality in social programs," which he described as "a cornerstone of our Party's philosophy."[220]

Indeed, Mulroney went to considerable lengths to emphasize his view that Canadian Conservatism was not a doctrine limited in its goals to retrenchment, efficiency and economy. He developed the other strain of Conservatism, what we have called the democratic tory strain, in a series of speeches such as the one he delivered in Kitchener, Ontario where he spoke of the "commitment of our party to fundamental fairness and justice."[221] And he spoke of the need for a "government which works with the people to build a society of dignity and compassion, a community where the strong help the weak and the fortunate help the disadvantaged."[222]

Was this cynical image-making and callous electioneering, or did it signify a more fundamental understanding of the goals he would pursue? There are good reasons for accepting Mulroney's sincerity. First, although he lapsed frequently into the sentimental in his recollections of his childhood as the "p'tit gars de Baie Comeau," his childhood experiences were clearly important to him, and he obviously had a deep sympathy for the dignity of the working poor. "I have so many memories of growing up in Baie Comeau, imperishable memories of a father who, during his entire life, held down two jobs to provide for the needs of his family with neither complaint nor regret."[223] Second, we can consider the influence of John Diefenbaker. With some symbolism Mulroney went to Prince Albert to make his first major policy statement of the 1984 campaign, and he spoke of the western spirit Diefenbaker had brought into the party and "which I felt first as a young man when I served as Vice-Chairman of the Convention for Youth."[224] Third was Mulroney's experiences as a labour lawyer and businessman. He was proud of his record at Iron Ore of Canada, which he described as "an attempt to introduce a new degree of civility, of understanding, of genuine fraternity into our relations, which we believed would ultimately benefit all associated with the company."[225] The democratic tory strain in Mulroney's political thought, we conclude, is not only present, but more deeply rooted than commentators have previously noted.

Mulroney's election victory, therefore, was important for a number of reasons. First, it emphasized the continued importance of principled differences between the major Canadian political parties over what constitutes the national good. Although all three political leaders in the 1984 campaign interpreted their own and their rivals' intentions in ways most likely to give themselves electoral advantage, they all agreed that important values divided them. This argument does not deny the existence of continued substantial areas of agreement at the heart of the parties' shared liberalism.

Second, it seemed possible that democratic toryism would reestablish a more visible presence in national life. The democratic tory's understanding of the nation as a whole, the sense of the past, the awareness of differences between individuals and regions, the acceptance of social advantages as long as those advantages bring commensurate benefits to those worst-off in society, all these values supplement liberalism's enduring commitment to the individual and to freedom. These values were in danger of being erased by the electoral strength of the Liberal Party over the past two decades.

Third, Mulroney gave the Conservative Party another opportunity to reestablish its contacts with Quebec. This has proved a decisive development, since there is considerable evidence that it was not wasted as it was in 1958 to 1962.

THE CONSERVATIVES IN ACTION

The battle about Mulroney's vision of the Conservative Party was to be fought sooner than anyone would have anticipated. The issue arose on November 8, 1984 when former leadership rival and Finance Minister Michael Wilson delivered a policy statement in which he suggested that it might be possible to change universal social programs in such a way that the savings might contribute to a reduction of the Government's budget deficit. This suggestion gave rise to an intense conflict within the Cabinet between the Health Minister, Jake Epp, generally seen as representing the democratic tory wing of the party, and Wilson. It also gave rise to heated criticism from both the Liberals and the NDP over what they portrayed as a betrayal of a fundamental principle of Canadian welfare policy, the maintenance of which Mulroney had referred to during the election campaign as a sacred trust.

The issue was seen as a symbolic one by both sides. Colin Brown of the National Citizens Coalition was worried that the Conservative Government was in danger of deviating from a strict free-enterprise outlook, and complained: "They've got so much pressure on them from those screaming bleeding hearts, they might give in."[226]

It proved impossible for Epp and Wilson to resolve this ideological issue between them, and it was left to the Prime Minister, whose credibility was increasingly involved in the matter, to intervene. As he put the matter in the House of Commons on December 17: "All we are trying to do is to share declining resources, modest resources, with those in our society who need it the most: the disadvantaged, the widows, those people who need assistance." Early in the new year, he reiterated these views, denying that he was aiming at a "tax revolution" of the sort that President Reagan was attempting. Instead, he wanted to rethink the tax and welfare systems "to aid the underprivileged, not reduce the deficit."[227]

The principles underlying the eventual outcome were those that had been enunciated by Jake Epp on November 15, 1984.

> Surely there can be only one workable definition of universality which is also consistent with the principle of fairness. That is that all individuals in the group designated for assistance should receive benefits. At the same time, however, the value of those benefits should surely be greatest for those in greatest need and least for those

whose needs are less. No one is to be excluded from universal programmes, but the value of the benefits received should be consistent with the level of need.[228]

This quarrel revealed quite sharply the major ideological divisions within the party. Michael Wilson, true to the business liberal desire to reduce the role of government, proposed a reduction in benefits with the aim in mind of reducing the deficit. Epp's position was that there should be no ultimate reduction in the level of government activity or expenditure on social welfare programs, but he accepted the democratic tory view that it was appropriate to treat people unequally, reducing the benefits to the wealthy and simultaneously increasing them for the underprivileged. The Prime Minister summed up his position on January 18, 1985. "I never varied....When I said universality was a sacred trust, that's exactly what it is. And there'll be no change. There was never any change contemplated, except in the minds of the NDP and the Liberals."[229]

The sacred trust debate was just the beginning of a long slide in Conservative popularity. Within the next eighteen months a series of scandals severely undermined credibility in the government. Defence Minister Robert Coates resigned after allegations that he had visited a sleazy bar in West Germany. Marcel Masse disappeared temporarily from cabinet over suspicions of electoral irregularities in the 1984 election, which were subsequently dismissed as unfounded. In September 1985 John Fraser resigned as Minister of Fisheries when it was found that his department had permitted the sale of tainted tuna. December saw the departure of Suzanne Blais-Grenier; and in May 1986 Sinclair Stevens, one of the most powerful ministers in the cabinet was forced to resign pending the outcome of a judicial inquiry to weigh charges that he had seriously breached conflict of interest guidelines. In the same month backbench MP Michel Gravel was indicted on fifty counts of corruption and influence peddling. In June the Prime Minister fired four more cabinet ministers who had proved ineffective in handling their portfolios. The political future had begun to look bleak indeed.

In the midst of this turmoil, however, Mulroney had unleashed a policy that was to prove a major factor in the restoration of his administration in the public esteem: free trade with the United States. On September 26, 1985 he announced that he had informed President Reagan of his interest in "pursuing a new trade agreement between our two countries."[230] What surprised many people was that this was a major reversal of the stand he had taken during the 1983 leadership campaign when he had roundly condemned John Crosbie's advocacy of the same policy. There were two main factors that effected this change.

The first was the pressures in the United States to take protectionist action against what the Americans considered unfair competition by foreign trading partners. An example of this was the punitive duty imposed by the U.S. on cedar shakes and shingles originating in Canada. By adopting a comprehensive free trade agreement, Mulroney hoped that he could exempt Canada from such countervailing tariffs. As he explained in response to a question in the Commons: "...we are concerned about the growth of protectionist sentiment which is now infesting many areas of American life....we want to ensure that those markets are secured for Canadian producers because they mean jobs...."[231]

The second major influence came from the publication of the report of the Royal Commission on the Economic Union and Development Prospects for Canada. Known as the Macdonald Commission after Donald Macdonald, the former Liberal finance minister who had been the chief commissioner, its report gave strong support to the idea of free trade, and backed its recommendation with detailed economic studies. As Mulroney explained to the House:

> Over a three-year period from 1982 to 1985 the Macdonald Commission analyzed options for Canada's economic future. It heard from hundreds of Canadians, individuals and institutions, held public hearings in 32 cities, in all 10 provinces, and sponsored three-day debates in major centres across Canada. Its research alone fills 72 volumes. In 1985 the Macdonald Royal Commission concluded that free trade with the United States would be "a prudent course which will help make us richer and, by making us richer, strengthen the fabric of our country and increase our self confidence."[232]

Although Mulroney responded relatively quickly after the release of the report he had, in fact, had a copy of the English text for several weeks before its release, and hence had been able to consider it carefully before making his reponse.

Although Macdonald was a Liberal, he stood, as we argued in Chapter III, on the business liberal wing of his party. For him as for Mulroney free trade represented an attractive measure, not just because it promised increased material prosperity, but all the more so because it carried the hope of lessening government involvement in the economy. For Mulroney, the idea was consistent with other aspects of his attempts to mitigate the effects of the welfare state. One aspect was known as deregulation. Although the Conservatives proceeded more slowly than most experts had thought they would, except in the area of airline transportation and energy, they did establish a general atmosphere in which it was expected that the government would henceforth exercise less influence over the general details of economic activity.

The other area involved the selling off of those Crown Corporations that were primarily economic rather than service oriented. Barbara McDougall was appointed Minister of Privatization. Although the Canadian Conservatives did not attack the issue with the same intensity as their British counterparts under Thatcher, who engaged in a dramatic restructuring of the balance between the public and private sectors, they did take some substantial steps. DeHavilland and Canadair, Polysar and Teleglobe were sold outright to the private sector. In 1988 the Government also announced that it would offer shares in Air Canada to the general public, though it would retain effective control. Nothing was done at that time with respect to Petro-Canada whose proposed privatization had been instrumental in the downfall of Clark's 1979 Government.

However consistent this business-liberal package might appear, it was obviously inconsistent with the tory traditions of the Conservative Party. From Macdonald through Bennett to Diefenbaker, Conservative Prime Ministers had used tariffs precisely to protect the country against American intrusions. This appeared to be a major reversal of traditional Conservative policy. As Conservative backbencher Alan Redway saw it:

> ...one of the most appealing cornerstones of the Progressive Conservative Party ... was its Canadian nationalism...[the 1911 Reciprocity Debate involved] a tariff barrier which stretched from sea to sea and created a Canadian industrial economy....you can imagine my feelings and the feelings of many other supporters of the Progressive Conservative Party when the government decided to embark upon a course of trade negotiations with the United States....[But] we realized the importance of trade to Canada...to protect jobs in the country. The only way we could do it would be to sit down and negotiate with the United States....[233]

As we have seen in the last chapter, these themes were to play a major role in the 1988 Liberal election strategy. Although both those who favoured and those who opposed free trade thought that they were defending the best interests of the country, it is clear that the nationalist position has moved away from the Conservatives into the Liberal camp. The main reason for this migration has been the declining importance of business liberalism under Turner's leadership and the rising significance of this ideology in Brian Mulroney's Conservative Government, which we examined in Chapter III.

For some of Mulroney's critics, however, this policy merely confirmed what they had suspected all along, based on the Prime Minister's background. After all, he had been raised in a company town, and still recounted with pride his memories of his song recitals given for the benefit of a visiting American businessman. He had also served as the President of Iron Ore of Canada, a subsidiary of an American-based company, and had presided over the closing down of their operation at Schefferville. From this perspective, it was not surprising that Mulroney possessed a branch-plant mentality, and was seeking to integrate the Canadian economy even more securely into the American.

One argument that free trade did not necessarily mean subservience to the United States comes from the area of defence and foreign policy. The June 1987 White Paper on Canadian defence policy put forward a comprehensive program for the rearming of the three military forces. The most controversial measure was the proposal to purchase a fleet of ten to twelve nuclear submarines with the main priority of patrolling the Arctic Ocean. Defence Minister Perrin Beatty believed this was necessary for two reasons. First, as matters stood, Canada had no presence in this area which it claimed as part of its sovereign territory; and consequently, American submarines operated there as the sole defence against their Russian missile carrying counterparts. Second, the Government was humiliated when the American ship *Polar Sea* sailed defiantly through the Northwest Passage without requesting Canada's permission. However, this stand was dropped after the 1988 election at the insistence of Finance Minister Michael Wilson, who feared the effect on the government's attempt to reduce the deficit. Beatty was eased out of Defence and became Health Minister.

In addition, as the *Economist* points out, Canada has pursued a foreign policy on many issues independent of the United States.

Canada stayed put when Britain and the United States withdrew from UNESCO. It joined other Commonwealth countries in favouring economic sanctions against South Africa when the Reagan administration, again supported by Britain, argued for a policy of "constructive engagement" to persuade the Botha government to phase out apartheid. Shortly after America introduced a trade embargo against Nicaragua, the Canadian government pointedly permitted Nicaragua to open a trade office in Toronto. It has remained aloof from America's star-wars programme. At bilateral meetings in the White House the American president is routinely scolded publicly for the pollution his country dumps on Canada.[234]

The other major initiative the Mulroney Government undertook was the Meech Lake Constitutional Accord. When Trudeau had met with the provincial premiers he was unable to achieve unanimous support for his 1982 package of patriation and a charter of rights and freedoms. Most particularly, Quebec had not agreed, and from a moral, if not a legal, point of view, "had not signed the constitution." For Mulroney, this was an unacceptable state of affairs, and after an all-night bargaining session at the Prime Minister's cottage on Meech Lake, he came up on June 3, 1987 with a set of constitutional amendments acceptable to all the provincial premiers.

The main provisions were as follows. First, the constitution was to be inter-preted in a manner consistent with the recognition of the existence of English-speaking and French-Speaking Canadians in all parts of the country, but it recognized that the latter were concentrated within the Province of Quebec and that the English-speakers predominated outside. This, it said, constituted the fundamental characteristic of Canada. It also provided that the Constitution was to be interpreted in a manner consistent with the fact that the Province of Quebec constitutes a distinct society within Canada, and recognized the role of the government of Quebec to preserve and promote Quebec's distinct identity.

The second major change involved two central federal institutions, the Senate and the Supreme Court. In both cases, the proposed amendments would give the provinces a role in the appointment process. The third change provided that the provinces would have a constitutionally protected role to play in the immigration process. A fourth allowed the province to opt out of shared-cost programs, but to receive reasonable compensation from the federal government as long as it carried on a program or initiative compatible with the objectives of the national scheme.

As we suggested in the last chapter, Trudeau's Charter represented a radical innovation in Canadian politics, which had been moderated by the constitutional and political necessity he faced in gaining substantial provincial agreement. The Meech Lake reforms represent a further adjustment. As the *Globe and Mail* summarized Mulroney's position:

> Mr. Mulroney argued that the accord does not represent a decentralizing thrust, as its opponents suggest, but is a "pragmatic representation of the reality" of Canada.
> "Compromises were made at Meech Lake, honorable compromises to improve as well as reflect the situation we inherited," he said, but there were no compromises as significant as those made in 1982.
> "In 1982, Canada achieved patriation and an entrenched Charter of Rights only at the price—the tremendous price—of a notwithstanding clause," he told the House. So while the most fundamental rights of Canadians were guaranteed in 1982, the Federal Government agreed that Parliament or provincial legislatures could override these rights by invoking the notwithstanding clause.[235]

Although eight provinces quickly ratified the amendment, it is significant that the two provinces which did not, New Brunswick and Manitoba, were both influenced by theoretical considerations put forth by Trudeau Liberals, that the Accord would weaken the capacity of the Federal Government to serve as an instrument of national unity. For the business liberals in the Conservative Party, however, its decentralizing tendencies were undoubtedly attractive features. For the democratic tories, what was significant was the recognition of the collective character of Quebec's identity.

The Mulroney Government also devoted considerable attention to tax reform. The various measures enacted by 1988, including the capital gains exemption and the main tax reform package announced in June 1987, exhibited a mixture of base-broadening and reduced tax rates typical of tax reform measures adopted by the business liberal governments of Great Britain and the United States, though the Canadian effort was less far-reaching. The companion measure to these changes, increased consumption taxes to replace lost revenue, was still pending until 1989 in the form of a value-added type of national sales tax. These measures all stem from an attempt to give market forces freer rein by diminishing the tax preferences and subsidies inherent in the current tax system. Their business liberal character is reinforced by their tendency to reduce the taxes of the better-off in the hope of stimulating capital formation and investment. The capital-gains tax exemption in particular was directed to this end.

GENERAL ELECTION OR
FREE TRADE REFERENDUM?

When Mulroney called a general election for November 21, 1988, his two major initiatives had been stalled. Meech Lake still awaited the required assent of the two provinces, and the free trade bill languished in the senate, held up there by the Liberal majority on the instructions of the leader of the opposition, who told his senate followers not to pass it until after an election had been held.

Buoyed by favorable polls, Mulroney called Turner's bluff. After that, little went according to plan. It was the Conservatives' strategy, as Jeffrey Simpson observed, to run the Prime Minister: "...around the country like a stuffed pigeon. This was the way those organizing the federal campaign had arranged former premier William Davis's campaigns in Ontario: keep things low-key, mechanical, folksy and if possible, dull."[236] Although he emphasized the FTA is his appearances, he also ran broadly on the issue of the government's record of achievement in economic growth and job creation and on the managerial competence of his cabinet compared with the Liberal alternative. In short, he emphasized the business liberal aspect of his party's tradition. It was John Turner's nationalistic attack on free trade that pointed out the error in this strategy.

Ironically, it had been Ed Broadbent who had drawn the clearest attention to this development when he attacked the government in the House of Commons.

> ...there is, for Conservatives of tradition, the importance of continuity and community and nation, of a sense of values based on a shared common past. According to this view, other values, like those of the market economy, are seen to be subordinate to the primacy of the historical common good of all in society. This view has been the kind of conservatism invoked by Disraeli in the 19th century when he made a critique of the ravages of industrialism. It was the conservatism of Sir John A. Macdonald who used government power to build a separate Canadian economy because he had a different vision of the future of this part of North America from what existed to the south of us. It is the conservatism that at one time supported the CBC and Air Canada....It was the conservatism of John Diefenbaker who brought in a national hospitalization program in this country because he knew if left to individual action in the market-place we would never have had such a plan.[237]

It was this sense of the whole that Mulroney lacked. His defence of free trade was almost exclusively in economic terms: jobs created, access to markets, the possibilities of economic growth, protection against retaliatory tariff action by the United States.

Just as in 1984, the televised debate between the three party leaders proved a key development during the campaign. Public opinion, especially on the free trade issue, was in a highly volatile state; and John Turner's assertions, (as we have seen in the last chapter) that the FTA threatened both Canada's sovereignty as well as its ability to maintain its universal social programs, was making inroads in

Conservative support. For Mulroney the Agreement was only "a commercial document that is cancellable on six months' notice."[238] In response to the charge that our social programs were among the key elements of our national life which distinguished us from the United States, Mulroney replied: "I believe the best social policy is a job....That is the motherlode of social programs. That is the growing economy, the new pool of wealth that allows us to pay for a lot of these social programs that Canada desires."[239]

In spite of the Conservatives' efforts to broaden the base of the campaign, the Liberals with the help of the New Democrats turned the election virtually into a referendum on free trade. This did not mean that democratic toryism was entirely overlooked. In his closing statement in the debate, Mulroney assured his audience that the "human values of caring and compassion and respect will be enlarged, not weakened, in the stronger Canada we will build together."[240] Nonetheless the 1988 election came as close to a pure ideological confrontation as any we have had in Canada.

It is difficult to draw conclusions from any election campaign and this one was no exception. Although the Conservatives were returned with 169 of the 295 Commons seats, a comfortable majority over the opposition parties, they had secured only 43% of the total vote, compared with over 52% for the Liberals and New Democrats who had each campaigned vigorously against the pact. In some sense, both sides could claim victory; but the Canadian constitution awards power on the basis of parliamentary seats and pays no explicit notice to the percentage of the popular vote for the parties.

Nonetheless, a couple of factors stand out. The first is that the business liberalism in the Conservative Party seems just as likely as the business liberalism of the Liberal Party in the days of King and St.Laurent to draw into closer economic ties with the United States. Therefore, how nationalistic the Conservative Party proves to be will depend largely on the strength of the democratic toryism emanating from the Quebec caucus, especially after the departure of David Crombie and the election loss of Flora MacDonald. This is still a relatively new factor in Canadian politics, but one that may prove increasingly significant as Quebec Conservative MPs gain more confidence, and are promoted to positions of ever greater influence in the cabinet.

How thoroughly the business liberals will dominate the political agenda is another matter that is unclear. Although it was not a major issue in the campaign, the budget deficit continues to worry many businessmen and economists. At least in the short term, it seems that those concerns have prevailed over those who would incline to greater generosity in areas such as child care.

One thing is certain; it is unlikely that the Conservative Party can establish itself as the dominant element in federal politics on such a narrow basis as business liberalism. Unless it can rediscover something like the toryism that was such an important constituent element of Canadian Conservatism for so long, it will remain susceptible to a challenge from the welfare liberalism we explored in the last chapter, and the collectivism inherent in socialism and nationalism that we examine next.

---

1. H. Macquarrie, *The Conservative Party* (Toronto: McClelland and Stewart, 1965), p. 1. See also, George Hogan, *The Conservative in Canada* (Toronto: McClelland and Stewart, 1963), p. xi.

2. P.L. McCreath, *The Canadian Party System* (Ottawa: n.p. 1969), p. 2.

3. E.C. Manning, *Political Realignment* (Toronto: McClelland and Stewart, 1967), pp. 11, 21, 72.

4. R.L. Stanfield, *Address to the Progressive Conservative Policy Conference,* Toronto, May 14, 1982, mimeo, p. 2.

5. *The Report and Despatches of the Earl of Durham* (London: Ridgways, 1839), p. 12. Reprinted by Methuen and Co. Ltd., London, 1902.

6. Michael Oakeshott, "On Being Conservative" in *Rationalism in Politics* (London: Methuen Press, 1962), p. 169 (New York: Basic Books, Inc., 1962).

7. *Ibid.,* p. 169.

8. *Durham Report,* p. 17.

9. Quoted in D. Creighton, *John A. Macdonald* (Toronto: MacMillan, 1966), Vol. 1, p. 199.

10. Quoted in L.J. Ladner, *The Progressive Conservative Party,* (n.p., n.d.), p. 1.

11. W.L. Morton, *Canadian Conservatism Now,* (Winnipeg: The Progressive Conservative Party 1959), p. 104.

12. *Ibid.,* p. 9.

13. L.F.S. Upton, "The Idea of Confederation: 1754-1858" in *The Shield of Achilles,* W.L. Morton, ed. (Toronto: McClelland and Stewart, 1968), p. 202.

14. Luther Hamilton Holton, *Parliamentary Debates on the Subject of the Confederation of the British North American Provinces* (Quebec: 1865), p. 147.

15. Taché, *ibid.,* p. 6.

16. *Ibid.*

17. T.W.L. MacDermot, "The Political Ideas of John A. Macdonald," *Canadian Historical Review,* XIV, No. 3, pp. 251-253.

18. J.I. Cooper, "The Political Ideas of George Etienne Cartier," *Canadian Historical Review,* XXIII, No. 3, p. 293.

19. Jacques Monet, "The Personal and Living Bond, 1839-1849" in *The Shield of Achilles,* p. 62.

20. Cartier, *Confederation Debates,* p. 60.

21. *Ibid.,* p. 60.

22. Taché, *ibid.*, p. 10.

23. Macdermot, p. 250.

24. Cartier, *Confederation Debates*, p. 61.

25. *Ibid.*, p. 62.

26. Macdonald, *Confederation Debates*, p. 35.

27. cf. the later statement, "In each of us there is something of the liberal as well as something of the conservative—the desire for change struggling with the love of the familiar." Hon. L. MacAulay, "History and Aims of the Conservative Party" in *Canadian Problems as Seen by Twenty Outstanding Men of Canada* (Toronto: Oxford University Press, 1933), p. 37.

28. Macdermot, p. 251.

29. Simpson, *Confederation Debates*, p. 234.

30. Stanfield, *Address*, May 1982, pp. 4-5.

31. *Ibid.*, p. 5.

32. See the "Liberal Platform of 1874" and the "Liberal Platform of 1882" in *Canadian Party Platforms*, 1867-1968, D.O. Carrigan (Toronto: Copp Clark, 1968), pp. 12, 18, 19.

33. "Liberal Conservative Platform of 1874" in Carrigan, p. 14.

34. "Liberal Conservative Platform of 1878" in Carrigan, p. 16.

35. Macdonald to Sir George Stephen, 31 March 1891. *Correspondence of Sir John Macdonald*, Pope, ed. (Toronto: n.d.), p. 485.

36. Macdonald to Stephen, 10 November 1890, Correspondence, *ibid*, p. 477.

37. Robert Laird Borden, *Letters to Limbo*, H. Borden, ed. (Toronto and Buffalo: University of Toronto Press, 1971), p. 167.

38. Borden, *Limbo*, pp. 166-167. See also, *R.L. Borden, His Memoirs*, H. Borden, ed., abridged and edited by H. Macquarrie (Toronto: McClelland and Stewart, 1969), Vol. II, pp. 127-130.

39. R.C. Brown, *Robert Laird Borden: A Biography*, Vol. II, p. 133.

40. From *Unrevised and Unrepented: Debating Speeches and Others*, by the Rt. Hon. Arthur Meighen, Copyright by Clarke, Irwin and Company Limited, 1949, p. 5. Used by permission.

41. John English, *The Decline of Politics: The Conservatives and the Party System*, 1901-1920 (Toronto: University of Toronto Press, 1977), p. 33.

42. R.C. Brown and Ramsay Cook, *Canada 1896-1921: A Nation Transformed* (Toronto, 1974), p. 186, quoted in English, p. 35.

43. Borden to R.P. Roblin, 2 August 1907, Borden Papers, v. 351, quoted in English, p. 35.

44. Quoted in Brown, *Borden*, p. 216.

45. Brown, *Borden*, p. 217.

46. English, *Decline*, p. 55.

47. R.L. Borden, "Manifesto to the People of Canada" in Carrigan, pp, 65-66.

48. From *Robert Laird Borden: His Memoirs* (Toronto: McClelland and Stewart, 1969, Vol. I, p. 152), by R.L. Borden, abridged and edited by H. Macquarrie, reprinted by permission of The Canadian Publishers, McClelland and Stewart Limited, Toronto. Italics in original.

49. Brown, *Borden*, I, p. 192.

50. Quoted in Brown, *Borden*, p. 110.

51. Quoted in Brown, *Borden*, II, p. 110.

52. Quoted in Brown, *Borden*, II, p. 169.

53. For a fuller discussion, see Roger Graham, *Arthur Meighan: A Biography* (Toronto: Clarke Irwin, 1960).

54. Meighen, p. 98.

55. *Ibid.*, p. 99.

56. Borden, *Memoirs*, Vol. II, p. 245.

57. E. Forsey, *The Royal Power of Dissolution* (Toronto: Oxford University Press, 1968), passim.

58. Roger Graham, *Arthur Meighen: A Biography* (Toronto: Clarke Irwin, 1963) Vol. II. and *The King-Byng Controversy*, (Toronto: Copp Clark, 1967), passim.

59. Macquarrie, *The Conservative Party*, p. 97.

60. Campaign speech of Mackenzie King, from Toronto *Globe*, in Carrigan, p. 104.

61. Meighen, p. 114.

62. *Ibid.*, p. 161.

63. *Ibid.*, p. 206.

64. George Hogan, *The Conservative in Canada* (Toronto: McClelland and Stewart, 1963), p. 10.

65. *Ibid.*, p. 9.

66. George Perlin, *The Tory Syndrome* (McGill-Queen's University Press, 1980), p. 42.

67. cf. Bennett. Q ...The constitution of the Conservative Party as a Conservative Party is inconsistent with state interference to any extent with the individual right. Mr. Bennett. "I would say that that is hardly the way you put it. With the development of public opinion, state regulation of individual activities has been and will continue to be a part of the programme of any Conservative Government. It was so with respect to restriction of hours of labour as against laissez-faire opinions of their opponents. The Conservative Party has always taken the view that the order of regulation of individual activity may be of interest in the government of the whole." "Democracy on Trial" in *Canadian Problems, op. cit.*, p. 30.

68. R.B. Bennett's Winnipeg Speech, June 9, 1930, in Carrigan, p. 111. Our italics. Reprinted by permission of The Progressive Conservative Party of Canada.

69. *Ibid.*

70. *Ibid.*

71. W.D. Herridge to R.B. Bennett, 13 September 1933. *Secret.* Reprinted in *The Bennett New Deal: Fraud or Portent*, J.H.R. Wilbur, ed. (Toronto: Copp Clark, 1968), p. 67.

72. W.D. Herridge to R.B. Bennett, 22 June, 1934, in Wilbur, p. 70.

73. *Ibid.*

74. W.D. Herridge to R.B. Bennett, 11 July, 1934, in Wilbur, p. 71.

75. See note 72.

76. W.D. Herridge to R.B. Bennett, 12 April, 1934, in Wilbur, p. 69.

77. *Ibid.*

78. *Ibid.*

79. See note 74.

80. See note 72.

81. Perlin, *The Tory Syndrome,* p. 46.

82. Bennett, "Democracy on Trial," p. 13 cf Meighen, "Whither are we drifting?" (1935), "...whether or not the people in mass who now under universal suffrage determine the fate of many nations are really cognizant of their responsibility as well as their power. You will apprehend already that I am somewhat doubtful myself." Unrevised, pp. 248-249.

83. Borden, *Limbo,* p. 163.

84. *Ibid.,* p. 164.

85. R.B. Bennett, *The Premier Speaks to the People,* (Ottawa: Dominion Conservative Headquarters, 1935), reprinted in Wilbur, p. 81.

86. *Ibid.,* p. 80.

87. Meighen, p. 253.

88. Bennett, *The Premier Speaks,* in Wilbur, p. 83.

89. *Ibid.,* p. 81. Our italics.

90. Quoted in Brown, *Borden,* II, p. 196.

91. Meighen, p. 317.

92. *Ibid.,* p. 320.

93. *Ibid.,* p. 437.

94. *Ibid.,* p. 443.

95. Grattan O'Leary, "Can the Conservatives Come Back," *MacLean's Magazine,* Dec. 1, 1942, p. 11.

96. *Report of the Round Table on Canadian Policy,* Port Hope Conference, 1942, p. 1.

97. Frances Flaherty, "A Conservative Philosophy," Saturday Night, September 19, 1942, pp. 10-11.

98. John Bracken, *John Bracken Says* (Toronto: Oxford University Press, 1944), p. 8.

99. *Ibid.,* p. 66.

100. *Ibid.,* p. 17.

101. *Ibid.,* p. 67.

102. Bennett, p. 17.

103. Bracken, p. 92.

104. George Drew, *Sydney Post Record,* June 9, 1949, in Carrigan, p. 188.

105. *Ibid.*

106. *Ibid.,* p. 192.

107. E.D. Fulton, "Introduction" to John Farthing, *Freedom Wears a Crown* (Toronto: Kingswood House, 1957), p. xvi. Leopold MacAulay in 1933, for instance, referred to Lord Hugh Cecil's study of English Conservatism, and observed that the "general characteristics of Conservatism in England are equally characteristic of the development of the Conservative Party in Canada." "History and Aims," *Canadian Problems,* p. 189.

108. *Ibid.,* p. xviii.

109. *Ibid.,* p. xix-xx.

110. *Ibid.*

111. E. Davie Fulton, "The Basic Principles of Conservatism" (1964) in L.J. Ladner, *The Progressive Conservative Party,* p. 6.

112. *Ibid.,* p. 7.

113. Fulton, "Dynamic Conservatism," *Report of the Macdonald-Cartier Conference,* 1959, (Ottawa: 1959), p. 24.

114. Donald Fleming, "Distinctive Conservatism" (Ottawa: The Progressive Conservative Party of Canada, 1956), p. 5.

115. *Ibid.,* p. 12.

116. From *Lament for a Nation* (Toronto: McClelland and Stewart, 1965), p. 12, by George Grant reprinted by permission of The Canadian Publishers, McClelland and Stewart Limited, Toronto, and the author.

117. From *Renegade in Power* (1963, p. xiv) by Peter Newman reprinted by permission of the Canadian Publishers, McClelland and Stewart Limited, Toronto, and the author.

118. *Ibid.,* p. xii.

119. *Ibid.,* pp. xii-xiv.

120. John Diefenbaker, *One Canada* (Toronto: Macmillan, 1975), II, p. 11.

121. David Lewis, *The Good Fight* (Toronto: Macmillan, 1981), p. 483.

122. John Diefenbaker, *One Canada,* (Toronto: MacMillan, 1975), I, p. 153.

123. John Diefenbaker, *One Canada,* (Toronto: MacMillan, 1975), II, p. 283.

124. Diefenbaker, *One Canada,* III, p. 7.

125. Diefenbaker, *One Canada,* II, p. 244.

126. Diefenbaker, *One Canada,* III, pp. 182-183. Our emphasis.

127. Diefenbaker, *One Canada,* I, p. 266.

128. Lewis, *The Good Fight,* pp. 482-483.

129. Diefenbaker, *One Canada,* I, p. 108.

130. Diefenbaker, *One Canada,* II, p. 31. Emphasis in the original.

131. *A New National Policy for Canada* (Ottawa: The Progressive Conservative Party of Canada, 1957) in Carrigan, p. 225.

132. Diefenbaker, *One Canada,* I, p. 133.

133. Diefenbaker, *One Canada,* II, p. 46.

134. Diefenbaker, *One Canada,* II, p. 320.

135. Diefenbaker, *One Canada,* II, p. 32.

136. Diefenbaker, *One Canada,* III, p. 209.

137. Diefenbaker, *One Canada,* III, p. 111.

138. Diefenbaker, *One Canada,* II, p. 15.

139. Diefenbaker, *One Canada,* III, p. 259.

140. Diefenbaker, *One Canada,* III, p. 298.

141. Diefenbaker, *One Canada,* III, pp. 284-285.

142. George Grant, *Philosophy in the Mass Age,* (Toronto: Copp Clark, 1959, 1966), p. 109.

143. Grant, *Lament,* pp. 66-67.

144. See G.C. Perlin, *The Tory Syndrome* (Montreal: McGill-Queen's University Press, 1980), chs. 7, 8 for a detailed discussion of the 1967 convention.

145. Geoffrey Stevens, *Stanfield* (Toronto:McClelland and Stewart, 1973), pp. 31-32.

146. E.D. Haliburton, *My Years with Stanfield* (Windsor, N.S.: Lancelot Press, 1972), pp. 13, 14.

147. Stevens, p. 238.

148. *Summary of Leadership Conventions* (Ottawa: n.d.), p. 11.

149. Progressive Conservative Policy Handbook (Ottawa: 1968) in Carrigan, p. 349.

150. Mimeo, p. 11.

151. *Ibid.,* p. 4.

152. *Ibid.,* p. 11.

153. From "The Relation of the Two Founding Peoples" in *Unfinished Business* (1967, p. 174) by Marcel Faribault, reprinted by permission of The Canadian Publishers, McClelland and Stewart Limited, Toronto.

154. *Ibid.*

155. Faribault, "Conservatism and Confederation" in *Unfinished Business,* p. 111.

156. Robert Stanfield, *House of Commons Debates,* Sept. 16, 1968, p. 59.

157. Robert Stanfield, *House of Commons Debates,* Feb. 28, 1974, p. 31.

158. Robert Stanfield, *Ibid.,* Vol. 117, no. 3, p. 47.

159. Robert Stanfield, mimeo, p. 9. Our emphasis.

160. *Ibid.*

161. Robert Stanfield, *House of Commons Debates,* Sept. 10, 1973, p. 6378.

162. Robert Stanfield, *House of Commons Debates,* May 8, 1974, p. 2155.

163. Robert Stanfield, *Memorandum to Caucus,* p. 3.

164. *Ibid.,* p. 2.

165. *Ibid.,* p. 4.

166. *Ibid.,* p. 5.

167. *Ibid.*, p. 7-8.

168. *Ibid.*, p. 8.

169. *Ibid.*, p. 9.

170. *Ibid.*, p. 11.

171. *Ibid.*, p. 12.

172. *Ibid.*, p. 13.

173. *Ibid.*, p. 14.

174. Perrin Beatty, "Letter to Hon Robert Stanfield," Nov. 18, 1974, mimeo, p. 3.

175. *Ibid.*, p. 4.

176. *Ibid.*, p. 5.

177. *Ibid.*

178. *Ibid.*, p. 7.

179. Jim Gillies, "Letter to Delegates," Progressive Conservative Leadership Convention, Feb. 1976, p. 4.

180. Perlin, *The Tory Syndrome,* ch. 9.

181. Perlin, p. 174.

182. Quoted in D.L. Humphreys, *Joe Clark: A Portrait,* (Toronto, 1978), p. 219.

183. Gillies, quoted in the *Globe and Mail,* August 27, 1979, p. 5.

184. David MacDonald, quoted in the *Globe and Mail,* February 7, 1980, p. 9.

185. Joe Clark, *House of Commons Debates,* Oct. 10, 1979, p. 40.

186. Humphreys, Clark, p. 207.

187. Humphreys, p. 146.

188. Joe Clark, *House of Commons Debates,* Oct. 10, 1979, p. 39.

189. Joe Clark, *House of Commons Debates,* Nov. 15, 1979, p. 1331.

190. Humphreys, Clark, p. 183.

191. Joe Clark, *House of Commons of Debates,* Oct. 10, 1979, p. 42.

192. Joe Clark, *House of Commons Debates,* Oct. 10, 1979, p. 42.

193. Jeffrey Simpson, *The Conservative Interlude and the Liberal Restoration* (Toronto, Personal Library Publishers, 1980), p. 118.

194. Aileen McCabe, "Workshops reveal deep party divisions," Ottawa *Citizen,* March 2, 1981, p. 7.

195. Stanfield, *Address,* pp. 2-3.

196. *Ibid.*, p. 7.

197. *Ibid.*, p. 8.

198. *Ibid.*, p. 8.

199. R.L. Stanfield, "Notes for Remarks before the Policy Conference of the Ontario Progressive Conservative Party," Constellation Hotel, Toronto, Sept. 24, 1983, mimeo, p. 3.

200. *Ibid.*

201. *Ibid.*

202. *Ibid.*, p.8.

203. See, for example, John Gamble's speech to the PC Leadership Convention, June 10, 1983, mimeo, pp. 9-10.

204. Joe Clark, "Transcript of an Address by Rt. Hon. Joe Clark to the General Meeting of the Progressive Conservative Association of Canada," Winnipeg, Jan. 28, 1983, mimeo, p. 2.

205. *Ibid.*

206. John Gamble, "Speech to announce his candidacy in the Leadership Convention of the P.C. Party of Canada," March 6, 1983, mimeo, p. 3.

207. Hon. David Crombie, "Speech to the PC Leadership Convention," Ottawa, June 10, 1983, mimeo, pp. 4-5.

208. *Ibid.*, p. 6.

209. Michael Wilson, "Speech announcing his candidacy," n.d., mimeo, p. 4.

210. John Crosbie, "Speech to the P.C. Leadership Convention," June 10, 1983, mimeo, p. 2.

211. Wilson, *ibid.*

212. Crosbie, *ibid.*

213. Joe Clark, "Speech to the Ontario Good Roads Association," Toronto, February 23, 1983, mimeo, p.3.

214. *Ibid.*, p.4.

215. Joe Clark, "Speech to the PC Leadership Convention," Ottawa, June 10, 1983, mimeo, p. 4.

216. Brian Mulroney, "Speech to the PC Leadership Convention," Ottawa, June 10, 1983, mimeo, p. 2.

217. *Ibid.*, p. 4

218. *Ibid.*

219. Brian Mulroney, "On the Issues," PC Party of Canada, Ottawa, July 1984, p. 33.

220. *Ibid.*

221. Brian Mulroney, "Notes for an Address," Confederation Club, Kitchener, August 10, 1984, mimeo, p. 1.

222. *Ibid.*

223. Brian Mulroney, "A View from Baie Comeau," extracts from *Where I Stand, PC Party of Canada*, Ottawa, 1984, p. 8. *Where I Stand* was published by McClelland and Stewart in 1983.

224. Brian Mulroney, Statement at Prince Albert, Sask., July 5, 1984, p. 1.

225. Brian Mulroney, "Civilizing Labour Relations," extract from *Where I Stand*, p. 4.

226. Quoted in the *Globe and Mail*, December 21, 1984.

227. Quoted in the *Globe and Mail*, December 18, 1984.

228. Charlotte Montgomery, "Debate confused by conflict in meanings of universality," *Globe and Mail*, Dec. 18, 1984.

229. Quoted in the *Globe and Mail,* January 19, 1985.

230. Charlotte Gray, *Saturday Night,* October 1988, p.16.

231. Brian Mulroney, *House of Commons Debates,* Vol. 5, p. 6398, September 8, 1985.

232. Brian Mulroney, *House of Commons Debates,* Vol.129, p. 19050, August 30, 1988.

233. Alan Redway, *House of Commons Debates,* Vol. 5, p. 5786, May 5, 1987.

234. *The Economist,* "Survey on Canada," p. 14, Vol. 309, No. 7571, October 8, 1988.

235. Graham Fraser, "Meech Lake bolsters Charter, PM tells House", *Globe and Mail,* June 15, 1988.

236. Jeffrey Simpson, "Tories out of focus," *Globe and Mail,* Nov. 16, 1988.

237. Ed Broadbent, *House of Commons Debates,* August 30, 1988, vol. 129, p.19070.

238. Brian Mulroney, in *Encounter '88,* transcript of the leaders' debate, October 25, 1988, p.43.

239. *Ibid.,* pp.36-37.

240. *Ibid.,* p.57.

CHAPTER V

Δ

CANADIAN SOCIALISM

A TWO-PARTY SYSTEM?

Many Canadians still have an image of Canadian politics as a "two-party system." Liberals and Conservatives, according to this view, are supposed to alternate in power, while other political groupings, third parties, rise and decline, playing a temporary role as agents of regional, linguistic or class protest. This understanding derives from several sources, the most important of which are the pattern of nineteenth-century British politics, transmitted through Walter Bagehot's classic study of the British Constitution, the practice of American politics since the Civil War and the experience of the Canadian party system from Confederation to the First World War. However, as we have suggested in our first two chapters, this model has had little relevance to Canadian politics since 1921 and perhaps even since 1911. In each of the twenty-one federal elections since 1917, at least three parties have been represented in the federal parliament, and the number has usually been higher.

In the 1988 election, twelve parties were registered with the chief electoral officer, but of these, only the Liberal, Conservative and New Democratic Parties had any serious chance of electing their candidates. Many more candidates ran, technically as independents; but in their own minds, or as described in their campaign literature, they were running as representatives of some party or other, usually one of their own creation and consisting of themselves, their family and perhaps a handful of friends. It is easy to dismiss these small parties with a laugh, and most of them indeed do not deserve serious attention.

A brief survey of Canada's electoral history in the twentieth century, however, will confirm that sometimes these smaller and apparently insignificant parties should be taken seriously, sometimes very seriously indeed. Throughout the country, there are instances of parties that began small, and then rose to prominence. In British Columbia, Social Credit and the New Democratic Party now vie for office in provincial elections. In Alberta, the United Farmers of Alberta and Social Credit in turn dominated provincial politics for about fifty years. Saskatchewan had the first democratically elected socialist government in North America, the CCF administration of 1944. Manitoba and British Columbia, too, have elected an NDP government. The CCF and the NDP have both been major forces in Ontario; and Quebec chose Union Nationale and Parti Québécois governments for by far the greater part of the period since 1935. Only in the Atlantic provinces have the Liberals and Conservatives alternated in office, but even here it is worthwhile to remember that Newfoundland's political parties date from only 1949, when the province entered Confederation, and their character was originally shaped by the struggle between those supporting Confederation with Canada and those opposing the union. In the federal legislature, there have been Nationalists, Progressives, United Farmers of Alberta, Social Credit, CCF, Reconstruction, *Bloc Populaire,* Labour-Progressive (Communist), *Union des Electeurs,* Creditistes, and the NDP, as well as a few variations on some of these themes.

Of all these only the CCF and the NDP have proven breadth and depth of appeal, as well as staying power. Continuously represented since 1935, they have, at one time or another in their history, elected at least one federal member from seven Canadian provinces; only Quebec, New Brunswick and Prince Edward Island have never chosen this option. Few of its supporters expect the NDP to form the government after a federal election; nonetheless, even before 1988, there were many who thought that their party would secure fifty or sixty seats on the way to becoming the official opposition. Voting NDP in either a federal or a provincial election remains a very real option for a large number of Canadians, even for many who from habit, inclination or a considered view of public policy eventually decide to cast their vote for another party.

A detailed history of Canadian socialism would be a daunting project. Even now there is a socialist party other than the NDP that contests federal elections: the Communist Party of Canada. Moreover, support for the NDP is often of a heterogeneous nature. One student of Canadian socialism has concluded that, in many instances, NDP supporters are not convinced that their party has the best answers to contemporary problems. He argues that "much of the support for the NDP is no more than a protest vote by those who feel that their interests are not receiving due consideration and who think that their claims to attention will be best served if on election day they support the leading protest movement in Canada."[1]

Even the title of this chapter, "Canadian Socialism," is misleading. It will be our argument that the CCF and the NDP have been the main carriers of the socialist tradition in Canada, and that these parties succeeded in developing a style of socialism that was reformist rather than revolutionary and was committed to democratic electoral practices and parliamentary government. Our contention will also be that this style of socialism was adapted to Canadian needs and circumstances and grew, to a considerable extent, out of deeply rooted Canadian forces as such as farmers' organizations, trade unions and Christianity. Yet socialism was never the only element within the CCF-NDP. Like the Liberals and the Conservatives, the CCF-NDP has for over fifty years been a coalition of ideological forces that have been generally more or less in harmony, but at times have been openly at war with each other in a struggle to dominate and to impose a narrower but more coherent and more sharply defined set of beliefs as the party's central principles.

More specialized studies have examined in greater detail the diversity of the party's socialism and its alliances with such ideologies as Progressivism, Social Credit, Communism and trade unionism. We will, for the most part, not pay close attention to subtle but important ideological alliances. Instead we will attend to the compromises Canadian socialism has made with the powerful strain in the Canadian ideological conversation to which we have previously drawn considerable attention, namely welfare liberalism. For it has been by creating a party in which the different strands of socialism ally with welfare liberalism that Canadian socialism has managed to escape the sterile doctrinal hairsplitting that marked its early history, and to transform itself into an enduring organization whose doctrines and policies are attractive to a considerable number of Canadian voters.

CANADA AND THE USA— A KEY CONTRAST

The relative success of socialist parties in Canada — the CCF, the NDP and more recently the Parti Québécois — contrasts strikingly with the United States, where socialist parties generally presented doctrinaire ideologies to an indifferent, indeed, often hostile, audience. Part of the explanation of this difference derives, as we argued in Chapter II, from Canada's tory tradition, which provided the elements out of which a native socialist movement could grow. The tory commitment to privilege provoked a sharp reaction, which gave a focus to the socialist demand for equality. Socialist views of equality also grew from the liberal commitment to formal or legal equality and equality of opportunity. Moreover, the collectivist element in toryism accepted trade unions and farmers' co-operatives as legitimate. This combination of collectivism and egalitarianism is what we mean by socialism.

In the nineteenth century, socialism in Canada was a latent possibility rather than a potent political force. Its development was stimulated, as we have also seen with regard to Canadian Liberalism and Conservatism, by Canada's continuing openness to external influences. In Norman Penner's words:

> When craftsmen from Britain began to pour into Canada at the end of the 19th and beginning of the 20th century they brought more than their industrial skills with them. They brought a trade-union consciousness from a country where the labour movement was already highly developed, and many also came with socialist ideas, which they proceeded to implant on Canadian soil. Socialist ideas also came at the same time from the United States, and somewhat later immigrant labourers from Eastern and Central Europe added to the strength of socialism in Canada.[2]

As an historian observes, most immigrants were of Anglo-Saxon or Celtic stock, and those "from the British Isles displayed a greater propensity to join socialist groups or agrarian protest movements in the prairies than did native Canadians."[3] Rejecting the sweeping revolutionary attack on existing political and economic institutions, which was favoured by some of the Central European immigrants, these British trade unionists and socialists found a plausible entry point into the Canadian political tradition through shared collectivist values.

This collectivism was a feature almost co-terminous with Canada. We have seen in the last chapter that the tory element in Canada contained a significant collectivist strain. In fact, the desire to use the state to further collective ends dates back as far as the French colonial regime. The succeeding British regime with its policy of canal-building and other public works made this an enduring feature of Canadian politics. After Confederation Macdonald continued to promote collectivist goals. The National Policy is perhaps as good as any overall description of Macdonald's plans, which included the use of a tariff strategy to foster industrial development, a partnership with business interests to build the CPR and the settlement of the Northwest to prevent its annexation by the Americans. Since Macdonald's time successive governments have been involved in extensive public enterprises, railways, broadcasting, banking, oil and gas pipelines and satellites, to name just a few.

All this is in sharp contrast to American individualism. In that country, from its eighteenth-century founding as a state, there were Bills of Rights and supreme court decisions to enforce them, which prevented the American state from joining in an active partnership to build the nation. It was not until the 1930s that supreme court decisions gave the central government power, which Canadians had always expected their government to exercise. These rival traditions of government activity are important for understanding the different receptions that socialism received.

In both world and Canadian terms, socialism is the newest of the ideologies we have considered to date. G.D.H. Cole, looking on Canadian socialism from an international perspective, wrote that "there was very little significant development up to 1914." Paul Fox also notes that the early Canadian socialist parties were slow to develop ideas appropriate to a Canadian setting, and instead relied heavily on classical Marxism as interpreted by Americans like E.V. Debs and Daniel De Leon. The lack of any agreement among the scattered socialist groups concerning the nature or goals of socialism, and their failure to build a nationally successful party, lend credence to the belief that at least until the end of the Great War, Canadian socialism was not a major force.[4]

THE IMPACT OF TRADE UNIONISM

One important factor that deprived Canadian socialism of early success in this country was the preference of most early Canadian trade-union leaders to ally with the previously existing parties rather than found a political movement to promote their interests. It was only in 1871 that the first rudimentary alliances of trade unions, the Toronto Trades Assembly, had been formed. A year later, that movement had its first major test in a strike against George Brown's *Globe* newspaper. Brown's liberal individualism rejected the essentially collectivist nature of trade unions, and Brown set out to break the strike of his newspaper by invoking the *English Combination Acts* of 1792 and 1800 which had been repealed in England but which were still law in Canada.

The consequence of this action, as with the later Taff Vale decision in England, was the opposite of what the employers hoped for. The working men's associations in Toronto organized public rallies, and the Conservatives, unwilling to let a golden opportunity slip from their hands, began to woo the workers. The egalitarian element in trade unions was intensely unpleasant to Victorian Canadian Conservatism; but collectivism was part of the tory inheritance, and Macdonald introduced legislation to "improve existing laws relating to Trades Combinations in Canada," following the lines of the British *Trade Union Act* of 1871.[5] The response of the working men was natural enough; they looked upon the Conservatives as their friends, and gave them their political support. The outcome had indicated a particularly important lesson: that labour could be politically influential, and more important, could secure significant gains for its members by alliances with existing parties.

Macdonald's shrewd political move had both "dished" the Liberals and taken the steam temporarily out of the trade-union movement as a political force. However, after a decade of inactivity, Canadian unionism was faced with a rapid series of imported American ideologies. The first Assemblies of the radical American organization, the Knights of Labor, entered Canada in 1881. This organization urged Canadian workers to take a broad view of their power, and to put an end to the "speculators, usurers, landgrabbers and other classes of idlers [who] live on the labour of other classes."[6] However, this doctrine of class division and conflict had no roots in Canadian social reality, and after a brief spell of importance, was on the wane by 1887.

Its decay coincided with a second American onslaught, this time leading to the founding of the first socialist parties in Canada: the Workingman's Party of British Columbia in 1886 and the American Socialist Labour Party of Daniel De Leon, a branch of which was established in Ontario in 1894. "The S.L.P. was doctrinaire Marxist in ideology and exhibited from the outset an extreme sectarian and anti-trade union orientation."[7]

Other socialist organizations arose soon after, such as the Canadian Socialist League of George Wrigley, which advocated a gentle Christian socialism.[8] However, it would be futile and redundant to trace the waxing and waning, the dividing and subdividing of these different socialist parties. Grace MacInnis, J.S. Woodsworth's daughter, describes the condition of the early socialist groups perceptively as follows:

> British Columbia's long tradition of Marxian socialism, European in origin, had been brought over by Britishers before the British Labour Party had become a major force. Labour parties rose and fell and rose again under other names. Each prairie city had its similar Labour Party, autonomous and almost unaware of the existence of its neighbour. In two or three Ontario cities both Marxian and Labour Party traditions lived through a multiplicity of tiny parties, each the centre of a ring of deviationists. Quebec and the Maritimes had practically no organization.[9]

The failure of these socialist parties reflected the important choice that Canadian trade unionism had made in the early 1870s: to ally with existing parties. This doctrine became known as Gompersism, after the American trade-union leader, Samuel Gompers, who succeeded in imposing it on the mainstream of the trade-union movement in that country. On the whole, Canadian unionists preferred this labourism to socialism; that is, they preferred that their trade-union organizations pursue primarily economic goals within the context of the existing society and economy. Just as the early unionists had welcomed the action taken by Macdonald's Conservative Government on their behalf, so later unionists were content to ally themselves with whatever political party seemed to be in a position to do them the greatest benefit.

It was neither accident nor corruption that led some of the pioneers of the Canadian labour movement into the government service. The Liberal Party of Laurier secured with the trade-union movement a success similar to that which they achieved with the Province of Quebec. Liberalism used its concern for liberty to persuade the latter that it would be better able to defend its culture under the Liberal doctrine of provincial rights. The trade-union movement also had much to gain from an increased liberty, hampered as it was by restrictive business practices and restrictive laws. Thus, when Laurier's government established a Department of Labour in 1900 it sought to staff the new department with men who could command the respect and support of trade unionists in the country. Daniel O'Donoghue was invited to become a fair wage officer and the young, prolabour Mackenzie King, whose welfare liberalism was to become such a powerful force in Canadian politics, became editor of the *Labour Gazette,* and, in 1909, Minister of Labour. By accepting such government posts, labour supporters could be more certain that the working man's case would be given sympathetic consideration. From the socialists' point of view, they were bolstering an oppressive system; but by their own lights, they were pursuing the only course that would lead to the bettering of the workers' condition.

THE EARLY SOCIALISTS

For the rest there were indeed socialists in Canada, although they had to await the founding of the NDP in 1961 for a formal union with labour. The socialists can be roughly classified as follows. There were the doctrinaires, who believed in socialism as a goal, a set of social relationships or institutions to be established, peacefully if possible, but who would resort to violence if the dominant class proved unmovable by other means. Robert Owen's communitarian followers established an Owenite community in Ontario in the 1850s, which failed like similar experiments in the United Kingdom and the United States. The First International had its followers in Ontario, as did the Socialist Labor Party of the United States led by Daniel De Leon. The influence of American union radicals such as E.V. Debs and Bill Haywood, who were to join with De Leon in 1905 to form the Industrial Workers of the World (IWW or the "Wobblies") was also felt.[10] Up to the beginning of the First World War, Canadian socialism was primarily working class in character,[11] and in Penner's view, its two significant accomplishments were "implanting and popularizing Marxist ideas, and building the trade-union movement."[12]

There was, however, another strain of socialism, which arose from elements that had already been thoroughly domesticated in Canada such as Christianity. G. Weston Wrigley's Canadian Socialist League, mentioned above, believed that "Christ was the first socialist."[13] Such socialists normally emphasized that "socialism is a way of life" rather than a series of institutional arrangements. To explore the distinction between these two styles of socialism more fully, we will first turn our attention to the early ideas of the man who was the spiritual father of the mainstream of socialism in Canada, J.S. Woodsworth. Then, by way of contrast, we will consider a notable manifestation of the rival conception of socialism, the One Big Union (OBU) and the Winnipeg General Strike of 1919.

J.S. WOODSWORTH

James Shaver Woodsworth was born in Ontario in 1874. His parents were Methodists, and interestingly from the point of view of our argument about the connection between toryism and socialism, his mother's ancestors were United Empire Loyalists. Even before birth, he was dedicated "to the service of the Lord";[14] however, as a young man he decided that his vocation lay in teaching rather than in preaching.[15] When dissatisfaction within the Church led him to offer his resignation, he was offered a more secular position as Superintendent of All Peoples' Mission in Winnipeg in 1907. From his experience there came his first book, *Strangers within our Gates* (1909). It was not a socialist tract, but rather a compassionate look at the problems faced by the immigrants who had come to Canada. In spite of its predominantly factual character, there is clear evidence in it of certain strains that were to become important later in Woodsworth's ideological understanding of Canada, and which he was also to share with the others with whom he was associated, first in the Ginger Group in the House of Commons in the 1920s and then in the CCF in the 1930s.

In some ways the young Woodsworth's social understanding reflected a microcosm of Canada as a whole. There is a tory strain that manifests itself in places in the book, especially in Woodsworth's obvious preference for a British Canada. On a higher level, the collectivism that he expresses here also shows a strong tory influence, since it is more concerned with the collectivist aspects of the nation as a whole than it is with placing emphasis on collectivist elements such as trade unions within the nation. Such a tory collectivism is clearly present in his fear that the "presence of incompatible elements [as a result of immigration] changes the entire social and political life of a country; it is a fatal barrier to the highest national life."[16]

Yet the pervasive influence of liberal individualism affected Woodsworth, too. His vision of Canada rejected the tory sympathy for diversity, in favour of early Canadian liberalism's drive for homogeneity. "There is an unfounded optimism that confidently asserts that all this mingling of the races is in the highest interest of the country."[17] His answer to the question "How are we to make them [immigrants] into good Canadian citizens?" was simple enough: "First of all, they must be in some way unified. Language, nationality, race, temperament, training, are all dividing walls that must be broken down." This doctrine, intolerant as it is, is surely the same individualism that is implicitly present in the liberalism exemplified by Pierre Trudeau.

Woodsworth came to this position by preferring to promote greater equality, in contrast to the liberal's emphasis on liberty. His analysis of the causes of immigration to Canada identified privilege as one of the most important forces: "the whole social system [in the immigrants' homeland] is iniquitous. Privileged classes prey on the masses. The state exists not for the good of the people, but to gratify the ambition of a few leaders."[18] His hostility to continued diversity in Canada stemmed largely from his belief that if immigrants retained their distinctive features, this might lead to the development of a class system in Canada:

> We can already perceive changes in Canada. The Westerner differs from the Easterner, not merely because East is East and West is West, but because of the mixed character of the population of the West. The character of Eastern cities, too, is changing. The people on the street differ in physique from those of a decade ago. Social distinctions, hitherto unknown, are being recognized. A hundred years from now who and what shall we be?[19]

This distaste for privilege and preference for an egalitarian society without class distinctions was the feature of Woodsworth's thought that prevented him from being either Conservative or Liberal, and which led him to develop a new social doctrine that contained prominent socialist features.

As with other clergymen in this period in the West, Woodsworth was strongly influenced by the Social Gospel movement.[20] In Avakumovic's words:

> On one point, however, these clergymen were all agreed: the Gospels did provide inspiration and guidance for anyone wanting to improve the lot of the unfortunate members of society. Sermons and prayers could not replace the need for social activism. It was up to the churches to show the way if mankind was to be saved and Christianity survive as a moral force. If the churches failed in this task, individual clergymen must set an example of social consciousness.[21]

With such other Social Gospellers as Salem Bland, William Ivens, William Irvine, A.E. Smith and Henry Wise Wood, Woodsworth played an extremely important role in developing this feature of Canadian socialism.

When he addressed the circumstances around him in Winnipeg, he found that the immigrants in Winnipeg posed a "challenge to the church" that required it "not merely to preach to the people," but to "educate them and to improve the entire social conditions."[22] Unless the church were willing to minimize the importance of doctrinal orthodoxy, an orthodoxy with which Woodsworth found it increasingly difficult to profess agreement, it would not be an important social force. Woodsworth urged it to participate, not in a revolution, but in an extensive program of education and social improvement.

By the time that he came to publish his next book, *My Neighbour*, in 1911, he was even more committed than he had been in *Strangers*. "Someone is responsible! Every unjustly treated man, every defenseless woman, every neglected child has a neighbour somewhere. Am I that neighbour?"[23] His work with the Mission in Winnipeg had begun to convince him that the increasing urbanization of the country would present society with problems that were becoming more difficult to solve. Moreover, these problems would be such that it was no longer possible to rely on virtues such as self-reliance and an individualistic morality. "Man has entered on an urban age. He has become a communal being." Cities differed from rural life because of the complex ties of interdependency. "City life is like a spider's web — pull one thread and you pull every thread."

The implications that Woodsworth was beginning to feel were that the type of work that he was doing in Winnipeg, charitable work through the church in an attempt to alleviate the distress of individuals, was no longer adequate to the new problems that were arising as a consequence of the increasing trend toward urbanization. "[Injured workmen] are part of a system as we are party of the same system. We as individuals cannot help them as individuals. The whole system must be reckoned with — possibly completely changed."[24]

In spite of the suggestion that complete change might be necessary, Woodsworth was neither at this time in his life, nor later, a revolutionary, the abuse heaped on him by men who called him "a dirty bolshevist" or a "red rabble-rouser in the pay of Moscow" notwithstanding.[25] Rather, he repudiated socialism of "the doctrinaire variety so dear to the hearts of the self-styled 'scientific socialists.' [His] was kin to the socialism of the British Labour Party, a movement which had been fed from religious, ethical, cooperative and Fabian streams....it was, in a new form, the building of the Kingdom of Heaven on earth." So Woodsworth tried to build an ideological understanding out of indigenous elements within Canada. His socialism would "spring from the soil of each locality, be rooted in its traditions and nurtured in its heart, adapt itself to its continually evolving mental and cultural climate."

As Woodsworth shrewdly appreciated, there was little to be gained by continuing to draw, as Canadian socialism previously had done, on foreign ideological doctrines, however appealing they might appear to intellectuals. Any effort to import the particular variety of socialism developed in Europe or elsewhere, he felt, would end only in futility and bitterness. Canadians must evolve their own type."[26] This understanding of socialism led him to reject the ideas of the more doctrinaire Marxists who had their utopias already sketched out. He did not want to discard what already existed if it could be made to work in the interests of the workers. "Our ideal ought to be not to create new organizations but rather to really socialize those already in existence." Only if this should prove impossible should they be relegated "to the scrap heap."[27]

As he became convinced that it was of central importance to the type of society he wished to see created in Canada that he enunciate a socialist political ideology, he grew increasingly concerned with developing a doctrine that would repudiate privilege with sufficient vigour, while at the same time avoiding the theories of class war that classical socialism taught.

We dream of a socialistic state and yet sympathize with Mr. Brooks when he says that "the Mecca of the Co-operative Commonwealth is not to be reached by setting class against class, but by bearing common burdens through toilsome stages along which all who wish well to their fellows can journey together." If there must be a fight then it is a fight for the rights of the many weak against the privileges of the strong few and we stand with the many weak. We believe in opportunism and compromise in securing practical reforms, but never when they involve the abandonment of the hope of attaining the ultimate goal, or the sacrifice of vital principles.[28]

This attack on privilege, partly shared with the welfare liberal strain within Canadian Liberalism, together with the defence of opportunism and compromise, was a significant element in the subsequent ideological composition of both the CCF and the NDP. In Gregory Baum's words:

The new society to be created was never regarded — as in Marx — as the final stage of history and the passage from the realm of necessity to the realm of freedom....This refusal to split radical politics and reformist plans became a characteristic of Canadian socialism....Woodsworth never accepted the view that reform is the enemy of radical change: he never wanted to magnify the contradiction of capitalism at the expense of the workers to hasten the coming of the great revolution.[29]

THE WINNIPEG GENERAL STRIKE

Woodsworth's impact on Canadian socialism still lay in the future. It was not until 1921 that Woodsworth was first returned to the House of Commons for a Winnipeg constituency. In the interim, he had resigned from his position with the mission, taken a position with the provincial government, and had been fired from it for his pacifist opposition to the Great War and, in particular, to conscription. The desperate financial condition he found himself in as a result led to his first and only direct participation in the life of the working men of Canada to whom he had dedicated his life; he worked for a time as a longshoreman in British Columbia. However, he soon began to give lectures, and it was as part of a lecture tour that he arrived back in Winnipeg on June 8, 1919, three weeks after the beginning of the Winnipeg General Strike.

The men who participated in the General Strike in Winnipeg can be divided into the three groups we identified earlier. First, there were the liberals, the orthodox trade-union leaders, who "approved of the existing system of trade unions, which they regarded as well designed to improve the position of labour. They envisaged no fundamental reconstruction of society but instead orthodox efforts to raise wages and reduce hours within the framework of capitalist free enterprise."[30] In the opinion of one of the leaders of the international union movement in Canada, Tom Moore, the error of the syndicalists in the One Big Union was that they had attempted to usurp the power of the international union executives. These latter preferred a "policy of negotiation and the using of the strike weapon as a last resort only."[31] The second group, to which we will turn in a moment, was composed of those socialists such as Woodsworth who supported the limited goals of the trade-union leaders.

Most controversial, however, was the vocal minority from the Socialist Party of Canada, which was founded in 1904 and drew most of its strength from the West Coast. Avakumovic describes their outlook as rigid and their view of the world as uncompromising.[32] David Lewis, speaking of the SPC in the thirties, confirms that "a rigidly interpreted Marxism reigned supreme" within the party, and comments that at times "the rigid, doctrinaire approach led the Socialist Party of Canada to ridiculous lengths."[33] Most of its leaders were born and raised in the British Isles and they brought to Canada certain ideas from British unionism and British socialism, especially "the Owenite tradition as a millenarian solution to working-class difficulties," ideas which "were at best utopian and visionary."[34]

It is in part because of the continuing influence of such men that we were unwilling in the second chapter to accept Horowitz's notion of congealment. Masters goes so far as to suggest that the "course followed by the western labour movement" could be regarded "almost as an extension of the British labour movement." In spite of the fact that the program of the One Big Union was considerably less radical than its American counterparts, the International Workers of the World (I.W.W. or "Wobblies") and the Workers' International Industrial Union, it could not have come onto the stage in an historical situation more likely to cause panic in both business and governmental circles.[35]

Not only was there widespread industrial unrest in Canada at this time as a consequence of the demobilization after the Great War; there was also the inspiration of the Russian Revolution, which "had aroused keen enthusiasm in the hearts of those who wanted direct and drastic economic action."[36] The government could not be reassured by suggestions put forward that the Russian Soviet system had been devised from the same source as the OBU. Nor would they feel secure when they heard the aggressive rhetoric of men such as Kavanagh when they explained the rationale behind the movement: "Political action comes through a political system and a political system is a class or slave system. Politics only exist where there are classes, and any act taken by a class in defence of its interests is political action....any action used to control political power in order to utilize it for the benefit of that class; that is political action, and it matters not what method it takes."[37] As Robin summarizes their ultimate goal, only "a One Big Union, the living embodiment of the class consciousness the socialist educators worked to create, could accomplish the revolution."[38] The preamble to the constitution of the One Big Union sets out clearly and concisely the social analysis that lay behind the movement.

> Modern industrial society is divided into two classes, those who possess and do not produce, and those who produce and do not possess....Between these two classes a

continual struggle must take place....In the struggle over the purchase and the sale of labour power, the buyers are always masters — the sellers always workers. From this fact arises the inevitable class struggle. Compelled to organize for self-defence, they are further compelled to educate themselves in preparation for the social change which economic developments will produce whether they seek it or not.

The One Big Union, therefore, seeks to organize the wage worker not according to craft, but according to industry; according to class and class needs; and calls upon all workers to organize irrespective of nationality, sex, or craft, into a workers' organization so that they may be enabled to more successfully carry on the everyday fight over wages, hours of work, etc. and prepare themselves for the day when production for profit will be replaced by production for use.[39]

All this was clear enough, but its very weakness lay in the vigour and the determination with which its supporters pressed it. It was not an ideology which was congenial to Canada. "Even a brief description of the OBU opinions will sound a number of notes familiar to students of proletarian history in western Europe and the United States."[40] But this similarity was exactly what Woodsworth had feared when he warned against any "effort to import the particular variety of socialism developed in Europe or elsewhere." Indeed, so far were the revolutionaries in the OBU from appealing to the ingrained beliefs of ordinary Canadians that Bercuson argues that their influence "was born as a result of a coup" and suggests that "it would be a great mistake, therefore, to consider the OBU as the sole or indeed the prime representative of the radical mainstream of Western Canada."[41]

Woodsworth's attitude was more in harmony with that of the effective leadership of the General Strike. "His was a practical approach to a concrete situation." Although he took a sufficiently active interest in the strike, particularly with regard to editing the *Western Labor News*, and was arrested (though he was never tried), he was strongly opposed to the basic approach taken by the OBU supporters. He favoured here, as ever, "a solution by peaceful legal means," and he "had no use for class war and repeatedly stated his belief that no society founded upon hatred could endure. Instead of wanting to fasten the dictatorship of the proletariat upon Canada, he talked of a new social order where each individual would have more freedom than was possible today."[42]

It was Woodsworth's approach, and that of the trade union leaders, that proved the more enduring, as it was securely founded in indigenous local roots. Within a year after the General Strike, the One Big Union was "no more than a small sect"[43] and within two years the Socialist Party of Canada "was reduced to a shambles of depleted, dispirited, and disorganized local groups."[44] Although the Communist Party of Canada, led by Tim Buck, was formed in 1921-1922, the events of the aftermath of the Winnipeg General Strike established that mainstream socialist opinion would follow the peaceful, pragmatic and opportunistic course of the British Labour Party rather than the class wars of the Marxist doctrinaires.

CANADIAN SOCIALISM—
PEACEFUL AND PARLIAMENTARY

Even if we accept this argument — that by 1921 Canadian socialism had chosen the road that it was to follow — it is clear that Canadian socialism had not selected the vehicle. "By 1921 there was a host of various labour parties in Canada, most with branches — some with headquarters — in the western cities." To name a few, there were the Dominion Labour Party, the Manitoba Independent Labour Party (ILP), the Saskatchewan ILP, the Farmer-Labour Party, the Canadian Labour Party, the Labour Representation League, the Federal Labour Party, the Workers' Party, and the Socialist Party of Canada. In spite of this wealth in numbers of parties, only twenty-nine labour-socialist candidates stood in the 1921 election, of whom only two, Woodsworth and William Irvine, were elected.[45]

The presence in parliament of these two men was not, of course, by itself a turning point for Canadian socialism. Although they both took radical stands on such subjects as civil liberties,[46] especially on issues like the repeal of Section 98 of the Criminal Code, and on matters concerned with public ownership in the economy, Woodsworth's pragmatic strategy in a parliamentary setting was such that it hampered the development of a consistent and coherent socialist doctrine. Because the Labour Party group was so small, it was not in a position to press home its policies or its programs. If it hoped to influence the course of events, it could do so only by pressing for measures that were within the ideological scope of the Liberal Party, as it did with old age pensions in 1926. In spite of this tactical manoeuvering inside parliament, at which Woodsworth became adept, like Stanley Knowles after him, he would not modify his principles or the public expression of his beliefs in order to curry favour with the electorate. Like King, Woodsworth was a democrat, but unlike the prime minister, the Labour leader had a radically different perspective on time. King was convinced that he had to maintain power, both to accomplish his policies, and to prevent the Conservatives from implementing theirs. For King there was no end to this process; there was no foreseeable point at which the process of governing would come to an end. On the other hand, although Woodsworth's vision was certainly not apocalyptic, he could image a time, once the Co-operative Commonwealth was established, when politics of the traditional sort would no longer be necessary. However, the post-political age could not be attained by a cynical manipulation of short-term electoral considerations, which Woodsworth consequently eschewed.

THE PROGRESSIVE MOVEMENT

This hostility to political parties, and the correlative preference for considering Canadian socialism as a movement came into Canadian socialism from the farmers' movements, such as the United Farmers of Alberta. In 1924 Woodsworth had succeeded in extending the ambit and influence of his leadership by forging increasingly close ties with a group of the more radical Progressives, the majority of whom came from Alberta; later they formed the Ginger Group. In an earlier chapter we pointed out that a majority of the Progressives, with Forke as their leader, were radical liberals, who could find a relatively congenial home in the Liberal Party of Mackenzie King, once the social and economic conditions in the farming areas had improved sufficiently to take the edge off the need for a new ideological perspective. However, the more radical group, mostly from Alberta, were supporters of the ideas of Henry Wise Wood. Irvine himself had written a book, *The Farmers in Politics* (1920), "expounding the ideas of group government better than those ideas had ever been presented by Henry Wise Wood himself."[47]

As Irvine saw it, the Great War had induced a dramatic alteration in social and economic circumstances in Canada, especially in the competitive system, for which the traditional parties were unable to present effective or compelling explanations. Farmers, Irvine believed, possessed a truly novel ideological vision. It was, therefore, "the privilege and duty of organized farmers to show the better way in politics and industry. All parties are alike to them....In their economic oppression and political wandering, the farmers have discovered the *new law* and *the new hope*. They do not seek to destroy, but to fulfil, governments; they do not want to compete with exploiters for the lion's share of the plunder, but seek true co-operation in all things for the highest common good."[48]

The farmer was the ideal representative of the nation, of "the highest common good," because he transcended all divisions. "The farmer, in reality, combines in his own profession the two antagonists. He is both capitalist and labourer." This union of the "two antagonists" was a symbol for the collectivism he pursued. His plan was to rely on this aspect of the farmer's nature to replace individualism by a philosophy that treats "group organization" as "the first democratic unit" and proceeds from there to "cohesion, concentration, solidarity, united action, and co-operation." Farmers, organized on a class basis, would not have to "shape their minds to a previously made platform"; rather they could "shape their platform according to their collective mind."

If collectivism was one lodestar of Irvine's political thought, equality was the other. "The History of Canada is the record of the rise, development, and supremacy of class rule." Just as the Ontario election of 1919 had presented a "formidable challenge to partyism and privilege," so the rise of a national farmers' movement would put an end to privilege throughout the country. "The group policy, logically followed, will prevent any class from dominating. Group organization does not imply class legislation. It is the negation of class legislation."

Although Irvine thought that his approach included everything that was valuable in bolshevism, syndicalism and guild socialism, the theory that he propounded in this book would not have been accepted by continental socialists as socialism at all. However, it was perhaps all the more appropriate in a Canadian setting for that. Irvine's theory of group government, although addressed to farmers in the first instance, was not exclusive, and the grounds on which he sought to make his appeal — collectivism and equality — were ideals that had an attraction for Canadian socialists as well as for some politically minded members of the Canadian labour movement. Of special importance was the fact that these ideas, like Woodsworth's, were quite congenial to theories of the radical members of the UFA and the Progressives. Throughout the 1920s, these men continued to work in increased harmony with the Ginger Group in spite of their diverse political backgrounds.

"By the end of the twenties some of the members [of the Ginger Group] had come to regard finance as the overshadowing issue of modern society. Unwittingly, by focusing public opinion in Alberta almost exclusively on the banking system, they were preparing the way for Aberhart and Social Credit."[49] Grace MacInnis's argument here, though plausible, is misleading. Irvine, whose beliefs by this time shared much in common with Social Credit,[50] was already inclined in that direction when he wrote *The Farmers in Politics.* More serious, however, is the overestimate implicit in this argument of the power of individual ideological thinkers or groups to effect a transformation of the ideological attitudes in the public at large. Although the repetition of the anti-banking theories of the Ginger Group throughout the 1920s would have prepared the ground for Social Credit to the extent that it began to familiarize the people of Alberta with that sort of argument, it is more likely that the Depression, rather than the Ginger Group, was the more important causal factor.

THE GREAT DEPRESSION

The Depression was significant in the context we are presently considering, not so much because it worked such havoc with people's lives — there had in the past been plagues, famines and other natural disasters that did not induce men to begin a process of ideological introspection — but rather because it was inexplicable; it perplexed people. Many of the assumptions of the old individualism were brought into question. The notion that there were "deserving poor" became more widespread. It became harder and harder to accept the belief that if a person were suffering, then it was the consequence of a lack of virtue — industry, prudence, thrift or the like. The Social Credit and socialist movements shared this in common: they both provided perspectives on what was happening that absolved the individual worker of the blame for his or her plight. There is no space in this volume to go into the ideas of Social Credit.[51] What concerns us here is the impetus that the

Depression gave to the congealing of the disparate socialist, labour and farmers' movements into the coalition that became known as the CCF.[52]

Woodsworth was the focus around which the movement centred. Throughout the twenties, and increasingly with the onslaught of the Depression, he spoke in defence of those who suffered, and against vested interests and privilege. In 1930 he contended that "the present system is failing to function,"[53] and by 1932 he was railing against the economic system as the cause of most of the evils that beset the nation: "The present capitalist system has shown itself unjust and inhuman, economically wasteful and a standing threat to peace and democratic government...." Just as he had been sceptical about the usefulness of individual action to rectify such miseries in *My Neighbour,* so now he continued to promote the idea that it was only through concerted group action that any alleviation was possible. The aims of the movement were the same that Irvine sought — collectivism and equality: "We therefore look to the establishment in Canada of a new social order which will substitute a planned and socialized economy for the existing chaotic individualism, and which, by achieving an approximate economic equality among men in place of the present glaring inequalities, will eliminate the domination of one class by another."

This hostility to capitalism was critical, because it was perhaps the only thing that united the different groups that met first in Calgary in 1932 and then in Regina in 1933. The Calgary Programme of 1932 was, for that reason, imprecise. The weakness of socialism in Canada prior to that time had not been that socialists believed in too little, but rather that they believed doctrinally in too much. Their ideological quarrels not only split them from the labour movement and the farmers' movements, but even from each other. Hence a federation, the object of which would be to "promote co-operation between the member organizations and to correlate their political activities," with the purpose of establishing in Canada "a Co-operative Commonwealth in which the basic principle regulating production, distribution and exchange will be the supplying of human needs instead of the making of profits," was not needlessly divisive.

THE REGINA MANIFESTO

At the famous convention in Regina the next year, 1933, the task was more difficult. There it was necessary to make a more complete statement about the nature of the Co-operative Commonwealth, without alienating the different elements that the founders hoped might join the coalition. Norman Penner identified these strands: the main elements of the Socialist and Labour Parties that started thirty or forty years earlier; the radical farmers' protest movement; the social reform tradition of the trade unions; and the concerns of the Social Gospel.[54] To this list should be added the more moderate co-operative movement, and an element eventually to prove of little significance to the CCF, Social Credit. The CCF also represented the first incursion of a significant number of academics into active politics, contrary to the tradition of detachment epitomized and given sustaining power by the University of Toronto political economist, Harold Innis, the most influential Canadian academic of the late thirties and forties.

How were these divergent strains to be united within a single political party? One method was organization. The CCF was established as a federal party, with many of the constituent groups retaining their separate identity.[55] Second, there was an appeal to nationalism, combined with a general sense of abandoning minor differences for the sake of a greater future. Woodsworth urged the delegates to discard the foreign elements in their ideologies, and reiterated his belief that only a socialism derived from native sources was likely to prove an electoral success.

> Undoubtedly we should profit by the experience of other nations and other times, but personally I believe that we in Canada must work out our own salvation in our own way. Socialism has so many variations that we hesitate to use the class name. Utopian Socialism and Christian Socialism, Marxian Socialism and Fabianism, the Latin type, the German type, the Russian type — why not a Canadian type?[56]

The third step, and clearly the most central, was the Manifesto, the positive statement of principles. At the request of the CCF national council, Frank Underhill, a University of Toronto historian, had prepared a draft program, which was revised and modified with the help of certain of his colleagues in the League for Social Reconstruction. This organization had been formed mainly by academics from the University of Toronto and McGill University. They hoped to play a role similar to the Fabian Society in the United Kingdom, namely to act as an independent group of socially conscious citizens concerned with social, economic and political analysis, and to urge policy proposals based on their studies.[57] However, the intellectuals in the LSR never succeeded in keeping their distance from the CCF, and were involved in plotting its course from the outset.[58]

The LSR draft manifesto that was presented to and endorsed by the convention in Regina was a relatively short and concise statement of the outlines of the Co-operative Commonwealth. For most Canadians, until the Winnipeg Declaration of Principles of 1956, the Regina Manifesto was the definitive statement of the aims and aspirations of Canadian socialism. Although the inspiration behind it came mostly from British sources, the *New Statesman,* the Left Book Club, Sidney and Beatrice Webb, Harold Laski, G.D.H. Cole, R.H. Tawney and John Strachey,[59] in the problems it addressed and the solutions it offered, it was clearly the answer to Woodsworth's desire for a Canadian style of socialism. If criticized by doctrinaires that the Manifesto was not socialism as it was known elsewhere, the CCF replied: "The C.C.F. is essentially socialistic. It does not wish to follow slavishly schools of thoughts [sic] in existence elsewhere but aims to develop a distinctively Canadian approach to socialism."[60] It is therefore worth looking for a moment at the details of the *Manifesto.*

The basic source of agreement between the diverse groups at Regina was a hatred of the excesses of capitalism, "the cancer which is eating at the heart of our society."[61] Two important things were wrong with capitalism, in addition to the fact that it did not appear to be an effective economic system in 1933. First, it rested on the premise that people were competitors, rather than co-operators; in the Co-operative Commonwealth, economic planning would "supersede unregulated private enterprise and competition." The second objection to capitalism was just as serious and just as radical. Capitalism had an inexorable tendency to develop in such a way that "our principal means of production and distribution are owned, controlled and operated for the private profit of a small proportion of our population." This system should, and could, be replaced "by a social order from which the domination and exploitation of one class by another will be eliminated."

All this was for the future, though in the moral outrage and heady optimism of Regina there were doubtless many who expected the movement to make rapid strides towards both power and success. On the whole, however, this was a vision of the green and pleasant land that would ultimately come. Other problems needed more immediate attention. This was recognized in 1933, and brought out more clearly at the Winnipeg Convention in 1934, which prepared the "CCF Immediate Programme."

At no time did the CCF endorse violent revolution as a legitimate means of social change. The most disturbing passage in it was its conclusion:

> No CCF government will rest content until it has eradicated capitalism and put into operation the full programme of socialized planning which will lead to the establishment in Canada of the Co-operative Commonwealth.

This passage was not in Underhill's original draft[62] and its insertion at the convention represented a compromise with some of the more extreme socialists who were concerned about the generally moderate and reformist tone of the document as a whole.[63] Although the passage was interpreted merely as the expression of a fond hope and a general, vague intention by most of those involved in the subsequent leadership of the party, the radical impression it created caused some serious difficulties for the CCF over the next twenty years.

Woodsworth clearly puzzled and disappointed many of his implacable opponents by omitting revolutionary rhetoric from his speeches. Nonetheless they often imputed violent designs to him. There can be no doubt at all, however, that Woodsworth believed deeply in peaceful change and in electoral and parliamentary politics. The Manifesto itself announced that the CCF did not believe in "change by violence." Its members preferred to wait until a majority of the electorate had been "inspired by the ideal of a Co-operative Commonwealth." Until then the party was content to make an appeal "for support of all who believe that the time has come for a far-reaching reconstruction of our economic and political institutions." Those who believed in the ideal had a responsibility to proselytize and educate until this goal could be achieved "solely by constitutional methods."

This approach rested on one of two hopeful assumptions. First, it could assume that ideological conversion on a wide scale was a likely outcome of the CCF's vigorous "educational" activities. Second, it might have been based on the presumption that the socialist strain in Canada was powerful enough in its own right to allow the CCF to secure widespread electoral support. This assumption could plausibly support the apparently sincere charge the CCF often made that the comparatively large sums of money available to the Liberals and Conservatives for election campaigns, obtained mostly from the business community, deceived the common voter. As we shall see, the CCF recognized both limitations implicitly in their frequent additions of liberal concepts to CCF doctrine.

The collectivist element in this program does not need comment here additional to what we made previously in this chapter. Worthy of note, though, is another feature the CCF shared in common with their enemies, the Conservatives. As Bennett was to reassert in his abortive New Deal, economic forces could no longer be allowed free play. Politics was the primary activity, and the state had the right and the duty to control economic consequences where necessary. The CCF affirmed its belief that "the welfare of the community must take supremacy over the claims of private wealth." The insistent and often repeated demands for economic order and centralized planning were central to the faith of Canadian socialists; they were also reassuring ideological explanations that offered an appeal to all who felt disoriented by the economic crisis through which Canada was passing.

A final important element in this ideological mix must be separated, not only because it was discordant, but also because it was extremely important for an understanding of the later development of socialism in Canada. That element is liberalism. The Conservative prime minister in the election campaign of 1935 declared that there "is no room in the same country for socialism and liberty."[64] Here Bennett was working, probably unwittingly but certainly not disingenuously, a grave injustice on Canadian socialism. The Manifesto came out strongly and clearly in favour of "Freedom of speech and assembly for all; repeal of Section 98 of the criminal Code; amendment of the Immigration Act to prevent the present inhuman policy of deportation; equal treatment before the law of all residents of Canada irrespective of race, nationality or religious or political beliefs." The goal of these freedoms was to be the traditional liberal one of "a much richer individual life for every citizen." Their most notable rival for the distinction of being the champions of the oppressed was the Liberal Party of Mackenzie King. As we have seen in Chapter III, King succeeded in 1919 in weaning Canadian Liberalism away from an exclusive reliance on business liberalism, and began to fashion the modern alliance of business and welfare liberalism that would last over half a century. This same problem concerned the CCF: "Genuine liberty for the masses of the people is impossible without economic equality."[65] The mistake that the CCF made, and one which caused them great heart-rending when they saw the Liberals implement what they thought were their policies, was to believe that they were the only party in Canada concerned, or even aware, of the preconditions of the welfare state. Although the requirement of "economic equality" was more radical than anything Mackenzie King ever spelled out, the CCF never made clear what they meant by that concept either, and we are left with the conclusion that it probably had no greater effective meaning for them than the equivalent notion of greater security might have had for King. What was important to the CCF was the belief that they were the only group in Canadian political life that cared about such matters. To achieve this, they charged that the "Liberal Party is, in fact, grooming itself to take the place of the Tories as the party of big business."[66]

Not only was the *Manifesto* an ideological compromise, it was also a social and economic compromise. If it hoped to have wide electoral support, the CCF had to include provisions that would appeal to farm elements, the labour movement and the socialists. This problem meant that the program had to contain a number of uneasy compromises, especially on matters relating to property holding. Although all groups could agree that finance and public utilities ought to be "socialized," it was very clear that the farmers, especially, were not in favour of an extensive policy of nationalization. Hence the program acknowledged that "the family farm is the accepted basis for agricultural production in Canada," though it went on to encourage an extension of co-operative institutions. Labour also had to be offered policies that were attractive in the short run, and the *Manifesto* promised a "National Labor Code to secure for the worker maximum income and leisure, insurance covering illness, accident, old age, and unemployment, freedom of association and effective participation in the management of his industry or profession."

SOCIAL PLANNING FOR CANADA

In spite of the breadth of the appeal, both ideological and class, the voters of Canada appeared to have agreed that the choice in 1935 was between King and chaos. The Liberals won a landslide victory in the election of that year and the CCF returned a very disappointing seven MPs, three from British Columbia, two from Saskatchewan and two from Manitoba. They were shut out of Alberta completely in the face of the Social Credit landslide, and in national terms, they were overshadowed by Social Credit's seventeen seats, although they more than doubled its popular vote. However if 1935 was not electorally a gratifying year, it was intellectually the high point of the CCF. It was in that year that the members of the LSR, particularly Frank Scott, Frank Underhill and Eugene Forsey, published what is probably the single most important socialist work in Canadian history, *Social Planning for Canada*. When Woodsworth wrote in the Preface to *Social Planning for Canada* that "on the whole this book is undoubtedly in line with the Regina Manifesto,"[67] he was doing no more than acknowledging that the men who wrote the latter had amplified their views into a "sustained academic critique that was a far cry from the more superficial criticisms of the farmers' organizations."[68]

There were, clearly, few doctrinal surprises to be expected from this work, but for the first time there was a document that would amplify and clarify the principles of Regina. Throughout the book, the two main conflicting ideologies were juggled and blended. The socialist aspects came out most clearly in the critiques of contemporary capitalism, "a luxury we can no longer afford."[69] In all advanced industrial countries, the argument went, the forces of production had a strong tendency to become concentrated in increasingly fewer hands. A handful of businessmen could "dominate enterprises covering almost every imaginable economic activity."[70] The consequence of this economic development was the creation of a small class of privileged property owners who dominated the economic and political life of the country. But the concentration of economic power was the fruitful source of the capitalists' downfall and the necessary precondition of the Co-operative Commonwealth, since it was relatively easy, given the development of "monopoly capitalism," for the state to take over the existing business and operate without the necessity of any far-reaching economic reorganization.[71]

At this point in the analysis, however, an important disagreement arose between the urban, intellectual socialists and the farmers' movement, whom the former acknowledged would, "because of voting power, be for a considerable time the senior partner."[72] The LSR thought that the economic state of affairs lent itself easily to placing "ultimate authority in the hands of the State."[73] The farmers' movements were not so sure that this was the right approach. As E.J. Garland said in the debate on the *Marketing Act* of 1934:

> ...the two most essential steps towards the building of a new state and a new social order in which through the encouragement and growth of cooperatives on one side, collectively owning the essential basic industries, and direction by the State of the other essential secondary industries, we will have brought about what we are proposing in our Cooperative Commonwealth Federation Manifesto....
>
> I am not a socialist, I have never been a socialist....
>
> The organization to which I belong, the United Farmers of Alberta, constitutes the largest and most powerful part of [the CCF]. Our whole philosophy is based upon the development of cooperatives.
>
> We do not, particularly those of the U.F.A. which is the most powerful body in the Canadian Cooperative Federation, regard it as essential to undertake, say, vast dislocating series of socializations or nationalizations of industries. We do not believe it is necessary....[74]

Woodsworth tried to split the difference on this issue. "[The CCF] does not advocate a bureaucratic state socialism. We recognize very clearly that there are certain matters which must be dealt with by the State; there are other matters that may be left to voluntary cooperative effort."[75] It is worth noting this disagreement because it indicates that right from the very beginning of the CCF there was a serious ideological division between those who leaned more to the egalitarian side of the ideological compromise and favoured extensive state activity to that end, and those whose primary goal was the more explicitly liberal one of enhancing freedom.

The latter element was by no means absent from the LSR's thoughts. They sought a "full realization of personal freedom," but argued that it could come about only through collectivism, through a "willing cooperation in concerted social action." True freedom could "only be enjoyed by people whose work and incomes secure against arbitrary disaster and afford them a reasonable chance of a decent living and leisure."[76] None of this was very far at all from the beliefs of welfare liberalism, an ideology the League believed had seduced "the disinherited groups." This "middle-class optimism" was all the worse because it rendered "impotent the finer impulses."[77] This false consciousness on the part of "the classes which suffer most from the present chaos of monopoly capitalism" meant that the CCF had a formidable task of education in front of it. "No system of socialism will work without the support of a determined and instructed public behind it, and this work of public education is the more necessary in a democratic movement which does not contemplate a violent or forcible transition to the new order."[78] Even the theorists of the LSR, then, could not imagine a successful appeal to the people which did not embody elements of the liberal ideology that had struck such deep and extensive roots in the Canadian ideological soil. Or perhaps even these theoreticians could not themselves escape from the ideological snare of liberalism. One of their most distinguished number, Frank Underhill, was to become increasingly an exponent of liberal ideas; and as we shall see, the trend of the development of the CCF, until its demise, was precisely the same as that of the Conservatives after Bracken: namely, towards a minimization of ideological differences with the Liberals.

COULD THE CCF WIN?

Between 1935 and 1940 the CCF moved increasingly into the control of the urban, Eastern forces in the party, who began to consider it a labour party allied with the farmers' movements.[79] But for the most part, the trade unions in Canada were content to continue the policy of avoiding specific commitments to any single party, a policy they had pursued since the nineteenth century. King's masterfully cynical timing of the 1940 election made things incredibly awkward for a party committed to domestic reform. Although the party as a whole did not endorse Woodsworth's consistently pacifist opposition to war, and announced that it was as determined "to bring the war to a successful conclusion" as the Liberals and Conservatives, it was faced with the unlikely eventuality that the people of Canada would abandon King's Liberals during such a crisis. Although it gained one seat, its share of the popular vote remained static.

After that, however, its popularity surged. As people began increasingly to turn their attention to the problem of postwar reconstruction, the attractiveness of choosing a CCF government to carry out this process of reconstruction became more appealing. The end of the war presented an opportunity, even more than had the Depression, of choosing between ideological visions. Great changes were bound to be underfoot, and the question was: what shape would the postwar nature of Canada take? The first taste of success was in October 1941, with a strong showing in British Columbia provincial election. This was quickly followed in 1942 when the CCF candidate, Noseworthy, defeated the redoubtable Arthur Meighen in South York in his attempt to reenter the House of Commons. The year 1943 was the high point. The CCF won thirty-four seats in the Ontario provincial legislature where it had held none previously, and a Gallup poll in September showed them leading both the Liberals and the Conservatives in popular support (29 percent —28 percent — 28 percent). Finally, in 1944 they scored what turned out to be their only enduring electoral triumph when they swept to power in Saskatchewan under the leadership of Tommy Douglas.[80]

M.J. COLDWELL

On Woodsworth's death in 1942, the party formally elected M.J. Coldwell as leader. He had been, in effect, party leader from the onset of Woodsworth's final illness in 1940. Described by David Lewis as "a very attractive person, full of natural charm and gentle sympathy,"[81] Coldwell had begun his political career in his native England as a Tory, but his traditional conservatism had "melted when he left his middle-class surroundings and confronted the abject poverty in some parts of England....he began to question the ethics of capitalism in terms of his religious beliefs."[82] As a young man he emigrated to Canada, where he settled in the West and became a schoolteacher. While in Saskatchewan he participated in labour politics at both the municipal and provincial level, and in 1935 he was elected to the Dominion Parliament. Coldwell had more of the politician's time perspective than had Woodsworth, the prophet. Under Coldwell's leadership the CCF lost some of its millenarian fervour and began to take into account more tactical electoral considerations. The successes of the early 1940s gave him and the other leading theorists of the CCF reason to hope that they were devising policies and drafting programs that they would very soon be in a position to implement.

In 1943 David Lewis and Frank Scott collaborated in writing *Make This Your Canada* which, Coldwell wrote, "presents a faithful outline of the principles, history and organization of the CCF."[83] In this work there is clear evidence that the liberal elements in the party's ideological mix were beginning to take on an increased importance under the new regime. Ironically, it was the more doctrinaire socialist elements in the party's economic analysis that drew them in that direction. Their understanding of the development of the Canadian economy taught them to isolate as a critical factor the remorseless tendency of that economic organization to concentrate power in the hands of increasingly fewer capitalists. If, as they speculated, the well-to-do Canada numbered no more than 10,500 families, or 0.6 percent of the population,[84] the overwhelming majority, the 99.4 percent of farmers, workers and middle class had a real and substantial interest in combining to end the rule of the wealthy. "Obviously, if the farmers, workers and middle class were allowed to recognize their common interests and to unite in an effective political party with a programme and a philosophy deriving from their own experience and needs, no power in the land could stop them from building together a free society based on the common welfare of all."[85] This analysis raises a difficult question: why include the middle class in this coalition, when according to the CCF's figures, farmers and workers together comprised 73.7 percent of the total population? The answer can only be that the socialism of the CCF had grown from the collectivist theories of the Western farmers' movements. The CCF preferred an analysis that would allow it to speak for virtually the whole country, rather than for class divisions within it. Provision had to be made within the doctrine and within the program for measures that would appeal to middle-class voters.

This development did not involve the leaders of the party in much personal soul-searching since, for the most part, they tended to be Eastern intellectuals, of a predominantly middle-class bent themselves. Their preoccupations were more those of the middle class to whom they sought to appeal than of the farmers to whom they did appeal, and upon whom they relied for the bulk of their parliamentary representation. They continued to strive for a society that would provide an "opportunity for all the people to build and work cooperatively in an environment of democratic equality and fellowship";[86] but their overriding goal was the fundamentally liberal one of increased freedom. A "dynamic, progressive society" to them was one that allowed all to "express their *individual* personalities and initiative in accordance with their talents and aspirations."[87] Although they emphasized that individual rights "are not absolute, but are qualified by their communal purpose,"[88] it is clear that they intended merely a statement that the freedom that concerned them was not the freedom of the capitalists in the unregulated use of control over their enterprises. What they were saying amounted to little more than the observation that the aims of positive liberalism could be attained better in an "organized society which reached far beyond the negative 'freedom from want.'"[89] Even the equality they pursued was influenced by individualist assumptions. "Democratic equality rests on the basic right and value of every personality."[90]

Although this ideological development took place as a consequence of dynamics that had been present in the party since its birth, this style of political thought had been foreshadowed earlier in the century in England by men such as L.T. Hobhouse. Hobhouse rejected the old *laissez-faire* argument that practices like child labour and the twelve-hour day were justified because they were based on freely-made contracts between employer and employed. He concluded that the state had to intervene to rectify injustices that resulted from the unequal bargaining power of the parties. When the liberal came to terms with this necessity, he was impelled to make modifications in classic liberal doctrine. "[I]ndividualism, when it grapples with the facts, is driven no small distance along Socialist lines. Once again we have to extend the sphere of social control."[91] Hobhouse was well aware that his position might be criticized as not being liberalism at all, and to that he retorted: "Pursuing the economic rights of the individual we have been led to contemplate a Socialistic organization of industry. But a word like Socialism has many meanings, and it is possible that there should be a Liberal Socialism, as well as a Socialism that is illiberal."[92]

It is our contention that although the CCF began at a starting point different from Hobhouse, it arrived at a similar ideological conclusion. Since it is this "Liberal Socialism" of which Hobhouse spoke that became the dominant form of liberalism in our society today, it is easy to understand why the CCF and later the NDP had a close, but jealous, relationship with the Liberal Party, and why the Liberals found it easy to adopt their rival's policies. Mackenzie King, whose beliefs led him in the direction of Hobhouse's liberalism, was the leader of a Liberal Party that included, even in the 1940s, many prominent supporters who were still concerned exclusively with business liberalism. The electoral threat the CCF from time to time posed to the Liberals allowed King to use the opportunity that this presented him to introduce modest doses of the welfare liberalism he preferred.

Coldwell's book, *Left Turn, Canada* (1944), took basically the same tack as Lewis and Scott. The individualism of the latter was there, but Coldwell, former schoolteacher as he had been, drew out even more the educational aspects of the CCF programme. Since socialism aimed at a new way of life, as well as new political and economic arrangements, Canadian socialists have long been concerned with education as a means of attaining it. It has become a traditional socialist policy in Canada to advocate that educational facilities ought to be expanded and opened equally to members of all social classes. As Coldwell explained, "The product of the school ought not to be a regimented automation, but a self-reliant, thinking and co-operative person. Such a society requires not only reliable information, but the ability of large masses of the people to make a critical analysis of known facts to provide the foundations for appropriate action."[93] The next year, 1945, saw the CCF's greatest electoral success, with 16 percent of the popular vote and twenty-eight members of Parliament, a number not exceeded by a social democratic party in Canada until the NDP's thirty-one MPs in 1972. The cautiousness of the approach in 1945 is indicated by the title given its program, *Security with Victory*. Here were no ringing denunciations of capitalism, only mild criticism of the "planlessness of capitalism and the restrictive power of private monopolies."Although it promised "to remove the glaring inequalities that still exist," the program made only the modest request for "a new mandate for a further advance toward the Co-operative Commonwealth." What was foremost in the strategists' minds and, they expected, in the fears of the voters, was the spectre of massive unemployment consequent to demobilization; to this end they made as their "central aim" the scarcely uniquely socialist pledge of "jobs and an adequate income for all."[94]

However, from David Lewis's point of view, *Security with Victory* represented "an important milepost in the never-ending ideological argument which has characterized democratic socialist parties since day one: the debate about the extent of public ownership which should be promised in the party's program and undertaken by a social democratic government. For the first time the CCF officially recognized the idea of a mixed economy."[95]

From 1945, the welfare liberal aspects of the party's ideology waxed while its electoral strength on the whole waned. Avakumovic speaks of this as a "definite retreat from the kind of socialism one associates with the Regina Manifesto."[96] Too little is known about the factors that induce voters to cast their ballots to come to any firm conclusions that there is a link between the progressive liberalization and the decline. There is, though, reason to suspect that the more doctrinaire socialists were shrewd in their appreciation that if the people of Canada wanted liberalism, they would prefer to give their support to the Liberals, rather than to the CCF. As Carlyle King of the Saskatchewan CCF observed earthily in 1952: "The trouble is that socialist parties have gone a-whoring after the Bitch Goddess. They have wanted Success, Victory, Power; forgetting that the main business of socialist parties is not to form governments but to change minds. When people begin to concentrate on success at the polls, they become careful and cautious; and when they become careful and cautious, the virtue goes out of them."[97]

The 1949 program *Security for All,* on which the CCF dropped to 13 percent of the popular vote and thirteen seats, was scarcely socialist at all. At least the socialist inspiration of many of the party's promises was heavily veiled behind liberal rhetoric. In fact the program sought to hide any differences that might prove offensive to voters. Instead of providing a clear ideological choice, it announced: "In a land of Canada's resources, no person should go without the basic necessities of life. *All parties agree, therefore they promise these necessities.*"[98] In place of the social and economic analysis that figured prominently in 1945 and before, the CCF in 1949 was content with the cheap and banal charge that the "Old Parties can't fulfil their promises because those who provide their election funds, and therefore control them, are unwilling to pay the price."[99]

Security for All was probably the high point of welfare liberal influence in the period in which the CCF was the vehicle for the expression of mainstream Canadian socialism. Walter Young has argued that the CCF's "liberalism kept them from being communists while their socialism prevented them from becoming liberals."[100] The 1953 election saw them winning twenty-three seats but falling to 11 percent of the popular vote. It was at this time that Young's Law (above) came into force, and the party veered away, at perhaps the last moment, from its assimilation course with Liberalism. *Humanity First* spoke in more traditionally socialist terms of an economy *"artificially* bolstered by war production" in which "no one's future is secure," and praised those "Canadians who are determined to put an end to the exploitation of the poor by the rich, of the weak by the strong— Canadians who believe in working cooperatively for the good of all instead of the dog-eat-dog method of every man for himself."[101]

The possibility that the CCF would be absorbed by the Liberals, as the moderate strain of the Progressives had been in the 1920s, was the more likely of Young's two possibilities. Individual members had, of course, changed sides, and Mackenzie King certainly was not above tempting leading members such as David Lewis with the prospect of a cabinet post.[102] The other possibility was less likely. We have seen that there was a conflict between revolutionary and reformist socialism, which was tentatively resolved in favour of the latter after the Winnipeg General Strike. The creation of the CCF had confirmed that the Canadian socialist movement would be peaceful and parliamentary, and would be in no way subordinate to the Soviet Union. The Communist party of Canada had opposed the CCF in the 1930s, hurling accusations that they were social fascists. Although Lewis opposed the communists with more vigour and effectiveness than many of his colleagues, he probably spoke for many when he wrote: "My position in the CCF and my close work with the labour movement put me in the forefront of the fight against communist disruption. I make no apology for it....I had had enough direct experience to understand the ruthless instructions which the Communist International issued for dealing with parties like the CCF and the slavish devotion with which the Canadian communists carried out those instructions."[103]

Nonetheless, the Labor-Progressives, led by Tim Buck, were a constant embarrassment to the CCF. Time after time CCF members felt compelled to deny the accusation that their movement was communistic, and the party platforms of 1949 and 1953 contained strong statements dissociating the CCF from the Labor-Progressive offers of electoral alliance. To prevent infiltration of the CCF by individual Communists, the CCF carried out periodic small-scale purges, and denied membership in their organization to any person who was already a member of another political party. Yet there can be little doubt that their position was misunderstood by many. The consistent agitation by Woodsworth and his allies against both the old Section 98 of the Criminal Code and the deportation powers the government had granted itself during the Winnipeg General Strike found a parallel in the CCF's opposition to the Liberal Government's desire to outlaw the Communist Party. The CCF realized the dilemma arising from its apparent support for the Communists from the electors' point of view, but felt that "democracy cannot exist where minorities do not have full protection against oppression, domination or encroachments on their legitimate freedoms."[104] With specific reference to Communism, and doubtless in full confidence that its position would be both misunderstood and cynically misrepresented, the CCF stated:

> Although the CCF abhors communism and will continue to fight it, the CCF does not support proposals to outlaw it. The CCF has always contended that the way to fight communism is not to outlaw it, but to correct those social and economic injustices and wrongs on which communism thrives. To outlaw communism and to engage in "McCarthyism" and witch-hunting is to weaken the very freedom we are trying to protect.[105]

THE WINNIPEG DECLARATION

Early in its history the CCF's leadership began to regret the inclusion of the call for the eradication of capitalism in the Regina Manifesto. It made the party seem more dangerously radical than it actually was, and as David Lewis had pointed out, by 1944 the CCF had publicly declared itself in favour of a mixed economy, a move which many of the more doctrinaire socialists considered a betrayal. Yet the Regina Manifesto was still the party's governing ideological statement, although work had begun as early as 1950 on a replacement. This was to be the *Winnipeg Declaration of Principles* of 1956,[106] which, said the CCF convention of that year, was "intended to supersede all other statements of principles which have been adopted by previous conventions of the CCF from its foundation to date."[107]

To what extent the *Declaration* is socialist was at the time, and continues to be, a matter of controversy. Avakumovic describes it as "a move away from traditional socialism"[108] and Norman Penner says it was a "shift to the right" and "a step backward."[109] David Lewis, on the other hand, admits to being annoyed by the presumptuous and superficial interpretation of the Winnipeg Declaration by some students of politics and political theory. "The comments of many of them gel into a few leaky capsules of wisdom. The language of the Declaration is less strident and menacing, therefore the document is less socialist."[110] In our view, the *Declaration* is the direct descendant of the Regina Manifesto, and we are content to accept its authors' identification of themselves as socialists. As Avakumovic has pointed out, "After 1945 Anthony Crosland and others popularized among socialists the concept of the mixed economy."[111] In this sense the CCF was participating in what was virtually a world-wide movement to revise certain of the main tenets of traditional socialism.

Clearly the intention of its drafters was to steer a course between communism and Marxism on the one hand, and pure liberalism on the other. There can also be little doubt that the document represents a fresh attempt to provide a satisfactory synthesis of socialism and welfare liberalism. Throughout the *Declaration* liberal and socialist concepts jostle one against the other. The first sentence speaks in terms of the "co-operative commonwealth" and presses the primary importance of "supplying human needs and enrichment of life." Yet the very next sentence goes on to laud the importance of the inherently individualist notion of equality of opportunity. The third and fourth paragraphs deal with inequalities, which the CCF claimed resulted "in a virtual economic dictatorship by a privileged few." But nowhere is there an attempt to explain how a society in which equality of opportunity operates could fail to produce inquality given the unequal distribution of talents within society, which is a primary justification for equality of opportunity.

Although the *Declaration* condemned Canadian society as "motivated by the drive for private profit and special privilege," it no longer sought a new form of property-holding to eliminate what it repudiated as "basically immoral." The CCF "recognized" that private enterprise could make a "useful contribution to the development of our economy." When David Lewis took stock in 1956 he rejected nationalization as a cure-all for social and economic problems. Instead of this traditional socialist policy, Lewis proposed a reliance on the Keynesian economic palliatives which had by then become the orthodoxy among the Liberal economists. He spoke of the "use of fiscal and financial policies to influence the volume and direction of investments, to redistribute income, and to stimulate purchasing power."[112] Here was a policy which would not have been uncomfortable to any but the most ardent supporters of business liberalism.

The *Winnipeg Declaration* was meant to breathe new life into the party; yet, within two years in the 1958 election, its parliamentary strength had been reduced to eight, its lowest level since 1940, and only one more than had been elected in 1935. Clearly the CCF had failed in Winnipeg, and a few clues to this failure can be gleaned from the party's *Share Canada's Wealth!* (1957). An ideology, as we argued in Chapter I, has to provide answers to certain enduring questions about the polity if it is to be an adequate guide for its converts in their political activities. It was in this area that the CCF failed most clearly. The following passage is most instructive:

> The CCF presents an alternative to the people of Canada. It offers a programme designed to ensure that every person — regardless of occupation, sex, colour or creed will have full opportunity to share in the nation's progress and to develop his talents in a society free from the exploitation of *man by man or class by class*.[113]

There is no clear answer in this passage to the question of whether individuals are to be competitors or co-operators. The ideal of the Co-operative Commonwealth would seem to imply the latter, as would the suggestion that individuals were to share in the nation's progress. Yet individualism and competition are present in the references to the development of talents and the insistence that prior membership in a group based on occupation (and this would have to be taken generally to include farmers and workers) is deemed harmful. Another question an ideology is supposed to treat — namely, the units of which society is composed — is also skirted. The focus is primarily economic, but the units involved might be individuals ("exploitation of man by man") or groups ("class by class").

There was, however, one clear area of difference between the CCF and the Liberals, and that was the question of the primacy of politics over economics. The Liberals, as we have seen, were content to allow the free play of economic forces in international trade, regardless of the consequences to such things as ownership of Canadian industry. The CCF was alarmed both at this attitude and at its consequences. It asserted that government had to play "a much more active part in the nation's economic life," especially to check the hold of American concerns in the Canadian economy, which threaten "our economic, and even our political independence." This latter problem was, as we shall see, to become a matter of increasing importance to Canadian socialism. For the time being, however, it is of importance only to the extent that it indicates how little the CCF had succeeded in providing Canadians with a real ideological alternative, for the Progressive Conservative platform of 1957, *A New National Policy*, also took the same stand. It, too, talked about the importance of the "nation builders who made Confederation" and worried that the policies of the Liberal Party had exposed "future generations to the possible loss of national independence." John Diefenbaker's liberal conservatism, with its concern for "that equality of opportunity [which] must be assured to our people in every part of Canada" had, for the time being at least, pre-empted the ground that could be occupied by a party in Canada interested in mixing a form of collectivism with liberalism. The crushing defeat the CCF suffered in 1958 was clear proof that the party had outlived its usefulness, and a new party movement arose soon after the defeat to effect a "fundamental political realignment through the creation of a broadly based people's political movement embracing the CCF, the labour movement, farm organizations, professional people, and other liberally minded persons interested in basic social reforms and reconstruction through our parliamentary system of government."[114]

FOUNDING A NEW PARTY

There were a number of advantages to founding a new party, rather than attempting to remould the remnants of the CCF into an acceptable ideological state. In the first place, it appeared that the socialist "touch" in Canada, of which Horowitz spoke (and which we explained in an earlier chapter), did not comprise a sufficient proportion of the population to guarantee the CCF adequate representation in the House of Commons. It therefore lacked the tinge of success that would have convinced voters of the vigour of the alternative it offered. Second, a new party would not be tied, as the CCF had been, by the ideological compromises that had been arrived at in Regina in 1933, which hampered the restatement of Canadian socialism in Winnipeg in 1956. Third, and perhaps most important from the point of view of practical politics, if not from an ideological perspective, was that for the first time a significant number of Canadian trade unions were willing to abandon their traditional Gompersism — the refusal to align with one particular political party — in favour of supporting the new party. The CCF, unlike the British Labour Party, had survived in the absence of this stable trade-union support, which provided for social democratic parties in the United Kingdom and elsewhere both continuing electoral and financial support, especially in the period between elections. The CCF was proud of this financial independence, which it believed gave it the freedom to promote social justice without fear of the consequent wrath of the large corporations; but its relative poverty, at least compared to the Liberals and Progressive Conservatives, left it barely able to perform the task of socialist education, which doctrine dictated was an essential precondition for social and economic transformation. Thus, the CCFers followed the dictates of their ideology to one of its possible conclusions, and put an end to the party itself.

This development was made more likely by the amalgamation in 1956 of the two leading trade-union groups in Canada, the Trades and Labour Congress and the Canadian Congress of Labour, into the Canadian Labour Congress. Before this time the Gompersism of the TLC was too strong. It objected to the support of any one political party, and advocated strongly that the trade-union movement support whomever was deemed most friendly to labour at the time. Yet the merging of these two bodies was not as fortuitous as it might seem. In Britain the Labour Party had been the creation of the trade-union movement. In Canada the politicians in the CCF had taken an active and perhaps leading role in the creation of the Canadian Labour Congress, and had thereby prepared the way for an alliance between the unions and a social democratic political party.

THE BIRTH OF THE NDP

The new party, subsequently christened the New Democratic Party at its founding convention in Ottawa from 31 July to 4 August 1961, was formed by the same groups that had founded the CCF in 1932: farmers, labour, socialists. But in 1961 the second element in the triad loomed far larger than it ever had previously in the history of socialism in Canada. Canada, by comparison with European countries, is not heavily trade unionized and the support of the trade unions for the NDP has never been total. All the same, the influx of large numbers of organized unionists had a major impact on party ideology. "A Job for Everyone" was the first item in the *Federal Programme*[115] adopted by the NDP's founding convention, reflecting, perhaps, Knowles's belief that unions are basically economic units.[116] The program went on to outline a whole range of policies on investment, Canadian ownership, trade, automation; a national health plan, retirement plan, labour standards, and education, "a matter of sound economics"; co-operative federalism, an entrenched bill of rights; and co-operation for peace.

Yet the real ideological difference the unions made was to alter the time perspective of Canadian socialism. Practical people, concerned with this world rather than the next, the unionists in the past had found the millenarian aspects of the CCF unappealing. Their wish was not to educate for socialism, but to agitate for better conditions for their members. Some writers, noting this different attitude in the NDP, would prefer to describe it as a social democratic, rather than a socialist, party. Others prefer to distinguish between socialism as a goal and socialism as a process. The NDP was clearly of the latter stamp. Stanley Knowles set the tone in his *The New Party* (1961). There he argued strongly that socialism did not strive for a fixed and static final goal; rather, it involved continual movement towards dignity, equality, social justice and economic and political freedom.[117] The conversion of the ideal of the Co-operative Commonwealth into an endless process was a vital part of the melding of socialism and trade unionism.

Knowles also succeeded, better than had anyone before him in Canada, in reconciling the liberal and socialist elements in the NDP's official ideology. He achieved this by what superficially appears to be a minor change, but which in reality is one of great significance. Instead of attempting to attain equality, the NDP was to be content with "greater equality." This phrase was satisfactorily vague in that the NDP was not forced to choose whether it meant by that a strict economic equality as the socialists had traditionally preferred, or equality of opportunity, as the liberals in the CCF had favoured. "Greater equality" was consistent with "economic security" and the "opportunity to develop the best that is in him,"[118] as well as with a "society in which human dignity might be the lot of all." Knowles's phrase indicated the importance of the value of equality, both to socialist theory and socialist practice in Canada without raising the issue in such a way as to be needlessly clear.

Clarity was provided by *Social Purpose for Canada,* essays by leading theorists such as George Grant, John Porter and Pierre Trudeau. However, a collection of essays could not be expected to have the same force as the League for Social Reconstruction's 1935 study, since the tendency of the writers was to tackle different problems from an independent point of view. As a consequence, Knowles's *The New Party* is a better statement of the NDP's ideological position than *Social Purpose for Canada* or any of the succeeding books published under the auspices of the University League for Social Reform.

Grant's essay in this volume was, as was usual with his work, a brilliant piece of philosophical writing in its own right. It pinpoints an essential problem that the NDP faced: did it still remain a socialist party? Grant's concern was to show the new party that its proper concern was equality, both material and moral. What Grant spoke of as "the old socialist ethic of egalitarian material prosperity," which the CCF had pursued, was still necessary to solve a number of the quantitative problems that continue to plague Canadian society. But increasingly, Grant argued, these quantitative problems would diminish in importance, and qualitative problems would loom large. The latter could not be solved by a society in which "production is inevitably directed to those things which can be produced privately at a profit at the expense of those goods which cannot be."[119] It was here that socialism was most important, because only socialism offers a "high and more realistic morality" that was "a better alternative to our present capitalist system and ethic."[120] The key to the new socialist vision of Canada would have to continue to be equality, rather than, as Grant showed in his later works, the liberal principle of freedom.

> Equality should be the central principle of society since all persons, whatever their condition, must freely choose to live by what is right or wrong. This act of choosing is the ultimate human act and is open to all. In this sense all persons are equal, and differences of talent are of petty significance.[121]

TOMMY DOUGLAS

There was some evidence that the NDP might chart a course that highlighted this greater moral equality. The party's choice for its first leader was the successful CCF Premier of Saskatchewan, T.C. Douglas, who was persuaded to leave provincial politics to contest the leadership of the new federal party. His chief rival for the leadership, Hazen Argue, indicated his dissatisfaction with the ideological direction of the new party by defecting to the Liberals soon after his defeat by Douglas.[122] A former Baptist minister, Douglas developed his political awareness in much the same way as Woodsworth: he came to the social gospel through a progressive dissatisfaction with the ability of the traditional church to do anything in a real way to alleviate suffering and hardship. To some extent, then, Douglas reintroduced into the party the millenarian aspects that had been progressively squeezed out under the Coldwell-Lewis regime. Yet even under Douglas, the new alliance with the trade movement kept the party from reversing its direction. And if not all trade-union leaders were liberals, there was little doubt that the bulk of the membership, reflecting the social composition of the country as a whole, was at least as sympathetic to individualism and increased liberty as it was to collectivism and equality.

In its first two elections, in 1962 and 1963, the NDP increased its share of the popular vote first to 13 percent and then to 14 percent, winning nineteen and seventeen seats respectively. Although its platforms were as comprehensive as those of its rivals, in its election campaigns the party tended to concentrate on a single major issue fundamental to its concept of social justice. In 1962 the campaign focussed on the issue of "the right to health."

We have seen that equality and collectivism are the key concepts that distinguish Canadian socialism from other ideologies. These two root ideas are reflected in the medical care plan that the NDP presented. It rejected, as the CCF had done many times in the past, anything that looked like a means test, on the grounds that such a requirement was always demeaning for those who had to apply: "Worst of all, it would be humiliating." This was an affirmation, as they saw it, of human dignity. Their plan would, therefore, not be a private one supplemented by government assistance to the needy: "It will be based on two fundamental principles." The first of these was equality: "Services must be available to every citizen when needed, regardless of income." The second was collectivism: "The cost must be spread over society as a whole, each person contributing on the basis of ability to pay."[123]

External events took the issue of the 1963 campaign out of the control of the NDP. The question of nuclear warheads for the Canadian armed forces had brought down the minority Diefenbaker government in the House of Commons, and the central issues revolved around questions of foreign policy and Canadian independence, the latter because of the intervention of senior American military and government personnel in the campaign on behalf of the Liberals. The NDP at the time advocated the rejection of these arms, and spoke strongly in favour of an internationalist approach to foreign policy, a doctrine that implied paying less concern to the sensibilities and interests of the Americans. But on this issue their stance, though more righteous, was not easily distinguished from that of the Conservatives, especially as presented by the Secretary of State for External Affairs, Howard Green. In the event, the voters preferred the continentalist defence policy of the Liberals.

There had, of course, been little time for ideological development between elections. The Liberals had moved more convincingly into the NDP's main campaign issue of the previous year, medicare. However the differences between the two plans are interesting. They indicate limitations on the theory that the NDP, and the CCF before it, function as a pressure group that spurs the Liberals on to enact progressive measures. We have seen that the NDP's plan relied heavily on principles we have identified as fundamental to Canadian socialism. In the same way, the Liberals advanced a medicare plan, but it was one which differed significantly from what the NDP had proposed, and those differences are directly traceable to the two concepts central to liberalism in this country, liberty and individualism. As the Liberals said about their plan: "There will be *no restrictive conditions*. The patient will be *free* to choose his doctor. The doctor will remain *free* to practise as he chooses. There will be no interference with the doctor-patient relationship....The doctor will continue to receive his income on a fee-for-service basis."[124] Comparison of the two schemes indicates that the Liberals could be pressed by NDP pressure to adopt a liberal medicare program, perhaps sooner than they might have otherwise; they could not be manoeuvred into bringing forth a socialist one.

A SOCIALIST CHALLENGE — THE WAFFLE MOVEMENT

The surprise election of 1965 saw the NDP still pressing the same issue. But its rise to 18 percent of the popular vote more likely reflected the dissatisfaction of some liberals with Lester Pearson's decision to call an election on the pretext that he needed a majority government. By 1968, however, things had changed significantly in all the major political parties in Canada. As we have seen, the Liberals and the Conservatives chose new leaders; the NDP was soon to follow in 1971. But for the time being, the party had to content itself with the arrival of a new faction called the Waffle movement. Because the most widely controversial aspect of the Waffle was its violent anti-Americanism, we shall analyze it as well in the next chapter; but it is appropriate to treat it here because it offered a rival conception of socialism.

Ironically, the Waffle movement probably owes its impetus to a task force Lester Pearson's Liberal government set up under the direction of Mel Watkins to investigate foreign ownership in the economy. After Watkins had submitted his committee's report in 1968, he began increasingly to associate with a group in the NDP who came to consider American ownership in the Canadian economy to be the most important barrier to the establishment of a socialist state in Canada. Their choice for an agent to break the power of the foreign corporations was the traditional socialist one, namely the state. Such a state, however, was sure to be a powerful institution, and to make sure that this powerful state was the servant and not the oppressor of the vast majority of the Canadian people, it would have to be a socialist state. The creation of "an independent socialist Canada" was their goal.

Their Marxist approach, and their strident, aggressive confidence in the correctness of their analysis and the appropriateness of their proposed solutions did not win them universal support within the party. Although party leader Tommy Douglas tolerated them, at least to the extent that he was unwilling to confront them in a possibly divisive showdown,[125] David Lewis's attitude was less than charitable. He wrote in his memoirs of the "poisonous antagonisms of internal strife on an organized scale" and of the "fratricidal animosities which deformed relationships and crippled the will to constructive thought and work during the Waffle period." Lewis described the activists in the Waffle as either "unscrupulous" or "egoists who consider their own branch of socialism so superior that the decisions of the majority are the stuff of ridicule...."[126]

In spite of these vigorous attacks on the Waffle, there can be little doubt that its members' desire to forge an ideological alliance between socialism and nationalism in Canada had deep roots. We can recall, to take one example, Woodsworth's appeal for a Canadian style of socialism at the Regina meeting of 1933. Moreover, when tactical circumstances permitted, the Communist Party normally took a determined anti-American line, especially with the development of the Cold War. Even Lewis was generally sympathetic to nationalism. For example, he spoke of the Liberal plan for the Trans-Canada Pipeline as "another, and by no means the last, example of a sickening pattern of continentalist sellouts for which Liberal governments were responsible, usually, but not always, with the support of the Conservatives."[127]

The Waffle only began to make its influence felt as a pressure group within the party at the Winnipeg Conference of 1969, but some of its preoccupations found their way into the platform upon which the party fought the election of the previous year. There it was announced, ignoring the earlier pronouncements of the CCF, that "New Democrats have become convinced that recovering our economic independence is a crucial step in securing our future prosperity. This is not narrow nationalism...."[128] The spirit of 1968 was clearly infectious and the party began to talk consciously again, and with renewed assurance that there was the possibility of ideological conversion in Canada, a "new society in a new world," one in which "excessive privilege and wealth for the few will be replaced by equal opportunities for the many." In spite of the vigour of the 1968 program, the NDP found themselves losing out to Prime Minister Trudeau's promise to establish a Just Society. They should not have been surprised however, because Trudeau's Just Society bore certain striking resemblances to that put forward in the 1968 Regina Programme, especially in regard to promises of greater equality of opportunity. The NDP dropped in 1968 from 18 percent to 17 percent of the popular vote, though its parliamentary representation rose from twenty-one to twenty-two seats.

It was in the aftermath of these events that the Waffle burst onto the scene, and the party experienced considerable difficulty in constraining it. Many of the more electorally experienced members were genuinely concerned that the Marxist rhetoric and anti-Americanism would prove to be as considerable a millstone around the neck of the NDP as the eradication of capitalism phrase had been for the CCF. The party responded with the resolution "For a united and independent Canada," unkindly dubbed the "Marshmallow resolution." In it, the convention accepted the argument that extensive American ownership and control were generally harmful to Canada, but responded in the Lewis tradition, which favoured a mixed economy and the use of the more limited techniques of monetary and fiscal policy to mitigate its influence.[129]

DAVID LEWIS

It was with this background that the NDP met in 1971 to choose Douglas's successor. Douglas had failed to make the electoral breakthrough for which he and the party had hoped in 1968, and he announced after the election that he would step down as party leader. The leadership convention was held in Ottawa in 1971, and it faced a range of choices comparable to that which the Conservatives had met in 1967 and the Liberals in 1968.[130] The leading candidate and heir-apparent was David Lewis, closely identified throughout his life with the trade-union movement, and an influential figure in Canadian socialism for forty years. His chief rival, who secured nearly 40 percent of the vote on the final ballot, was the representative of the Waffle movement, James Laxer, a relative newcomer to NDP politics, but one whose opinions had a strong appeal for the younger members of the party. John Harney, a York University English professor, was also a strong candidate, whose main appeal lay in the belief that he would have strong support in Quebec. He, in fact, became leader of the Quebec NDP in the late 1980s. Ed Broadbent, an early supporter of the Waffle, had severed his links with it in an attempt to create a position for himself at the party's centre between Lewis and Laxer; Broadbent's hope to secure the votes of both welfare liberals and socialists was a failure. The last candidate in terms of delegate support was the British Columbia member, Frank Howard, who exemplified the party's traditional compassion and concern for human dignity.

The surprising strength of Laxer as the Waffle candidate was a clear indication that the fragile doctrinal unity the party had always cherished was in danger of breaking down. The more doctrinaire socialists in the party — or, to put it less contentiously, those who believed more in socialism as a goal than as a process — had normally been discontented with the compromises the party had customarily made with the aim in mind of attracting large segments of the liberal centre. These socialists were under no delusion concerning the difficulty of effecting ideological conversions. They were aware that the process we described in Chapter I involved enormous expenditures of time and effort on what they chose to call educational activity; but they argued, as the CCF had argued in the 1930s, that only such an ideological conversion, and only a party elected by a majority of the citizenry, which had previously been persuaded of the correctness of their positions, could succeed in achieving a socialist society. On this ground they were in clear conflict with the more pragmatically inclined trade unionists, who represented, for the time being anyway, a substantial portion of the NDP's electoral strength and a growing portion of its finances.

This is not the place to deal in detail with the events that led to the final destruction of the Waffle within the NDP in 1972. The new leader was concerned that he could not fight an election campaign with the party in ideological disarray, especially in view of the tendency of the leaders of the Waffle to make ideological pronouncements at considerable variance with the party's established position. Lewis decided on the dangerous tactic of suppressing it as a separate movement within the party, and the task was effectively handled by his son Stephen. Some of the Waffle left the NDP to form the Movement for an Independent Socialist Canada under Laxer's leadership, but their party received a derisory 2500 votes in the 1974 election.

When the 1972 election was called, Lewis was firmly in control of the party. He stated his own general approach in *The Good Fight*:

> In my view, the essential aim of democratic socialism is not a certain economic or social structure. Although that structure may be necessary for its achievement, the aim is to enrich the life and free the creative spirits of those who have only their labour, skills, and talents to contribute to society and without whom little could be produced to meet human needs, even in this age of technological wizardry. The achievement of this goal requires change in economic and social relationships that will give workers the power to make, or at least to affect, decisions which shape their lives. At bottom these objectives involve a struggle for power with those groups and institutions which own and control or manage the capital resources of society. And the trade unions, even the conservative ones, are daily participants in this struggle, on the same side as the democratic socialist. Organized labour is, therefore, the natural ally of a social democratic party, whether one defines the contest in terms of a class struggle or in any other terms.[131]

In the campaign itself, however, Lewis chose to reunite the party by concentrating on an enemy agreed on by welfare liberals, social democrats, and socialists, namely the "corporate welfare bums," the corporations, many of which were foreign-owned or -controlled, that received grants and subsidies from the federal government.

This appeared to be a good issue to heal the divisions within the party, but Lewis also had reason to hope that it would have a wider appeal to the country as a whole. An attack on foreign-owned corporations was sure to be received sympathetically by those who had supported and sympathized with the Waffle. After all, the Waffle manifesto had complained: "Canadian development is distorted by a corporate capitalist economy. Corporate investment creates and fosters superfluous individual consumption at the expense of social needs."[132] The Waffle might support this attack for both socialist and nationalist reasons. Nonetheless, the issue was perfect because it did not involve Lewis in a compromise with them. By concentrating on the corporations, he was choosing an issue that would not take him too far away from the mainstream of his party's preoccupations, nor was he likely to alienate the support of the trade-union leaders. Lewis justified his stance by attacking the privileges that business had acquired: "[G]ross inequities have continued to exist in our social and economic structure. We have laboured to make Canadians aware of these inequities."[133]

Of perhaps even greater interest than the substance of Lewis's tilting against the corporations was an admission he made near the end of his book concerning the difficulties of ideological change in Canada. The Waffle had urged the NDP to strive above all for an ideological victory: "The development of socialist consciousness, on which can be built a socialist base, must be the first priority of the New Democratic Party."[134] Lewis, conscious of the problems that democratic socialism has always faced in Canada — that ideological conversions take place only slowly, and only when the people can be persuaded that their previous understanding is no longer adequate — put the problem shrewdly and eloquently:

> Every day of our lives we arrive at a crossroad. Every day we make decisions that will affect the course of our lives to a greater or lesser degree. To choose the right road, we must first know where we want to go. We must identify our destination. Otherwise, we stand paralyzed at the crossroad, without progress in any direction.
>
> No decision of any moment is simple or without conflict. But no achievement of any merit was ever accomplished by shirking decision, by apathy, by timidity or lack of commitment to desired goals. Canadians must confront themselves with the evidence. They must weigh it carefully, because justice is not blind. Justice comes only to those who work for it, demand it, shout for it and proclaim its worth above other considerations.[135]

This passage, almost more than any other, points out the difficulties inherent in the task of converting a basically liberal country such as Canada to socialism. Although there are in this land socialist and tory touches, as Horowitz's argument outlined in Chapter II shows us, we are left with the conclusion that our argument in Chapter I is basically correct, and that the political parties in Canada, different though they are in their ideologies, are fundamentally limited, in the short run in any event, by the social, economic and political beliefs already in the country. Lewis's vigorous campaign brought the party thirty-one seats, its highest total to date, but its percentage of the popular vote rose to only 18 percent, the same level as the party had achieved under Douglas in 1965.

The overall election results transformed this success into a dilemma. Nationally, Pierre Trudeau's Liberals suffered a serious electoral setback, ending up with only two seats more than Robert Stanfield's Conservatives. The NDP held the balance of power in parliament, but the party was faced with danger as well as opportunity. We have touched earlier on Avakumovic's hypothesis that a substantial proportion of NDP support is not motivated by an acceptance of socialism, but looks to the party as an agent of general discontent. Seen from the perspective of these supporters, if the NDP kept the Liberals in power it would lay the party open to a charge which the Conservatives sometimes put forward with effect, namely that a vote for the NDP is indirectly a vote for the Liberals. However, the leadership also had to take into account their own principles and those of their ideologically committed supporters.

There is little doubt that most of the NDP caucus would have found Robert Stanfield an acceptable prime minister. Stanfield, as we showed in the last chapter, accepted the democratic tory tradition of his party, and his social compassion and his essential moderation were all qualities with which the NDP could live. On balance he was almost certainly preferable to Pierre Trudeau. However, as we have also pointed out, the Conservative Party is an ideological coalition, and not only did Stanfield necessarily have to compromise with his powerful business liberal wing, but on certain key matters of policy, he might have been dominated by them.

Weighing these considerations, the New Democrats decided to sustain the Liberals in office, hoping that they could extract a sufficient number of policy concessions to satisfy both groups of their supporters. In policy terms, they had limited, though real, success. The Foreign Investment Review Agency (FIRA), an institution which for a time was to prove much more effective in moderating the Americanization of Canadian business than its originators had expected, satisfied the nationalistic urges which, as we have seen, were running strong in the NDP at this time. In addition, the previous Liberal government had created the Canada Development Corporation (CDC) in 1971, a measure congenial to the NDP's mixed-economy approach, since it appeared to give government the opportunity to extend its influence in various sensitive areas of the economy without requiring widespread nationalization. Finally, this initiative was later extended with the creation of Petro-Canada, which allowed the government to expand its influence further into the oil and natural gas industry, one almost exclusively controlled at the time by multi-nationals. Petro-Canada was to be of critical importance during the 1979 minority Clark administration and the 1980 election campaign.

By 1974, the New Democrats had extracted as many concessions as they thought likely from the Trudeau government, and the Liberals, confident that they had regained some of the popularity lost in 1972, were not anxious to make additional compromises. The minority Liberal government fell on a vote on Finance Minister John Turner's budget, but the election itself was a disappointment for everyone except the Liberals, who were returned with a majority. To some extent the New Democrats were a victim of their own success. By pushing through the measures mentioned above, they defused nationalist sentiment temporarily, and the issue that became the central one on the 1974 campaign, wage and price controls, left them uncomfortably between the Liberals and the Conservatives. In principle, they could support the policy, though they had genuine fears that wages rather than prices were likely to be the more strictly regulated. In the election they dropped to 15 percent of the popular vote and sixteen seats, and as in 1968 when Tommy Douglas lost his own seat, in 1974 David Lewis went down to personal defeat. Like Douglas, Lewis announced that he would step down from the leadership, and a convention was held in 1975.

The departure of Lewis meant that the intimate personal connection between the CCF and the NDP was finally severed. Douglas and Lewis had both been deeply involved in the CCF continuously from the 1930s, but henceforth the leadership of the party would be in the hands of those whose political consciousness had been formed not by the conditions and disputes of the 1920s and 1930s, but by post-World War II circumstances. The revolt of the Waffle against the party leadership had been in part a generational conflict within the Canadian socialist movement. Although Canadian socialists had opposed virtually unanimously the Vietnam war and indirect Canadian involvement in support of the Americans, the Waffle movement appealed to and was influenced by the New Left, whose strength culminated in the widespread student disturbances of 1968.[136]

We have seen that David Lewis strongly affirmed the traditional socialist position that an alliance between a socialist party and the trade-union movement was an indispensable condition for either electoral success or conversion through the process of socialist education. The failure of the CCF to make any significant national electoral breakthrough was generally attributed in CCF circles to the party's failure to win the enduring support it felt it deserved from Canadian trade unionists. Various explanations ranging from capitalist manipulation of the media, the control of the American headquarters over the Canadian locals of the international unions, and the machinations of Communist activists in key unions were offered to account for this hiatus between the trade-union movement and the chief electoral arm of Canadian socialism.

Many younger socialists were not convinced that the alliance with labour was necessarily correct strategy. The party's finances and organization were more soundly based than ever before, but the elections of 1968 and 1974 had been a considerable cause to doubt the radicalness of Canadian trade unionists. Although the newly powerful public-sector unions were proving more aggressive and politically conscious than their industrial counterparts, the Canadian union movement still seemed a rather staid affair. The New Left movement had identified other groups in society who appeared more likely to be the cutting edge of radical social and socialist reform. In the United States, Blacks had led the way, but Amerindians, young people, and women all had their advocates as major oppressed groups in society whose social conditions might be significantly enhanced by major social, economic and political changes. In Canada, the growing strength of the separatist movement in the province of Quebec marked French Canadians as another important social group whose frustrated aspirations might spill over into support for a more far-reaching social reorganization.

ED BROADBENT

In the 1975 leadership convention, these various strains were all represented. Douglas Campbell, the most radical of the candidates, was not a serious option for the convention in spite of his previous three attempts at the Ontario leadership and his prior attempt at the national leadership. Campbell represented the Marxist strand of Canadian socialism which, as we have seen, has never had a strong hold over the leadership of the NDP. He argued that Cuba, Portugal and Vietnam were teaching us "how to stand up to the last bastion of decaying capitalism — the U.S.A. and its colonies — Canada, Britain etc." and called for Canadians to "unite with our progressive sisters and brothers of this planet and break the chains of capitalism. We have nothing to lose but our chains."[137] John Harney's address was also in a crisply socialist vein; he spoke of creating a society that "strives toward the virtual equality of all its citizens in all the essential conditions of life" and told the convention that it was the responsibility of the leader "to convince the nation that it needs and wants a socialist party for government."[138] Although Harney wanted "to struggle toward an independent, socialist Canada," words that echoed the Waffle movement's desire in the previous leadership convention, he was not willing to rely solely on the trade-union movement, and argued instead for "the freely chosen solidarity of all its peoples, the English-speaking and the French-speaking, the naturalized Canadian and the native peoples." Lorne Nystrom, a young but experienced parliamentarian from Saskatchewan, represented the prairie strain in Canadian socialism, one which had for most of the history of the CCF/NDP provided the bulk of its seats, though not by any means as high a proportion of its national popular vote. However, the main opposition to the recognized front runner, Ed Broadbent, came from Rosemary Brown, a black member of the British Columbia legislature. Indeed it was only on the fourth ballot that Broadbent succeeded in defeating her, though even here she showed surprising strength, winning over 40 percent of the vote on the final ballot.

Avakumovic attributes part of Brown's appeal to the fact that 1975 was International Women's Year;[139] however, it is more likely that the delegates were attracted both by her aggressive attempt to restate certain of the fundamental elements of Canadian socialism, as well as by the sentiment that the traditional approach of Douglas and Lewis, which Broadbent seemed likely to continue, had not been a notable success. Brown spoke in favour of the Canadianization of the oil and natural gas industries, and lashed out against Canada's role as both client of and participant in American imperialism. She also advocated Canadian withdrawal from NORAD and NATO, and urged Canadians to join "with other people who are struggling, like ourselves, for independence and social justice."[140]

Although Brown identified several social groups, such as tenants and children, who, she suggested, suffered considerable hardship from the continuation of capitalism, she singled out women as a leading group in the establishment of socialism in Canada. "I believe that even though the concept of feminism may be radical, and even threatening at first to those who have not fully understood them [sic], there is an integral connection between feminism and socialism. Until women take their place alongside their men, the achievement of a socialist society is impossible."[141] In general, she proposed that Canadian socialists come to power by forging an alliance between the poor, the workers, the farmers, her "socialist comrades in Quebec," native Indians and women, and she finished her appeal to the convention by giving it a solemn pledge:

> That I will never forget that our party has its roots in the prairie soil, where it grew in spite of dust and depression, fed by sweat and tears and the passionate hatred of injustice; that I will never forget that we are the party of the working people, and that our task and our duty is to bring them legal and moral justice in the face of attacks from power and privilege; that I will be unbending in my stand against every form of oppression which deforms and crushes people and prevents them from the fulfillment of their lives; and that as leader of our New Democratic Party, I will be answerable to the members of this party as we go forward to become the government that will build a truly socialist, truly humane society — here in Canada.[142]

While Rosemary Brown represented the radical strand within the NDP and was supported by both those who agreed with her ideological position and those who were generally out of sympathy with the party establishment, Ed Broadbent clearly identified himself with the dominant mainstream of the party. "Under the leadership of J.S. Woodsworth, M.J. Coldwell, Tommy Douglas, David Lewis, we have in forty years succeeded in quite literally revolutionizing social legislation in Canada. It is a proud record."[143] In a way that would appeal to welfare liberals as well as to traditional social democrats. Broadbent identified what he described as "the socialist challenge" or "what I have called the economic question," and he urged: "Corporate power must be broken. This is the socialist issue of our time."[144] Although he concluded his address with an appeal to "build a nation with a sense of compassion, a sense of community and above all a sense of equality,"[145] he continued to reassure the welfare liberals and the trade unionists that their ideological concerns would not be overlooked in a party under his leadership. At the end of his address, he spoke of "democratic socialist objectives," and he emphasized the pragmatic, rather than utopian, nature of his objectives. "We will be on our way to political power in Ottawa, and we will be able to measure electoral victory in years, not decades."[146]

Unlike Rosemary Brown, who had argued that the NDP should take a radical stance and build a new coalition out of groups she identified as oppressed within Canadian society, Broadbent aimed at more moderate objectives, offering a party that would continue to be an alliance between socialists and welfare liberals. The record of the New Democratic Party under Broadbent's leadership shows ambiguous results from this strategy. Although Broadbent himself rated very high in popularity polls for most of his leadership and ran substantially ahead of his party, and indeed, often ahead of the leaders of the Liberals and Conservatives, the radical image of the socialists within the party continues to frighten many Canadian voters.

The election of Broadbent assured the continuation of the NDP in the path that it had trod since Regina. We should not forget, however, that although the NDP is the incarnation of electorally successful socialism in Canada, it is not now the only socialist presence, just as the CCF was not the only Canadian socialist party in the 1930s.

The Moscow-oriented Communist Party of Canada and its more radical counterpart, the Communist Party of Canada (Marxist-Leninist), have fielded a substantial number of candidates in federal general elections, although they secured a tiny portion of the total vote. The Communist Party has never been a major electoral force in Canada, though it did succeed in electing a member under the Labor-Progressive Party banner; however, that member later proved to be a ringleader in the Russian spy network in Canada that was uncovered by the Gouzenko disclosures of 1946. In spite of systematic electoral failure, Canadian communists and their sympathizers have had a slight but real influence on the CCF/NDP and a more direct and immediate impact through the trade unions.[147] We have seen that David Lewis fought strenuously against both aspects of communist influence in Canada, and he, more than any other single Canadian, is probably responsible for the extremely limited impact that Canadian communists have had on domestic socialism.

THE INFLUENCE OF MARXISM

Although Marxism in its communist variant had had little impact since the founding of the Communist party in 1921-22, it has had slightly more appeal among academics. However, in no sense are we suggesting that these Marxists and neo-Marxist university professors have any sympathy for the Communist party. First, in the 1930s, Marxist ideas were generally popular amongst intellectuals in Europe, the United States and in this country. In the circumstances of the Great Depression, some academics, looking for an explanation of the crisis that capitalism was experiencing, found the Marxist analysis persuasive. The League for

Social Reconstruction, in the words of its historian, "was not ignorant of the works of Karl Marx"[148] though as he points out, "most of its members were not well acquainted with it and they saw no need to improve the acquaintance." The index to their major work, *Social Planning for Canada,* has three references to Lenin, one to Engels, but none to Marx. Nonetheless, it is generally fair to describe the overall approach of the work as vaguely Marxist. However, in Canada as in most of the Western world, the appeal of Marxism waned during the Second World War, and fell further with the upsurge in the economy and with the extension of Russian influence into Eastern Europe after the War.

It is difficult to say exactly what led to a revival of interest in Marx in the late 1960s and early 1970s among Canadian academics, particularly economists, sociologists, political scientists and some historians. Marxism itself on a world-wide scale showed some creativity at this time with the members of the Frankfurt School and Herbert Marcuse, guru of the New Left in the United States, as leading thinkers. In addition, there was the fact that the unpopular war in Vietnam was being fought against a regime that was formally Marxist. Finally, there was the survival of the political economy tradition in Canada. Its centre had been the University of Toronto, the institution that provided such a large number of the new university professors to the expanding universities of the 1960s. Toronto's Political Economy Department before that time had been an amalgam of economists, political scientists, geographers, sociologists, anthropologists and commerce professors, presided over from the mid-1930s until 1952 by a thinker whose interests were as synoptic as the department, Harold Innis. Innis had fought a lifelong battle against neo-classical economics and against the increasing mathematization of economics as a discipline, and had produced works that attempted to integrate findings from a vast range of social sciences and other studies, scientific and humane, into a general understanding of Canadian problems.

The younger generation of the sixties admired Innis but rejected both his liberalism and his hostility to nationalism. Instead, many were strongly influenced by C.B. Macpherson, at the time of Innis' death a relatively junior colleague, but by the 1960s an established scholar of international stature. Macpherson's restrained and liberal interpretation of Marxism had a considerable influence both through his writings and through his graduate seminars. The late 1960s and the 1970s saw the production of a number of books written or edited by academics such as Kari Levitt, Mel Watkins, R.M. Laxer, G. Teeple, Ian Lumsden, Stanley Ryerson and Daniel Drache that combined a neo-Marxist analysis with Canadian nationalism.[149] Since much of their driving force was their nationalism, their contribution will also be discussed in the next chapter. Suffice it to note here that except for Levitt and Watkins, their writings are little known outside the academic community, and their influence on the development of the mainstream of Canadian socialism, the NDP, has been slight.

SOCIALISM IN QUEBEC

Marxism, however, has had more effect in the Province of Quebec, both with French-Canadian intellectuals and on the development of Quebec socialism. In Chapter III, we discussed the development of liberalism in Canada and suggested that it had made slow progress in Quebec because it was seen by many Quebecers as an alien doctrine, associated with the British conquest of Canada and with Protestantism. Laurier's great triumph had been to reconcile French Canadians to at least a toleration of liberalism, but it remained a minor factor in Quebec provincial politics until the victory of Jean Lesage in 1960. The history of socialism in Quebec is an extremely complex topic, and without much more in the way of detailed studies, it would be imprudent to venture anything more than a few general comments about its development.

The first thing to be noticed about socialism in Quebec is that the CCF and the NDP have never been major political forces in that province. Much of this is explained by the fact that Quebec saw the CCF as an English-Canadian and Protestant phenomenon. As David Lewis explains, "[T]he CCF, born in the west and led by English speakers who knew no French, came into Quebec from outside, greeted enthusiastically by a few English-speaking people in Montreal, but unnoticed or stared at as a foreign plant by the French-speaking community. The prospects were bleak from the start."[150]

Lewis went on to note that they "were made even more bleak by the intervention of the church." In Gregory Baum's words, this took the form of a joint pastoral letter in May 1933 in which the bishops of Quebec "condemned every form of socialism and defended the capitalist system."[151] As Baum argues, the influence of the Catholic hierarchy was decisive in characterizing the CCF as an illicit political option for many Quebecers, despite the fact that other hierarchies, such as the British, took a more tolerant view of peaceful, parliamentary socialism. These two factors, combined with others such as the preference of the CCF for a strong central government in Canada, combined to arrest the party's growth from the outset.

The anti-socialist forces in Quebec also had the advantage of a skilled and ruthless leader in the form of Union Nationale Premier Maurice Duplessis. Having been successful in harnessing the forces of Quebec nationalism for his own political purposes, he played an active role in suppressing most radical forms of dissent both within society and within the universities. Although trade unionists like Jean Marchand, journalists like Gerard Pelletier and academics like Trudeau allied to fight against his regime, they generally made little headway against Duplessis's genuine political popularity, combined as it was with ruthless and unscrupulous political tactics. The death of Duplessis in 1959 unleashed the swelling tide of liberalism in Quebec; and, as we argued in Chapter II, the tardy but powerful presence of liberalism in that province, faced with the declining power of the feudaltory strain that had prevailed from the Conquest to 1960, contained the seeds to generate an indigenous style of socialism. At first, it was not clear what direction socialism would take. Lesage's electoral victory occurred at a time when the influence of the church was in dramatic decline, and the Quebec provincial regimes of the 1960s took the opportunity of secularizing educational and welfare services that had hitherto been in the hands of the church. As in English Canada before the Winnipeg General Strike, the first thrust of the socialist movement in Quebec was revolutionary and Marxist. The most celebrated radicals of the 1960s were the FLQ theorists Pierre Valliéres and Charles Gagnon, who combined Quebec nationalism with a fairly heterogeneous collection of radical notions such as syndicalism, anarchism and a belief in technocracy.

The FLQ cells that kidnapped British trade commissioner James Cross and Quebec cabinet minister Pierre LaPorte hoped that their terrorist acts would either break the nerve of the Quebec government, or provoke massive repression on the part of the federal government. In the latter event, they expected to be able to mobilize popular opinion in Quebec by arguing that the actions of the federal government revealed its true nature as oppressor of Quebec and they hoped, at the least, that the general situation would be one highly conducive to revolution. To their great surprise, although the federal government acted repressively, its invocation of the *War Measures Act* and use of troops to maintain public order in Quebec not only failed to generate revolutionary sentiments, but was generally popular. In the light of this, thinkers like Valliéres rejected the revolutionary path to an independent socialist Quebec and chose to work through democratic and electoral means.

The vehicle that became the agent of Quebec nationalism and the focus of democratic socialism was the Parti Québécois, led by former Quebec Liberal cabinet minister René Lévesque, and formed of an alliance between Lévesque's *Mouvement Souveraineté-Association,* the socialist *Rassemblement pour l'Indépendence National* (RIN), and the more conservative *Railliement National* (RN). From its outset, the PQ revealed itself to be, as well as a nationalist party, a social democratic one. At its creation in 1968, Lévesque's "opening address was less a call for independence than a cry for a new society, a form of participatory democracy that would lead to a revolt against all outdated and rigid social, economic, and political structures."[152] In the subsequent elections of 1970 and 1973, it continued to put its commitment to social democracy in the forefront, claiming at least equal place for its call for social reform with its desire to achieve some form of independent status for the province of Quebec. When it achieved its victory in the 1976 election, its platform "described by Lévesque as social democratic, remained the same on social and economic policy as in 1973."[153] Although there

were, in Saywell's words, "many ultra-socialists in the party," Lévesque was successful in projecting a moderate social democratic image for the party.[154] Most
commentators outside Quebec are in agreement that the PQ's moderate socialism,
perhaps even more than its nationalism, combined with the unpopularity of
Bourassa's Liberals, was the main factor in the 1976 election results. At least in
the short term, the success of the PQ convinced all but the most radical of Quebec
socialists that the parliamentary route was the one to follow.

However, the success of one socialist party does not necessarily translate into
good news for another. As Avakumovic puts it: "the Parti Québécois (PQ)'s rise
and successes reduced whatever prospects the NDP had in that province."[155] The
success of the PQ put the leadership of the NDP in an awkward position. Although
many of the members of the Waffle had shown themselves actively in favour of,
or at least prepared to acquiesce in Quebec independence, the formal position of
the NDP leadership and the vast majority of NDP supporters has been to retain
Quebec within the Canadian federal framework. The NDP is thus torn between
sympathy for the PQ's social programs and distaste for its avowed goal of separation. Consequently, those Péquiste supporters who are attached to its nationalism
often see little reason to support any federal political party, let alone one that does
not share an aspiration they deeply feel.

The failure to make gains in Quebec not only lessens the chance that the NDP
can form a national government, but also considerably detracts from its claims to
be a national political party. The federal election that had been widely expected in
1978 was postponed until 1979 because the Liberals were aware of their widespread unpopularity outside Quebec. When the election was finally called, Ed
Broadbent's New Democrats were facing a new Conservative leader, but one who
had failed to convince many Canadians that he was suited for the job of Prime
Minister. The NDP entered the 1979 election campaign with considerable enthusiasm, hopeful that with their popular leader they would finally make substantial
electoral gains. Indeed, although they realistically expected only to hold the balance of power as they had done in 1972, they anticipated that this time around they
would have a substantially increased number of MPs.

COULD BROADBENT MAKE A BREAKTHROUGH?

It was in 1979 that the coalition between the NDP and the Canadian Labour Congress came to its fullest fruition to date. The CLC ran a parallel advertising campaign using the slogan "The Perfect Union: Me and the NDP," with the particular
intention of persuading union members and union households to support the NDP.
It was not a particularly successful campaign in these terms.[156] Overall, the NDP
received only 18 percent of the popular vote, its 1974 total, and less than 25 percent of union members voted NDP.

These results were bound to prove a disappointment for Broadbent. His strategy had been based on two considerations. First, with the obvious Liberal weakness in western Canada, it looked as if the Canadian Liberal Party might be ready to be squeezed out of the centre of Canadian politics as the British Liberal Party had been some sixty years earlier. The Liberals were going into the 1979 election in a weakened state, with a leader whose popular appeal seemed at its nadir.

Second, Broadbent appeared convinced that the time had come to reorient the NDP's general strategy and image, changing it from a party that was the agent of general protest and dissatisfaction to one that looked more like an alternative government. As Sandra Gwyn explained in *Saturday Night*:

> The gamble he's been taking these past three years is that the NDP can slowly and painfully be transformed from the idealistic, evangelist movement it's been for nearly half a century into a tough-minded party seeking and understanding power. Which means hammering away, Johnny One Note Fashion, about unemployment and inflation to the point, if need be, of stupefaction. We've got to get it across that the social democratic philosophy doesn't simply mean more handouts. That what it means, ultimately, is a redistribution of economic power relationships. We've got to do a hell of a lot more than simply adopt the rhetoric of economic planning. We've got to develop industrial strategies that will show, in concrete terms, how a modern industrialized economy can be made to work.[157]

Or as Bob Rae, then an NDP federal member and subsequently leader of the Ontario NDP, put it: "[W]e will become a majority party only when we change ourselves and our self-image, only when we recognize that the voters of Canada are expressing their interests as they see them and are not necessarily suffering from massive false consciousness."[158]

These considerations governed the NDP's election campaigns in both 1979 and 1980. In both instances, Broadbent and the party strategists were convinced that the party could make substantial headway by addressing itself to the problems associated with the economy, inflation, unemployment, high interest rates, and in general the economic strategy of the two major parties.

This approach has survived the mitigated failure of the 1980 election results in which, although the Liberals were returned with another majority government, the NDP increased slightly their number of MPs. Speaking in St. John's in January 1982, Broadbent told his audience: "We don't need a government that blames the poor and the unemployed for unemployment; who punish workers for fighting inflation and cut taxes for the rich so they can profit from it. Let the Liberals and Tories take their stand with the banks; we'll stand with you."[159] As he put it to the OFL Political Education Conference, "[f]or trade unionists and social democrats, this is a time when there are sharp differences between us and North America's corporate elite and their political friends.[160] Similarly, the NDP's position paper on Mega-projects, which Broadbent released on May 5, 1982, continued on the same theme: "The NDP believes that only through strong government presence can we give direction to resource development and provide guarantees to maximize Canadian benefits. This, coupled with a plan to restore our manufacturing sector, will enable us to reindustrialize the Canadian economy."[161] Gone from most of Broadbent's speeches was the heady radical rhetoric, and missing as well, except for addresses to some trade union and party gatherings, was much emphasis on socialism or social democracy.

Broadbent's strategy for securing the political centre in Canada by emphasizing the welfare liberal elements in his party's tradition was, in its early stages, neither a signal success nor a spectacular failure. He concentrated on policy matters, which were also of concern to socialists, and kept his coalition together by steering clear from too detailed discussions of matters of principle. Nonetheless, there continued to be critics within the party. *Canadian Dimension* was especially caustic about the 1979 Convention, which it claimed "was planned to help the party move toward the Liberal centre."[162] According to Jim Turk, the Left Caucus decided to fight "the Federal Council's 'liberal' industrial strategy in favour of a more socialist approach,"[163] and division prevailed throughout the convention. "Of the six issues on which the Left fought, it won three and lost three."[164] In spite of this determined opposition, Broadbent's strategy prevailed:

> Bruised, but with his programme largely intact, Broadbent closed the Convention by trying to make the best of the situation he had found so distasteful. "I am very glad that this debate took place. I have friends on both sides of the debate....It brought joy to my heart."[165]

There can be little doubt that he experienced minimal joy over the divisions within his party on the question of patriating the constitution and entrenching a new charter of rights and freedoms, which Prime Minister Trudeau made the major political issue of 1981. Broadbent himself, in a debate on national unity in 1979, had indicated that he considered the crux of the problem economic, and spoke of the need to chart "a course in which Canadians would gain economic control of our country."[166]

Several of his colleagues in the House of Commons were not as convinced as Broadbent of the correctness of supporting the Liberal government's constitutional proposals. They saw the chance for pursuing the alternative strategy, which we have mentioned above in connection with Rosemary Brown, that of attempting to put together a new radical coalition. Hence, they would in future rely less on the trade union movement and on workers and emphasize the potentially radical nature of other groups within society. As Pauline Jewett explained in the House:

> This order consists of groupings of individuals, economic groupings, cultural groupings based on ethnicity, religion or sex. These are powerful, dynamic and democratic groupings of people whose points of view we, as legislators and parliamentarians, ignore at our peril.[167]

For Jewett, the most serious defect in the charter was that it did not protect women's rights to equality, and in her view, this deficiency was "so enormous that no women in the country, or indeed any other group which had not hitherto been equal, could feel equality was being guaranteed."[168] Svend Robinson was perhaps the most radical of the NDP MPs in his criticism of the inadequacies of the proposed charter. He was not at all concerned with the drive for middle-of-the-road respectability that some said motivated Broadbent. As Robinson saw the moral responsibility of the NDP, it was the party's task to stand for those who were oppressed regardless of whether their cause was a popular one.

> In fact, had the charter of rights been entrenched, in many ways Canadians would have been worse off. There was no protection in that charter for the handicapped; there was no recognition of the rights of equality for women; there were no provisions for remedies in that proposed charter of rights. *The War Measures Act* could have been enacted tomorrow under this charter of rights in exactly the same terms. Above all, there was nothing in that charter of rights to recognize the rights of the aboriginal peoples of the country.[169]

In the face of continued pressure such as this, especially from his colleagues from Western Canada, Broadbent eventually compromised with his caucus and formally adopted many of their concerns. As he said in the House in November 1981, "Finally, in recent years our party has become aware, at long last, of the moral claims of Canadian women and the native people of our land."[170] And he went on to integrate these concerns into a more general statement of the NDP's overall position: "[W]e said, along with others, that now is the time to act and create a fully independent Canada within a political framework that would make possible the creation of a society that is at once just and exciting, a society that is at the same time peaceful and human."[171]

The divisions within the party have not been settled, and we can confidently expect that they will arise again in the future. As we have seen, ever since the creation of the CCF in 1932, the mainstream of the Canadian socialist movement in Canada has been a coalition of several diverse elements. Before that time, the rival socialist parties and factions were separate and often warred both with each other and, even more seriously, internally. The NDP inherited this legacy of internal divisions and strong differences of opinion continue as to the correct strategy for an electorally committed social democratic party in Canada.

The debate on the *Charter of Rights and Freedoms* brought some of these concerns to the surface. As Broadbent admitted to the NDP's eleventh biennial convention in 1981: "There have been other judgments within the Party on this issue. The differences have been keenly felt and the differing opinions honestly held."[172] Yet the Broadbent/Rae strategy remains uppermost in the party's approach to the 1980s. Putting the matter somewhat disingenuously, Broadbent claimed that "there is no disagreement among New Democrats about what this nation's leading priorities are," and then went on, for most of his remaining speech, to address himself to jobs, interest rates, housing, the oil companies, and the tax system. Only at the end did he turn to women's rights, native peoples and the environment.

THE NEW REGINA MANIFESTO

Although both the other parties sought to improve their electoral fortunes by changing their leaders, the New Democratic Party settled for a new statement of principle. The twelfth Federal NDP Convention took place in 1983, fifty years after the meeting that had approved the CCF's most famous document, and in commemoration of that event, the NDP also held their meeting in Regina. It is almost certainly true that some who initially approved the drafting of a new manifesto started to have very serious reservations as the discussions surrounding the preliminary version progressed. As we saw earlier, under Broadbent's leadership the NDP made a determined effort to establish itself as the welfare liberal alternative to the Conservatives, in the hope that Trudeau's departure would open up the possibility of a significant realignment in Canadian politics. Consequently Broadbent systematically minimized the prominence of both socialism and radical rhetoric in his public appeals. Yet the NDP, as we have seen, contains a coalition of welfare liberals, social democrats and socialists, as well as a significant number of individuals who are more concerned with single issues such as the environment, nuclear disarmament and women's issues than they are with broader questions of public policy.

For Broadbent, then, many of the aspects of the Preliminary Draft must have been unnerving, since the document was written in language sufficiently radical to frighten the majority of Canadians. It spoke of the welfare state's "concessions won from a free enterprise capitalist economy,"[173] and argued that the current economic crisis "may prove to be even deeper than that of the 1930s."[174] Economies were becoming increasingly dependent upon trans-national corporations, and rapid technological change meant that "the skills of workers are being fed into the memory banks of machines."[175] All these developments were dangerous because "managed by the corporate elite, technological change will serve only to extend the power of the powerful and the wealth of the wealthy."[176]

The draft, then, went on to specify the party's objectives as peace, "equality, not just in the legal sense, but equality in the fullness of human experience," a broadened and extended democracy, a commitment to civil liberties "combined with a social order in which wealth and power are justly shared," the replacement of "private gain and competition as the guiding principle of social and economic life with the spirit of the co-operative commonwealth," and finally it recognized "an obligation to preserve the natural environment and to pass on to future generations a better world, not an ecological debt."

Clearly these goals, taken together, constituted a more radical program than Broadbent had been offering to the electorate, and some policies, such as the progressive extension of "democratic control over the major means of production and distribution" were far more than a party attempting to attract moderate welfare liberals could safely offer. The official statement of principles that was adopted in Regina was much more restrained, at the price of being less incisive and somewhat vague. Thus the official version intoned that "as peace must prevail over war, so must cooperation and mutual responsibility prevail over private gain and competition as the guiding principles of social and economic life. We seek a compassionate and caring society, serving the needs of all."[177]

Although the Statement acknowledged that a society based on equality was the major aim of democratic socialism, it quickly affirmed as well that democracy and freedom "are at the very heart of democratic socialism." And for those who might have been worried by the Preliminary Draft's dangerous talk about increasing social ownership, the statement affirmed "the preservation of the family farm, other family enterprises and small businesses" as NDP policy.[178]

In the section on means, the statement was also a moderate document. It declared again the belief in democracy and the desire to extend it, without becoming needlessly explicit. Next, and more significantly, it affirmed the importance of planning, but it did not demand nationalization as a major element in the extension of social control. The Preliminary Draft had spoken, following the lead of the French socialist government, of selective nationalization in the financial sector.[179] However the Statement was more modest. Although it acknowledged the importance of the safer term "social ownership," it preferred to emphasize "decentralized ownership and control...and progressive democratization of the workplace."[180] As an acknowledgement both of the debt the NDP owed to the CCF, but also as an affirmation that it wished to press in a somewhat different direction from its predecessor, the Statement concluded by echoing the famous phrase from the 1933 document that: "No CCF government will rest content until it has eradicated capitalism and put into operation the full program of socialized planning which will lead to the establishment in Canada of the Co-operative Commonwealth." In its place, the 1983 Statement said: "The New Democratic Party will not rest content until we have achieved a democratic socialist Canada, and we are confident that only such a Canada can make its rightful contribution to the creation of a more just, democratic and peaceful world."[181]

For Broadbent, once begun, the whole process proved at best an exercise in damage containment, and to this end he was reasonably successful. The 1933 Statement had exaggerated the CCF's radicalism and had given its opponents an easy weapon to harm the CCF's electoral chances. The 1983 Statement avoided a similar mistake, but it lacked inspiration, and for some in the party it smelled of shameless electoralism. In the event little was subsequently heard of the *Manifesto*, and it has played no significant role in the subsequent development of the NDP.

THE 1984 ELECTION

There were rumblings about Broadbent's leadership at Regina, and these grew increasingly ominous as NDP popularity sank to historic lows in the public opinion polls in the summer of 1984 as Canadians faced the general election. When the 1984 election was called the public opinion polls were showing the Liberals with the support of about 46 percent of voters, the Conservatives favoured by about 40 percent and the NDP facing an electoral disaster with 13 percent. Yet when the votes were counted, the Conservatives had won 50 percent of the popular vote, the Liberals had fallen to 28 percent and the NDP had risen to 18 percent, and had secured thirty seats to the Liberal's forty. This astonishing transformation of electoral fortunes had occurred in a campaign in which there were no major issues of either foreign or domestic politics that might occasion significant shifts, or might be expected to create a volatile electorate. Even more dramatic than the national results was the picture in Quebec. In 1980 the Conservatives had elected only a single member, and had secured only 13 percent of the provincial vote. In 1984 they swept the province with fifty-eight members and 50 percent of the vote.

For some observers, these results would prove beyond question the unimportance of ideology in Canadian politics. However, as we understand the events, they bear strong testimony to the continuing strength of ideology in Canadian affairs.

As we explain in Chapter VII, the NDP under Broadbent's leadership had pursued a strategy of emphasizing its welfare liberal principles, and of keeping its more socialist members from frightening the middle ground of the electorate. By the early summer of 1984, it looked as if this policy had been a disastrous failure. Broadbent's leadership was increasingly questioned within his caucus, and there were some who would have been delighted had he stepped down before the election. However Broadbent had prepared his ground against a Liberal Party led by John Turner. Indeed nothing could have suited his strategy more satisfactorily than Turner's accession.

With Turner taking a predominantly business liberal line throughout the leadership campaign and in the early stages of the election, the possibility was there for Broadbent to portray the NDP as the representatives of decent, caring, compassionate Canadians, committed to the welfare state and the host of established programs that gave most Canadians such a strong incentive to favour the continuation of welfare state capitalism. Adopting a traditional CCF/NDP position of alleging that the two old line parties were fundamentally indistinguishable —

John Mulroney and Brian Turner, as similar as Visa and MasterCard, the difference between the Bank of Commerce and the Royal Bank — Broadbent attempted to present the NDP as the only party that could be counted on to speak for the concerns of the poor and the underprivileged. However, he was also at pains to reassure the comfortable middle class that they would not be expected to take a commando role in the war against want. Neither were they the enemy. Instead, taking his lead from David Lewis's Corporate Welfare Bums campaign of 1972, Broadbent suggested that the welfare state could be preserved and enhanced by a fairer distribution of the tax burden and increased taxes for the wealthy and the large corporations.

Although the NDP returned only thirty MPs in 1984, Broadbent was gratified with the outcome. The once powerful Liberal Party had secured a mere ten more than the NDP. For the first time this put the NDP within striking distance of official opposition status. The next parliament and the succeeding election might prove decisive in creating the breakthrough the party had sought.

TRYING TO BECOME NUMBER TWO

After the Government's initial honeymoon period, the NDP's electoral fortunes began to advance dramatically. This was a result of two factors we outlined earlier. The first was the difficulties John Turner experienced in solidifying his hold over his party after the 1984 electoral debacle. Polls showed that he was generally neither liked nor trusted as a leader, and he regularly came third when people were asked who would make the best prime minister. The second consideration was the dramatic decline in popularity of the Conservatives. The series of scandals we mentioned in the last chapter reduced the Conservatives at one point to 22 percent in the opinion polls, in third place. This was an enormous turnaround from the results of the election. The NDP found itself in an unaccustomed place, either leading in the polls or a close second to the Liberals.

However, broad ideological considerations affected the NDP's strategy. The Broadbent-Rae strategy involved moving the party closer to the ideological centre of the country in the hope of transforming it into the primary vehicle for welfare liberal ideas in Canada. To succeed here meant constantly jockeying with the Liberals for credibility as welfare liberals. As Broadbent predicted to his caucus after the 1984 election, "the Liberals would move to the left, and ...the challenge for the NDP was to avoid moving farther left to what he called a position of 'comic-book' leftism, and to keep articulating its true position as a social democratic party. As a result, [Broadbent's] campaign against Liberal Leader John Turner would hinge on Mr. Turner's credibility as a reformer."[182]

Another factor was the NDP's understanding of the nature of Mulroney's conservatism. Most in the party feared that the established programs of the welfare state would be threatened by the new regime. They thought that they would have to engage in a rearguard action to protect such measures as the Family Allowance payments, unemployment insurance, medicare and the like. In the contemporary phrase, they suggested that the Conservative government had a "hidden agenda," a set of policies it intended to implement, but which it had not openly explained during the election campaign.

> ...Broadbent drew attention to the fact that Finance Minister Michael Wilson admitted in an interview...that during the election campaign the Progressive Conservatives concealed their plans to cut spending and review social programs. "The Conservatives weren't telling the people what they intended to do because they would not have voted for them," Mr. Broadbent said. Prime Minister Brian Mulroney, he added, "did not come clean with the people of Canada."

During the campaign for the September election, the Conservatives promised that jobs would be a top priority, Mr. Broadbent said, but after they were elected they immediately moved to cut spending. "Instead of jobs, jobs, jobs, we got cuts, cuts, cuts."[183]

The NDP Biennial Convention, which met in Ottawa over the Canada Day holiday in 1985, confirmed this resolve towards moderation. It was described as a "love-in" by the party's out-going president, who summed up the meeting as follows: "Even on divisive questions, there is in fact, if not unanimity, a pretty strong consensus about our positions."[184] As Broadbent's biographer Judy Steed saw the situation: "Broadbent's pleasure was heightened by his perception that, as he puts it, 'the caucus has been wonderfully disciplined, working together as a team.' He felt his MPs had matured; they were keeping their cool in the midst of Tory scandals and Liberal shifts to the left."[185]

One minor development threatened to disturb the NDP's harmony and calm. This was the decision by B.C. MP Svend Robinson to announce that he was homosexual. In itself the matter of Robinson's homosexuality was not of great importance, though it had two possibly dangerous implications. The first was that the party might seem to be encouraging homosexuality rather than merely tolerating it. The second was that this declaration might contribute to the view that the NDP was really a coalition of radical causes such as feminism, gay rights, environmentalism. This view had been advanced earlier by Rosemary Brown, and following the slogan of the American Democratic presidential candidate Jesse Jackson, it was described as building "a rainbow coalition." Not surprisingly, it was this approach Robinson himself preferred against his leader's mainstream strategy, and which he exemplified in his involvement with the Haida Indians of the Queen Charlottes in their attempt to stop logging on South Moresby. This was an attempt to combine a concern for the environment with support for native rights.[186] As matters turned out, neither Robinson's homosexuality nor his controversial activities had much impact on the party's fortunes.

The major issue that might have seriously harmed the NDP was the Meech Lake Constitutional Accord. In 1981 there had been a serious split, particularly between Ontario and some of the Western members over patriation and the Charter of Rights. As Judy Steed explains:

> Meech Lake could have been a bomb....Instead of jumping in to support the deal ...[Broadbent] conducted long, thoughtful caucus meetings and heard everyone out, going round the table, drawing forth opinions, making notes, articulating the pros and cons.[187]

Opposition revolved around a number of issues. One was the process by which the deal had been concluded, by the provincial premiers and the prime minister behind closed doors. This genuinely offended some in the party because of its lack of democratic openness. There were also more substantial grounds for opposition. It was suggested the Accord weakened the force of the equality rights provision in the Charter, and therefore that it harmed the position of women. There was also opposition on the grounds that it did little if anything to clarify and protect the position of native rights. Finally, there was the objection that Meech Lake harmed the interests of Canadians in the territories, especially because it created more difficulty for the territories to attain provincial status. These concerns all came to the surface in the British Columbia NDP, which voted to condemn the Accord.[188]

However, the Accord contained one crucial agreement around which the party could rally: the distinct society clause. This declaration had been at the heart of Quebec's opposition to the homogenizing provisions of the Charter. By acknowledging Quebec to be a distinct society and its government to be the agent that protected that distinctiveness, the federal government and the other premiers reassured Quebec that its unique character was not meant to be threatened by the new constitutional arrangement. According to Ed Broadbent, it "allows us to recognize Quebec's contribution to Canada's history. It recognizes what is already implicit...that Quebec is a distinct society within the Canadian family."[189] We have emphasized throughout the collectivism that forms such an important part of the NDP's ideological understanding, and this is what was so helpful to the party in accepting the idea of Quebec as a distinct society, as a collectivity within Canada whose collectiveness did not, in itself, threaten the larger whole, which was Canada.

Although it was by no means the party's principle reason for supporting the Accord, it would also be true to suggest that there were pressing tactical reasons as well. Two factors — the CCF/NDP's English-speaking and Protestant heritage, and its traditional commitment to a strong central government — had severely limited its appeal in French-speaking areas of the country. During its tenure in office, the Parti Québécois had succeeded in rendering social democracy an acceptable political option. Its defeat and apparent collapse offered the NDP its first good opportunity to make electoral strides in this area. As Broadbent explained:

> ...the growth of the NDP [is] a reflection of the changes in Quebec society. "It reflects the social democratic development in Quebec, which has been somewhat different in its development compared to other provinces," Mr. Broadbent said. He suggested that the social changes brought about by the Quiet Revolution in Quebec during the sixties were so rapid and so great that they resulted in support for the NDP from a wider range of occupations in the province.[190]

The possibility that the NDP might make, for the first time, significant electoral gains in the province of Quebec was buoyed by public opinion polls, which regularly showed the NDP at historic levels of popular approval. It remained to be seen whether the party could overcome the organizational hurdles it faced in its attempt to secure a substantial foothold.

The free trade agreement, by contrast, presented the party with a dilemma, since it was initially popular in Quebec, and had the strong and enthusiastic support of Quebec Premier Robert Bourassa. However, here as elsewhere, ideology took pre-eminence over brokerage politics. In Chapter III we have seen that the welfare liberals in the Liberal Party developed a vision of the country that increasingly identified the construction of the welfare state in Canada, such as medicare and the Canada pension plan, with the Canadian national identity. Their co-ideologues in the NDP concurred in this analysis even more strongly, since they were supported by the party's socialist element also.

This was the position Broadbent advanced in his major speech on the Free Trade Agreement (FTA). His major premise was that the Conservative Party had abandoned the nation-building tradition "that would distinguish our country from mainstream U.S.A."[191] In his view, the business liberal tradition in the Conservative Party had completely swamped the tory element. The consequences of this change were privatization and deregulation, and indifference to the "claims of Canadian culture precisely because these matters are totally subordinate to the claims of the market-place...."[192] As for the Prime Minister, he suggested:

> I believe that his life experience — and we can debate about this — as a former branch plant manager has so internalized the values of the market-place as being pre-eminent that, unlike Sir John A. Macdonald and John Diefenbaker, he sees no possible contradiction between the national good and the continental market good.[193]

Although the address was a curious one in some ways, since it appealed regularly to John A. Macdonald and John Diefenbaker rather than to the figures on the left who had been more traditional occupants in the pantheon of the NDP, it was consistent with the strategy we have described earlier of trying to move the NDP more securely into the centre-ground of Canadian politics. The aim can be seen even more clearly when Broadbent came to state the positive principles upon which his party was based:

> Our vision of Canada as a social democratic party is based on fairness for average Canadians and their families. We want a fair deal for the many, not a special deal for

the few. Our vision of Canada is rooted in what I believe has become a modern Canadian tradition of compassion and justice....Instead of rejecting the past, we want to build upon it. Instead of restricting the notions of liberty, equality and community, we want to expand them.[194]

Nationally, the party was at its highest-ever standing in the polls; Broadbent himself outstripped the other party leaders. The 1988 election would be the final test for his strategy.

THE 1988 ELECTION — BREAKTHROUGH OR BREAKDOWN?

From the incipient annihilation that had threatened the New Democratic Party in March 1984 when it stood at 11 percent in the polls, through the heights that showed Ed Broadbent clearly the most-liked and most-respected leader in the country, and his party challenging for first place among decided voters, the question always remained whether he would be able to transmute his popularity into his party's seats. The 1988 election was to prove a decisive test for the strategy of seeking a place in the centre of Canadian politics.

In the view of Goldfarb and Axworthy, this strategy rested on a tenuous foundation. In the first place, it did not commend itself to Broadbent's own supporters.

With 45% of the delegates classifying themselves as social democrats and 30% as socialists, more than three-quarters of its delegates rejected the idea that they "present a more moderate image to the general public." A majority of the delegates (55.6%) wanted the NDP to move "more clearly to the left."[195]

The second problem would be to broaden the basis of NDP support beyond that of their traditional 15 percent to 20 percent:

Ed Broadbent has a wide personal dominance in comparison with Mulroney and Turner, but several NDP policy positions are anathema to Canadians....Broadbent's political trick will be to articulate Canadian concerns strongly enough to maintain his electoral advantage (send them a message), but not so strongly that the next election can be polarized around the theme of free enterprise versus socialism.[196]

As the campaign developed it became clear that Broadbent had chosen the second course over the first. In order to appeal to his general popularity, NDP signs regularly boasted the message "Ed's Team," and ignored any prominent reference to the party itself. As well, Broadbent laid out, soberly and cautiously, a series of policy proposals appropriate for a party that might actually have to implement them within the foreseeable future. He also moderated the party's foreign policy stance, which had been overwhelmingly re-affirmed at its last convention, that Canada would withdraw from NATO. That would remain NDP policy, but the timing would be at the discretion of an NDP Government, and would not likely occur during that party's first period in office.

This strategy came unstuck at the hands of John Turner's one-issue campaign. On the question of free trade there was little to separate the position of the two men. As Broadbent said in his opening statement in the leaders' debate:

...Mr. Mulroney failed completely to answer criticisms that his trade deal threatens out families, our environment, our medicare, and pensions; that it jeopardizes regional development and sets back programs for our farmers. The truth is that Mr. Mulroney signed a trade deal that goes beyond the exchange of commodities between Canada and the United States. It affects virtually every aspect of Canadian life. And the truth is also that, time after time, Mr. Mulroney gave the Americans what they wanted but failed to get what Canadians wanted.[197]

The key question for many voters quickly became: if free trade is the important issue, and if Turner and Broadbent both oppose it, which of them represents the most effective instrument? The answer that many gave was that Turner, who opposed it with energy and passion, rather than the calmer and more balanced Broadbent seemed the better bet. Whatever effect the debate had on the election as a whole, there can be no doubt that it clearly established John Turner as the chief rival to the Conservatives, and quickly reduced the NDP to its customary status.

The 1988 election results proved a crushing disappointment to the NDP, although it secured the largest number of seats in its history. The party had been certain, that this was the year it would establish itself as the leading opposition. Matters turned out otherwise; John Turner's blend of welfare liberalism and nationalism proved a potent electoral weapon which, although it was not strong enough to overtake the Conservatives, was adequate to the job of fending of the challenge for the position as chief spokesman for welfare liberalism in Canada. The NDPs feel the loss all the more intensely because it senses it might have missed a unique opportunity. This feeling was sharpened by Ed Broadbent's decision in March of 1989 to step down as NDP leader. Broadbent was, without a doubt, the most popular leader the CCF or NDP has had, and his departure may make reproducing the opportunity difficult.

Regardless of who succeeds Broadbent, the central question the party will want to resolve is its ideological complexion. The rise in the 1988 election of other parties of protest such as the Christian Heritage Party and the Reform Party led by Preston Manning was made possible in part by the NDP's decision to move closer to the mainstream of Canadian politics. This made it less appealing to voters who were seeking an instrument to indicate their dissatisfaction with the status quo. As we have seen above, there is also discontent within the party that, by becoming too moderate, it is losing its reason for existence. It will be interesting to see whether, as it has in the past, it will veer away from its current assimilation course with liberalism under its new leader and reassert the socialist tradition that has been such a powerful part of its heritage.

1. Ivan Avakumovic, *Socialism in Canada: A Study of the CCF-NDP in Federal and Provincial Politics* (Toronto: McClelland & Stewart, 1978), p. 247.

2. N. Penner, *The Canadian Left: A Critical Analysis* (Toronto: Prentice-Hall Inc., 1977), p. 1.

3. Ivan Avakumovic, *Socialism in Canada,* p. 14.

4. Paul Fox, "Early Socialism in Canada" in *The Political Process in Canada,* J.H. Aitchison, ed. (Toronto: University of Toronto Press, 1963), pp. 79, 98.

5. Doris French, *Faith, Sweat and Politics* (Toronto: McClelland and Stewart Limited, 1962), pp. 22-30.

6. *Palladium of Labour,* January 5, 1884. Quoted in Martin Robin, *Radical Politics and Canadian Labour* 1880-1930, (Kingston: Industrial Relations Centre, Queen's University 1968), p. 22.

7. James Harding. "The New Left in British Columbia" in *The New Left in Canada* (ed.) Roussopoulos (Montreal: Our Generation — Black Rose Books, 1970), p. 19; Robin, p. 34.

8. Robin, p. 34.

9. Grace MacInnis, *J.W. Woodsworth: A Man to Remember* (Toronto: Macmillan, 1953), p. 6.

10. See Avakumovic for a more detailed discussion, pp. 18-19.

11. Penner, pp. 39, 42-45.

12. Penner, p. 76.

13. Robin, p. 34.

14. MacInnis, p. 11.

15. Kenneth McNaught, *A Prophet in Politics* (Toronto: University of Toronto Press, 1959), p. 43; MacInnis, p. 17.

16. J.S. Woodsworth, *Strangers Within Our Gates* (Toronto: Missionary Society of the Methodist Church, 1909), p. 217. Reprinted 1972 by the University of Toronto Press.

17. *Ibid.,* pp. 217-219.

18. *Ibid.,* pp. 206, 279.

19. *Ibid.,* p. 219.

20. See Richard Allen, *The Social Passion: Religion and Social Reform in Canada 1914-1928* (Toronto: University of Toronto Press, 1971) for a full discussion of this movement.

21. Avakumovic, p. 29.

22. Woodsworth, *Strangers,* p. 311.

23. J.S. Woodsworth, *My Neighbour* (Toronto: Methodist Book Room, 1911), p. 20. Reprinted 1972 by The University of Toronto Press.

24. *Ibid.,* pp. 29, 26, 21.

25. McNaught, p. v.

26. MacInnis, p. 124.

27. Woodsworth, *Neighbour,* p. 332.

28. *Ibid.,* p. 88.

29. G. Baum, *Catholics and Canadian Socialism: Political Thought in the Thirties and Forties* (Toronto: James Lorimer and Co., 1980), p. 36.

30. D.C. Masters, *The Winnipeg General Strike,* Copyright, Canada, 1950 by University of Toronto Press, Toronto, pp. 17-18.

31. Robin, p. 184.

32. Avakumovic, p. 20.

33. David Lewis, *The Good Fight* (Toronto: Macmillan, 1981), p. 93.

34. David Bercuson, "Western Labour Radicalism and the One Big Union: Myth and Realities," in Clark, Grayson and Grayson, eds. *Prophecy and Protest: Social Movements in Twentieth Century Canada,* (Toronto: Gage, 1975), pp. 251-252.

35. Robin, p. 177, Masters, p. 8.

36. MacInnis, p. 124.

37. "The Origin of the O.B.U." Verbatim Report of the Calgary Labour Conference, 1919, p. 47. Quoted in Robin, p. 176.

38. See generally Robin, pp. 174-176.

39. Quoted in Robin, pp. 187-188.

40. Master, pp. 20-21.

41. Bercuson, p. 254.

42. MacInnis, pp. 147, 214.

43. Robin, p. 192.

44. Fox, p. 98.

45. Walter Young, *The Anatomy of a Party* (Toronto: University of Toronto Press, 1969), p. 23.

46. Baum attributes this commitment to civil liberties and democracy to the British tradition, and suggests that the anti-religiousness of Marxism is an important reason why it never appealed to British trade unionism on a large scale. Baum, p. 63.

47. McNaught, p. 157.

48. From *The Farmers in Politics* (1920), pp. 98-99, 101, 158, 157, 167, 198, 193, 207, 202, 208, by William Irvine. Reprinted by permission of the Canadian Publishers, McClelland and Stewart Ltd., Toronto. Our emphasis.

49. MacInnis, p. 223.

50. Young, p. 34.

51. See John Irving, "The Evolution of the Social Credit Movement," Clark, Grayson and Grayson, eds., pp. 130-152.

52. See Young, pp. 34-36.

53. J.S.Woodsworth, *A Plea for Social Justice* (Ottawa: CCF, 1933), pp. 4, 78, 79.

54. Penner, p. 216.

55. Young, p. 34.

56. Quoted in MacInnis, p. 274.

57. *Canadian Forum,* XII, No. 139, April 1932, p. 250.

58. For an excellent study of the LSR, see Michiel Horn, *The League for Social Reconstruction: Intellectual Origins of the Democratic Left in Canada 1930-1942* (Toronto: University of Toronto Press, 1980).

59. See Horn, pp. 61, 100-101.

60. Grace MacInnis and Charles Woodsworth, *Canada Through C.C.F. Glasses* (Ottawa: CCF, 1935), p. 58.

61. This and following quotes until otherwise noted are taken from the CCF program, Regina, 1933.

62. Horn, p. 46.

63. See Penner, p. 196.

64. Carrigan, p. 119.

65. CCF Platform of 1935.

66. *Ibid.*

67. J.S. Woodsworth, Preface to *Social Planning for Canada* (Toronto: Thomas Nelson and Sons, 1935), p. v.

68. Young, p. 71.

69. League for Social Reconstruction, *Social Planning for Canada,* p. 53.

70. *Ibid.,* p. 85.

71. *Ibid.,* pp. 101, 266.

72. *Ibid.,* p. 475.

73. *Ibid.,* p. 266.

74. *House of Commons Debates* (1934), pp. 2558, 2559, 2563.

75. *House of Commons Debates* (1932-1933), p. 7.

76. LSR, *Social Planning,* p. 225.

77. *Ibid.,* pp. 32, 37.

78. *Ibid.,* p. 465.

79. See Young, Chapter 4.

80. For the preceding, see Leo Zakuta, *A Protest Movement Becalmed* (Toronto: University of Toronto Press, 1964), pp. 154-156.

81. Lewis, p. 87.

82. Lewis, p. 89.

83. M.J. Coldwell, "Introduction," David Lewis and Frank Scott, *Make This Your Canada* (Toronto: Central Canadian Publishing Co., 1943).

84. Lewis and Scott, *Make This Your Canada,* p. 96.

85. *Ibid.,* pp. 99-100.

86. *Ibid.,* p. 34.

87. *Ibid.,* Our emphasis.

88. *Ibid.,* p. 194.

89. *Ibid.,* p. 34.

90. *Ibid.,* p. 195.

91. L.T. Hobhouse, *Liberalism* (Oxford: Oxford University Press, 1911), p. 54.

92. *Ibid.,* p. 87.

93. M.J. Coldwell, *Left Turn, Canada* (New York: Duell and Sloane, 1944), pp. 180-194.

94. *Security With Victory* (Ottawa: C.C.F., 1945). Reprinted in Carrigan, pp. 143-50. To get the ideological moderation of this program in perspective, it is worth noting that the Liberal platform of the same year promised equality of opportunity, "a wide-open chance to make a real success of [one's] life." In concert with the CCF's emphasis on industrial development, the Liberal platform asked, "Isn't that what you want — a chance to make your own way. In your own way?"

95. Lewis, 249, 250.

96. Avakumovic, p. 69.

97. Quoted in Young, p. 127.

98. *Security for All* (Ottawa: CCF, 1949). Our emphasis. Reprinted in Carrigan, pp. 168-178.

99. *Ibid.*

100. Young, p. 137.

101. *Humanity First* (Ottawa: CCF, 1953). Reprinted in Carrigan, pp. 198-205.

102. Lewis, p. 336.

103. Lewis, p. 298.

104. *Ibid.*

105. *Ibid.*

106. *Winnipeg Declaration of Principles of the Co-operative Commonwealth Federation* (Montreal: CCF, 1956). Reprinted in Carrigan, pp. 215-222.

107. Quoted in Lewis, p. 442.

108. Avakumovic, p. 162.

109. Penner, 237.

110. Lewis, p. 445. There is no suggestion that Lewis had Avakumovic or Penner in mind when he wrote those words, but we think that their comments typify the kind of observation about which Lewis was complaining.

111. Avakumovic, p. 70.

112. David Lewis, "A Socialist takes Stock" in *Politics: Canada,* 3rd ed., Paul Fox, ed. (Toronto: McGraw-Hill Ryerson, 1970), pp. 238-241.

113. *Share Canada's Wealth!* (Ottawa: CCF, 1957). Our emphasis. Reprinted in Carrigan, pp. 217-222.

114. The wording is that of the Canadian Labour Congress Resolution, 1958, which can be found in CLC-CCF Joint National Committee, *A New Political Party for Canada* (Ottawa: CLC, 1959). See also, Stanley Knowles, *The New Party* (Toronto: McClelland & Stewart, 1961), p. 20.

115. *The Federal Program of the New Democratic Party* (Ottawa: NDP, 1961). Reprinted in Carrigan, pp. 271-283.

116. Knowles, p. 113.

117. *Ibid.,* p. 93.

118. *Ibid.,* 102.

119. George Grant, "An Ethic of Community" in M. Oliver, ed. *Social Purpose for Canada* (Toronto: University of Toronto Press, 1961), p. 9.

120. *Ibid.,* pp. 16, 17.

121. *Ibid.,* pp. 20-21.

122. Though, at the time, his crushing defeat was seen as a "major blow to the left-wingers." Avakumovic, p. 192.

123. Campaign Leaflet, (Ottawa: NDP, 1962). Reprinted in Carrigan, pp. 283-286.

124. *The Policies of the Liberal Party* (Ottawa: 1963). Reprinted in Carrigan pp. 294-302.

125. Avakumovic, p. 200.

126. Lewis, p. 387.

127. Lewis, p. 432.

128. *New Democratic Party Program* (Regina: NDP, 1968). Reprinted in Carrigan, pp. 342-348.

129. For a more complete discussion of the Waffle and its critics, see Avakumovic, pp. 197-204, and Penner pp. 238-240.

130. It was also faced, as has become customary for the mainstream of socialism in Canada, with a raft of advice about how it should develop. *Essays on the Left,* ed. LaPierre et al, contained a brilliant paper by Charles Taylor titled "The Agony of Economic Man," which, along with Taylor's *Pattern of Politics* (Toronto: McClelland and Stewart, 1970) constitute two of the most significant recent contributions to Canadian socialist thought. Taylor's penetrating critique of modern socialist thought begins with a rejection of the ubiquitous notion that modern society and social organization exist for the sole purpose of "transforming the surrounding natural world" and goes on to argue for a society in which contemplation rather than production is deemed the "highest activity of man." To this end Taylor calls for a rewriting of socialist theory "as complete and far-reaching as that of Karl Marx a hundred years ago." Taylor, "The Agony of Economic Man" in *Essays on the Left,* edited by J.T. McLeod and L. LaPierre (Toronto: McClelland and Stewart, 1971), pp. 221-225.

131. Lewis, pp. 142-143.

132. "Waffle Manifesto" in *Politics: Canada,* ed. Fox, pp. 242-243.

133. David Lewis, *Louder Voices: The Corporate Welfare Bums* (Toronto: James, Lewis and Samuel, 1972), p. v.

134. "Waffle Manifesto," Fox, p. 242.

135. Lewis, pp. 117-118.

136. For a fuller discussion, see Avakumovic, pp. 235-236; Penner, pp. 239-259.

137. "Nomination Speech of Douglas K. Campbell, NDP Leadership Candidate, Winnipeg Convention, July 4-7, 1975," mimeo, p. 3.

138. *Notes for an Address* by John Harney, mimeo.

139. Avakumovic, p. 240.

140. "Rosemary Brown for NDP Leader," July 6, 1975, mimeo, p. 3.

141. Brown, p. 10.

142. Brown, p. 12.

143. "The text of a speech by Ed Broadbent given at the eighth biennial convention of the New Democratic Party," mimeo, p. 1.

144. Broadbent, p. 3.

145. Broadbent, p. 6.

146. Broadbent, p. 6.

147. See, among others, Irving Abella, *Nationalism, Communism and Canadian Labour* (Toronto: University of Toronto Press, 1973); Ivan Avakumovic, *The Communist Party in Canada* (Toronto: McClelland & Stewart, 1975); Norman Penner, *The Canadian Left: A Critical Analysis* (Toronto: Prentice-Hall, 1977), ch. 4, 5; Norman Penner, *Canadian Communism: The Stalin Years and Beyond* (Toronto: Methuen, 1988), and the works of the Canadian Communist leader, Tim Buck.

148. Horn, p. 101.

149. See Penner, pp. 240-245.

150. Lewis, p. 457. See also Baum, pp. 175, 187; Horn, pp. 112-115.

151. Baum, p. 119.

152. John Saywell, *The Rise of the Parti Québécois, 1967-1976* (Toronto: University of Toronto Press, 1977), p. 21.

153. Saywell, p. 140.

154. Saywell, p. 141.

155. Avakumovic, p. 213.

156. For a fuller discussion, see Irving Abella, "The Imperfect Union," *Canadian Forum*, September 1979, p. 8.

157. Sandra Gwyn, "Ed broadbent on a fast track," *Saturday Night*, September 1978, p. 20.

158. Bob Rae, *Canadian Forum*, September 1979, p. 12.

159. Ed Broadbent, "Notes for a Speech," January 15, 1982, mimeo, p. 9.

160. Notes for a speech by Ed Broadbent, OFL Political Education Conference, March 3, 1982, mimeo, p. 1.

161. NDP Position Paper on Mega-Projects, May 5, 1982, mimeo, p. 9.

162. Jim Turk, "Left Debates," *Canadian Dimension*, Vol. 14, June 1980, p. 22.

163. Turk, p. 23.

164. *Ibid.*

165. Turk, p. 24.

166. Ed Broadbent, *House of Commons Debates*, January 25, 1979, p. 2555.

167. Pauline Jewett, *House of Commons Debates,* March 4, 1981, p. 7897.

168. *Ibid.*

169. Svend Robinson, *House of Commons Debates,* Feb. 23, 1981, p. 7593.

170. Broadbent, *House of Commons Debates,* Nov. 20, 1981, p. 13053.

171. *Ibid.*

172. Ed Broadbent, "Notes for a Speech," July 3, 1981, mimeo, p. 5.

173. New Democratic Party, "Principles and Objectives, Preliminary Draft for discussion," January 1983, mimeo, p. 2.

174. *Ibid.,* p. 3.

175. *Ibid.*

176. *Ibid.,* p. 4.

177. NDP, "Resolutions passed by the 12th Federal NDP Convention, Agridome, Regina," June/July 1983, mimeo, p. 26.

178. *Ibid.*

179. "Preliminary Draft," p. 7.

180. "Resolutions," p. 27.

181. *Ibid.,* p. 28.

182. Graham Fraser, "NDP in Quebec", *Globe and Mail,* December 24, 1987.

183. *Globe and Mail,* Dec. 14, 1984

184. Barbara Yaffe, "NDP love-in marked by consensus on issues, celebration", *Globe and Mail,* July 1, 1985.

185. Judy Steed, *Ed Broadbent: The Pursuit of Power* (Markham, Ontario: Viking, 1988), p.319

186. Steed, p. 321

187. Steed, p.301

188. John Cruikshank, "Party united on Meech Lake despite vote, Broadbent says," *Globe and Mail,* April 11, 1988.

189. Paul Korning, "Broadbent decries 'nonsense' on pact", *Globe and Mail,* June 15, 1988.

190. Graham Fraser, "NDP in Quebec", *Globe and Mail,* Dec. 24, 1987.

191. Ed Broadbent, *House of Commons Debates,* August 30, 1988, vol. 129, p.19070.

192. *Ibid.*

193. *Ibid.,* p.19071

194. *Ibid.,* p.19072.

195. Martin Goldfarb and Tom Axworthy, *Marching to a Different Drummer: An Essay on the Liberals & Conservatives in Convention* (Toronto: Stoddart, 1988), p. 134.

196. Goldfarb and Axworthy, p.134.

197. Ed Broadbent, *Encounter 88,* transcript of the leaders' debate, October 25, 1988, p. 1.

CANADIAN NATIONALISM

The mixture of business liberalism and toryism in the Conservative Party and of welfare liberalism and socialism in the CCF/NDP reflect the need and the desire of politicians to ally with the pervasive liberalism of Canada rather than to establish a permanent, but small, tory or socialist party. Toryism or socialism possesses a sufficiently comprehensive vision of society to sustain a continuing political party; it does not enjoy sufficiently comprehensive support to sustain a successful political party. The position of nationalism is in some ways the reverse.

Nationalism, concerned with the important but limited question of national identity and independence, is a less comprehensive ideology than liberalism, conservatism, or socialism — it accounts for a narrower range of social and political phenomena and provides answers to fewer questions. There is no distinctive nationalist approach to many important political concerns, from local government to social policy and protection of the environment. While its concern for national identity or independence may have some relevance to many areas of policy, and may even dominate some — foreign policy or ownership and control of industry or natural resources — it is not sufficiently comprehensive to stand alone as a descriptive or prescriptive account of political phenomena in general.

In consequence, nationalism has never been permanently embodied in a particular political party in Canada. There has never been, nor is there likely to be, a Nationalist Party in Canada, though there are parties with attitudes that can consistently be described as liberal, liberal-tory, or liberal-socialist, even if the fit between party and ideology is not perfect. Rather, nationalism has influenced all political parties at different times and in varying degrees, thus remedying its lack of comprehensiveness and creating nationalist variants of liberalism, conservatism and socialism as well as liberal, conservative and socialist forms of nationalism. Specifically, nationalist political groups have been special-interest or pressure groups, such as the Canada First movement, the *Bloc Populaire* in Quebec of the Second World War, or the more contemporary Committee for an Independent Canada or The Council of Canadians, existing for only a relatively short time. The electoral success and relative permanence of the Parti Québécois since its founding in 1968 is due in part to its position as the bearer of democratic socialism in Quebec.

The bicultural nature of the Canadian state has produced a distinguishably Canadian variant of the nationalist pattern, which can be properly understood only by examining the nature of modern nationalism. A full study is beyond the scope of this book, since nationalist doctrines are ubiquitous in the modern world and have, in Europe at least, a history stretching back over 150 years. A sketch of the outlines, however, shows that nationalist beliefs and attitudes in Canada fall between two poles.

The first is what might be called "full-blown" nationalism, or, in Carlton Hayes's term, "integral nationalism."[1] The most cogent and lucid account of this variety is the brilliant study, *Nationalism,* by Elie Kedourie (which, incidentally, had an important influence on Pierre Trudeau's attitude to nationalism). Kedourie defines nationalism as the doctrine that "holds that humanity is naturally divided into nations, that nations are known by certain characteristics which can be ascertained, and that the only legitimate type of government is national self-government."[2] In his view, nationalism presents a truly ideological way of viewing the world, limited and incomplete. It sees the world in terms of a division into nations, and seeks to remake politics in that image, regardless of the claims of history, economics or geography.

For Kedourie, this nationalism has roots in philosophy, specifically in the Kantian argument that the essence of moral behaviour is the free individual acting in accord with an internalized moral law, the categorical imperative. As we suggested in Chapter I, although philosophy does not claim direct political application, it is always open to others to take philosophy's teachings and to apply them for better or worse in the practical world. This is what happened to Kant's doctrines. His ideas were first put to the service of liberalism when some of his successors emphasized that the self-determination of the individual should be the hallmark of political morality. Subsequent thinkers like the German philosopher, Fichte, shifted the emphasis to the group and claimed that the universal rather than the individual consciousness was the source of order and rationality.

The final step in the conversion of this philosophic idea into a political doctrine came with the rise of romanticism. Especially in Germany, men like Herder and von Humboldt praised the value of ethnic diversity and inspired extensive ethnological and philological research. These inquiries persuaded many that there were natural divisions of mankind marked out by linguistic differentiation. For such nineteenth-century romantics, preserving and fostering these differences was the highest cultural value.

When this idea was joined to the doctrine of the moral value of group self-determination, it produced the nationalism that Kedourie describes: the overriding commitment to the realization of national self-determination. This doctrine, that any group sharing the same language and culture ought to be self-governing, and that such groups or "nations" are sovereign, embodying the highest earthly values for their members, has had a potent appeal. The moral strenuousness of Kantian moral philosophy, which nationalism absorbed, tended to give it a spiritual or even quasi-religious appeal, a point that has been well made in C.J.H. Hayes' *Nationalism: A Religion,* which documents the sacralization of the nation and its various symbols — flag, anthem, heroes — as well as the "nationalization" of previously universal institutions like the Christian church. It is this appeal that provides the basis for nationalist fanaticism, which subordinates all other moral considerations to nationalist criteria, and has resulted in numerous instances of terrorism, war and violence in the name of the nation and its freedom.

This view of nationalism is not, however, universally accepted, and many object that while it is valid in some circumstances, it ignores genuine varieties of nationalist thinking that take a less extreme view, both of the definition of the "nation" and of the status of the moral claims the nation makes on its citizens. Thus, nation or nationality might be defined in terms of a common political allegiance or domicile in a particular country rather than in more restrictive ethnic or linguistic terms. Likewise, the degree of identification of individual and nation and the claims made by the nation on the individual's loyalties may be considerably less than absolute.

This sort of thinking is, by Kedourie's definition, hardly nationalist at all. It bears a greater resemblance to the universal human propensity to love one's native land; in short, patriotism, what Robert Stanfield has called "simply a feeling for the nation."[3] Patriotism in this sense is not as exclusive or demanding as the more rigorous forms of nationalism, because it is neither tied to a particular or restrictive view of the nation, nor is it invested with any special moral claims on the individual. It is merely one loyalty among others. As the late George Heiman put it:

> ...nationalism as opposed to patriotism, commands the ultimate loyalty and devotion to the nation-state. Patriotism, on the other hand, is pluralistic in its inclinations. A patriot can have ties with other associations besides those he has with the nation. He may show loyalty towards a religious group, a political party, a trade union, not to

mention the traditional ties of family and kin. These loyalties are not looked upon as being incompatible with the loyalty he shows towards the nation. Where patriotism rather than nationalism prevails, the political structure of the native land, the nation-state, does not encompass or subjugate all of the individual's interests.[4]

The moderate type of nationalism is more appropriate to a multi-ethnic and bilingual state like Canada. The more extreme nationalist doctrine that calls for one state with one language is clearly incompatible with the basis of the present Canadian Confederation. It has been taken up only by those who have sought some sort of radical change, which would extinguish the cultural diversity and linguistic duality of Canada: by English Canadians who wish to assimilate or suppress the French, by French Canadians who wish to separate.

Both the extremes of English assimilation and French separatism are profoundly ideological in nature; they attempt to remake the existing situation in the light of the limited perspective of nationality. It is the magnitude and revolutionary character of the change they seek that has led most Canadians to reject these more extreme nationalist options. This has doubtless reduced the intensity and strength of nationalist feeling in Canada because it has separated ethnic and linguistic loyalties from national loyalty. Canadian nationalists have had to appeal for support either to patriotic affection for the land and a shared past, or to the negative argument that Canadian nationalism is desirable to protect or preserve certain other Canadian values, such as bilingualism or our social-welfare policies. This tendency to moderation in most Canadian nationalism has been reinforced by the absence of ideological uniformity, as we noted in Chapter II. Thus, unlike the identification of liberalism with "Americanism" in the United States, national and ideological loyalties in Canada have remained quite separate.

This moderate mainstream notwithstanding, some French-Canadian nationalists have pursued the goal of national self-determination and of an independent French-speaking state; some English Canadians have sought linguistic and cultural uniformity through assimilation. Lord Durham proposed assimilation in his report but the imperial government pursued that policy only half-heartedly and by the 1850s had abandoned it entirely. Pressure for full-scale assimilation became a significant political force only in the last quarter of the nineteenth century. In the decade following the Riel Rebellion of 1885, an atmosphere of racial hostility was produced by the crisis over Riel's execution, the conflict over separate schools in Manitoba and the recognition of the French language in the Northwest Territories. Some English Canadians advocated outright assimilation of the French or, failing that, at least a gradual reduction of the importance of the French fact in Canada.

Charles Mair, one of the original members of the Canada First movement, spoke for many English Canadians in opposing the extension of any French-language rights to the Northwest Territories: "How, then, if we wish ever to become a homogeneous people, can we extend the parliamentary use of a language which is limited of right to a certain Province?"[5]

THE IMPERIAL FEDERATION MOVEMENT AND THE DEVELOPMENT OF CONSERVATIVE NATIONALISM

Canada First, however, despite its concern for cultural and racial uniformity,[6] was overshadowed in its zeal for a British Canada by the imperial federation movement, which rapidly gained momentum in the 1880s. Dalton McCarthy, president of the Imperial Federation League, led a vigorous battle in 1889-1890 against French-language rights in the Northwest Territories, as well as the successful campaign for the abolition of separate schools in Manitoba. National unity demanded unity of language and the complete assimilation of the French: they must "learn to cherish, not merely our institutions, but our glorious past, and to look forward with us to a still more glorious future."[7] Not all of those connected with the imperial federation movement were hostile to the French. George Munro Grant, for example, was tolerant of French Canada and admired its conservative society — but even he was convinced that the French fact in Canada was bound to be a declining force.[8]

The problem of cultural duality was not the only one faced by Canadian nationalism. If the approach of the imperial federationists could not provide a theory that accounted satisfactorily for the aspirations of the major language groups in Canada, their theories provided more compelling answers to other problems. The imperial federationists are the direct ancestors of most modern Canadian nationalists and made a contribution to the development of nationalist thought in Canada, which is still felt today. This may well appear paradoxical to a reader who associates "imperialism" with colonial subordination and wonders what possible connection this can have with nationalism. However, the movement for imperial federation — that is, the closer integration of Britain and the self-governing colonies with greater colonial participation in the imperial government — was a repudiation of colonial status. Canada, its authors reasoned, had outgrown colonial status and was ready to assume greater responsibilities in the world; the Empire of which she was a part was the vehicle through which this enhanced national stature would be realized. The time had come for Canada to take her place in the world alongside the mother country, eventually with the same status and responsibilities. To become a co-imperial power, Canada had to assume a proportionate share in the governance of the Empire. This was hardly colonialism; as Stephen Leacock, a convinced imperial federationist, stated: "I am an imperialist because I will not be a Colonial."[9]

The counter to this view was that Canada's growing national stature ought more properly to result in independent national action. The imperialists rejected this suggestion outright — Canada, though maturing, was too small and weak to play a meaningful role in the world outside the imperial context. The imperialists correctly equated advocacy of greater Canadian independence from the Empire with a desire for isolationism, a stance they believed unworthy of Canada's rising stature. R.B. Bennett clearly drew this conclusion in a speech of 1914:

> How can you and I think of independence, how can we be concerned about an independent Canada? Eight or nine million people could not discharge the responsibilities that have come down to us....An independent Canada means this, that we Canadians are afraid of responsibility and obligation of power....[10]

Not only was isolation unworthy of Canada; it was also dangerous. To abandon Europe and the Empire meant to abandon the British make-weight to the power and expansionism of the neighbouring United States. As the poet Wilfred Campbell pointed out, Canada had a choice between "two different imperialisms, that of Britain and that of the Imperial Commonwealth to the south";[11] the option of Canadian independence was a spurious one, merely disguising a move into the American orbit. Sir John A. Macdonald himself was in no doubt on this score: "As to independence, how long could we stand as an independent republic...?"[12] The lasting contribution of the imperial federation movement to Canadian nationalism was a strong sense of the separate identity of Canada within North America and of the dangers to it from continentalism. Campbell, for example, thought that entry of Canada into the American imperial system would mean "sheer annihilation of all our personality as a people."[13]

For the imperial federationists, this Canadian identity could not be based on linguistic or ethnic uniformity, for the logic of linguistic or ethnic unity pointed towards continentalism. The arguments of proponents of a united "Anglo-Saxondom," such as Goldwin Smith, demonstrated this. The imperial federationists relied to a degree on the uniqueness of the Canadian physical setting, and particularly our northern climate, but placed most weight on ideological differences between Canada and the United States. They saw the United States as a land in which liberty ran riot, producing lawlessness, social disorder, and political corruption. Canada, on the other hand, had inherited from Britain a greater sense of social order and stability and respect for law and authority. This social conservatism in Canada, about which the imperialists were so enthusiastic, fitted closely with their own conservative leanings, for they were the embodiment at the time of the tory strain in the Canadian ideological structure. It is no accident that the imperial federation movement was closely connected with a great revival of interest in the United Empire Loyalists. Interestingly enough, the conservatism of the imperialists tended to soften their potential hostility to French Canada, for men like George Munro Grant thoroughly approved of and even idealized the rural and conservative society of Quebec, in sharp contrast to the liberal criticisms of French-Canadian society mounted by liberals such as Lord Durham and Goldwin Smith.[14]

This alliance of nationalism and toryism was not ideologically difficult, for both share a common concern for the collective aspects of political life. In practice, the willingness of tories to subordinate economic considerations to politics lent itself admirably to the achievement of nationalist ends. The effectiveness of this alliance and the strength of conservative nationalism were strikingly evident in the first half-century of Confederation, not only in the theoretical arguments of the imperialist federationists but in the practical politics of the Conservative Party. The nation-building policies of Macdonald, the National Policy and the CPR, and his adamant opposition to continentalist policies of reciprocity were all products of this school of conservative nationalism.

ROBERT BORDEN AND THE DEVELOPMENT OF NATIONAL STATUS: THE HIGH POINT OF CONSERVATIVE NATIONALISM

If Macdonald's policies were primarily internal and domestic, Sir Robert Borden's aspirations were to raise Canada's status in the world. Borden's drive for greater Canadian autonomy and influence represented the high point of the imperial federation movement and the most significant realization of its nationalist goals. To begin with, Borden (like Macdonald) was convinced that Canada could maintain and develop her autonomy only by remaining at arm's length from the United States through association with the Empire. He characterized the decision on reciprocity in the 1911 election as a choice between "the spirit of Canadianism or of Continentalism," and declared that rejection of the latter was a vote for "the maintenance of our commercial and political freedom, for the permanence of Canada as an *autonomous* nation within the British Empire."[15]

Canada's status demanded more than merely negative steps to repel external threats; national status within the Empire required that she assume the duties of a nation and receive the privileges that went with responsibility. In particular, Borden felt that Canada should assume a fairer share of the burden of imperial defence. Answering Laurier's reluctance to move in this direction and his willingness to shield Canada behind the Monroe Doctrine, Borden retorted: "...if we have assumed that status of a nation in one respect, shall we adhere to the status of a Crown colony in other and still more important respects?"[16] National "self-respect" required that Canada avoid the "humiliating" and "degrading" position of relying on Britian for her own defence, or worse, in "an appeal to the charity...of a great neighbouring nation"; rather, she ought to "stand proud, powerful and resolute in the very forefront of the sister nations."[17]

In return, Borden and other imperialists expected a corresponding share in imperial decision making on an equal basis with Britain. As we saw in Chapter IV, Macdonald had distinguished between being British and being a tool of

English foreign policy. Indeed there were those among the imperialists who took this a stage further, looking to the day when Canada would surpass Britain in size and power, and Ottawa would become the imperial capital. Borden's consistent pressure on Britain after 1911 for a greater Canadian voice in imperial foreign policy and in the conduct of the War and for proper recognition of Canada at the Versailles Peace Conference in 1919 is too well detailed to require further treatment here.

Conservative nationalism succeeded, then, in arguing that a distinctive Canadian nation existed and that it should begin to assume the powers and responsibilities that went with this status. This position, however, while genuinely nationalist, was not entirely satisfactory, for it stressed the Britishness of Canada to an extent that practically excluded the French Canadians. This, in turn, was potentially so disruptive to national unity as to negate the ends that the conservative nationalists sought. They were not content merely to stress the value of British political institutions, which most French Canadians acknowledged. They went further and saw Canada as essentially British or English in language and culture: if only a minority were systematic assimilationists, then even those most sympathetic to French Canada, like G.M. Grant, accepted the likelihood of a steady decline in French culture and language. Their vision of Canada was basically unicultural. Finally, their desire for active Canadian participation in world affairs in the framework of the Empire ran up against deep isolationist current in French Canada, which was heightened by the lack of any emotional ties between French Canadians and the Empire.

THE DECLINE OF
CONSERVATIVE NATIONALISM

In time, though, despite the racial friction it caused, conservative nationalism might have become the dominant form of Canadian nationalism, but for external events that doomed the imperial federation movement and many of its ideas. The Great War allowed Canada to exercise to the full her new-found national responsibilities, to consolidate her autonomy and her sense of national pride and identity. But the horrors of the Western Front led to a deep aversion to any outside commitments and a strong tendency to isolationism. The ethnic conflict engendered over conscription during the war ended any possibility that the French Canadians might come to accept the attitude of the conservative nationalists as to the proper position of Canada in the world. Furthermore, by encouraging more vigorous French-Canadian nationalism, the war dashed any hopes that the social conservatism common to French Canada and to the imperialists might bridge the other gaps between them. In this competition of ideologies, nationalism proved stronger than conservatism.

Above all, the war marked the beginning of an inexorable decline in the position of Britain in the world and diminished the attractiveness of the Empire as a field for the exercise of Canadian autonomy and national status. In the long run, the imperialist argument was irretrievably lost, but the fact of Canadian nationhood, which the imperialists had done so much to establish, remained. The particular national identity and place in the world, which they had asserted, was a casualty of time and fortune. Canadians were forced to find a new focus for their nationalism after 1920, and the "new nationalism" of the 1970s and 1980s is part of this search. That so much time passed without a resolution of the issue, and that it has fallen on the nationalism of the last two decades to make such a significant contribution, can be attributed in large part to the deficiencies of the successor doctrine that was waiting in the wings.

LIBERAL NATIONALISM FROM KING TO ST. LAURENT

This alternative doctrine was basically an alliance of business liberalism and nationalism and it was associated almost exclusively with the Liberal Party. Just as the nation-building policies of Macdonald, the National Policy and the CPR, and Borden's nationalist opposition to Unrestricted Reciprocity were shaped by the conservative willingness to subordinate economics to politics, so the nationalism of Laurier and King was expressed in terms of the Liberal Party's commitment to liberty and individualism.

When King became leader in 1919, the Liberal Party had only begun to explore "positive" liberty and to fashion its commitment to welfare liberalism. When it did so fully in the 1960s and later, the implications for Canadian nationalism were substantial. Welfare liberalism, as we saw in Chapter III, allied itself with a defence of central government power and championed the ability of the federal government to intervene in the economy. In contrast, business liberalism looked for the removal of intervention and restriction by government. The brands of nationalism each produced were similarly different. The "business liberal" nationalism, as we call it, of Laurier, King and St. Laurent was preoccupied with removal of perceived restraints imposed by ties to Britain. The "welfare liberal" nationalism of Pearson, Trudeau and Turner was concerned with government intervention for preserving Canada's freedom of action in the face of American economic and cultural pressures. Paradoxically, what the former helped to create by ignoring American domination was the perceived threat to Canadian identity and independence in the 1960s, which called the latter into existence.

The marriage of liberalism and nationalism has always been somewhat uneasy, for the primary focus of nationalism is on the nation as a collective rather than on the individuals of whom the nation is composed. Nationalists often argue that individual welfare can be understood only in terms of the collective whole. This nationalist tendency to subordinate individual interests to the interest of the nation does not sit well with the liberal concern for individual liberty. There is, however, a point of contact between the two ideologies, insofar as national status and freedom are seen as indirectly fostering individual liberty, and Canadian liberals have supported nationalist goals on this ground.

Canada's position in the Empire was a case in point. To many nineteenth century liberals, Canada's subordination to Britain was an offence to liberty because imperialism in any form implied the control of one nation and, by extension its citizens. Business liberal nationalists therefore sought greater autonomy and enhanced national status solely to advance the cause of liberty. Unlike their imperialist contemporaries, who looked to greater national power and status through Canadian participation in the Empire on a more equal basis, the business liberal nationalists preferred withdrawal from imperial ties. If anything, they favoured outright isolationism.

The liberal suspicion of imperial entanglement involved, as Borden's reminiscence in Chapter IV revealed, a dislike for certain features of the European ideological mix. As Hartz has pointed out, Europe was ideologically diverse, possessing strong elements of privilege, hierarchy and collectivism. This repelled liberals who saw Europe as, in Laurier's words, "a vortex of militarism," created by a privileged aristocratic minority with nothing but contempt for individual liberty. When Europeans rejected aristocratic privilege, they often espoused socialism, which was not much more acceptable to Canadian liberals in the nineteenth century. All in all, Europe was to be kept at arm's length. Liberals saw the Canadian imperialists' desire for participation in imperial affairs as an attempt to extend this nefarious system to the purer new world of North America. If the conservative nationalists thought largely in imperial terms, their liberal counterparts were as naturally attracted to the thoroughly liberal American model, and turned in reaction to the United States and a continental perspective.

This anti-British orientation won the sympathy of French Canadians, who saw the conservative nationalists' desire for close imperial ties as evidence of their desire to anglicize Canada. The business liberal nationalists' opposition to imperial involvement coincided with the natural inclinations of the French Canadians and overcame any misgivings that the conservative French might have had about their liberalism. Laurier cemented this alliance and since his time the Liberal Party used it to claim a unique competence in preserving national unity.

Continentalism was not only a product of Canadian liberal sympathy for the eminently liberal society of the United States, but also coincided with the business liberal unwillingness to subordinate economics to politics. We examined in Chapter III the consistent opposition of Liberals from Brown to Laurier and beyond to the Conservative policies of economic nationalism, despite feelings of patriotism and national pride felt by most Liberals. The logical drift of liberal thinking without the counter-pressure of patriotic sentiment was the annexationism of Goldwin Smith, a sentiment that did not remain entirely academic; for as we have seen, as prominent a Liberal political figure as Sir Richard Cartwright could entertain the possibility of continental union in the 1880s. Nationalist feeling may also have restrained the tendency in pure liberalism to be insensitive to ethnic or linguistic differences. A growing feeling of national pride in Canada's bicultural makeup, reinforced by the strong Quebec wing of the Liberal Party and support for language rights on an individual-rights basis, produced this result, although it has not made Liberals any readier to accept the collective aspects of cultural duality, as Pierre Trudeau's views and the opposition of many Liberals to the Meech Lake Accord demonstrate.

This inherent tension in Liberalism between continentalism and nationalism undoubtedly contributed to the party's relative lack of success before 1920, since in those years it was in competition with a nationalism that possessed a more compelling vision of the national identity and a more consistent approach to achieving it. For the majority of English Canadians, the distinctiveness of Canada lay in its Britishness within North America, and the Conservative Party offered the most clear and consistent defence of that national identity. It enjoyed power for the greater part of that period and even during the Laurier period, its nationalist polices were substantially maintained. Indeed, in 1911 when Laurier attempted to diverge from them in his naval policy and in support of reciprocity, he met defeat at the polls.

After the Great War, the decline in British power and prestige made the British-oriented ideas of the conservative nationalists increasingly irrelevant, and the racial rift that opened up in the conscription crisis of 1917 revealed the inadequacy of their views to ensure national unity. The imperial federation movement disappeared almost without trace. However, the Conservative Party under leaders like Meighen approached the areas of nationalist concern as if nothing had changed; for this, they paid the supreme political penalty. They ignored the changing pattern of Canadian trade and foreign investment in an increasingly continentalist direction and could produce no improvements on the National Policy of 1879. Not surprisingly, Conservative nationalism in Canada gradually atrophied and was replaced, except for pangs of nostalgia for the British connection, by the burgeoning forces of the business liberal strain in the Conservative Party, a development we have analyzed in Chapter IV.

In the years between 1920 and 1957, this brand of nationalism was dominant. It saw Canada as a primarily North American nation sharing a common set of liberal values with the United States. In this view, Liberal governments were supported by the continentalist school of Canadian history led by the late Frank Underhill and following in the traditions of Goldwin Smith, of whom Underhill was a keen student. Canada's destiny was to escape entirely from the evils of Europe and to realize the liberal values epitomized by such American leaders as Franklin Roosevelt and John Kennedy. The thrust of Canadian foreign policy under King, shaped by O.D. Skelton's almost pathological suspicion and dislike of Britain, was to escape from imperial or other international commitments into a North American fortress. Domestically, there was a steady policy of reducing ties (after 1931, ties of form rather than of substance) with Britain. This was not entirely unattractive to conservative nationalists, for they too had wished greater autonomy for Canada, though in a different world context. Thus, Louis St. Laurent's decision to end judicial appeals to the Privy Council in civil cases in 1949 was an extension of R.B. Bennett's similar decision in respect of appeals in criminal cases in 1933; and the inauguration of a separate Canadian citizenship in 1947 was the logical development of a more limited form of separate status established by the Meighen government in 1920. *The Statute of Westminster* of 1931, the legal recognition of complete Canadian independence, was passed by Britain and accepted by Canada during Bennett's term in office.

In the area of trade and investment policy, there was no replacement for Macdonald's National Policy and the national east-west economic system it produced, no initiative to influence the flow of trade or the flow of investment, both of which were rapidly turning to a north-south orientation. By 1957, Canadian trade was predominantly with the United States rather than Britain and Europe, and American investment had displaced European in importance, rapidly attaining a level of ownership and control in Canada reached nowhere else in the world. This process of economic integration into the United States was tolerated, if not encouraged, by the King and St. Laurent governments. The attempt of the latter's chief lieutenant, C.D. Howe, to railroad through parliament a measure to aid the exploitation of Canadian gas resources by Texas interests in the notorious "pipeline debate" of 1956 was only a dramatic reminder of a common occurrence. The process of north-south integration forecast and acclaimed by Goldwin Smith appeared to be well on the way to completion.

The abandonment of the attempt to preserve a national economic identity by the Liberals illustrated the shortcomings of business liberal nationalism in that period. Liberalism had great difficulty in articulating any clear sense of national identity. The very notion of a nation, of a collective entity and interest superior in some respects to the individual, was suspect and, to a doctrine that placed supreme reliance on individual rationality, the values of history and tradition upon which nationalism or patriotism was based were of dubious theoretical value. In particular, business liberals found it difficult in the 1940s, 1950s and early 1960s to perceive any clear differences from their co-ideologists to the south. Preoccupied with escaping British ties, they were blind to the new bonds they were forging. The liberal commitment to individual liberty made them loath to restrict it for collective, nationalist ends. They consistently opposed restrictions on economic liberties, which a policy of economic nationalism involved. Liberals at the time could not see the ends and denied themselves the means to pursue economic nationalism.

As a substitute, or surrogate, for a national economic development policy, Liberal governments after 1945 committed themselves to the construction of a national social welfare system, including family allowances in 1944, an enhanced old-age pension system in 1952 and a variety of shared-cost programs in the health-care field, culminating in the hospital insurance plan of 1957. This product of welfare liberalism also satisfied nationalist feeling that national minimum standards should be available to all Canadians. As we noted in Chapter III, it helped to confirm and strengthen a habit of government intervention, which the Liberal Party was to turn to more clearly nationalist uses in the 1970s and 1980s.

Despite the long predominance of business-liberal nationalism, however, the Canadian people were not uniformly liberal and the liberalism of many was tempered by shadings of the doctrine from other sources. By the mid-1950s, American economic penetration and American influence in various fields of Canadian life, from culture (radio, TV, books and magazines) to politics (the attempts of McCarthyites in the United States to investigate Canadian foreign-service officers) aroused increasing concern. John Diefenbaker's proposals for a Macdonald-style national development policy and trade diversification away from the South in 1957 met a sympathetic response and were major factors in his upset victory.

FRENCH-CANADIAN NATIONALISM

At the same time, a new wave of French-Canadian nationalism was developing in Quebec and burst forth in the Quiet Revolution of the 1960s. French-Canadian nationalism, as we argued above, has tended to run at cross purposes to Canadian nationalism, for it asserts the existence of a distinctive French-Canadian nation based on a common language and ethnic origin and draws, in varying degree, the nationalist conclusion that this nation enjoys rights of self-determination. This is a potentially revolutionary claim, for it threatens the basis of the existing Canadian state, which is the belief that a political community can exist independently of linguistic and ethnic uniformity. Paradoxically, French-Canadian nationalism flared up again in the 1960s at a time when English Canada was apparently laying to rest the remnants of the assimilationist ideas that had previously threatened the Canadian state from the opposite direction.

The roots of nationalism run deep in the history of French Canada. The rebellion of the Patriots in 1837 was in part an expression of resentment against alien, English domination, though partly also a conservative reaction to the impingement of a liberal society and people on conservative Quebec. As early as 1846, Etienne Parent, in a speech to the *Institut Canadien,* was urging French Canadians to organize their approach to political questions along nationalist grounds: "Our national consciousness must constantly be our beacon, our compass, our guiding star, as we pick our way through the stumbling-blocks of politics." This was not only a nationalist approach; it was a truly ideological stance — for Parent, nationality was the key, the window through which all political questions ought to be viewed, the ultimate standard against which to judge political priorities: "Our nationality should be our prime concern, then all the rest will automatically fall into place."[18]

At about the same time that Confederation was creating a political union of French and English, Mgr. L.-F.-R. Laflèche linked language and nationality, and identified a distinctive French-Canadian nation. Arguing on Biblical grounds, Laflèche maintained that before the Flood and the Tower of Babel, man was "able to maintain unity of language and therefore national unity." The multiplication of tongues after these events naturally created a variety of nationalities, a work in which he saw the hand of Providence, for he quoted with evident approval the opinion "that God himself created different nationalities." Applying this to French Canada, Laflèche had no difficulty in concluding that:

> French Canadians in this country are a real *nation,* and the vast expanse of territory irrigated by the majestic St. Lawrence is their own legitimate *homeland.*
> For here we have a population of close to one million rising up as one man upon hearing their name called out, speaking the same language, confessing the same faith.
> ...we French Canadians have become a *nation.*[19]

The final factor in the nationalist equation, the call for self-determination for this French-Canadian nation, had appeared by the turn of the century. The successive French-English conflicts surrounding the Riel Rebellion and the Manitoba schools crisis doubtless contributed to this process by providing proof for extreme nationalist claims that English Canada was bent on assimilation. As J.-P. Tardivel put it in 1904:

> The partisans of a great, unified Canada, whatever their political affiliation, Liberal or Tory, want to make the Dominion of Canada an exclusively English-speaking country with English customs and English traditions...when they act, it is always with a view toward the anglicizing of the great whole.[20]

This militant English nationalism Tardivel found "quite natural"; his answer was to encourage French nationalism to the ultimate end of separation:

> We have been working...toward the development of a French-Canadian national feeling: what we want to see flourish is French-Canada patriotism; our people are the French-Canadian people;...*the nation we wish to see founded at the time appointed by Providence is the French-Canadian nation.*[21]

By the 1920s, following the further crises over conscription and Regulation XVII in Ontario, separatism was advocated explicitly. J.-M.-R. Villeneuve in 1922 identified nationality closely with race and language. The four elements combined to form a nation, "origin, language, territory, and form of government," but "these elements are of unequal importance: the first two are the soul, the last two the body, of a nation. As the soul by far transcends matter, so must unity of origins and community of language be much more important."[22] For Villeneuve, the differences between English and French in Canada were insurmountable—"there is not the slightest meeting-point between our languages, social traditions, religious aims, habits of mind, spiritual formation, public institutions, or civil laws,"[23] and separation was inevitable: "Whether we like it or not, Canada is bound to split up."[24] National self-determination for French Canada was now a real possibility: "That a French and Catholic State should, during the course of the present century be established in the St. Lawrence valley is, according to many people, no longer a utopian dream, but a viable ideal, a hope founded in reality."[25] Furthermore, separation by Quebec would be in the best interests of the French minorities outside Quebec: "A strong French State, practically homogeneous and completely free in its activities, would be the surest guarantee of the survival and integrity of our people of the Diaspora."[26] Antonio Perrault, writing about the same time and, like Villeneuve, connected with the conservative and clericalist *Action Française* movement, also stressed the gulf between English and French in Canada (both attributed this in part to the growing Americanization of the English provinces) and unequivocally stated the goal of their group: "the establishing of a French State in eastern Canada."[27]

The influence of separatist nationalism in Quebec waned after the 1920s, perhaps because of the increasingly conservative and Catholic cast of nationalist thinking, which justified French Canada's existence as much on grounds of religious vocation as linguistic differentiation, and which ignored or attempted to repel the intrusions of liberal and technologically dynamic social forces into Quebec. The concern of the traditional nationalists for the Catholic vocation of French Canada and their inability to speak to the needs of a secular, urban, industrial society made them appear increasingly irrelevant. During the 1940s and 1950s, the nationalists fought the battles of the past; the federal government and its supporters seized the initiative in attacking pressing social and economic problems. Nationalism in Quebec was on the defensive, within the ramparts of the "siege mentality," and the movement towards independence became a rearguard action to protect the existing position of the government of Quebec under the leadership of Union Nationale Premier Maurice Duplessis.

Nationalism in French Canada took the offensive again when it succeeded in forging new ideological alliances that allowed it to rectify its previous weaknesses. As we argued in Chapter II, as Quebec became increasingly integrated into the liberal economic structure of North America, the traditional "feudal" or conservative ideology was largely displaced, either by the dominant liberalism of North

America or by socialism, which developed from the collectivism of the older beliefs. Nationalism followed suit, and largely exchanged its conservative ally for either liberalism or socialism. Thus rearmed, nationalism returned to the battle immensely reinforced, as English Canada came to realize after 1960. Its new liberal and socialist weapons allowed it to make great inroads among the economic, political and intellectual elites of Quebec and to reverse the defensive posture of the government of that province.

Throughout these changes, however, the fundamental nationalist concern remained the nation as defined in terms of language and ethnicity. The 1979 White Paper on the Quebec Referendum produced by the Parti Québécois government spoke of "the essential elements that characterized our people; its language, its customs, its religion." Similarly, the conclusion drawn from the premise of the existence of the nation is the same — it must possess a very substantial degree of political self-determination: "Quite simply, a people must have the right to conduct its affairs as it pleases. The time has come for us to be our own masters."[28] What is new is the determination to include within the purview of nationalism what Jean-Marc Léger called the "fundamental realities of the economic and social sphere"[29] and to promote state intervention, whether along the lines of socialism or welfare liberalism.

The main vehicle of the new nationalism was the Parti Québécois, the product of a merger of earlier separatist movements. The PQ's electoral success in the 1976 and 1981 provincial elections was due not only to the united front it presented and to that attractiveness of its leader, but also to the new ideological alliances it had forged. The PQ united nationalism with that mixture of socialism and welfare liberalism most commonly known as social democracy.

As we have already argued, such alliances are necessary for any nationalist ideology to remedy its inherent lack of comprehensiveness. The PQ was fortunate in broadening its ideology in a way that had a wide appeal, particularly among the young and in urban areas. It combined the long-standing nationalist concern for the ethnic-linguistic nation with this new concern for its economic and social, as well as cultural, development. Traditional nationalist concerns were reflected in *Bill 101,* the charter of the French language, which makes French the only official language in Quebec, and which was designed to require immigrants to Quebec to educate their children in French. But independence to the PQ also promised the means of rectifying the economic and social shortcomings of Quebec society. The new nationalism sought to employ all the powers of the modern state:

> In the economic realm as in others progress requires that this fundamental condition for an appropriate policy be first realized: ONE complete government, given the whole range of powers and machinery required for the development of a society at once modern and unique.[30]

The Lévesque government, in consequence, adopted a social democratic policy stance very similar, nationalism aside, to that of provincial NDP governments in English Canada. Broader social welfare measures, government automobile insurance, limited nationalization, broad planning and land-use controls and a more sympathetic approach to the labour movement marked the PQ's years in power. Thus, the PQ succeeded in reasserting an all-encompassing ideological view of politics by providing a set of overriding nationalist goals to guide political action:

> Quebec nationalism, which inspires the programme of the Parti Québécois, possesses a profound function to restore to Quebecers the consciousness of a national homeland, to open to them all possible opportunities to assert themselves on the national and international levels, to make a modern nation of a territory still prey to the constraints of a colonial domination.[31]

By combining nationalist ideas with socialism and welfare liberalism, the PQ broadened its electoral appeal and also gave itself a reason to exist, whether the goal of separation was reached or even if it were rejected. Thus, the defeat of sovereignty association in the referendum in May 1980 did not prevent the PQ from achieving a convincing victory in the provincial election a few months later. This is not to downgrade the dominant nationalist element of the PQ ideological mix: the rank-and-file members of the PQ consistently resisted suggestions that the party leadership back away, even in emphasis, from the goal of independence. When René Lévesque in 1984 retreated from his committment that the next provincial election be fought on the sovereignty issue, he precipitated a major split in the PQ. This was undoubtedly a factor both in the defeat of the PQ in the 1985 provincial election (by then, under the leadership of Lévesque's immediate successor, Pierre-Marc Johnson) and the eventual choice of Jacques Parizeau, an unrepentant nationalist and separatist, as PQ leader in 1988.

The rejection of separatism in the 1981 referendum, and the defeat of the Parti Québécois in 1985, were seen by some as an indication that French-Canadian nationalism was in decline. This was reinforced by the continued high standing of the Bourassa government in the polls and the apparent development of a new business class in Quebec with apparently typical business liberal attitudes, including rejection of collectivist nationalist restrictions on individual freedom. The controversy arising from the Supreme Court of Canada's decision in December of 1988, that the restrictions on the use of English in commercial signs in Quebec were unconstitutional, showed that such conclusions were premature, to say the least. The dispute over the issue of language in signs attracted increasing public attention in Quebec as it proceeded through the courts and promoted public demonstrations reminiscent of the 1960s and 1970s and there were isolated instances of vandalism directed at English-language signs. The Bourassa Government apparently anticipated a significant hostile public response to the decision and made elaborate preparations for its response to the decision. Bourassa's decision to enact new legislation prohibiting the use of English in any signs visible from the outside of a store, which required invocation of the "notwithstanding" clause in the Charter of Rights and Freedoms, was criticized by French Canadians, for the most part, only because it did not reenact the complete ban on the use of English contained in the Charter of the French language. The overwhelming support among French Canadians for Bourassa's position, or for a more strongly nationalist position, is a good indication of the continuing power of nationalism in French-Canadian society. We have already discussed in Chapter III the impact of the French Canadian on the provincial Liberal Party in Quebec, which has always been the chief bearer of liberal values at the provincial level in Quebec.

Isolated acts of violence at the time of the Supreme Court's decision on the sign-language issue were a reminder that others in Quebec were not always as patient as the *péquistes* with their attachment to moderate reforming measures. Chief among these more extreme nationalists was the *Front de Libération du Québec* (FLQ), one of whose cells kidnapped the British trade commissioner James Cross in October 1970. Another cell kidnapped and murdered the Quebec cabinet minister Pierre Laporte. The FLQ had been engaged in sporadic acts of terrorism since 1963.

Yet the main focus of their leading theorist, Pierre Vallières, was socialist rather than nationalist: "It is a question of making men equal, not only in law but in fact."[32] The felquistes were nationalists, not from intrinsic reasons but because, contingently, Quebecers happened to be, in their view, a particularly oppressed class. Vallières makes it clear that nationalism, for him, was a means rather than an end in itself. In *L'Urgence de choisir,* published in 1971 after he had repudiated the FLQ's violent road to Quebec independence he wrote: "In Quebec, the establishment of a national independent state is the necessary condition for all economic development and all social progress."[33] His support for the Parti Québécois stemmed from his belief that: "In fact, from the permanent confrontation of social struggles and political crises in Quebec in the last ten years, there has only arisen one type of coherent political action, as a real alternative to gain power for the white niggers of Quebec, and that's the Parti Québécois."[34]

A rather different, and often ignored, branch of French-Canadian nationalism developed among the Acadian people of New Brunswick. The *Parti Acadien,* which was formed in the early 1970s, combined the ethnic-linguistic focus of classical nationalism with both the traditional collectivism of the Acadian people (represented by the Catholic Church and the church-inspired institutions such as the *caisses populaires*) and moderate democratic socialism. Its nationalism consisted mainly in a call for a separate Acadian province carved out of northern and eastern New Brunswick, but the party attracted little mass support among the Acadian population. It is not clear whether this was a result simply of a weak nationalist sentiment or of a general belief among the Acadians of the unlikelihood of Acadian independence or even separate provincehood. The *Parti Acadien* has shown no particular enthusiasm for the Parti Québécois either because of its own greater moderation or because of the long-standing Acadian resentment of the patronizing attitude of Québécois in general to their co-linguists in Atlantic Canada.

THE RESURGENCE OF CANADIAN NATIONALISM: 1957 TO 1989

The transformation of nationalism in Quebec has been paralleled by the resurgence of a wider Canadian nationalism, whose stirrings were seen in the Diefenbaker campaign of 1957. This "new" nationalism, which has been an increasingly important feature of Canadian politics since 1957, incorporates a number of different stands. At bottom, it is rooted in simple patriotic sentiment, love of the country and its past, and concern for its present and future. It is important to realize that this is patriotic, and not in the extreme sense of the word, nationalist feeling, for there has been little attempt to give it any particular ethnic or linguistic bias. The existence of this sentiment in itself is not a sufficient explanation of the new nationalism, for patriotism is probably a permanent feature of human nature and society and is certainly widespread in the Canadian population. Other influences have shaped its contemporary form, its intensity and the particular demands it has made on politicians.

One of the most important was the old conservative nationalist tradition with its sense of a distinctive Canadian identity within North America. It should not be surprising that the architects of this view have been found primarily among historians, for a sense of national identity is largely the result of an appreciation of national history, of the process through which the nation became what it is. What is mildly surprising is that the first of these architects was an economic historian, Harold Innis, though surprise should perhaps be tempered by recalling that conservative nationalists like Macdonald or Borden were deeply concerned with economic questions.

Innis flew in the face of the prevailing economic orthodoxy and argued that east-west economic links that followed national rather than continental lines were just as "natural" as those along a series of north-south axes. In particular, Innis offered an economic justification of the economic system developed under the National Policy of the east-west national economy, which tied the St. Lawrence-Great Lakes area to the hinterlands of the East and West. Innis's defence of a national economic identity, in turn, exercised a powerful influence on general historians and, in particular, on Donald Creighton, who placed this identity in a wider historical context. This "empire of the St. Lawrence" was in Creighton's view the foundation upon which Macdonald built, and provided a major theme for his definitive biography of Macdonald.[35] Creighton's writing evoked a sense of both national destiny and pride, restated the old conservative nationalist doctrine and criticized liberal nationalism.[36] In addition, Creighton and another leading conservative historian, W.L. Morton, stressed the ideological differences between Canada and the United States and by implication our ideological diversity. Morton's *The Canadian Identity* (1961) pointed out both the greater respect for order and authority in Canada and the collectivist strain that has been apparent in our politics. Creighton's plea in *Canada's First Century* (1970) for government intervention that would increase our economic independence reflected the old conservative willingness to subordinate economics to politics. Like their imperialist predecessors, they attributed much of the distinctiveness of Canada from United States to its British past and to inherited British institutions and both were strong defenders of the Canadian Crown.

Although some people found this aspect of the new conservative nationalism difficult to accept, especially as emotional ties to Britain dwindled, their insistence that Canada is not simply a North American nation, that there is a Europeanness (if only partly British) about Canada has found wide acceptance. Support in the 1970s and 1980s for multiculturalism, for the mosaic rather than the melting pot, draws heavily on the conservative toleration for diversity, ideological and ethnic, which we noted in Chapter IV. The collectivist willingness of the conservative nationalists to see the state intervene in key areas of national life has also made an important contribution to contemporary Canadian nationalism. This, of course, represents only one of the strands in the Conservative Party, the tory element, and because of the strength that the business liberal strand in the party has enjoyed in recent years, it has been far from dominant in the party.

Another important force in the new nationalism is the other bearer of collectivism in the Canadian political tradition, socialism. As we have argued, toryism, socialism and nationalism all share a common collectivist orientation in various forms. Socialists are predisposed to appreciate the value of group or collective ties among individuals as well as to use collective means to protect and further group interests, and when nationalist or patriotic sentiment led them to see the nation as one of the more important of such groups or ties, socialist nationalism quickly developed. Socialist hostility to privilege has contributed to this process in Canada, for socialists have consistently identified privilege with the interests of business, and as Canadian business became increasingly foreign-owned and -controlled (especially from the United States), nationalism was seen to be an effective means of attacking privilege.

Socialism has been a serious political force, as we have seen, only since the 1930s, and its commitment to Canadian nationalism has usually been strong. The strong strain of welfare liberalism, with which electorally successful Canadian socialism has always been allied, has generally, as today, stemmed from the trade-union movement. It is not surprising that the more nationalist unions are also the most socialist. The relative increase in socialist feeling in Canadian labour almost certainly guarantees a continuing nationalist orientation in the NDP as long as that party remains formally allied with the labour movement.

The balance of power in the Canadian Labour Congress has tipped steadily away from the international (that is, American-dominated) craft unions and towards the national unions (such as the public-service unions and the Canadian Auto Workers) and the more nationalist-inclined international unions, such as the Steelworkers. These changes resulted in the secession of the craft unions from the CLC in 1981 and has doubtless, in turn, weakened anti-nationalist forces in both the labour movement and the NDP.

The last factor in the nationalist revival is liberalism itself, despite its tendency to reject the collectivist element at the heart of nationalism. However, liberals who for many years had been preoccupied with freeing Canada from any vestiges of a colonial relationship with Britain belatedly began to realize that the new relations they had forged, or allowed to develop, with the United States bore an uncomfortable similarity to the colonial status they had so long fought. This feeling has not been universal among Canadian liberals, least of all among business liberals in the Liberal and Conservative Parties, but combined with rising patriotic feelings has given birth to a nationalist wing in the Liberal Party, whose growth in the 1970s and 1980s we examined in Chapter III.

French Canada has provided both an opportunity and a problem for the new nationalism. On one hand, the French fact has become recognized as an important part of the Canadian identity, and protection of Canada's cultural duality has become an important nationalist goal. On the other hand, extreme French-Canadian nationalism is diametrically opposed to the interests of Canadian nationalism. Efforts by Quebec to obtain greater autonomy are resented by Canadian nationalists, for they promise to reduce the power of the national government to protect the Canadian identity. The consequent feelings of frustration have led some nationalists to advocate drastic solutions: some, like Creighton or Morton, would have upheld federal power in direct conflict with French-Canadian nationalism if necessary; others, like the Waffle group in the NDP in the late 1960s would have maintained a strong national government by granting Quebec special status, or acquiescing in secession, while increasing Ottawa's power in relation to the other provinces. In 1987 and 1988, some nationalists in the Liberal Party opposed the Meech Lake Accord because they felt the price of accomodating French-Canadian nationalism in the Accord was too high.

Many French Canadians, however, have rejected French-Canadian nationalism, at least in its more extreme forms. As emotional ties with Britain have faded and English Canadians have become more responsive to the French fact, it has been easier for French Canadians to embrace a wider Canadian nationalism. Henri Bourassa consistently took such a position more than eighty years ago and today most French-Canadian "federalists" would see little to criticize in Bourassa's classic reconciliation of French-Canadian and wider Canadian national interests (made in answer to the extreme nationalism of Tardivel in 1904):

> Our own brand of nationalism is Canadian nationalism, based on the duality of the races and the special traditions this duality imposes. We are working towards the development of Canadian patriotism, which in our eyes is the best guarantee of the existence of two races and of the mutual respect they owe each other. Our people...are the French Canadians; but the Anglo-Canadians are not foreigners, and we view as allies all of them who respect and desire, as we do, the full maintenance of Canadian autonomy. Our homeland is all of Canada....The nation we want to see develop is the Canadian nation, made up of French Canadians and English Canadians, that is, two elements separated by their language...but united by brotherly affection and a common love for a common homeland.[37]

Finally, some French Canadians see Canadian nationalism as an effective means of combatting separatism. A Canada prepared to assert and protect its identity and independence would, they argue, be an inherently more attractive focus of loyalty for French Canadians, particularly since nationalist efforts in this direction would be directed against the same American influences that threaten French-Canadian society.

The various strands that make up the new nationalism were all beginning to emerge in 1957; the defeat of the essentially anti-nationalist Liberal government in that year was due, in part, to the success of John Diefenbaker in appealing to nationalist feeling. By 1957, the areas of nationalist concern were becoming clear, and the most obvious disquiet concerned the erosion of Canadian political sovereignty. The attempts of American McCarthyites to hunt out suspected communists in the Canadian diplomatic service in the 1950s, the virtual fusion of continental defence efforts, and American attempts in the 1960s to forbid the Canadian subsidiaries of American corporations to trade with Cuba and China all threatened Canadian political independence.

Others pointed out that political independence could not be separated from cultural or economic independence. In 1951, the Massey Commission emphasized the importance of cultural factors to national identity and survival:

> It is the intangibles which give a nation not only its essential character but its vitality as well. What may seem unimportant or even irrelevant under the pressure of daily life may well be the thing which endures, which may give a community its power to survive.[38]

In 1956, the Gordon Commission on Canada's economic prospects warned of the foreign domination of the Canadian economy[39] and Walter Gordon was later to become the leading nationalist in the Pearson cabinet.

Nationalist hopes focussed on Diefenbaker in 1957 were largely dissipated by the time of his defeat in 1963 by the almost complete inaction of his administration in this area. Even those who supported his stand against American interference in the 1963 election campaign (against Diefenbaker's refusal to accept American nuclear warheads for Canada's Bomarc missiles) damned with faint praise. George Parkin Grant, for example, in *Lament for a Nation* (1965) made it clear that Diefenbaker did not really understand the complexities of the problem of Canadian independence and had totally ignored economic and cultural factors, which in effect rendered nugatory the purely political question. Grant's brilliant study served further to stimulate the growing debate on economic and cultural nationalism, which accompanied the career of Walter Gordon as Minister of Finance in the Pearson government from 1963 to 1965.

The Liberals had returned to power with a nationalist wing headed by Gordon. His presence set off an intra-party conflict over nationalism, which at times broke into open conflict. During the 1960s, the nationalists were clearly in the minority. Pearson's liberal suspicions of nationalism were reinforced by his experience as a diplomat. Indeed, one of the first concerns of his government was to restore the tradition of "quiet diplomacy" with the United States, which had been shattered by Diefenbaker's confrontation over nuclear weapons.

Nationalist economic legislation passed under Pearson between 1963 and 1968, which restricted foreign ownership of banks and certain other financial institutions, newspapers, and broadcasting, and which provided minor incentives to increase Canadian equity participation in foreign-controlled corporations, owed its success largely to Pearson's tendency to compromise between the warring sections of the cabinet.

By the early 1970s the arguments that the nationalists had been making, particularly in the key area of economics, were clearly beginning to strike home. The fundamental premise of economic nationalism was that foreign (largely American) penetration and influence of the Canadian economy would weaken both the Canadian identity and Canadian sovereignty. In short, a degree of economic independence was essential to a separate national existence for Canada, sharing as it does a continent with a huge and powerful neighbour.

The argument for economic nationalism has several facets. Foreign ownership and control drain profits out of the country and make it possible to alter the terms of trade between foreign parent and Canadian subsidiary, so as artificially to lower the price of Canadian exports or raise the price of imported goods, technology or services. Foreign ownership may result in a reliance upon imported technology and a neglect of Canadian research and development. In an age when technology is more and more the key to economic prosperity, such reliance may mean effective economic serfdom. In addition, it may restrict the career prospects for Canadians in many fields or force them to emigrate. Indeed, when foreign control results in integration of industry on a continental basis, many high-level jobs may be closed to those Canadians who are un-

willing to spend much of their lives outside of Canada. The continental integration of economic elites, which often follows on foreign control, threatens
large-scale assimilation or the breaking down of Canadian values and attitudes
in an important segment of the population. More directly, it may mean the extension of foreign domestic law, extra-territorially to Canada, through foreign
parent corporations.

These specific arguments were joined by a more indeterminate conviction that
economic integration with the United States was bound to lead to eventual political integration and the destruction of Canada as an independent state. The close
relationship of economic and political independence perceived by Macdonald in
the 1880s was put concisely in the mid-1960s by George Ball, at the time a senior
American diplomat and proponent of continental union:

> Sooner or later, commercial imperatives will bring about free movement of all goods
> back and forth across our long border. When that occurs, or even before it does, it
> will become unmistakably clear that countries with economies so inextricably inter-
> twined must also have free movement of the other vital factors of production—capi-
> tal, services, labour. The result will inevitably be substantial economic integration,
> which will require for its full realization a progressively expanding area of common
> political decision.[40]

It was precisely this argument, and the suspicion of many Canadians that it was
correct, that underlay much of the opposition to the Canada-United States Free
Trade Agreement of 1987.

One of the most effective stimulants for economic nationalism was the energy
crisis that followed the Yom Kippur War of 1973. The twin convictions that government intervention was essential to ensure energy supplies, and that the multinational oil companies were exploiting the crisis for their own profit, produced a
climate of public feeling that provided the political underpinnings for the establishment of Petro-Canada in 1975 and the National Energy Program of 1980.

A number of ideologically divergent approaches to economic nationalism
have been advanced. In the late 1960s, Eric Kierans, whose career spanned the
presidency of the Montreal Stock Exchange, membership in the Trudeau cabinet and candidacy for the federal Liberal leadership in 1968, developed a nationalist economic policy within the existing framework of the private enterprise
system, which would use incentives to induce market forces to generate a greater
degree of economic sovereignty.[41] Kierans advocated the elimination of tariffs so
that foreign producers would find it unattractive to establish uneconomic branch
plants in Canada, and called for reduced corporate tax rates for Canadian-owned
and -controlled companies. He also criticized the extensive system of tax allowances available to resource-exploitation companies, which encouraged investment in an industry that provided few permanent jobs, and which further
encouraged the squandering of natural resources in return for short-term gains.

This preference for the use of market mechanisms to achieve nationalist ends and the reluctance to see government intervene directly combine a liberalism verging on the radical with a belief in the indispensability of the business community for realizing economic independence, and a faith that it will seek that end, given proper incentives.

Walter Gordon's *A Choice for Canada: Independence or Colonial Status,*[42] published in 1966, provided a model for economic nationalism that has predominated ever since. Gordon, like Kierans, accepted the existence of a private enterprise, capitalist economy, and sought to modify it rather than to replace it along socialist lines. That this should be the dominant Canadian approach is hardly surprising, since both the Conservatives and the Liberals accept a capitalist economy even though they might differ at times on its regulation. Gordon's solution, however, placed less faith in the operations of the market and more in direct government intervention and supervision. He favoured the following: a government agency to ensure that pricing and purchase policies, profit margins and export policies of foreign-controlled companies were in the best interests of Canada; direct measures to discourage foreign takeovers; and the establishment of a Canada Development Corporation to funnel Canadian savings into Canadian equities. Though Gordon often appeared to be a prophet crying in the wilderness in the 1960s, almost all of his proposals had been adopted in one form or another by 1980: the Canada Development Corporation was established in 1971, the Foreign Investment Review Agency (FIRA) in 1973, and the National Energy Program, which applied a number of Gordon's ideas (specifically in the energy sector), in 1980.

The development of Canadian economic nationalism, then, has reflected fairly closely the ideological mix of the country; its desire for an economy, both capitalist and Canadian, through a moderate degree of government intervention mirrors the way in which the dominant liberalism is tempered by both conservatism and nationalism. Kierans's unique reinterpretation of business liberal nationalism stood a little to one side and the full-blown socialist variety, which we will examine shortly, a good deal to the other.

This dominant strain of Canadian economic nationalism, found its intellectual roots in the report of a federal task force, inspired by Gordon and headed by Mel Watkins, an economist who had achieved a certain notoriety by challenging conventional academic *laissez-faire* ideas. Its report, *Foreign Ownership and the Structure of Canadian Industry,* which appeared in 1968, suggested a way to create a new, forward-looking liberal nationalism. We have seen that liberal nationalism was preoccupied with the question of freedom from foreign control and that traditional Liberal policy had pursued this goal with systematic vigour, especially against the remnants of British influence in Canada. By the 1960s, though, these issues had ceased to have any relevance.

Watkins suggested that new restrictions on Canadian national autonomy and liberty of action had arisen from the increasing foreign (mainly American) control of Canadian businesses, that Washington and Wall Street were plausible modern substitutes for Whitehall and the City. The multinational corporation, shifting production, investment research and development from country to country as its global interest dictate, represented a novel but serious threat to the development of a vigorous, independent economy. The Watkins Report, with its recommendations for a government regulatory agency, the establishment of the Canada Development Corporation, tariff reductions, stricter anti-trust laws to control multinational oligopolies and measures to encourage Canadian research and development, probably represented the limits to which liberal nationalism could be pushed without submerging the liberal elements in the mix.

For some, including Watkins himself, it was ideologically inadequate. Only the NDP endorsed the report, despite the fact that it contained few, if any, distinctively socialist measures. However, though the party's stand satisfied the nationalist feelings of its liberal wing, it was rejected by the more radical socialism of the emerging Waffle faction.

The Waffle group, as we argued in Chapter V, grew out of frustration with the moderate liberal-socialist mix of the NDP. It sought to replace the party's ideological diversity with socialist purity, to make the NDP "a truly socialist party," which would seek a "socialist transformation of society." For the Waffle, this end was inextricably connected with nationalism. National independence and socialism went together: "Our aim...is to build an *independent* socialist Canada." The primary obstacle to the realization of this goal was the threat posed to Canada's very existence by the domination of the Canadian economy by "American corporate capitalism."[43] This tied Canada to the American empire, committing her to American foreign politics, which were both racist and militaristic and to a domestic capitalism that subordinated human needs and the general good of the Canadian community to the profit motive and the value-system that accompanies it. Both nationalism and socialism had a common interest in breaking the bonds of the American empire and to this extent they were allies: "Canadian nationalism is a relevant force on which to build to the extent that it is anti-imperialist." Indeed, the Waffle believed that real nationalism was impossible without that socialism, for the ideas of individual economic liberty and the primacy of individual private gain implicit in capitalism effectively counteracted the nationalist commitment to the national collectivity. Consequently it rejected policies that merely sought to replace foreign capitalists with Canadian capitalists.

This mixture of socialism and nationalism based on a common collectivism was not restricted by the need to reconcile nationalism with capitalism, and the Waffle was able to put forward an unambiguously nationalist set of proposals. Such a potent combination had probably not been seen since Macdonald's blending of conservatism and nationalism, and Macdonald had been restrained by the need to conciliate the liberal elements in the Liberal-Conservative Party. The Waffle had no ideological need to persuade, entice or reward Canadian capitalists to act in nationalist ways; they were simply to be replaced by direct and sweeping state intervention. The Canadian economy was to be recaptured by frontal assault, with "extensive public control over investment and nationalization of the commanding heights of the economy, such as the key resource industries, finance and credits, and industries strategic to planning our economy." Regulatory agencies, takeover taxes and tax credits were merely redundant.

The Waffle believed that their combination of socialism and nationalism would also solve the problem of national unity by forging new ideological bonds between English and French. Both had a common interest in repelling American capitalism, and this common perception of "two nations, one struggle," while not extinguishing linguistic and cultural differences, would at least create "common aspirations that would help tie the two nations together once more." The watering-down of the traditional socialist hostility to nationalism and its commitment to internationalism was a good indication of the strength of the nationalist appeal to the Waffle and the genuineness of the alliance it forged between nationalism and socialism.

The NDP rejected the Waffle attempt to turn the party sharply to the left and to undo the party's traditional mixture of socialist and liberal elements at the party's biennial convention in 1969, and the Waffle formally disbanded in 1972. In leading the attack of the more moderate majority, David Lewis rejected the ideological uniformity of the Waffle — it would put the NDP into an "ideological strait-jacket" — and attacked its pure socialist doctrine as foreign to the Canadian experience in terms strikingly reminiscent of Woodsworth:

> To bury this central problem of independence in a general statement of analysis, to bury it in words which are foreign to the Canadian people, to clothe it in incomprehensible language and to put around it a lot of other issues is...to confuse the people of Canada.[44]

And, Lewis might well have added, alienate those NDP supporters who were attracted by its strand of radical welfare liberalism.

The NDP's rejection of the Waffle served to reinforce the conclusion that the mainstream of economic nationalism in Canada was to continue to be restrained by the powerful influence of the liberal substratum in the Canadian political tradition.

This did not, however, prevent the NDP from maintaining the position that it had assumed in the 1960s as the most consistently nationalist of the three major parties.

NDP AND NATIONALISM

As early as 1961, the NDP had called for legislation forcing minimum Canadian-ownership levels in all industries. In 1965, it proposed a Canadian Development Fund for the purpose of repatriating foreign control (by 1969, renamed the Canada Development Corporation) and in 1969 it sought public control over foreign takeovers, anticipating FIRA.[45] The 1971 federal convention deplored foreign ownership of resource industries and protested "the continentalist energy deal with the US and the sell-out of our resources to that country" and called for increased public ownership of resource industries.[46] In 1974, the party's Federal Council welcomed the Trudeau government's acceptance of the principle of establishing Petro-Canada but asserted that "its size, its powers, and the range of its activities must be substantially greater."[47] After FIRA, Petro-Canada and the CDC were established, the NDP continued both to defend them and to press for an extension of their role.[48]

In advocating a new national industrial strategy, the 1979 national convention called for "securing a Canadian-controlled presence in all significant sectors of the economy" and for gradually phasing out all Canadian operations of the multinational oil companies.[49] The 1981 convention specifically proposed that Petro-Canada take over Imperial Oil, the Canadian subsidiary of Exxon Corporation.[50] Consistent with these stands, the NDP supported the National Energy Programme. After the Conservatives returned to power in 1984, the NDP continued to criticize on nationalist grounds, measures such as the dismantling of the NEP, the converting of FIRA into Investment Canada and the sale of the de Havilland aircraft firm to U.S. interests. As we have seen, the NDP vigorously opposed the 1987 Free Trade Agreement, both in Parliament and in the 1988 election campaign.

In the early 1970s, the cause of the new nationalism was endorsed in a number of quarters, including the Conservative policy conference of 1969,[51] and a House of Commons committee, chaired by Liberal backbencher Ian Wahn, which reported in 1970.[52] They added little of substance to what had become the established agenda of economic nationalism: controls on foreign takeovers of Canadian business, the Canada Development Corporation and restrictions on foreign investment, particularly in resource and cultural industries.

The Wahn committee also dealt with the neglected area of foreign control of Canadian unionism through international (in effect, American) unions, and concluded that "the development of a fully independent Canadian identity and the need that Canadian interests be always uppermost in every sphere of activity require that Canadian branches of international unions quickly gain the fullest possible autonomy and freedom of action." While not recommending specific legislation to reach this end, the committee did set certain "general objectives," including recognition of separate Canadian sections of international unions, election of Canadian officers by Canadian sections, and complete autonomy over funds, staff and collective bargaining.

COMMITTEE FOR AN INDEPENDENT CANADA AND THE COUNCIL OF CANADIANS

The upsurge in nationalist feeling has also produced two significant inter-party nationalist organizations, the Committee for an Independent Canada (CIC) and the Council of Canadians. The CIC was formed in 1970 to promote nationalist measures on a non-partisan basis. It was based on the premise that the nationalist concern for Canadian independence was sufficient grounds for common action by those otherwise divided by party allegiance:

> We have enough in common in our concern for an independent Canada to work together effectively on a concrete programme to reduce foreign control of the economy, foster the creative arts, assure more Canadian content in the media and in our educational system, and counter the deterioration of our environment.[53]

Like other interest groups, the CIC attempted to impress its views on government both from within and by means of publicity and educational campaigns, including public meetings and forums, and publications such as *Independence: The Canadian Challenge* (1972). The problems of maintaining an independent organization consisting mostly of politically partisan individuals and the very successes achieved by the nationalist cause in the 1970s, however, led to a gradual attrition and the CIC eventually folded quietly in the early 1980s.

The Council of Canadians was formed in 1985, apparently in response to the perceived threat posed by free trade to Canadian sovereignty. While the Council was concerned with a wide range of nationalist issues, including economic, cultural and social matters, in practice most of its attention until 1989 was focussed on the fight against free trade. The Council was seen as a re-creation of the CIC, with, however, a more broadly based membership. The Council claimed support from many unions, the National Farmers Union, cultural organizations and single issue pressure groups such as the Canadian Coalition on Acid Rain. Many individuals who supported the CIC and in particular the Edmonton publisher, Mel Hurtig, were active in the Council, although other Conservatives who had been CIC members, such as Flora MacDonald and Joe Clark, presumably held aloof because Council membership would have been incompatible with membership in the Mulroney cabinet. The relative absence of any formal Conservative participation in the Council is probably a reflection of the dominance of business liberal ideas in the Conservative Party in the late 1980s, which were generally hostile to nationalism.

THE TRUDEAU GOVERNMENT

The growth in nationalist feeling without doubt contributed to the increasing willingness of the Trudeau government to undertake nationalist policies after about 1970. As we have seen in Chapter III, the liberal desire for independence, the increasing dominance of welfare liberalism in the Liberal Party and the habit of government intervention all contributed to this movement. The period of minority government from 1972 to 1974 accelerated the trend, since part of the price of NDP support was nationalist legislation, pre-eminently the Foreign Investment Review Act of 1973, which established FIRA. The Canada Development Corporation had been established in 1971, and restrictions were placed on foreign ownership of uranium mining.

While these measures were considered by some to be mere sops to nationalist pressure or concessions made merely to hold on to power, they had greater impact than originally expected. The Canada Development Corporation, which began by assuming certain existing government shareholdings in Polymer Corporation, developed into a major holding company particularly strong in the resource area before falling on bad times when energy policies declined after 1982. The sale of a minority interest in CDC to private investors provoked a clash over the Trudeau government's plans in 1980-1981 to use the CDC as a tool of government policy for restructuring other areas of Canadian industry. The criticism was not antinationalist, but capitalist: the CDC should be allowed to maximize profit for its Canadian owners, rather than serve as a device to promote political or public policy goals.

The conflict, essentially one between business liberalism and the welfare liberal brand of intervention (which was in the ascendant in the Trudeau cabinet) was an interesting illustration of the complex ideological forces at work in Canadian politics. Pressure from the market community was sufficiently strong that the business liberals won; in early 1982, the Trudeau government announced that the CDC would in future operate in an ordinary, commercial way, and that government ownership would continue to decline. FIRA was also criticized initially for not controlling new investment but only takeovers of existing businesses, and for general ineffectiveness. In 1975, FIRA review was extended to new investments and subsequently FIRA successfully expanded its jurisdiction to include indirect takeovers. These occurred when the foreign parent of a Canadian subsidiary was itself taken over by another foreign owner and were sufficiently frequent that FIRA's area of operation was significantly expanded. In practice, FIRA used this jurisdiction most visibly to force Canadianization of several publishing enterprises, which it considered particularly sensitive for reasons of cultural nationalism.

Nationalist intervention in the economy received its greatest single boost from the energy crisis, which first hit the Western world in 1973. It produced widespread public feeling that foreign-controlled oil companies exploited the crisis for their own profit and that an important part of the solution lay in government intervention. The Trudeau government pursued a policy of government intervention from the outset and between 1973 and 1984, oil and natural gas prices in Canada were effectively controlled by the federal government, subject to pricing negotiations with the oil-producing provinces. In 1975, a further nationalist element was added when Petro-Canada was established. Through subsequent acquisitions, Petro-Canada has become a national, fully integrated oil company, and has pursued a major exploration program in frontier and offshore areas. The Liberals resisted plans, such as those of the Clark government in 1979, to allow private Canadian investment in Petro-Canada and made it a major issue in the 1980 election campaign. Despite some pressure from the oil industry and the business community in general, the Mulroney government had apparently made no decision about privatizing Petro-Canada at the end of 1988.

In the 1980 election campaign, the Liberals under Trudeau promised to pursue increasingly nationalist policies, particularly in the energy area and through a strengthened FIRA. This promise was redeemed in full when the National Energy Programme was enacted and significant steps taken to meet the goal of 50 percent Canadian ownership by 1990. In particular, a system of direct government grants in respect of exploration and development expenses replaced depletion allowances under the income tax system. Unlike depletion allowances that were available for all, the Petroleum Incentive Programme (PIP) grants under the NEP increased with the level of the recipient's Canadian ownership, and most grants were denied to foreign-controlled entities. This created a powerful incentive either to increase the level of Canadian ownership or to transfer the resource property to another company with high Canadian ownership.

The initial wave of Canadianization in the energy industry encouraged by the government and rewarded by the NEP, however, came to a shuddering halt in the credit and interest rate crisis of 1981-1982 and the NEP itself was finally dismantled by the Mulroney government.

As might be expected, these policies were supported by the NDP, though with the proviso that they did not go far enough. The NDP's consistent position in this area confirmed it in the vanguard of Canadian economic nationalism. The Conservative Party was generally hostile, a stance that reflects the strong and aggressive strain of business liberalism within the party, together with that party's opposition to the centralizing policies of the federal Liberal Party. When returned to power in 1984, however, the Conservatives did not dismantle wholesale the nationalist measures adopted in the previous decade and our analysis of the history and ideological complexion of that party indicates that such a development would be unlikely.

THE CONSERVATIVE PARTY AND
NATIONALISM: STANFIELD TO MULRONEY

The Conservative Party's attitude to nationalism in the 1970s reflected the mixture of toryism and business liberalism in the party and the growing strength of business liberalism in the 1980s. In 1969, a Conservative policy conference endorsed the suggestion of Eddie Goodman, a prominent figure in the party (and later a member of the CIC), that controls be placed on at least some foreign investment in Canada.[54] When the Trudeau government introduced the FIRA legislation in 1973, the Conservative response was to agree that foreign ownership should be reduced, but also to press for incentives to promote greater Canadian investment rather than relying on government controls. In the House of Commons, Paul Hellyer (a Conservative at the time), reviewing levels of foreign ownership of Canadian business, concluded that "we are in trouble" but characterized FIRA as "a pitifully inadequate response." Sinclair Stevens declared that "most Canadians are in favour of economic nationalism" but contrasted the "negative nationalists" of the Liberal and New Democratic parties with the "positive nationalists" in the Conservative party. Stevens's formula was a combination of tax and other investment incentives to encourage Canadian investment and entrepreneurship.[55]

In 1975, when Part II of FIRA extended the review process to new investment as well as takeovers and was proclaimed in force, the Conservatives took a similar position. Jim Gillies declared that "the need for proclamation is there" but once again put forward the "positive nationalism" of Stevens:

> Much of the need for this legislation would be reduced if the government were only to take a more positive attitude toward business in this country. Foreign ownership regulations are really only a short-term answer to the overall problem of foreign investment and the development of the Canadian economy. The real answer to our problem lies in the generation of a healthy Canadian business climate.[56]

The Clark government's much misunderstood policy towards Petro-Canada reflected the same approach. By reducing some of its functions, such as its role as the government's agent for offshore oil purchases, it wished to give Petro-Canada the same status as an ordinary corporation. By selling off part of the government's equity, it intended to allow private Canadian capital to participate. At no time, however, did it contemplate that Petro-Canada could or would be allowed to fall under foreign control.

This policy approach was similar to that proposed by Eric Kierans in the late 1960s and was clearly influenced by the business-liberal element in the Conservative Party, which favours private rather than state enterprise. When allied to nationalism and to the remaining inheritance of traditional Conservative nationalism, business liberalism has at times produced an approach to nationalism in Canada

distinct from the amalgams of welfare liberalism and socialism with nationalism advanced by the Liberals and the NDP. Despite its differences of approach,
it is still correctly described as nationalist. While most Canadian nationalists and
the Liberal and New Democratic Parties vigorously opposed the Canada-U.S. Free
Trade Agreement as a denial of Canadian national interests and a major step in
continental integration, it is possible also to rationalize support of free trade from
the same perspective. Free trade arguably enhances the ability of Canadian entrepreneurs to compete in world markets and may generate national wealth that can
be used to strengthen national identity and institutions.

WESTERN SEPARATISM

It is doubtful whether the succession of separatist and quasi-separatist groups that
developed in Western Canada from the late 1970s — the Western Canada Party,
the Confederation of Regions Party, Western Canada Concept or the Reform Party
of Canada — were in any sense nationalist. While sometimes advocating or coming close to advocating an independent state in the West, these groups have just as
often been sympathetic to union with the United States. It is difficult to avoid the
conclusion that their motor force, ideologically, is not nationalism at all, but an
extreme business liberalism mixed with prairie populism. This ideological combination is deeply hostile to the welfare liberalism and perceived elitism of Eastern-
dominated parties, and draws on feelings of regional identity and grievance in the
West. Our view, therefore, is that these groups cannot properly be described as nationalist in any meaningful sense.

CULTURAL NATIONALISM

Another area of increasing concern from the late 1960s was cultural nationalism.
The report of a cabinet task force headed by Herb Gray in 1971 broke new ground
by examining the relationship of economic to cultural dependence. It argued that
the question of cultural identity could be separated from economic dependence:
"There is no such compartmentalization. There can be little doubt that economic
activity, as organized in the modern corporation, has a profound impact on culture."[57] A vicious circle existed; cultural similarity between Canada and the
United States facilitated American investment, yet that same investment strengthened and emphasized those common features. American social, cultural, political
and economic ideas were exported to Canada along with American investment and
technology to the detriment of other facets of the Canadian ideological mosaic. The
technologies of production or management rarely take local needs or values into

account and produce a standardized product. The incompatibility of this process with nationalist respect for the values of national identity and diversity is obvious.

The cultural duality of Canada poses a special problem for cultural nationalism. Classical nationalism traced cultural differences between nations to linguistic divisions, and drew the conclusion that all who spoke the same language should belong to the same state. Modern Canadian cultural nationalists clearly want to avoid just that consequence. Yet because French and English in Canada share a common state but not a common culture, they pull back from pursuing the cultural differences between Canada and the United States, for fear of clarifying the equally obvious differences between English and French Canada.

One solution to this dilemma was increased government support for the arts and letters throughout Canada, advocated by the Massey Commission in 1952. The Commission report was not a nationalist document, but exhibited a concern for the arts in their universal rather than their strictly Canadian forms, and was limited to "high culture" — classical music, ballet and the like — rather than the sum of all the traditions, customs and attitudes that constitute Canadian culture.

The logic of cultural nationalism has pushed beyond this concern for public support of high culture to protection of a whole complex of institutions that contribute to a national culture. Understandably, a good deal of interest has been focussed on the various communications media, particularly in view of the flood of American content in books, magazines, films, radio and television.

Broadcasting was one of the first targets of cultural nationalism, and in 1968 the *Broadcasting Act* was amended so as to prohibit most financial ties between Canadian and foreign broadcasters and to strengthen the regulatory agency (the CRTC), which would enable it to enforce stricter Canadian content rules. Since then, the CRTC has vigorously pursued both objectives, though often it has been forced to slow down the planned increase in Canadian content in television because of financial problems experienced by private broadcasters. The predominance of the commercial element and profit motive in Canadian broadcasting, which gives advertising demands a heavy influence on program content, is a prime cause of this problem. Since many advertisers are American-controlled corporations intent on maximizing the sale of consumer goods, programming has tended to be "bland, slick, escapist, intellectually timid and uninventive, repetitive and essentially unrepresentative of the national life and culture."[58]

Prior to 1968, legislation was also passed that prohibited foreign ownership of Canadian newspapers and discouraged foreign magazines from draining advertising revenue from Canadian ones. In 1975, exemptions from the latter measure in respect of the Canadian editions of *Time* and *Reader's Digest* was repealed. When the FIRA was replaced by Investment Canada in 1985, special restrictions on foreign ownership of cultural industries such as publishing were retained and these restrictions were specifically protected in the Canada-United States Free Trade Agreement.

In the late 1980s, foreign dominance of the Canadian film distribution business became a significant issue, because of its possibly inhibiting effect on the production and distribution of Canadian-made films. In response to this pressure, the Mulroney government introduced the *Film Products Importation Act* in June 1988 which, however, died on the order paper when Parliament was dissolved for the 1988 election. The legislation was designed to force multinational distributors to give fair access to Canadian films in Canadian theatres and was introduced by Flora MacDonald, then Minister of Communications, and former member of the CIC. Conservative sensitivity to the strength of nationalist sentiment in this area may also have contributed to the Mulroney government's decisions in 1988 to support the CBC by upholding the CRTC's decisions to grant it the right to operate an all-news television channel and to construct new production facilities in Toronto.

Next to the communications media, the Americanization of the Canadian education system has been a prime concern of cultural nationalists. The widespread use of American textbooks and teaching materials at the primary and secondary school levels tended to go along with a neglect of specifically Canadian subjects, particularly Canadian history. The result was a spate of nationalist demands for more and better teaching of Canadian subjects. This, in turn, called attention to the Canadian publishing industry, which includes a large number of subsidiaries of American companies. Government intervention in this area has included provincial government insistence on the use of Canadian teaching materials, the use of FIRA as discussed above, and government financial assistance, including loans and the purchasing of Canadian books for distribution abroad. A Federal Crown Corporation, the Canadian Film Development Corporation, was also established to encourage the growth of a Canadian film industry, and generous tax incentives were put in place in the 1970s to stimulate investment in Canadian-made films.

In the universities, concern mounted in the late 1960s over the large number of non-Canadians on Canadian university faculties. It was estimated that the proportion of Canadians on university faculties declined from 75 percent in 1961 to closer to 50 percent by 1968[59] as the result of substantial immigration necessary to satisfy the needs of the rapidly expanding universities. Further, foreigners were concentrated in culturally sensitive areas. Demands for preferential treatment for Canadians or quotas were at that time resisted by many academics, some of whom genuinely feared a nationalist "witch-hunt." The debate, without doubt, made those responsible for hiring much more sensitive to the situation, and this pressure, together with the sharp reduction of the demand for new faculty, alleviated the problem to a large extent. By the late 1970s, the bulk of the new appointees were

Canadians and the overall balance was on the way to being righted. This trend was reinforced by the federal government's use of immigration regulations to discourage the hiring of foreigners when qualified Canadians were available.

CONCLUSION

Canadian nationalism has become steadily more active and influential during the last twenty years and there are few signs of any immediate decline in its popularity. General public reaction to Petro-Canada, the NEP and FIRA and sympathy for their nationalist goals were undoubtedly a factor in the Liberal election victory of 1980. Public misgivings about free trade, largely on nationalist grounds, were the driving force behind opposition to free trade in the 1988 election, which focussed traditional nationalist concern. This concern, as we have argued, is not new — nationalism as an ideology in both French and English Canada has deep roots from the nineteenth century, and the questions that Canadian nationalism raises today are in substance, if not in detail, the same as those that Canadians faced in 1878 over the National Policy, in 1891 over commercial union, in 1911 on reciprocity and in 1988 on free trade. Nationalism also remains, today as then, an ideology of limited comprehensiveness, raising questions and providing answers on a fairly limited range of concern and is forced to seek alliances with other ideologies. The future course and nature of Canadian nationalism will depend to a considerable extent on the nature of the alliances it makes. Nationalism in Canada's first half-century had a predominantly conservative flavour. Today, it enjoys close relations with its ideological half-brothers, conservatism and socialism, and its formerly estranged liberal cousins.

Paradoxically, this weakness of nationalism, its need for allies, has probably widened its influence, for through alliances it has been able to appeal in one way or another across the whole ideological spectrum in Canada. Indeed, the alliance of welfare liberalism and nationalism, dating from the 1960s, which we have described above and in Chapter III, has probably been the most significant development for Canadian nationalism in recent years. It has allowed nationalism to tap the mainstream ideological current in Canadian society in a manner that has been much more fruitful than the uneasy alliance with business liberalism in the nineteenth and early twentieth centuries. While only an intermittent participant in the ideological conversation, nationalism has contributed a good deal to its vitality by raising questions about Canadian identity and independence to which all of the other participants have been forced to address themselves. This nationalist contribution has been particularly marked in the last two decades and has been the major factor in producing the debate about the nature and purpose of Canadian policy, which is the central preoccupation of our ideologies and our politics today.

1. See C.J.H. Hayes, *Essays on Nationalism* (New York: Russell, reprint of 1926 edition) and *Nationalism: A Religion* (New York: Macmillan, 1960).

2. E. Kedourie, *Nationalism* (London: Hutchinson & Co., 1966), p. 9.

3. Robert Stanfield, Notes for 1978 Josiah Wood Lectures, "Nationalism: A Canadian Dilemma," Mount Allison University, Feb. 7-8, 1978, First Lecture, p. 3.

4. George Heiman, "The Nineteenth Century Legacy: Nationalism or Patriotism" in P. Russell, ed. *Nationalism in Canada* (Toronto: McGraw-Hill Ryerson, 1966).

5. Charles Mair, "The New Canada: Its Resources and Productions" in *The Canadian Monthly and National Review* (August, 1875), p. 160.

6. See C. Berger, *The Sense of Power* (Toronto: University of Toronto Press, 1969), p. 66. Berger's incisive study of the imperialist movement in Canada before 1914 and its nationalist overtones provides an invaluable insight into this period.

7. Berger, p. 135 (*Equal Rights Association of Ontario: D'Alton McCarthy's Great Speech Delivered at Ottawa, December 12th, 1889,* Toronto, n.d.).

8. See Berger, *op. cit.,* pp. 135-147.

9. Stephen Leacock, "Greater Canada: An Appeal," in *University Magazine,* Vol. II, no. 2, April 1907, p. 133.

10. *Empire Club of Canada: Address Delivered to the Members During the Sessions of 1912-3 and 1913-4* (Toronto: 1915) in Berger, p. 231.

11. Wilfrid Campbell, "Imperialism in Canada," Empire Club Speeches: Being Addresses Delivered Before the Empire Club of Canada During its Session of 1904-5, Toronto, 1906, in Berger, p. 170.

12. *Empire,* 2 October 1890, reprinted in Berger, p. 169.

13. Wilfrid Campbell, *op. cit.,* in Berger, p. 170.

14. *See* Berger, pp. 136-147.

15. From campaign message, Halifax, 19 September 1911, in *Robert Laird Borden, His Memoirs* (1969, Vol. I, p. 157), by R.L. Borden, abridged and edited by H. Macquarrie, reprinted by permission of The Canadian Publishers, McClelland and Stewart Limited, Toronto.

16. *House of Commons Debates,* 29 March 1909, p. 3523, 1st Session—11th Parliament, Vol. XC.

17. *House of Commons Debates,* 12 January 1910, pp. 1747, 1761, 2nd Session, 11th Parliament, Vol. XCIII.

18. Etienne Parent, "Industry as a Means of Survival for the French-Canadian Nationality," *Le Répertoire National* Montreal, 1893, translated and reprinted in Ramsay Cook, ed., *French-Canadian Nationalism* (Toronto: Macmillan, 1969), p. 84.

19. Mgr. L.-F.-R. Laflèche, *Quelques Considérations sur les rapports de la société civile avec la religion et la famille* (Trois Rivieres: 1866) translated and reprinted in Cook, pp. 93, 96.

20. J.-P. Tardivel, in *La Verite,* 1 June 1904, translated and printed in Cook, p. 151.

21. *Ibid.,* p. 147

22. J-M.-R. Villeneuve, "Et nos frères de la dispersion" in *Notre Avenir Politique: Enquête de L'Action française,* Montreal, 1923, translated and reprinted in Cook, p. 208.

23. *Ibid.,* pp. 207-7.

24. *Ibid.,* p. 204.

25. *Ibid.,* p. 202.

26. *Ibid.,* p. 205.

27. Antonio Perrault, "Enquête sur le nationalisme" in *L'Action française,* February, 1924, translated and reprinted in Cook, p. 220.

28. "Quebec-Canada: A New Deal — the Quebec Government's proposal for a new partnership between equals: sovereignty association," *Globe and Mail,* 2 November 1979.

29. Jean-Marc Léger, "Le Néo-nationalisme, où conduit-il?" in *Les Nouveaux Québécois,* Quebec, 1964, translated and reprinted in Cook, p. 310.

30. La Solution: Le Programme du Parti Québécois présenté par René Lévesque (Montreal: Jacques Herbert, 1970), p. 20. Our translation.

31. *Ibid.,* p. 7

32. Pierre Vallières, *White Niggers of America* (Toronto: McClelland and Stewart, 1969), p. 57.

33. Pierre Vallières, *L'Urgence de choisir* (Montreal, Éditions Parti Pris, 1971), p. 40. Our translation.

34. *Ibid.,* p. 117.

35. D.G. Creighton, *John A. Macdonald,* 2 vols. (Toronto: Macmillan, 1952, 1955).

36. See D. Creighton, *Empire of the St. Lawrence* (Toronto: Macmillan, 1953); *Canada's First Century* (Toronto: Macmillan, 1970).

37. Henri Bourassa in *Le Nationaliste,* 3 April 1904, translated and reprinted in Cook, *op. cit.,* pp. 149-150.

38. *Report of the Royal Commission on National Development in the Arts, Letters and Sciences 1949-51* (Ottawa: King's Printer, 1951), pp. 4-5, Reproduced by permission of *Information Canada.*

39. *Report of the Royal Commission on Canada's Economic Prospects* (Ottawa: Queen's Printer, 1957).

40. George Ball, *The Discipline of Power* (Boston: Atlantic-Little, Brown, 1968), p. 113.

41. See Eric W. Kierans, "Towards a New National Policy" in *Canadian Forum,* Jan.-Feb. 1972, pp. 52-55.

42. Walter L. Gordon, *A Choice for Canada* (Toronto: McClelland and Stewart, 1966).

43. Resolution 133, New Democratic Party Federal Convention, Winnipeg, 30 October 1969.

44. Debate at NDP Convention, 30 October 1969, reprinted in Godfrey, pp. 115-116.

45. *Ibid.,* p. 7.

46. *New Democratic Policies 1961-1976* (Ottawa, 1976), p. 47.

47. *Ibid.,* p. 5.

48. See, for example, the energy resolution of the 1979 national convention.

49. *NDP Convention Resolutions 1979* n.p., n.d. p. 8.

50. *NDP Convention Resolutions 1981* n.p., n.d. p. 4.

51. Recommendations of sub-committee at Niagara Falls Progressive Conservative Conference, 12 October 1969, reprinted in Godfrey, pp. 190-192.

52. 11th Report of the Standing Committee on Defence and External Affairs.

53. A. Rotstein and G. Lax, "Introduction," in *Independence: The Canadian Challenge,* (Toronto: McClelland and Stewart, 1972), pp. xii-xiii.

54. See footnote 51.

55. *House of Commons Debates,* March 30, 1973, p. 2783 ff; April 3, 1973, p. 2918 ff.

56. *House of Commons Debates,* July 18, 1975, p. 7713 ff.

57. Gray Report, *Canadian Forum,* December 1971, pp. 30-32.

58. F. Peers, "Oh, Say Can You See," in I. Lumsden, ed. *Close the 49th Parallel: The Americanization of Canada* (Toronto: University of Toronto Press, 1970).

59. See J. Steele and R. Mathews, "Universities: Takeover of the Mind," in Lumsden, pp. 170-177.

CHAPTER   VII

Δ

CONCLUSION

In considering the arguments of this book, the reader might have come to the conclusion that all of Canadian politics has been a battle over ideology. Or, to put it another way, that individuals have wrangled over issues and fought for things for ideological reasons only, and that they had not been moved by the attractions of leaders or candidates, or by gut issues such as employment, regional differences and inflation, or by emotional matters relating to considerations of race, religion, language, sex and the like.

Politics is no more all ideology than it is all psychological, or emotional or driven by the relationship of citizens to the means of production. It has been our argument that contemporary Canadian ideologies cannot be properly understood without considering their European origins. Two facts stand out. First, the Canadian ideological structure contains the same elements as the European, but the balance among liberalism, toryism and socialism is strongly in favour of liberalism in this country. Most of the emigration to Canada from Britain took place after liberal ideas had risen to considerable prominence there. However, the pattern of immigration in the nineteenth century helped to reinforce the ideological structure that had early been established in Canada. On balance, those who inclined more toward toryism found a more congenial atmosphere in Canada, while those more liberal preferred the United States. Nonetheless, most immigrants who came to Canada in the late eighteenth and nineteenth centuries accepted important elements of liberalism. Second, although Canada is the product of a European culture, the ideas brought by the settlers were modified in the course of their encounter with their new conditions.

In its North Americanness, Canada is like the United States, but the differences between this country and its neighbour are even more striking than the contrast between Canada and Europe. Unlike British immigrants to the United States in the sixteenth and seventeenth centuries, those who settled in British North America were not a persecuted and dissenting liberal minority. They reflected more fully the powerful tory or conservative strand in British political culture. Many were Catholic Scots and Irish, bearing a faith that was fundamentally hostile to liberal individualism. As well, many consciously identified with the Victorian conservatism of Disraeli and the Second Tory Party. This attachment to toryism was more true of the United Empire Loyalists who fled the United States after the Revolution, although even in their political thought liberalism was still significant. The presence in Canada of this tory element, although weaker than in Britain, created the conditions out of which an indigenous socialism could arise. This climate was enhanced in the late nineteenth and early twentieth centuries by immigration from Britain and continental Europe after socialist ideas had developed there, and this further contributed to the rise of a successful socialist movement in Canada.

Another important difference between Canada and the United States was the existence of French Canada. Many of the immigrants to New France had left France at a time when liberal ideas were virtually non-existent, and hence they brought with them to the new land an attitude to the state and to society that was more tory-feudal than liberal. When liberal ideas were introduced, they were brought through the medium of the English-speaking protestants who came to settle after the Conquest and who were commercial as well as religious rivals of the French. It was such a situation that Lord Durham reported. He sought to impose on Quebec an authoritarian form of government, fearing that if Quebeckers were given democratic rights in the mid-nineteenth century, they would use their power to prevent the development of a liberal society.

It was to be a long time before liberal ideas were accepted in Quebec. Laurier's famous speech on political liberalism was a major step in the reconciliation of French Canadians to liberalism, but the best that even Laurier was able to accomplish was to persuade many of his fellow French Canadians that liberalism was not anathema. He combined his moderate liberalism with a provincial-rights approach to the nature of the Canadian state, suggesting in effect that Quebeckers could vote Liberal in federal elections without creating a federal government that would use its powers to impose liberalism on the people of that province. Quebeckers could then vote for provincial regimes that were more ideologically acceptable to them, and the province would continue to enjoy full powers over those areas of law, religion and culture that were so important to it. It was not until the 1950s that liberalism became a strong ideological force in Quebec provincial politics, in part because of the journalistic activities of Pierre Trudeau. Against this background, heavily imbued with tory-feudal ideas, the advent of a powerful, indigenous liberalism soon generated a successful socialist movement in the Parti Québécois. Socialism and nationalism conjoined in their shared commitment to collectivism, and the PQ came to power in 1976. By the late 1980s the New Democratic Party was a legitimate contender for seats in the province.

Hartz has argued correctly that it is characteristic of fragment societies to be intolerant of rival ideologies. Our argument is that Canada is not a fragment society, but exhibits the ideological diversity of European societies, although it has a more liberal cast. This toleration, born of the necessity to live with and listen to the other voices in the ideological conversation, has deeply affected Canadian political life. Thus, we have noted a willingness in all of the major Canadian ideologies to be open, sometimes too open, to developments elsewhere. Canadian Liberalism had, by the 1919 convention, accepted the modifications of liberalism suggested in Britain by Green and Hobhouse, and had begun to develop a form of welfare liberalism in this country. The Conservative Party willingly accepted the lead of Disraeli and the British Tory Party in the nineteenth century. More recently, it has turned its attention to the United States, where it has been influenced by the "conservatives," first under the leadership of Barry Goldwater in the 1960s and more recently by the neo-conservatism of Ronald Reagan and George Bush.

Canadian socialists have always looked abroad for inspiration. Early Canadian socialism was a mixture of socialist ideas from various inheritances: religious, Marxist, central European and British, among others. However, under the leadership of Woodsworth, Canadian socialism sought its own domestic roots, though it still took the British Labour Party and the Fabians as its main guide and inspiration even in this quest. Subsequently it has paid attention to successful socialist movements in Europe, particularly the Swedish, the German and, most recently, the French experiment of François Mitterand. This openness of all the major Canadian ideologies to external influences has meant that the Canadian ideological mix, like the Canadian economy, lacks autonomy and, some would say, individuality. Canadians too often have let others do their thinking for them, and have accepted too much from abroad without considering carefully enough how suitable these ideological imports are to the needs of Canada.

Even so, there are blessings in this: it has prevented Canadians from becoming too parochial. At times, though, such openness, particularly to the allure of the powerful liberal strains in the United States, has threatened to destroy the integrity of Canada. Fortunately, both French-Canadian and English-Canadian nationalism have acted as correctives.

There is not, however, always universal agreement that Canada needs three major parties to represent this ideological diversity. Consider the following exchange that took place during the 1988 leadership debate.

MR. TURNER: I think Canadians have always supported broadly based progressive parties. The Liberal Party has been the overwhelming choice for most of this century. I want to ask Mr. Broadbent if he really believes that he wants to reduce the system to a two-party system? When he finishes third in this election, will he disband the New Democratic Party?

MR. BROADBENT: Mr. Turner, you are in third place, sir; not me. Your party is running third. So, I think it is more likely that you will be facing that question.[1]

From the point of view of many New Democrats, the alliance between business and welfare liberalism in the Liberal Party is under considerable strain, and the Free Trade Agreement provided exactly the right sort of conditions to separate these two elements in the Liberal Party. In this view, the NDP's welfare liberalism gives it an entrée into the centre ground of Canadian politics, where a majority of voters is found. By minimizing the party's socialist rhetoric, and indeed the extent of its commitment to an egalitarian society, they hope to pry substantial numbers of welfare liberals away from the Liberal Party. To do so, the NDP's socialism would have to be considerably moderated, and the socialists within the party would have to be content to remain a minority voice. The success of this strategy is inhibited both by the continuing presence in the NDP of more doctrinaire socialists and more radical trade unionists, and the failure of the strategy to secure increased electoral support in 1988, despite apparently ideal circumstances. Goldfarb and Axworthy succinctly put the party's continuing dilemma: "Ed Broadbent must retain the social-democratic vision of his activist core while broadening the party's appeal to a larger constituency."

From the other side, many Conservatives see a similar opportunity. In their analysis, the position of business liberalism in the Liberal Party has been deteriorating since the Trudeau years, presenting the opportunity to build on the centre ground they occupied in 1984 and to detach a significant portion of the business liberals from the Liberal Party. Their hope is that, reduced to a rump of welfare liberals, the Canadian Liberal Party would fade into the oblivion of the British Liberal Party.

All of these strategies reckon without the response of the Liberal Party itself. It has undoubtedly been the most successful of all Canadian political parties in the twentieth century. Its strategy was first established by Mackenzie King, who presided over the fortunes of the party for almost thirty years, and who led it from success to success by holding a balance between the welfare and business liberal wings of the party, as electoral circumstances dictated. Only when his successor, Louis St. Laurent, under the influence of C.D. Howe, allowed the Liberal Party to be narrowed in its ideological scope to a heavy reliance on business liberalism did the party experience defeat at the polls. This reverse was painstakingly overcome by Lester Pearson and Pierre Trudeau, who reestablished and strengthened the importance of welfare liberalism in the central vision of the party. Whether the

Liberal Party in the 1990s will follow their lead and continue to balance the two interpretations of the meaning of liberalism, or whether it will allow itself to be narrowed to one remains to be seen. However, all the current indicators suggest that it is pointing in the direction of redefining itself predominantly as a welfare liberal party. As Goldfarb and Axworthy note:

> It was a party trying to re-define its place in the political spectrum. It was a party that wanted to return to its traditional small "l" liberal, left-of-center roots in terms of social-policy orientation. It was a party that continued to be nationalistic and that continued to support strong, centralist government.[3]

What is clear is that there has been some sort of partial ideological realignment in Canada over the past decade. The virtually universal support of the business community for the Progressive Conservatives in the 1988 election, save for those sectors that would be adversely affected by free trade, points to the increasing stranglehold that business liberalism has taken over the heart of that party. John Turner's strident opposition to free trade in the name of welfare liberalism and nationalism is almost a concession that the Liberal Party has abandoned business liberalism, at least for the immediate future.

There is one factor that must, however, always be remembered, and that is the continuing impact of the *Charter of Rights and Freedoms*. After the 1984 election the Conservative government behaved in some areas in ways that were, ideologically, curious. For instance, the Minister of Defence announced that the role of women would be expanded in the armed forces; and just before the 1988 election, the government introduced a major plan to provide day-care places. It would be possible to give many more instances of this sort. What they amount to is a belief on the part of all Canadian parties that the Charter represents some sort of policy agenda, which must be fulfilled by any government, regardless of its political stripe. Rather than using the "notwithstanding" clause to allow him to pursue his own policy agenda, Prime Minister Mulroney made it clear that he does not believe this to be a valid option. In his view, he is forced to abide by the Charter in areas such as abortion, even though it might force him into a policy he opposes. Since most other major political figures share this belief, it is clear that there are limits on the ideological polarization that can take place in Canada.

There is another whole range of issues involving very important ideological questions, which we have largely left aside. These are, for the most part, highly contentious issues such as capital punishment, abortion, sexual orientation, prostitution and AIDS — issues on which the major parties have not themselves chosen to take a position. The capital punishment debate was an important case in point. In spite of overwhelming support for the restoration of the death penalty, a coalition of Conservatives, Liberals and New Democrats, including the three party leaders, allied to prevent its reintroduction. On abortion, the matter was even more confused. Here the government declined even to introduce a bill, but instead offered parliament a series of choices from which it was to choose broad principles. After this had been accomplished the government proposed to introduce a bill based on these principles, at which time MPs would be freed from party discipline and would be allowed to vote according to their own best view of the matter. However, since parliament was unable even to agree on the first step, the matter was withdrawn until after the election.

To some in the country, it seems as if the leadership of the three main parties form a conspiracy to prevent matters of urgent public interest from being discussed, let alone acted upon. The 1988 election saw the rise of two new parties. The more important, the Reform Party, sought to raise the question of the character of the Canadian nation, a topic that threatened to reopen the compromises that had arisen over such matters as bilingualism. The Christian Heritage Party, which drew its strength mostly from rural areas and localities where the Christian Reform Church was strong, declared itself in favour of the return of capital punishment and against a liberal abortion law.

It might be possible to argue that some tories who believe that they no longer have a home in the Progressive Conservative Party are important elements in these new formations. On this matter, it is too early to tell whether they are new stars in the constellation of Canadian politics, or merely ephemeral meteors who briefly light up the sky before disappearing forever into oblivion. In any event, it is worth remembering that nearly 5 percent of Canadian voters were sufficiently dissatisfied with what the three main parties had to offer that they abandoned them.[4]

The presence of these minor parties lends added credence to the continuing importance of ideological differences in Canadian political life. The 1988 election campaign would be clear proof of this. The major issue, free trade, and several lesser issues such as tax policy, Meech Lake, and deficit reduction, were defined and argued in ideological terms. As well, when the issues of Canadian identity and sovereignty were raised within the context of the free trade debate, distinctive ideological positions were obvious. The clearest of these was the favouring of collective or state activity by both Turner and Broadbent, which they also advanced as an important part of the identity they sought thereby to preserve.

In view of this, it is important to keep the 1988 election in perspective, because none of the three major parties acquitted themselves well in this regard. The Liberals and New Democrats consistently charged that the Free Trade Agreement was the Sale of Canada Act, that it abandoned the levers of economic control and would lead eventually to the political integration of Canada into North America once economic integration had been achieved. Although their rhetoric frightened many, especially those who feared social welfare programs might be threatened, they were short on analysis as to exactly why political union was a necessary consequence of this particular commercial arrangement.

For their part, the Conservatives showed little sense of their party's or their country's history. The Turner and Broadbent campaigns revealed that a residual fear of absorption by the United States continued, and a desire to maintain a separate political identity in North America. In their pre-occupation with business liberal values, the Conservatives lost sight of the commitment to the whole, which had been part of their party's heritage from Macdonald to Clark.

The ideological diversity we have described in this book is part of a wider theme, perhaps the dominant one in Canadian history: the assertion and survival of a distinctive Canadian identity in North America. Canada was shaped by a number of groups for whom survival was the most important goal. French Canadians, defeated on the Plains of Abraham, American Tories fleeing the victorious Republic, Highland Scots crushed at Culloden, Acadians painfully returning from the expulsion of 1755 — all were determined to survive and to build a society in which their identity and values would persevere. It was from this determination that a distinctive political society developed in the northern half of North America, a society which by necessity and by choice shared in the liberalism of the United States, but did not accept it wholly.

From the beginning, the influence of the liberal individualism of American society has been tempered by an insistence that Canadian society reflect an overarching social order: an order imposed and achieved through the collectivity, and an order based on an explicit recognition of the value of the whole, whether nation, region or community. In toryism, this concept of order took a more traditional and hierarchical form; in socialism, an egalitarian cast; in nationalism, it looked to a linguistic or ethnic basis. In all three cases, there existed the vision of a society ordered by imperatives beyond the sum of the desires of its individual members.

The ideological conversation we have described, then, is fundamental to the Canadian identity, as is the determination of Canadians to remember that there are other values than those held dear in the United States. From Laura Secord and Susanna Moodie, through John A. Macdonald and Robert Borden, to John Diefenbaker, David Lewis, Walter Gordon, George Parkin Grant and countless others, there has been a sense that we have created in the northern half of North America a society we love, not just because it is our own, but also because it brings its citizens closer to the Good that Plato has called "an irresistible beauty the source of knowledge and truth, but which itself exceeds them in beauty."[5] If these men and women are right, then we must persevere, and pray with Richard Hooker that "[w]e have not loosely through silence permitted things to pass as in a dream."[6]

This book is offered as a contribution to the preservation of that identity and those memories. We have tried to show that beyond geography and language there is something profoundly unique about Canada; an ideological conversation over the centuries has created a tradition of political civility that amply justifies our efforts to preserve it.

1. *Encounter 88,* transcript of the leadership debate, October 25, 1988, p.50.

2. Goldfarb and Axworthy, *Marching to a Different Drummer,* p.136.

3. Goldfarb and Axworthy, p.123.

4. We owe this observation to Professor George Alkalay of Trent University.

5. Plato, *Republic,* 509A. Our translation.

6. Richard Hooker, "Preface" to *The Laws of Ecclesiastical Policy* (1593).

Select Bibliography

PRIMARY SOURCES

GENERAL

Blair, R.S. and J.T.McLeod, eds. *The Canadian Political Tradition: Basic Readings.* Toronto: Methuen, 1987.

Durham. *Lord Durham's Report.* Edited by G.M. Craig. Toronto: McClelland and Stewart, 1963.

Forbes, H.D., ed. *Canadian Political Thought.* Toronto: Oxford University Press, 1985.

Waite, P.B., ed. *Confederation Debates in the Province of Canada.* Toronto: McClelland and Stewart, 1963.

LIBERALISM

Chrétien, Jean. *Straight from the Heart.* Toronto: Key Porter, 1985.

Johnston, Donald. *Up the Hill.* Montreal: Optimum Publishing International, 1986.

King, Mackenzie. *Industry and Humanity.* New York: Houghton Mifflin, 1918.

Pearson, Lester B. *Mike: The Memoirs of Lester B. Pearson,* 3 vols. Toronto: University of Toronto Press, 1972.

Pickersgill, J.W. *The Liberal Party.* Toronto: McClelland and Stewart, 1962.

Robert, John. *Agenda for Canada: Towards a New Liberalism.* Toronto: Lester & Orpen Dennys, 1985.

Smith, Goldwin. *Canada and the Canadian Question.* Reprinted with introduction by C. Berger. Toronto: University of Toronto Press, 1971.

Trudeau, P.E. *Federalism and the French Canadians.* Toronto: Macmillan, 1968.

CONSERVATISM

Diefenbaker, J.G. *One Canada: Memoirs of the Right Honourable John G. Diefenbaker.* 3 vols. Toronto: Macmillan, 1975.

Faribault, Marcel. *Unfinished Business.* Toronto: McClelland and Stewart, 1967.

Hogan, George. *The Conservative in Canada.* Toronto: McClelland and Stewart, 1963.

Meighen, Arthur. *Unrevised and Unrepented.* Toronto: Clarke, Irwin, 1949.

Stanfield, R.L., "Conservative Principles and Philosophy" in Paul Fox, ed. *Politics: Canada,* 6th ed. Toronto: McGraw-Hill Ryerson, 1987, pp.376-387.

Wilbur, J.R.H., ed. *The Bennett New Deal.* Toronto: Copp Clark, 1968.

Report of the Round Table on Canadian Policy, Port Hope Conference, 1942.

SOCIALISM

CCF. *Regina Manifesto,* Regina: CCF, 1933.

CCF. *Winnipeg Declaration of Principles.* Montreal: CCF, 1956.

Irvine, William. *The Farmers in Politics.* Toronto: McClelland and Stewart, 1920.

Knowles, Stanley. *The New Party.* Toronto: McClelland and Stewart, 1961.

League for Social Reconstruction. *Social Planning for Canada.* Toronto: Thomas Nelson & Sons, 1935.

Lewis, Davis and Frank Scott. *Make this Your Canada.* Toronto: Central Canada Publishing Company, 1943.

Lewis, David. *The Good Fight: Political Memoirs 1909-1953.* Toronto: Macmillan, 1981.

LaPierre, L., J.T. McLeod, C. Taylor, and W. Young, eds. *Essays on the Left.* Toronto: McClelland and Stewart, 1971.

Woodsworth, J.S. *My Neighbour.* Toronto: Methodist Book Room, 1911. Reprinted 1972 by the University of Toronto Press.

NATIONALISM

Borden, R.L. *Robert Laird Borden: His Memoirs.* 2 vols., ed. H. Macquarie. Toronto: McClelland and Stewart, 1969.

Cook, R. ed. *French Canadian Nationalism.* Toronto: Macmillan, 1969.

Creighton, Donald. *Canada's First Century.* Toronto: Macmillan, 1970.

Grant, George Parkin. *Lament for a Nation.* Toronto: McClelland and Stewart, 1965.

Lévesque, René. *Option for Quebec.* Toronto: McClelland and Stewart, 1968.

Russell, Peter, ed. *Nationalism in Canada.* Toronto: McGraw-Hill Ryerson, 1966.

Vallières, Pierre. *L'Urgence de choisir.* Montreal: Editions Partis pris, 1971.

Vallières, Pierre. *White Niggers of America.* Translated by J. Pinkham. Toronto: McClelland and Stewart, 1971.

INTERPRETATIONS

GENERAL

Bell, David and Lorne Tepperman. *The Roots of Disunity: A Look at Canadian Political Culture.* Toronto: McClelland and Stewart, 1979.

Glazebrook, G.P. de T. *A History of Canadian Political Thought.* Toronto: McClelland and Stewart, 1966.

Goldfarb, Martin and Thomas Axworthy. *Marching to a Different Drummer.* Toronto: Stoddart, 1988.

Horowitz, Gad. *Canadian Labour in Politics.* Ch. 1. Toronto: University of Toronto Press, 1968.

Manzer, Ronald. *Public Policies and Political Development in Canada.* Toronto: University of Toronto Press, 1985.

Perlin, George, ed. *Party Democracy in Canada: The Politics of National Party Conventions.* Scarborough: Prentice-Hall, 1988.

Wearing, Joseph. *Strained Relations: Canadian Parties and Voters.* Toronto: McClelland and Stewart, 1988.

Winn, C. and J. Mcmenemy. *Political Parties in Canada.* Toronto: McGraw-Hill Ryerson, 1975.

LIBERALISM

Careless, J.M.S. *Brown of the Globe.* 2 vols. Toronto: Macmillan, 1959, 1963.

Dawson, R.M. and Neatby, B. *William Lyon Mackenzie King: A Political Biography,* 3 vols. Toronto: University of Toronto Press, 1976.

Grant, George Parkin. *Technology and Justice.* Toronto: House of Anansi, 1986.

Hutchison, B. *The Incredible Canadian.* Toronto: Longmans Green, 1952.

Laxer, J. and Laxer, R. *The Liberal Idea of Canada.* Toronto: James Lorimer, 1977.

Morton, William. *The Progressive Party.* Toronto: University of Toronto Press, 1950.

Newman, Peter. *The Distemper of our Times.* Toronto: McClelland and Stewart, 1968.

Skelton, O.D. *Life and Letters of Sir Wilfrid Laurier,* 2 vols. Toronto: McClelland and Stewart, 1965.

Wearing, Joseph. *The L-Shaped Party: The Liberal Party of Canada 1958-1980.* Toronto: McGraw-Hill Ryerson, 1981.

CONSERVATISM

Creighton, Donald. *Sir John A. Macdonald,* 2 vols. Toronto: Macmillan, 1952, 1955.

Graham, Roger. *Arthur Meighen,* 3 vols. Toronto: Clark Irwin, 1960, 1963, 1965.

Granatstein, J.L. *The Politics of Survival.* Toronto: University of Toronto Press, 1967.

Newman, Peter. *Renegade in Power.* Toronto: McClelland and Stewart, 1963.

Perlin, G.C. *The Tory Syndrome: Leadership Politics in the Progressive Conservative Party.* Montreal: McGill-Queen's University Press, 1980.

Taylor, Charles. *Radical Tories.* Toronto: House of Anansi, 1982.

SOCIALISM

Avakumovic, Ivan. *Socialism in Canada: A Study of the CCF-NDP in Federal and Provincial Politics.* Toronto: McClelland and Stewart, 1978.

Baum, Gregory. *Catholics and Canadian Socialism: Political Thought in the Thirties and Forties.* Toronto: James Lorimer & Co., 1980.

Clark, S.D., J. Paul Grayson and Linda M. Grayson, eds. *Prophecy and Protest: Social Movements in Twentieth-Century Canada.* Toronto: Gage, 1975.

French, Doris. *Faith, Sweat and Politics.* Toronto: McClelland and Stewart, 1962.

Horn, Michiel. *The League for Social Reconstruction: Intellectual Origins of the Democratic Left in Canada 1930-1942.* Toronto: University of Toronto Press, 1980.

Masters, William. *The Winnipeg General Strike.* Toronto: University of Toronto Press, 1950.

Penner, Norman. *Canadian Communism: The Stalin Years and Beyond.* Toronto: Methuen, 1988.

Penner, Norman. *The Canadian Left: A Critical Analysis.* Toronto: Prentice-Hall, 1977.

Robin, Martin. *Radical Politics and Canadian Labour.* Kingston: Centre for Industrial Relations, 1968.

Steed, Judy. *Ed Broadbent: The Pursuit of Power.* Toronto: Viking, 1988.

Young, Walter. *The Anatomy of a Party: The National CCF, 1932-1961.* Toronto: University of Toronto Press, 1969.

Zakuta, L. *A Protest Movement Becalmed: A Study of Change in the CCF.* Toronto: University of Toronto Press, 1964.

NATIONALISM

Berger, C. *The Sense of Power.* Toronto: University of Toronto Press, 1969.

Creighton, Donald. *Canada's First Century.* Toronto: Macmillan, 1970.

Godfrey, D. and M. Watkins, eds. *Gordon to Watkins to You.* Toronto: New Press, 1970.

Grant, George Parkin. *Technology and Empire.* Toronto: House of Anansi, 1969.

Kedourie, E. *Nationalism.* London: Hutchinson, 1966.

Rotstein, A. and G. Lax, eds. *Independence: The Canadian Challenge.* Toronto: Committee for an Independent Canada, 1972.

Saywell, John. *The Rise of the Parti Québécois, 1967-1976.* Toronto: University of Toronto Press, 1977.

INDEX

cut here

STUDENT REPLY CARD

In order to improve future editions, we are seeking your comments on *Political Parties and Ideologies in Canada*, Third Edition, by W. Christian and C. Campbell.

After you have read this text, please answer the following questions and return this form via Business Reply Mail. *Thanks in advance for your feedback!*

1. Name of your college or university: _____

2. Major program of study: _____

3. Are there any sections of this text which were not assigned as course reading? _____
   _____ If so, please specify those chapters or portions:

4. How would you rate the overall accessibility of the content? Please feel free to comment on reading level, writing style, terminology, layout and design features, and such learning aids as chapter objectives, summaries, and appendices.

5. What did you like *best* about this book?

6. What did you like *least*?

If you would like to say more, we'd love to hear from you. Please write to us at the address shown on the reverse of this card.

cut here

-------------------------------CUT HERE-------------------------------

$\vdots$ CUT HERE

-----------------------------FOLD HERE-----------------------------

**BUSINESS
REPLY MAIL**

No Postage Stamp
Necessary If Mailed
in Canada

Postage will be paid by

7115

Attn: Sponsoring Editor, Social Sciences

The College Division
McGraw-Hill Ryerson Limited
330 Progress Avenue
Scarborough, Ontario
M1P 2Z5

TAPE SHUT